LITERARY CRITICISM AND MYTH

YEARBOOK OF
COMPARATIVE CRITICISM

VOLUME IX

Literary

Criticism

and Myth.

Edited by

Joseph P. Strelka

THE PENNSYLVANIA STATE
UNIVERSITY PRESS
University Park and London

Library of Congress Cataloging in Publication Data

Main entry under title:
Literary criticism and myth.
  (Yearbook of comparative criticism ; v. 9)
  Includes index.
  1. Myth in literature—Addresses, essays, lectures.
2. Mythology in literature—Addresses, essays, lectures.
I. Strelka, Joseph, 1927–   II. Series.
PN56.M94L57   801'.95   79-15111
ISBN 0-271-00225-5

CONTENTS

PREFACE

When the protagonist in Goethe's novel *Wilhelm Meisters Wanderjahre* enters the utopian "pedagogic province," he is among other things informed about the way talented young people are taught creative writing: they are simply told "myths, traditions and legends"[1] and then they are watched to see what they make of them. It seems that this method is not so far from the basic way to create literature in general. When Harry Slochower pointed out the mythopoetic qualities of literature, he took as examples works of Aeschylus and Sophocles, Dante, Shakespeare, Cervantes, Goethe, Dostoevsky, and Melville.[2] The mythical impact on literature seems limited neither to ancient classical works of world literature nor to myth itself. Ethnological, anthropological, and psychological studies of myth have not only provided new insights into the relationship between literature and myth but have sometimes had a direct impact on modern literature too, as was shown by John B. Vickery in his investigation of the influence of Frazer's *Golden Bough* on the works of Yeats, T.S. Eliot, D.H. Lawrence, and James Joyce.[3] Indeed the influence of myth scholarship on literature and on literary criticism, as represented for example by F.M. Müller and Karl Kerényi, Joseph Campbell, Mircea Eliade, and Ernesto Grassi, is as wide in scope as it is far-reaching in its consequences.[4]

There exists as little agreement about the concept of myth as about most other important concepts in literary criticism. The concept of myth is used in at least three different ways. First, it has the meaning of an often-ancient concept pointing at some phenomena of nature, the origin of man, or the costumes and rites of people, mostly involving the exploits of gods and heroes. In this sense Northrop Frye has called it the "union of ritual and dream in a form of verbal communication" and stated that "the structural principles of literature are as closely related to mythology and comparative religion as are those of painting to geometry."[5]

A second possible meaning of the term "myth" is the original Aristotelian meaning of plot or narrative scheme in a literary work.

A third basic meaning applied especially since the seventeenth and eighteenth century has pejorative connotations: myth stands for a statement or concept with which many people agree or pretend to agree, although it does not hold true. It sometimes can be a sort of euphemism for a lie. Roger Bauer, for example, used it quite deliberately in this sense when he wrote about French poets of the early nineteenth century: "They loved, they revered a Germany which they did not know, which perhaps does not exist, a dreamed one, a Germany for which they longed, a utopia, a wished-for illusion, a myth."[6]

It is mainly the first of these three meanings in which the term myth is used and treated here. However, there is a certain link between meaning number one and meaning number three: both of them refer to a concept of myth that cannot be entirely comprehended in a rational way. Their relation to each other is like the relation between real, "genuine" myth and fake or phony myth.

Wellek and Warren, in the *Theory of Literature*, supply two definitions that try to bridge the differences between meanings one and two and one and three. First, myth is used in a wider sense as "any anonymously composed *story* telling of origins and destinies: the explanations a society offers its young of why the world is and why we do as we do, its pedagogic images of the nature and destiny of men."[7]

Second, Wellek and Warren point out that in modern times the anonymity might be limited: "We may be able to identify the creators—or some of the creators of a myth; but it may still have the qualitative status of myth if its authorship is forgotten, not generally known, or at any event unimportant to its validation—if it has been accepted by the community, has received the 'consent of the faithful.' "[8]

Although aware of the relativity and the differences involved, I should like to specify this definition in order to distinguish between meanings one and three of the term myth. In this respect, who created it and what kind of community consented to a certain myth seem less important than the specific structure of the myth itself.

The difference lies between the concept of "myth" versus "logos" and the concept of "myth" versus "truth." In other words, true myth is connected with genuine religion, although it might be explained psychoanalytically. For this reason many critics, from Wellek and Warren to Luc Benoist, stress the fact of the relation between myth and ritual.[9] False myth, on the other hand, rests upon a total secularization of the mythical realm. In other words, true myth by its very nature transcends the logical sphere or the realm of outward manifestations, while false myth either reduces the infinite to the finite or applies infinite qualities to the finite. The myth of the great mother goddess may serve as an example for the first, while the last is nicely represented by the above example of the French "myth" of nineteenth-century Germany.

Even if one limits the term myth to the first of the three meanings, as I am trying to do, there exists a wide range of possible literary manifestations of it and many different kinds. Northrop Frye, for example, distinguishes between "canonical" and "apocryphal" myths in relation to a given historical situation: "For most poets of the Christian era who have used both the Bible and Classical literature the latter has not stood on the same plane of authority as the former, although they are equally mythical as far as literary criticism is concerned."[10] He also distinguishes between the learned and subtle myth on one hand and the primitive and popular myth on the other hand, although both tend toward one center of imaginative experience.[11] He distinguishes finally between myth and naturalism as the two poles of a wide range within which the literary design unfolds. On this scale he refers to the different degrees or shades of the tendency to displace myth in a human direction and yet, in contrast to "realism," to "conventionalize content in an idealized direction":

> The central principle of displacement is that what can be metaphorically identified in a myth can only be linked in romance by some form of simile: analogy, significant association, incidental accompanying imagery, and the like. In a myth we can have a sun-god or a tree-god; in a romance we may have a person who is significantly associated with the sun or trees. In more realistic modes the association becomes less significant and more a matter of incidental, even coincidental or accidental, imagery. In the dragon-killing legend of the St. George and Perseus family, of which more hereafter, a country under an old feeble king is terrorized by a dragon who eventually demands the king's daughter, but is slain by the hero. This seems to be a romantic analogy (perhaps also, in this case, a descendant) of a myth of a waste land restored to life by a fertility god. In the myth, then, the dragon and the old king would be identified. We can in fact concentrate the myth still further into an Oedipus fantasy in which the hero is not the old king's son-in-law but his son, and the rescued damsel the hero's mother. If the story were a private dream such identifications would be made as a matter of course. But to make it a

plausible, symmetrical, and morally acceptable story a good
deal of displacement is necessary, and it is only after a comparative study of the story type has been made that the metaphorical structure within it begins to emerge.[12]

According to some theorists, like the novelist Hermann Broch,
myth itself in its pure, original form is neither really known to us
nor can it be grasped or reconstructed: all we know are literary
manifestations of myth.[13] Other critics, like Richard Chase, trying
to pinpoint possible sources for the deeper rhythms of fiction,
hold that myth is literature as a "narrative resurrection of a primeval reality," and that we are able—in spite of the unbridgeable
distance from this primeval reality—to realize its older and newer
literary variations from its psychological angle as the fundamental
clash between the ego and the objective world with the alternat-
ing attempts of the one to "coerce" the other.[14]

Indeed Hermann Broch, a most consciously myth-oriented writer, went so far as to claim that "myth is the archetype of every
phenomenal cognition of which the human mind is capable."[15]
This might explain the innumerable aspects of myth in general, as
well as of myth in relation to literature, which appear in the classical anthologies from Pierre Maranda to John B. Vickery.[16] Thus it
is impossible to treat all the implied facets of *Literary Criticism
and Myth* in this one volume. A scholar of the stature of Philip
Wheelwright shows how images and image clusters function within a mythic context in a way that leads to a myth-oriented study of
metaphor and hence to the very heart of poetic meaning and the
structure of literature in general.[17] Wheelwright's treatment of the
rhythms and cyclic character of nature and ritual and its mythical
impact on literature, or Northrop Frye's mythical theory of archetypal criticism, covers so much ground that several books
could be devoted to each of these problems.

Since the step was taken from a simpler, more naive approach to
myth, with merely allegorizing and euhemeristic methods, to a
more complex and modern approach of multileveled and pluralis-
tic perspectives, as reflected in the change from the perspective of
the Venetian sixteenth-century humanist Natalis Comes to Giambattista Vico's *Prinicipii di una scienza nuova* . . . in 1725, the
analysis and hermeneutics of myth itself have grown increasingly
complicated. The latest development of its interchange with literature and the development of newer literary criticism has multiplied the difficulties. Not only myth but mythopoeic expression
and not only the artist as myth-maker but the artist himself as

myth exemplify some of the basic aspects of the broad scope and the complexities involved.

Haskell Block, whose excellent essay "The Myth of the Artist" opens the general, theoretical part of this book, shows the problems implied in the opposite extreme positions of a general mythic tradition vis-à-vis a totally private and personal myth, both of them encompassed by almost nothing else but myth-making as an inherent human need. In a similar way, starting from seemingly limited positions of only two authors, Sem Dresden makes the paradoxical dialectics of myth and antimyth visible as two overlapping forms, neither of which exists by itself alone in its extreme entirety. The genuinely sacred myth that becomes a recurrent and essential part of literature must again and again be recreated and therefore admit to its bosom the so-called antimythologizing of parody and criticism. Lillian Feder, using examples from modern poetry, presents a cross section of many different possibilities between the two poles of the mythical level of discourse and its imaginary transcendence of empirical reality on the one hand, and the mythopoeic level with its actual transcendence on the other hand, in the light of various theories from Frye's "criticism as myth" to Toshihiko Izutsu. John J. White advocates the analysis of myth in literature from the epistemological perspective of concentrating on the reading process in order to deepen the appreciation of the particular ways in which myths have been used in modern fiction.

The second part of our anthology is devoted to special problems and individual examples. It begins with a study by Helen Adolf of a few Rilke poems, especially one of his greatest early poems, "Der Schauende," which treats in a special way the mythical story of Jacob's wrestling with the angel. The change of the biblical original of the mythopoeic expression of Rilke's poem is analyzed as a change of the archetype. Heinrich Dörrie, concerned with the other mythical tradition most important for Western civilization, shows the indispensability of myth for the classical literature of the Greeks and Romans. Georges Dumézil compares mythic traditions in different ancient epics in order to establish an essential difference within the outraged states of mind of warrior-heroes in the *Iliad*. His comparison enables him to distinguish between the still-human "fury" on the one hand, and the diseased, rabies-like, inhuman outrage of a hybris-generated "madness" on the other hand. The two different poles of warrior-outrage shed new light on the meaning and structure of the *Iliad*. Although it concen-

trates on just one author, Kurt Weinberg's essay on Mallarmé deals
with such basic considerations that it could well have been placed
in the theoretical part of the book, had the author not stretched the
concept of myth almost to the breaking point. Weinberg demonstrates, in a most impressive way, the structure of a Mallarmé
sonnet as self-referential myth.

The third part of the book gives some insights into myth criticism
in different countries: Patricia Carden, concentrating on structuralist approaches, deals with Russian models and methods. Eva
Kushner takes French theories, mainly of Claude Lévi-Strauss, A.J.
Greimas, and R. Trousson, and shows them applied to Greek myths
in modern drama. John B. Vickery, one of the most respected ex-
perts on myth criticism, gives an overall view of the most important
Anglo-American perspectives. This essay too is of such broad scope
that it would fit equally well in the theoretical part of the book.
Klaus Weissenberger, finally, provides a comprehensive view of
German myth criticism.

E.W. Herd is correct when he warns that so-called myth criticism has at times strayed too far from literary criticism, and that it
has sometimes produced work in which the emphasis has been on
matters other than the function of myth in a work of literature.[18]
Yet it is necessary to examine mythical structures in literature not
only because "modern authors have been fascinated by the possibilities of myth and literature,"[19] but also because time and again
there has been a direct inner link between literary language and
the codes of myths and dreams.

The psychologist Erich Fromm demanded more impartial and
careful study of our dreams, which are put forward in the same
symbolic language as myths.[20] This symbolic language, he believes, is the only foreign language everyone need learn. It will
give us insights into the significant sources of wisdom, of myth,
and of our own personality. Dreams as well as myths, he holds, are
important messages that come from our inmost self, and, we may
add, myth-oriented literature is written in the same language. Progressive attempts to understand this "forgotten language" will
open up new insights not only into hidden literary structures and
forms of imagination but into human life. If it were neglected,
some of the most interesting parts of life as well as of literature
would remain misunderstood, underdeveloped, and lost.

JOSEPH STRELKA

Notes

1. Goethe's *Sämtliche Werke* (Jubiläums-Ausgabe) (Stuttgart and Berlin, 1902–7), 20:13.
2. *Mythopoesis* (Detroit, 1970).
3. *The Literary Impact of The Golden Bough* (Princeton, 1973).
4. Cf., for example, Burton Feldmann and Robert D. Richardson, eds., *The Rise of Modern Mythology* (Bloomington, 1972); Mircea Eliade, *Le mythe de l'eternal retour* (Paris, 1961); Mircea Eliade, *Myths, Dreams and Mysteries* (New York and Evanston, 1967); Joseph Campbell, *The Hero with a Thousand Faces* (Cleveland and New York, 1956); Karl Kerényi, ed., *Die Eröffnung des Zugang zum Mythos* (Darmstadt, 1967); Ernesto Grassi, *Kunst und Mythos* (Hamburg, 1957).
5. *Anatomy of Criticism* (New York, 1966), pp. 106, 134–35.
6. *Das Bild des Deutschen in der französischen und das Bild des Franzosen in der deutschen Literatur* (Bonn, 1977), p. 6.
7. René Wellek and Austin Warren, *Theory of Literature* (New York, 1956), p. 191 (italics added).
8. Ibid., p. 191.
9. Ibid., p. 191; Luc Benoist, *Signes, Symboles et Mythes* (Paris, 1975), pp. 95–112.
10. Frye, p. 54.
11. Ibid., p. 117.
12. Ibid., pp. 136–37.
13. "Die mythische Erbschaft der Dichtung," in *Dichten und Erkennen*, ed. Hannah Arendt (Zurich, 1955), pp. 239–48.
14. Richard Chase, *Quest for Myth* (Baton Rouge, 1949).
15. "The Style of the Mythical Age," in *Dichten und Erkennen*, p. 253.
16. Pierre Maranda, ed., *Mythology* (Harmondsworth-Baltimore, 1972); John B. Vickery, ed., *Myth and Literature* (Lincoln, 1966).
17. *The Burning Fountain* (Bloomington and London, 1968).
18. "Myth Criticism: Limitations and Possibilities," in *Mosaic* 2:3, pp. 69–77.
19. Ibid., p. 70.
20. *The Forgotten Language* (Chicago, 1955).

GENERAL THEORETICAL PROBLEMS

Haskell M. Block

THE MYTH OF THE ARTIST

The concept of personal myth is a commonplace of twentieth-century literary criticism. Study after study purports to deal with the myth of this or that individual writer, based on the assumption that the artist can and does create his own myth. At first glance, this concept would seem to be paradoxical and highly suspect, for most students of the subject have viewed myth as the common property of a culture or a people, with its very existence dependent on its collective character. The notion of the writer's personal myth suggests a special definition not only of myth but also of literary art. Relatively little attention has been given to the myth of the artist from the standpoint of writers who set forth the concept of personal myth or who proclaimed poetic theories and aims that moved toward this formulation. Their theoretical and sometimes programmatic statements may help us better understand not only the writer's view of his own art, but also the relation of poetic theory to artistic expression. If many twentieth-century literary critics seem to take the notion of personal myth for granted, it should be recognized that this is a relatively recent development and is the consequence of a number of important anticipations.

The notion of personal myth is essentially a Romantic attitude, attesting to the dramatic enlargement of personal consciousness in literature of the late eighteenth and early nineteenth centuries, and the refusal to accept abstract and uniformitarian views of human nature, which were attributed by the Romantics to the philosophical and critical thought of the eighteenth century. In retrospect, however, we may see that the scholars of the enlightenment who explored primitive society and religion, in their quest for the origins of modern culture, pointed the way to a recognition of the special place of myth as the groundwork of literature. As early as 1725, Vico asserted the essential unity of poetry and myth, rooted

not in rite or belief, but in the nature of language, and hence a
residual and universal property of human expression. This view
was to become of crucial importance in the following centuries,
but it had no significant impact on its own time.[1] It was the special
contribution of Herder to define for his contemporaries and successors the unity of poetry and myth and the imaginative power
inherent in myth as a symbolic expression of primal experience.[2]
Herder's approach to mythology is primarily that of the student of
early poetry and religion. While he recognized the poetic power of
Greek mythology, he saw all mythology as the source of a new
national poetry, at once sacred and patriotic.

Herder's first and perhaps most important programmatic statement of the relationship of myth to literature is his essay of 1767,
"Vom neuern Gebrauch der Mythologie."[3] Here Herder insists
that ancient mythology can serve as a source of inspiration for
modern art, provided that the modern poet employs the materials
of classical mythology not mechanically but "auf eine neue Art,"
animating the myths of the past "mit einer neuen schöpferischen,
fruchtbaren, und kunstvollen Hand."[4] Herder recognizes above all
the role of poetic transformation in giving life to myth, for scholars
are not necessarily poets, and a command of the details of ancient
mythology is no guarantee of poetry. The modern poet must not
merely transcribe or narrowly imitate an ancient model, but
should draw on myth as a basis of new and personal expression.
Herder seems to pose no limits to the freedom of the modern
poet's appropriation of ancient myth. At the same time, he admits
that capacities of invention and synthesis (Zusammensetzung)
rarely come together in the same individual, hence the great difficulty for the poet "eine ganz neue Mythologie zu schaffen."[5] It is
significant that Herder at least accepts the theoretical possibility
of the creation of new myth, and also that he sees myth-making as
a synthesizing and coalescing activity. The modern poet, he contends, should appropriate myth for his own ends and with his own
skill, "als Hausherr und Besitzer." At times Herder seems to view
myth more as a reservoir of material for the poet than an inherent
element of poetic creation, but he argues boldly and programmatically for the independence of the poet in his expression of myth,
and thereby moves significantly toward the notion of personal
myth.

Herder's assertion of the interrelatedness of poetry and myth was
markedly extended by Friedrich Schlegel.[6] In a fragment of 1799,
he insists that the essence of poety is *mythos,* and in this inherent

sense he defines all poetry as mythic.[7] In his view of contemporary poetry, however, Schlegel contends that the core of spiritual cohesion provided by mythology in ancient or medieval times is now lacking. The crucial programmatic text is the *Gespräch über die Poesie* of 1800, a direct expression of the intense speculation concerning the nature and function of myth on the part of Schlegel and his circle. The central statement of the dialogue of 1800 is the "Rede über die Mythologie," set forth by the character Ludovico, who has been equated with the philosopher Schelling.[8] According to Ludovico, the modern poet lacks a foundation that can direct him in the shaping of his art. The old mythologies have lost their imaginative power, and no new order has arisen in their place. The predicament of the modern age is summed up in a single phrase: "Wir haben keine Mythologie."[9] The most urgent task of modern poets is thus the production of a new mythology, a total synthesis of human activity in a collective and indeed infinite poem, to be shaped "aus der tiefsten Tiefe des Geistes," and to serve as the embodiment of all future poetry. In an idealistic or mystical sense, all individual poems will be manifestations of the vast cosmic poem constituted by the new mythology. It is in fact to the philosophy of idealism that Schlegel looks for the new center of collective energy that will provide poets with a large symbolic frame of reference. The new mythology will serve as a hieroglyphic expression of nature, a concrete representation of the infinite in its dynamic movement. The inner life of this mythology is "Beziehung und Verwandlung," the seizing of the active interplay of opposites as both personal and cosmic forces. The spiritual revolution of a new mythology would recover the magical and imaginative power of ancient myth of the occident or orient and would perforce issue in a new poetry appropriate to the modern age.

Implicit in Friedrich Schlegel's manifesto is the view that each age or culture creates its own mythology. Thus the Middle Ages were distinguished by "eine eigene Mythologie, aber auf die nordische gegründet."[10] The revitalization of the poetic spirit is seen by Schlegel as a collective effort, but he declares that in unusual circumstances it is possible for a supremely great poet to create a personal myth. After his urgent plea for a new mythology, Ludovico cites Dante as a model of cosmic poetry. Andrea, in extending the view of Dante as myth-maker, defines the Italian poet's achievement as the creation of a personal myth: "Gewiss ist Dante der einzige, der unter einigen begünstigenden Umständen durch eigene Riesenkraft, er selbst ganz allein, eine Art von Mythologie,

wie sie damals möglich war, erfunden und gebildet hat."[11] Clearly
this achievement is almost a miracle, yet it offers an example to
the modern poet. At least theoretically, it can be accomplished
again by an artist of similar synthesizing power.

It was the philosopher Schelling who, at about the same time as
Friedrich Schlegel, formulated the most categorical statement of
the concept of personal myth of German Romanticism. The crucial
text is the *Philosophie der Kunst;* although not published until
1859, the lectures were presented and circulated in manuscript in
the early years of the nineteenth century, and they reinforced
similar views set forth in Schelling's earlier published writings.[12]
Like Friedrich Schlegel, Schelling sees mythology as the origin
and essence of art, "die notwendige Bedingung und der erste Stoff
aller Kunst."[13] For the philosopher, the universe itself is an absolute and total work of art, whose divinity can be expressed only
symbolically. Schelling asserts a neo-Platonic parallelism between
the realm of nature and the human mind. Thus at the end of his
System des transcendentalen Idealismus, he declares: "Was wir
Natur nennen, ist ein Gedicht, das in geheimer wunderbarer
Schrift verschlossen liegt."[14] Myths are symbolic expressions of
the absolute. They constitute a symbolization of ideas in endless
process of realization. Schelling's formulation of the interdependence of myth and symbol was restated in the massive study of
Creuzer of ancient mythology and religion,[15] which in turn was to
be of major importance in shaping speculation on the nature and
function of the literary symbol in nineteenth-century France.

Art for Schelling is perforce collective and symbolic in both
origin and function, but the totality of vision of great epochs of the
past, and notably that of ancient Greece, is absent in the modern
world. Modern poetry is lacking in both largeness of substance
and wholeness of integration. Universality can be achieved only
in a poetry of cosmic synthesis. In the modern world, the highest
art is attainable only through the creation of a personal mythology:
"Universalität, die notwendige Forderung an alle Poesie, ist in
der neueren Zeit nur dem möglich, der sich aus seiner Begren-
zung selbst eine Mythologie, einen abgeschlossenen Kreis der Poesie schaffen kann."[16] Thus not only may a writer create a personal myth; he must do so if his art is to transcend the limits of his
own experience. In the hands of a great synthesizing artist, the
personal becomes the universal. Without personal mythology,
Schelling insists, there can be no great art.

For Schelling the supreme modern poets are myth-makers:

Dante, Shakespeare, Cervantes, Goethe. Dante fully exemplifies the achievement of the modern poet in creating "eine eigene Mythologie"; his figures, while taken from history, will be viewed as mythic in all time to come. The mythic dimension is a direct expression of the perspective and power of the poet. Thus Schelling adds: "Auch Shakespeare hat sich seinen eignen mythologischen Kreis geschaffen." The great poet creates his own world of consistency and wholeness, and in so doing, expresses the innermost essence of an age. Don Quixote and Sancho are "ewige Mythen," and Goethe's as yet only partially published *Faust* is "ein wahrhaft mythologisches Gedicht." Schelling goes even farther than Friedrich Schlegel in asserting the freedom of the myth-making artist and the necessity of personal myth: "Jedes wahrhaft schöpferische Individuum hat sich selbst seine Mythologie zu schaffen, und es kann dies, aus welchem Stoff es nur immer will, geschehen."[17] His freedom is absolute, subject only to the condition of endowing his myth with "ein unabhängiges poetisches Leben."

In his late writings Schelling seemed to despair of the creation of a new mythology and of the creation of great art in the modern world, and suggested that the mythic dimension of art has vanished forever.[18] In his earlier writings, however, the notion of personal myth was central to the philosopher's view of the nature of poetry and the function of the poet. Some of Schelling's readers felt that he had abused the notion of myth,[19] and even at the very time he set forth his position, it was vigorously attacked by August Wilhelm Schlegel in his Berlin lectures. Schlegel agreed with Schelling in viewing myth as a collective and unconscious fiction, but insisted that this could not be the work of a single person.[20] Thus Schlegel contended that Milton's *Paradise Lost* suffers from the effort of the poet to impose a private myth in the composition of the poem. It is impossible, Schlegel argued, "eine gültige Mythologie willkührlich zu stiften, da diese nur eine unabsichtliche allmählige Dichtung einer Nation, eines Zeitalters seyn kann."[21] No poet, according to this view, can create his own mythology.

Subsequent German speculation on the nature of myth is closer to A.W. Schlegel than to Schelling, even though Schelling's analysis of the myth-making imagination is a striking anticipation of twentieth-century views. Both critics agree on the essentially symbolic character of artistic expression as the representation of the infinite in the finite, and both point clearly to the formulation of myth that we find in Wagner and Nietzsche, and which the latter in turn transmitted to the twentieth century. Like his Romantic predecessors, Wagner sees myth at the center of artistic creation, but the artist is at best a mediator between art and the archetypal myth. Wagner's programmatic effort to recover the conditions underlying the creation of Greek art in no way depends on Greek mythology. As Theodore Ziolkowski has pointed out, Wagner is the primary source of the German transformation of the concept of *mythos* from "Göttererzählung primitiver Völker" to "bildhafte lebenerneuende Idee."[22] *Mythos* for Wagner constitutes elemental and eternal truth; it is the source of cultural vitality, unity, and organicity, and determines the form of art of a given epoch. Nowhere does Wagner assert the notion of personal myth. Since myth is necessarily common to a whole people, it cannot be the arbitrary creation of any individual artist. In "Eine Mitteilung an meine Freunde" (1851), Wagner admits the right of the poet to transpose mythical material in his own way, but the creation of art must properly be viewed as that of a whole people: "das Volk selbst dichtete, als es eben noch Dichter und Mythenschöpfer war."[23]

Nietzsche was to extend this view of myth to a sweeping indictment of modern culture. Indeed, for Nietzsche, the very investigations in such fields as psychology, the history of religion, ethnology, and folklore, which sought to systematize and explain the universal presence of myth, were in fact an assault on the dynamic power of *mythos* as a spiritual force in modern life.[24] In *Die Geburt der Tragödie,* Nietzsche argues that abstraction and rationality have displaced the mythical foundation of experience, leaving man homeless and rootless:

> Und nun steht der mythenlose Mensch, ewig hungernd, unter allen Vergangenheiten und sucht grabend und wühlend nach Wurzeln.... Worauf weist das ungeheure historische Bedürfnis der unbefriedigten modernen Kultur... wenn nicht auf den Verlust des Mythus, auf den Verlust der mythischen Heimat, des mythischen Mutterschosses?[25]

The recovery of a living relationship between the individual and his culture is possible only through a collective transformation that will accomplish a rebirth of the German *mythos.* For Nietzsche, no individual solution is possible in the face of the fragmentation and alienation of modern man.

Nietzsche's searching critique of modern life and his insistence on the totality of the relationship between an individual and his culture gave a new importance to myth as the expression of collective, archetypal, and unconscious values. The Nietzschean perspective is dominant in twentieth-century German views of myth. It is central to the reflections on myth of Thomas Mann, even though the novelist developed his attitudes at a relatively late stage of his career,[26] chiefly in connection with the composition of the *Joseph* tetralogy. However, Mann's interest in comparative mythology and the relationship of myth to fiction entered into his early development as well, and it grew with the passage of time.[27] His consciousness of the role of myth in his own art is perhaps most strikingly formulated in a passage added in 1919 to his essay of 1910, "Der alte Fontane." Here Mann defines the creation of fiction as the opposition and interplay of "Mythus und Psychologie," myth as a conservative and traditional force, psychology as an instrument of democratic enlightenment.[28] André von Gronicka has sensitively examined the fictional expression of these elements in Mann's art.[29]

For Mann, the symbolic and monumental values of art depend on a mythic ordering of experience. In his essay "Freud und die Zukunft" (1936), which he might have entitled "Freud und der Mythos," Mann discusses the creation of the *Joseph* novels as a way of clarifying the interplay of tradition and originality. Some artists are myth-oriented and others are not, but the mythic elements of a writer's art are, he insists, extrapersonal and unconscious, even though the writer may view them as personal and unique. For Mann, it is not possible for the artist to create myth, but he may revitalize it in his own way. The mythic perspective can thus become subjective and can view itself as a fresh and personal restatement of collective and unconscious experience. To be sure, this mythic perspective is to some extent an expression of choice on the part of "der mythisch orientierte Erzähler," but as the work of Freud demonstrates for Mann, this perspective is in no way limited to writers of fiction. In his discussions of myth with the historian of religion Karl Kerényi, as in the essay on Freud, Mann describes his own development as marked by "den Schritt vom Bürgerlich-Individuellen zum Mythisch-Typischen."[30] This distinction is developed by Mann in a lecture of 1942 on the *Joseph* novels, in which he sees the mythical as already present in the typical and elemental experiences of life, deriving its form from timeless and recurrent situations that are collective and unconscious.[31] The mythical dimension is thus a constant in human experience, but the artist, through his use of tradition, can willfully develop and cultivate the "mythisch-typische Anschauungsweise." Mythic styliza-

tion is thus a consequence of the writer's act of choice. His essential
task, "die Erfüllung der Tradition mit aufregender Neuigkeit," demands the interplay of tradition and originality. The constants of
human experience must reemerge as a personal synthesis if the
writer is to create living art. In this restricted but no less definite
sense, Mann reasserts the role of the artist as myth-maker and
admits of a large if not exclusive place to the artist's subjective
processes.

Mythopoesis in twentieth-century literature and criticism has
been dominated directly or indirectly by the German Romantics
and their spiritual descendants, but the notion of personal myth
was also set forth in England and France, generally in a context
less philosophical than in Germany, and more intimately related
to the poet's view of his own art. In nineteenth-century France it
was Victor Hugo's work that most significantly asserted the mythic
character of poetry,[32] but Hugo did not himself formulate the notion of personal myth, even though twentieth-century critics have
often interpreted his art in this perspective. Hugo, like virtually
all the French poets of his time, was keenly aware of the rich
tradition of mythological speculation in late eighteenth- and early
nineteenth-century France, which even before Creuzer, as in the
Illuminist doctrine of Saint-Martin, fused the notions of symbol
and myth.[33]

Ballanche's epic prose-poem, *Orphée* (1829), reflects his assimilation of Vico's triadic pattern of history as well as concepts of myth
prefigured in Herder, Schelling, and Creuzer. 1830 is indeed an
early date for reference to these writers in France.[34] *Orphée* is in no
way a restatement of narrative events associated with the archetypal poet. Ballanche views Orpheus solely as a symbolic representation of myth: "J'ai dû prendre les mythes pour des mythes, tout en
rendant à ce mot son acception primitive, qui est emblême de la
vérité."[35] The fable of the poem, Ballanche insists, is wholly his
own invention. Perhaps the only function of the title is to call attention to the mythic and prophetic rather than descriptive character of
the poem. In subsequent comments on his panoramic account of
cosmic history, Ballanche insists that traditional narrative would
not have enabled him to present the constrasting characteristics of
the human race and their religious implications: "J'ai dû faire un
mythe."[36] In *Orphée*, the recurrent pattern of action is the killing of
the initiator by the initiated. The crucifixion of Christ is set within
the contrast of parallels drawn from ancient myths. In functioning
as speculative anthropologist and historian of religion in his poem,

Ballanche declares: "Je n'ai point dissimulé que j'avais en quelque sorte inventé un mythe, toutefois comme on invente une telle chose, c'est-à-dire en pénétrant le plus possible dans les entrailles même des croyances."[37] Ballanche describes his "poëme antique" as a personal myth by way of insisting on the uniqueness and originality of his work, but it is clear that despite its curious mixture of cosmic history and prophecy, *Orphée* is more akin to traditional myth than Ballanche was willing to allow. For Ballanche as for other Romantics, myth embodies a vast synthesis of human experience, "une histoire condensée et pour ainsi dire algébrique."[38] He adds that each generation must create its own epic poetry and thereby make its contribution to a vast collective "mythe de l'humanité." Personal myth in this sense is a contribution to the universal poem created in time and space by the poets of all ages.

Ballanche's assertion of the poetic and prophetic values of his personal myth is unusual in nineteenth-century France. The symbolists were keenly aware of Victor Hugo's sustained preoccupation with myth and the synthesizing power of his poetry, but their theoretical formulations emphasize the mythic as typical rather than personal. All the same, in recent criticism, Nerval, Baudelaire, Mallarmé, and their followers have all come to be viewed as creators of personal myth. A representative statement is that of Marie-Jeanne Durry on Nerval: "Il va vers les mythes les plus variés, historiques, géographiques, légendaires, et il leur ôte leurs caractères historiques, géographiques: il les fait invinciblement aboutir à son mythe personnel."[39] It must be added, however, that the notion of "mythe personnel" does not seem to enter consciously into the poet's view of his own work.

Baudelaire and Mallarmé were both deeply preoccupied with the concept of myth. In keeping with the long tradition of symbolic interpretation in France, Baudelaire declared in his essay on Théodore de Banville (1861), "La mythologie est un dictionnaire d'hiéroglyphes vivants."[40] His view of the subject underwent considerable change, from his early conception of myth as a reservoir of allegories and ornaments, to his later notion of myth as a vast symbolic dictionary embodying collective and archetypal experience.[41] The impact of Wagner is particularly evident in Baudelaire's insistence that myth is the spontaneous and anonymous creation of a whole people.

Mallarmé's conception of myth was similar to Baudelaire's, but it received much fuller elaboration in the course of the poet's career.[42] As early as 1871 Mallarmé conceived the project of a

"livre de mythologie" and in 1880 published *Les Dieux antiques,*
an adaptation of a manual of mythology by George William Cox,
which was itself based on contemporary German scholarship.
Mallarmé seems to have been familiar with Max Müller's theory of
solar myths and with his view of the inherently mythic character
of language. For Mallarmé, the mythology of *Les Dieux antiques*
constitutes a vast poem of nature, condensing the impulses and
experiences that animate the modern poet.[43] All poetry is but a
fragment or a reflection of the cosmic poem to which Mallarmé
gave the name of "le Livre." Myth as a universal constant is the
eternal subject of "le Livre." It is not subject to individual creation, but each true poet perforce expresses its mystery and purity
in his art. Mallarmé's glorification of myth as "la matière éternelle
du poème" was transmitted to his symbolist disciples, who were
keenly attracted to the ambiguity and polyvalence of myths, to the
point where mythical configurations sometimes lost any semblance of traditional value. The poets of the young symbolist generation employed myth freely as a definition of both personal and
universal experience.[44]

For readers of English poetry, the preeminent myth-making artists are William Blake and W.B. Yeats, and it is in large part through
them and their interpreters that the concept of personal myth has
gained widespread diffusion. Blake's visionary and prophetic writings constitute an implicit assertion of a poetics of personal myth.
The "unwritten poetics"—to use Renato Poggioli's phrase—of
Blake's art are boldly subjective and individualistic. We may see
Blake speaking through Los in *Jerusalem* in declaring:

> I must Create a System or be enslav'd by another Man's.
> I will not Reason & Compare: my business is to Create.[45]

What we may view as Blake's "system" is a total explanation of
cosmic experience, for which "vision" or "myth" would be a more
appropriate term. Blake was sharply critical of any mode of abstract symbolization. Ancient myth he saw as originally poetic but
degraded through codification.[46] His own art, as he describes it in
the Notebook of 1810 to "A Vision of the Last Judgment," is an
effort to recapture the imaginative power of primal poetry:

> Let it here be Noted that the Greek Fables originated in Spir-
> itual Mystery & Real Visions, which are lost & clouded in
> Fable & Allegory.... The Nature of my Work is Visionary or
> Imaginative; it is an Endeavor to Restore what the Ancients
> call'd the Golden Age.[47]

Like many other modern poets, Blake urges a recovery of the values present in the origins of pagan art rather than a mere restatement of classical mythology. As he declares in the "Preface" to *Milton:* "We do not want either Greek or Roman models if we are but just and true to our own Imaginations."[48] His view of the debasement of ancient myth through allegorization underlies his assertion of a personal mythology.

Nineteenth-century editors and critics of Blake's poetry drew repeated attention to the privacy of his mythology. In the preface to his edition of *Songs of Innocence and Experience* (1839), James Wilkinson regretted that Blake rejected the traditional symbolism of Christianity for "the loose garments of Typical or even Mythologic Representation." He described Blake's poetic method as marked by privacy and radical subjectivity: "Copying the outward form of the Past, he has delivered to us a multitude of new Hieroglyphics."[49] Later commentators restated this view of the poet as myth-maker in a more favorable light. Thus R.H. Hutton declared in 1863 that Blake at times combines the "mysterious depth of Wordsworth with the grand symbolism of the primeval world," and Swinburne, in his important study of 1868, saw Blake's mythology as the body of the poet's mystical soul, the form assumed by his faith. The reading of Blake, he insisted, demands a special perspective on the part of the reader, a receptivity to "the curious habit of direct mythical metaphor or figure peculiar to Blake."[50] Swinburne saw this habit as the source of private symbolism and deep obscurity in Blake's poetry: "Blake was not incapable of mixing the Hellenic, the Miltonic, and the Celtic mythologies into one drugged and adulterated compound."[51] Ultimately this peculiarity constituted for Swinburne a crucial weakness in Blake's art. Subsequent readers of Blake, including Yeats, were also to contend that Blake's personal myth owed much to a variety of traditional mythologies, but viewed this syncretism in an altogether favorable light.

While Blake is unusual among the English Romantic poets in his bold expression of a personal myth, a deep awareness of mythical values in poetry is common to the major English poets of his time.[52] Wordsworth in *The Excursion,* especially in Book Four, proclaims the vitality of myth in the language of poetic idealism.[53] Coleridge was probably aware of Schelling's concept of myth, but did not give it the special importance it held for the German philosopher.[54] As Yeats was to recognize, among the English Romantics Shelley is the closest to Blake's position. In "A

Defence of Poetry" Shelley views myth as an essential element
of epic poetry, capable at its best of a large and unified panorama
of events, reflecting both the shaping art of the poet and the life
and culture of his time: "The Divina Commedia and Paradise
Lost have conferred upon modern mythology a systematic
form."[55] The supremely great poet, according to Shelley, gives
vitality and order to the myths of his particular time and place.
For poets at the end of the nineteenth century, Shelley reinforced the image of the poet as myth-maker derived mainly from
the example of Blake.

Both in his poetry and his literary criticism, Yeats expressed his
deep preoccupation with the relationship of poetry and myth. His
many writings on Blake are a key to his own artistic direction as
well as an illumination of Blake's work. It is not possible to separate Yeats the critic from Yeats the poet; the two activities are so
intimately interrelated that we can see the writer at every phase of
his career redefining the principles of his own art even while
interpreting the work of others or exploring large questions of the
nature and function of literature.

The edition of Blake published by Edwin Ellis and W.B. Yeats
in 1893 is by present day standards idiosyncratic and uneven, but
its contribution to the understanding and appreciation of Blake at
the turn of the century was immense.[56] Blake's impact on Yeats is
no less important. Yeats's mythical transformation of his predeces-
sor is unmistakable in his contention that Blake was of Irish descent and a member of the order of the Golden Dawn.[57] The
"Memoir" in the first volume of the edition, evidently written by
Ellis but with the active collaboration of Yeats, connects Blake's
allegedly Irish origins with the notion of personal myth as well as
with Irish mythical tradition:

> The very manner of Blake's writing has an Irish flavour, a lofty
> extravagance of invention and epithet, . . . and his mythology
> brings often to mind the tumultuous vastness of the ancient
> tales of god and demon that have come to us from the dawn of
> mystic tradition in what may fairly be called his fatherland.[58]

These remarks on old Irish myth may help us understand Yeats's
view of his own art as well as the alleged parallel of ancient myth
and the prophetic writings of Blake. Yeats developed the mythic
view of Blake's art at some length in his account of Blake's "symbolic system," included in the first volume of the edition. In a
note of 1900, Yeats indicated that the greater part of this section of

the edition is his writing.[59] Here Blake is assimilated fully into a framework of symbolist poetics, with its correspondent vision and its assertion of the world as a vast hieroglyphic dictionary, which the poet deciphers in his art. Yeats insists on the consistency and intelligibility of Blake's "system." The Prophetic Books, Yeats contends, are "records of one great Myth," whose fragments and images are tied together in a continuous pattern.[60] It is through the interrelation and synthesis of the elements of his cosmic vision that Blake defines himself as a myth-making poet:

> It is the charm of mythic narrative that it cannot tell one thing without telling a hundred others. The symbols are an end-lessly inter-marrying family. They give life to what, stated in general terms, appears only a cold truism, by hinting how the apparent simplicity of the statement is due to an artificial iso-lation of a fragment, which, in its natural place, is connected with all the infinity of truths by living fibres.[61]

The aim of Yeats's commentary on Blake is precisely that of en-abling the reader to translate Blake's personal myth into an intelli-gible imaginative order. Yeats contends that with the aid of his interpretations, the reader can himself arrive at a grasp of the coherence of Blake's art.

Underlying this approach to Blake is Yeats's conviction that Blake's work expresses a completely elaborated mystical system. In his essay of 1897, "William Blake and the Imagination," Yeats defines Blake's system as a personal myth: "He was a symbolist who had to invent his symbols; . . . He was a man crying out for a mythology, and trying to make one because he could not find one to his hand."[62] Blake's subjectivity and obscurity are explained by Yeats as the consequence of the inability of the poet's culture to provide fit models for his art. In other times and places such a writer would have been far less obscure "because a traditional mythology stood on the threshold of his meaning and on the margin of his sacred darkness." Clearly Yeats's view of the poet bereft of myth and hence of an organizing center for his art corre-sponds closely to Nietzsche's diagnosis of the predicament of modern man generally, and it is quite possible that Nietzsche's radically subjective view of experience had a direct impact on Yeats's concept of a personal myth.[63] Yeats was to remark in a letter of 1902 to Lady Gregory, "Nietzsche completes Blake and has the same roots."[64] The essay of 1897, giving full and an-guished expression to the necessity of personal myth, has been frequently reprinted; it is probably the principal source of the idea of the poet as myth-maker in twentieth-century English and American criticism.

The mediation between the claims of traditional and personal myth defines Yeats's poetic strategy throughout the whole of his career. The young poet was deeply disturbed by his sense of fragmentation and disorder. Late in life he set forth the injunction by which he sought to guide his literary art: "Hammer your thoughts into unity."[65] His concern with Irish myth and his sustained study of Irish popular tradition and legend attest to his deliberate search for an "inherited subject-matter known to the whole people" in which might reside "something called 'Unity of Being.' "[66] This programmatic search for a mythology was carried out by Yeats with a direct view to poetic practice. He declared in a letter of 1899: "I have worked at Irish mythology and filled a great many pages of notes with a certain arrangement of it for my own purposes; and now I have a rich background for whatever I want to do and endless symbols to my hands."[67] Irish myth provided the poet not only with the substance of much of his poetry and drama but also with a rich pattern of correspondences between mythic and individual experience. Through such symbols the poet gives utterance to the racial or collective memory in which resides the primal unity of a people. In this way the modern poet can overcome the besetting forces of rootlessness and subjectivity around him. In his essay of 1900, "The Philosophy of Shelley's Poetry," Yeats develops the notion "that our little memories are but a part of some great Memory that renews the world and men's thoughts age after age."[68] Individualistic and highly subjective art must seize on ancient and polyvalent symbols if it is to approach universal value. Increasingly Yeats came to see that the privacy of "the great myth-makers and mask-makers" is purchased at a very high price. Poets like Blake, he declares in his *Autobiographies,* "have imitators, but create no universal language."[69] Similarly he came to feel that the doctrines and art of the symbolist poets encourage the creation of symbols out of the poet's imagination, without any root or support in traditional and collective truths. Like many of his contemporaries, Yeats viewed the symbol as the center of poetic expression, but insisted that the symbol cannot be gratuitous or locked within a wholly subjective mind.

The central problem of the modern poet as Yeats defines it is that of reconciling the conflicting claims of tradition and innovation, of authority and individual freedom. The distinction he makes in a letter of 1901 between objective and subjective myth should be viewed in this context. In warning Fiona Macleod of the dangers of excessive expression of personality in fiction, Yeats declares, "In your simplest prose, the myths stand out clearly, as something objective, as something well born and independent. In your more elaborate prose they seem subjective, an inner way of looking at things assumed by a single mind."[70] Yeats admits of the validity of personality in art only to the extent that personal emotion is "woven into a general pattern of myth and symbol."[71] On occasion Yeats could express an impersonal theory of art as thoroughgoing as that of Flaubert,[72] but in less categorical terms he sees his own art as an embodiment of the interpenetration of the personal and the universal.

It is this interplay which Yeats extols in his explanation of the mystical system set forth in *A Vision*. In the foreword to the 1925 edition, he declares: "I wished for a system of thought that would leave my imagination free to create as it chose and yet make all that it created, or could create, part of the one history, and that the soul's."[73] While Yeats points to the Greeks, Dante, Swedenborg, and Blake for examples of similar elaborations, it is clear that *A Vision* must be viewed within the context of personal myth, as a revelation of secret and private knowledge of universal truth.[74] In his preface, Yeats insists on the originality of his vast systematization of human history and destiny: "I am the first to substitute for Biblical or mythological figures, historical movements and actual men and women."[75] Yet despite their historicity, Yeats's examples take on an essentially fictive and symbolic character in his myth. His effort to guarantee their validity as part of the communal "great mind and great memory" does not alter in any essential way the dependence of *A Vision* on the poet's myth-making imagination. Yeats's reader may regard *A Vision* as a wholly representative expression of Phase Sixteen of Yeats's system, in which he locates William Blake and which "has no thought but in myth, or in defence of myth."[76] This phase is closely akin to Phase Twenty-Three, whose adherents are similarly tormented by the pressures of subjectivity. Yeats's examples here are such major twentieth-century writers as Pound, Eliot, Joyce, and Pirandello. Their work testifies to the total separation of myth and fact, to the point "that man understands for the first time the rigidity of fact, and calls up, by that very recognition, myth—the Mask—which now but gropes its way out of the mind's dark but will shortly pursue and terrify."[77] Yeats deleted this judgment of modern literature from the edition of *A Vision* of

1938, but in that work as well it is clear that he considers the major poetic accomplishments of the age as marked by a total absence of unity and order. The anarchy of twentieth-century culture is the groundwork of personal myth.

All of Yeats's work may be viewed as an effort to restore to literature the living power of myth.[78] According to Yeats, myth that is wholly personal may and indeed must arise in certain cultural situations, but ideally myth should be both personal and traditional, at once a center of imaginative energy and spiritual revelation. The poet is prophet and mage, recreating universal truths in a language expressive of both personal and collective values. Yeats's keen awareness of the claims on the modern poet of personal myth is accompanied by a deeply felt realization of the paradoxical and contradictory character of this notion. Ultimately Yeats came to place primary emphasis on the traditional and collective elements of myth rather than on their subjective appropriation. In his longing for cosmic wholeness, for a total synthesis of the history and destiny of man and his universe, Yeats represents the modern artist animated and driven by the quest for myth.

Yeats's effort to define the nature and function of myth in literature was taken up by many of his younger contemporaries. Perhaps the most influential formulation of its time was that of T.S. Eliot in the 1923 essay on Joyce entitled "Ulysses, Order and Myth."[79] Here Eliot contends that Joyce in *Ulysses* has created a new art through mythic transposition, and he declares programmatically: "In using the myth, in manipulating a continuous parallel between contemporaneity and antiquity, Mr. Joyce is pursuing a method which others must pursue after him."[80] Eliot's account of "the mythical method" is close to the older view of myth as a thematic repository, and the "continuous parallel" would seem nearer to allegory than to myth. William Righter is altogether correct in viewing Eliot's "mythical method" as "little more than a figure of speech."[81] Nevertheless, in 1923 Eliot claimed that "the mythical method" can offer a response to the absence of a center of order and significance in modern life. It would seem, however, that Eliot is more concerned with the use of myth than with the creation of myth through literature. In a postscript of 1964, Eliot admits that in some details his essay of 1923 is naive; all the same, at that time it was an influential statement on behalf of the shaping and directing power of myth in art that reinforced the role of the artist as myth-maker. The manipulation of the continuous parallel that Eliot describes in *Ulysses* is perforce the work of the individual writer, who reshapes the myth as he recreates it in his art. Eliot's view of myth emerges as yet one more statement of the necessary interplay of tradition and originality.

The formulation and expression of myth in Eliot's criticism and poetry had a marked impact on the younger writers of his time, most strikingly perhaps in the work of the American poet Hart Crane. Much of Crane's reflection on his art can be viewed as a sustained dialogue with Eliot in the light of twentieth-century American experience. The consciousness of the mythical dimension of art permeates Crane's poetry. In his essay of 1925, "General Aims and Theories," Crane declares of one of his major compositions: "When I started writing 'Faustus and Helen' it was my intention to embody in modern terms (words, symbols, metaphors) a contemporary approximation to an ancient human culture or mythology."[82] The deliberate parallels between ancient myth and the circumstances of his poem reflect Crane's awareness of Eliot's "mythical method." For Crane, as for Eliot, the modern world is devoid of myth. The turbulent and disordered life of the present "has no formulated mythology yet for classic poetic reference or for religious exploitation." The poet must therefore provide his own myth. He does so, Crane contends, through a language at once autonomous and seemingly illogical, grounded on a "logic of metaphor" that creates its own dynamic movement.[83] Blake is an important antecedent for Crane's approach to his art. In Crane's poetry, myth is itself a recurrent theme, associated with both spatial and temporal movement, with openness, radiance, and joy. In "The Visible the Untrue," the poet looks to the creation of a new wholeness in his art:

> The silver strophe . . . the canto
> bright with myth. . . .[84]

Crane's most ambitious poem, "The Bridge," is replete with similar allusions. The whole poem for Crane is a celebration of "that great Bridge, or Myth." In a letter to Otto Kahn of September 1927, Crane describes his poem as "a symphony with an epic theme," a re-creation of "the Myth of America."[85] In his theories as well as in his epic poem, Crane invokes the precedent of Walt Whitman as a model for the fusion of the disparities of American life "into a universal vision."[86] For Crane, the poet must come to terms with the enormous variety and disorder of modern life. Poetry, he insists, must "absorb the machine, i.e., *acclimatize* it" naturally and casually if the poet is to fulfill his function. The achieved synthesis of experience into an ordered vision, at once history and prophecy, constitutes the poet's myth. Crane made large claims for "The Bridge," but in retrospect we may regard his lyric poems as even more powerful assertions of his art. A poet of "the broken world," his best poetry imposes a passionate assertion of value amid the fragmentation of modern life. The notion of the poet as myth-maker and the imperatives of a personal myth are writ large in the astonishing achievement of Crane's major poems.

One could extend considerably the account of twentieth-century literature attesting to the widespread and powerful force of personal myth, particularly in the novel.[87] The most striking achievement, however, transcends all traditional notions of genre: Joyce's *Finnegans Wake*, a cosmic dream at once almost hermetically private and archetypal, grounded in the polyvalence and ambiguity of words, the interplay of languages, and the recurrent processes of human experience. The programmatic assertions as well as the literary art of our time have facilitated the dissemination of the notion of personal myth. In English and American criticism, studies of the individual writer as myth-maker appear with increasing frequency, sometimes marked by a solipsistic conception of private myth that sees the world view of one writer as totally incommensurate with that of anyone else. In France the psychoanalytic approach of Charles Mauron, as defined in his book *Des métaphores obsédantes au mythe personnel* (1963), issues in a sharp distinction between collective and personal myth. Mauron's textual analyses are of individual schematizations that reflect the unique unconscious experience of each writer as expressed in patterns of obsessive images. Myth for Mauron is the image of the unconscious personality. Each writer perforce creates his own myth, objectively definable.

The formulations of the relationship of myth to literature that we have examined express a variety of perspectives. For some writers, myth is inherent in language: to create imaginative literature is to reassert the vitality of myth. For others, myth is essentially collective and archetypal, although a recent survey of myth-oriented criticism suggests that the "collective mysticism" of nineteenth-century formulations is thoroughly discredited.[88] A balanced view must take account of the interplay of tradition and originality present in any significant work of art. It has been forcefully argued that a private myth "cannot but be a contradiction in terms; and Blake's prophetic books and Yeats's *Vision* ought properly to be labelled pseudomyths."[89] As we have seen, however, writers themselves have insisted on the validity of their own consciousness of myth and their capacity for the creation of myth. The notion of personal myth need not depend on the assumption of *tabula rasa*.[90] Even the most seemingly private of writers will embody large traditional elements in their art. "Personal myth" must be viewed as a matter of degree, the reflection of an emphasis rather than an absolute. There is after all no inherent reason why seemingly private and public—or personal and traditional—myths may not intersect in the same artistic configuration. Even the most traditional classical myth can become personal through individual modification. Varying degrees of individualism may find expression in this process. At the extremes of privacy, personal myth may be seen as a demythologizing of literature.

Roland Barthes has convincingly argued that the creation of an artificial myth, as in *Bouvard et Pécuchet,* is a rejection of literature as a mythical system, "un meurtre de la Littérature comme signification."[91] Myth thus turning in on itself is a reconstitution with its own means of demystification and is in this sense a countermythical work. All assertions of personal myth imply a break with tradition and with a view of art as progressive and cumulative experience. The arbitrary character of personal myth must seem coarse and even chaotic to a scientifically minded investigator. In its extreme form it may be esoteric, private, even solipsistic. It frequently manifests a high degree of self-reflexiveness and abstraction. The literature of personal myth moves perforce toward coterie literature, yet its arbitrariness is fundamentally no different from that of language itself.

Language, to say nothing of themes, forms, and structures, is common property; it is the groundwork of the life of literature. Myth-making is an inherent human need.[92] The notion of personal myth is a modern restatement of the urge toward coherence, synthesis, and generalizing power that has been the property of all literature. As such, it has been a significant incentive for the writer in quest of an organizing center to his art. The achievements of the writers at hand are impressive validations of their claims.

Notes

1. René Wellek, *A History of Modern Criticism* (New Haven, 1955), 1:135–36.
2. See Fritz Strich, *Die Mythologie in der deutschen Literatur* (Halle, 1910), 1:118.
3. Reprinted in Herder, *Sämmtliche Werke*, ed. Bernhard Suphan (Berlin, 1877), 1:426–49.
4. Ibid., 1:428–29.
5. Ibid., 1:444.
6. See Wolff A. von Schmidt, "Mythologie und Uroffenbarung bei Herder und Friedrich Schlegel," *Zeitschrift für Religions- und Geistesgeschichte* 25 (1973):32–45. For a fuller discussion of German Romantic concepts of myth, see the works of Strich and Wellek cited above, and the illuminating survey of Klaus Ziegler, "Mythos und Dichtung," in Werner Kohlschmidt and Wolfgang Mohr, eds., *Reallexikon der deutschen Literaturgeschichte* (Berlin, 1965): 2:569–84.
7. Friedrich Schlegel, *Literary Notebooks, 1797–1801* (Toronto, 1957), Fragment No. 1574, p. 159.
8. Strich, 2:48.
9. Friedrich Schlegel, *Kritische Schriften* (Munich, 1956), p. 307.
10. Friedrich Schlegel, *Literary Notebooks, 1797–1801*, Fragment No. 2146, p. 213.
11. Friedrich Schlegel, *Kritische Schriften*, pp. 316–17.
12. Cf. Jean Gibelin, *L'Esthétique de Schelling* (Paris, 1934).
13. Schelling, *Sämmtliche Werke* (Stuttgart, 1859), 5:405.
14. Ibid., 3:628.
15. Cf. Jacques Matter, *Schelling* (Paris, 1845), pp. 172–73.
16. Schelling, 5:444.
17. Ibid., 5:445–46.
18. See Jochem Hennigfeld, *Mythos und Poesie* (Meisenheim am Glan, 1973), pp. 131–32.
19. Cf. Gibelin, p. 105.
20. Cf. Wellek, 2:44.
21. A.W. Schlegel, *Vorlesungen über schöne Literatur und Kunst* (Heilbronn, 1884), 2:206.
22. "Der Hunger nach dem Mythos," in Reinhold Grimm and Jost Hermand, eds., *Die sogenannten zwanziger Jahre* (Bad Homburg, 1970), pp. 176–77.
23. Cited in Anni Carlsson, "Das mythische Wahnbild Richard Wagners," *Deutsche Vierteljahrsschrift für Literaturwissenschaft und Geistesgeschichte* 29 (1955):250. Cf. Erich Ruprecht, *Der Mythos bei Wagner und Nietzsche* (Berlin, 1938), p. 21.
24. Ziolkowski, p. 184.
25. *Werke* (Munich, 1954), 1:125. For Nietzsche's concept of *mythos*, see Ruprecht, pp. 64–81.
26. Cf. T.J. Reed, *Thomas Mann: The Uses of Tradition* (Oxford, 1974), pp. 317–59.
27. See Herbert Lehnert, "Thomas Mann's Early Interest in Myth and Erwin Rohde's *Psyche*," *PMLA* 79 (1964):297–304.

28. Mann, *Adel des Geistes* (Stockholm, 1948), p. 558. Cf. Reed, p. 329; also, Thomas Mann-Karl Kerényi, *Gespräch in Briefen* (Zürich, 1960), pp. 97–98.
29. André von Gronicka, " 'Myth Plus Psychology': A Style Analysis of *Death in Venice*," *Germanic Review* 31 (1956):191–205.
30. Mann, *Adel des Geistes*, p. 578; Mann-Kerényi, p. 41.
31. Mann, *Neue Studien* (Frankfurt am Main, 1948), p. 162.
32. See Pierre Albouy, *La création mythologique chez Victor Hugo* (Paris, 1963).
33. Ibid., p. 38.
34. See Ballanche, *Œuvres* (Paris, 1830), 4:35, 51. Herder is cited in *Essais de Palingénésie sociale* (Paris, 1827), 1:125.
35. *Œuvres*, 1:68.
36. Ibid., 4:12.
37. Ibid., 4:55, cited in Albouy, p. 49.
38. *Œuvres*, 4:6.
39. Marie-Jeanne Durry, *Gérard de Nerval et le mythe* (Paris, 1956), p. 102.
40. Baudelaire, *Critique littéraire et musicale* (Paris, 1961), p. 312.
41. See Yoshio Abé, "Baudelaire et la mythologie," *French Studies* 25 (1971): 281–94.
42. See Pierre Renauld, "Mallarmé et le mythe," *Revue d'histoire littéraire de la France* 73 (1973):48–68.
43. Mallarmé, *Œuvres complètes* (Paris, 1956), p. 1168, cited in Renauld, p. 57.
44. See Pierre Brunel, "L' 'au-delà' et l' 'en-deçà': place et fonction des mythes dans la littérature symboliste," *Neohelicon* 2 (1974):11–29.
45. Cited in Hazard Adams, *Blake and Yeats* (Ithaca, 1955), p. 124.
46. See Albert J. Kuhn, "Blake on the Nature and Origins of Pagan Gods and Myths," *MLN* 72 (1957):563–72.
47. Blake, *The Complete Writings*, ed. Geoffrey Keynes (New York, 1957), p. 605.
48. Ibid., p. 480.
49. Cited in Deborah Dorfman, *Blake in the Nineteenth Century* (New Haven, 1969), p. 50.
50. Swinburne, *William Blake* (London, 1868), p. 101.
51. Ibid., p. 192.
52. See M.H. Abrams, *The Mirror and the Lamp* (New York, 1953), pp. 290–97. For a broad survey of mythical values in Romantic and modern English and American writers, see Kimon Friar, "Myth and Metaphysics," in Kimon Friar and John Malcolm Brinnin, eds., *Modern Poetry* (New York, 1951), pp. 421–43.
53. Douglas Bush, *Mythology and the Romantic Tradition in English Poetry* (Cambridge, Mass., 1937), p. 60.
54. See Wellek, 2:175. For the function of myth in Coleridge, see I.A. Richards, *Coleridge on Imagination* (New York, 1935), pp. 164–86.
55. Shelley, *Critical Prose* (Lincoln, 1967), p. 25.
56. See Dorfman, p. 192.
57. Adams, pp. 46–47; Richard Ellmann, *W.B. Yeats* (New York, 1948), pp. 116–17.
58. Blake, *Works* (London, 1893), 1:3–4.
59. See Adams, pp. 47–48.
60. Blake, *Works*, 1:370, 381.
61. Ibid., 1:382–83.
62. *Essays and Introductions* (London, 1961), p. 114.
63. See Richard Ellmann, *The Identity of Yeats* (London, 1954), pp. 94–95.
64. *Letters* (London, 1954), p. 379.

65. *If I Were Four-and-Twenty* (Dublin, 1940), p. 1, cited in Ellmann, *W.B. Yeats,* p. 237.
66. Yeats, *Autobiographies* (London, 1955), p. 190.
67. *Letters,* p. 322.
68. *Essays and Introductions,* p. 79.
69. P. 550.
70. *Letters,* p. 357. Cf. Ellmann, *W.B. Yeats,* p. 55.
71. Cited in Adams, p. 155.
72. Cf. Yeats, *Autobiographies,* p. 332.
73. *A Vision* (London, 1925), p. xi.
74. Cf. Ellmann, *W.B. Yeats,* p. 234.
75. *A Vision,* pp. xi–xii.
76. Ibid., p. 73.
77. Ibid., pp. 211–12.
78. Cf. Peter Ure, *Towards a Mythology: Studies in the Poetry of W.B. Yeats* (London, 1946); and Morton I. Seiden, *William Butler Yeats: The Poet as Mythmaker 1865–1939* (East Lansing, 1962).
79. Reprinted as "Myth and Literary Classicism," in Richard Ellmann and Charles Feidelson, Jr., eds., *The Modern Tradition* (New York, 1965), pp. 679–81, with a postscript by Eliot dated January 1964.
80. Ibid., p. 681.
81. *Myth and Literature* (London, 1975), p. 123.
82. *The Complete Poems and Selected Letters and Prose* (London, 1968), p. 217.
83. Ibid., p. 221.
84. Ibid., p. 176.
85. *Letters* (New York, 1952), p. 305.
86. *Complete Poems,* p. 263.
87. See John White, *Mythology in the Modern Novel* (Princeton, 1971), p. 8.
88. K.K. Ruthven, *Myth* (London, 1976), p. 70.
89. Harry Levin, "Some Meanings of Myth," in *Refractions* (New York, 1966), p. 28.
90. See Gerhard Schmidt-Henkel, *Mythos und Dichtung* (Bad Homburg, 1967), p. 256.
91. Roland Barthes, *Mythologies* (Paris, 1957), p. 243.
92. See Erich Kahler, "Das Fortleben des Mythos," in *Die Verantwortung des Geistes* (Frankfurt am Main, 1952), pp. 201–13.

Sem Dresden

THOMAS MANN AND MARCEL PROUST: ON MYTH AND ANTIMYTH

In modern, comparative, and general literary scholarship, hardly any subject is so widely discussed and at the same time so vague as the relationship between myth and literature. From ancient times mythology and art have been very closely linked; many artists turned to myth for inspiration. From the Greek dramatists to the Renaissance there is an almost unbroken line of myths manifested not only in literature but also (and perhaps especially) in the plastic arts. The tragedies of French classicism take up again partly mythological motifs, and German and English Romantic writers do the same, even though in the eighteenth century one detects a certain turning away from myth. From the beginning of the nineteenth century, Eastern myths were added to the literary inventory, and in the twentieth century one may find in the works of Sartre, Giraudoux, and many others an abundance of modern versions of old myths.

The study of literature had to take into account this multiplicity of data, and thus there came into being the vast quantity of scholarly works that concern themselves with Narcissus in French literature, with Prometheus, Cain, Orpheus, Oedipus, and so many others. Even if such studies were to display the utmost precision, it is still practically unavoidable that a certain vagueness would occur in respect to the conception of "myth" itself. The manifold use of the term "myth" is the chief reason for this. But precisely because there seems to be a relationship, or even, according to some, an identity between religion and poetry (or literature in general), the crossings of borderlines become more frequent and necessary. Because of this the flexibility of the concept of myth unavoidably becomes greater, and the precise use one can make of it becomes smaller. Eventually the elasticity of the term disappears and it really becomes useless.

To this we must add three facts that probably give pause to those who would like to use the term myth in surveys of literature. The use of the word is rendered difficult not only by the vast number of investigations but also by the influence of psychoanalysis. Studies concerning myth and allegory have naturally played an important role since late antiquity. These subjects never afterward disappeared from Western culture. During the eighteenth century there was much interest in mythology, despite the disdain of certain critics, and the value that Friedrich Schlegel and Schelling attribute to it is well known. From the beginning psychoanalysis, for example, with Hanns Sachs and Otto Rank, explored this same domain in an entirely different fashion. Psychoanalysis has led to a greater understanding of myth, but it is not without certain dangers. Whether we are dealing with the orthodox doctrine of Freud, or with the analytic psychology of Jung, or with other theories, there is at present an overabundance of explanations that analyze mythological motives psychologically. Bodkin, Trilling, Lesser, Holland, Kris, Greenacre, and Politzer are but a few of dozens, perhaps hundreds, who could be named. Most of them have done important work, yet precisely for this reason the concept of myth is increasingly being stretched and is ever more vaguely defined. Moreover, the spread of psychoanalysis did not restrict itself to scholarly research in mythical literature. One could perhaps sustain the view that the opposite is true. Many creative artists, including the most important of those who have participated in the development of twentieth-century literature, have consciously or unconsciously assimilated psychoanalytical data in their novels. With Schnitzler, Joyce, Kafka, and Mann, among many others, a renewal and an enrichment of literary myth has taken place. In their creations, however, it has become ever more difficult to determine what precisely is a myth. Finally, the desire to discuss myth in literature has become so great that the word seems to imply a certain praise for works about literature that include the term. Certainly no one today is surprised when the mythical world of Rabelais, of Balzac, or even of Zola is being discussed. On the contrary, many will consider this to be the only legitimate approach to the interpretation of the works of great artists.[1]

If the student does not wish to be discouraged by the incredible spread of literary myth, which moreover went many different directions, then he will need to impose upon himself the severest restrictions. Even then he will soon observe that he is still confronted by a superabundant quantity of material and documents. Moreover, in spite of all these restrictions, problems of a general nature will present themselves sharply and demand a solution. Two writers will serve here as examples, of whom at least one is extremely well known because of his intensive interest in the mythical, although the mythical world of the other has also regularly been mentioned. By myth I understand in the first instance a sacred tale, which has a religious function in a certain community but which also functions socially. I deliberately omit for the time being the problem of the realistic content of such a story. We are concerned with finding out in the first place whether the sacred story manifests itself in the work of a few writers, and if so how; what were their intentions; and finally, how the "sacred" can turn into something entirely different, or even opposite.

Here I am able to clarify but a few aspects of Thomas Mann's relationship to myth.[2] Even were I completely to renounce discussing the development of Mann's interest in myth and the mythological, a subject that has been repeatedly studied, we can keep as a systematic starting point the information he himself communicated to Kerényi. In a letter dated February 20, 1934, Mann writes: "Actually in my case the slowly increasing interest in matters of myth and religious history is a symptom of aging. It corresponds to a taste which develops over the years away from the middleclass-individualistic interest in the typical, the general and the human."[3] It is of no importance in this context whether Mann is correct in speaking about a symptom of aging, whether the perspective on his own work can be called correct, or whether various interpretations of what can be found later in his novels do not reflect earlier ones in which the same or at least similar situations and concepts can be found. Nor is our concern now with contrast, or with what might be called the important distinction between the individual and the general human. What is here of interest is that the mythical and the typical come so closely together. It is not important whether that happens more generally, and whether in religious studies such a rapprochement is usual or permissible or debatable.

Mann never claimed, in the case of *Joseph and his Brothers*, for instance, to make a contribution to religious studies. However great the importance of these novels may be, however curious the insight they afford, they are not of a scholarly nature and do not wish in the least to be that. To be sure, this tetralogy and other works make plain what Mann himself intended and wished to see, and they are characteristic for his concepts. The mythical is for him the typical, and this in the sense that they are one and the same: there is no myth without a fundamental ingredient of the typical; never is anything typical without myth playing an essential role. In contrast with this we have everything that must be called *bürgerlich* and individual. It now becomes easy to attach considerations to my argument that would place Thomas Mann in a development of literature. The contrast between individual and type has always, and particularly since the Romantic period, had a great significance. This contrast is not absent in Mann's work, but it did change its essence because the nature of the typical has changed. It has become richer and different because it has been coupled to, is perhaps identical with, the mythical and has obtained a form, but not more than a form, of sanctity.

It is a remarkable fact—and after *Joseph* even more remarkable—that the title of the second chapter in *The Magic Mountain* runs as follows: "About the baptismal bowl and the grandfather in a two-fold shape." It is just as remarkable that as a child Hans Castorp showed such a great interest in the baptismal bowl and particularly in the platter on which it rests, and in the names of the proprietors that were inscribed in it. His father's name is there, his grandfather's, his great-grandfather's, "and then the prefix 'great' doubles, triples, and multiplies." Thus comes into the boy's existence a mixing of his own life with a long past to which he belongs, because the object that belongs to him originates in a distant past, a kind of ancient past. That is but one element; another and perhaps a more important one is the fact that the grandfather appears in a twofold function. We have a phenomenon here that is characteristic of Mann's conception of the mythical, which for lack of a better word I shall provisionally call *geminatio*, meaning that a situation and even a character appear twice. In the two appearances they are not identical, yet they remain the same. That which is seemingly the same is nevertheless double and leads a double existence; that which appears to be double can be reduced to a unity. Fine examples of this may be found in the last chapters of *Lotte in Weimar*, in which differing situations do ultimately become one, and of *Felix Krull*, the novel of a swindler who leads a double existence, but also the novel that brings back to unity the doubling of mother and daughter as objects of love.

The mythical-typical often manifests itself in Mann's work in such doublings of unity. The best comparison to make this clear would be with twins and twin situations, which have much and in fact everything in common and yet are not completely the same.

With this *geminatio* the mythical in Mann's work is not yet, however, completely unfolded in the systematic use he makes of it. This really only happens in the *Joseph* novel. In that novel the doubling is once again a special case of a general multiplication in which the unity is comprised but not dissolved. The most famous example here is naturally Eleazar, who is Abraham's servant and at the same time the servant of many others. He (and along with him many other characters in the novel) does not find his identity solely and surely not primarily in himself, but in the multiple Eleazars who preceded him, who will follow him, and who are at the same time with him.[4] To Eleazar will also apply that which at a given moment is said explicitly in connection with Reuben: "He was not the man to be the only one in the world unaware of the significance of the question who one was, in whose footsteps he was going, and to which past he related his present in order to manifest it as reality."[5] If one wishes to have a clear idea of the constituent parts of the mythical—which thus signifies for Mann the typical and general human—then these few sentences afford a splendid opportunity. It is first of all apparent that the starting point is established by the question as to the identity of the human personality. The answer to this question is then immediately suggested by the words that follow and that make clear what does *not* constitute the identity for these mythical figures and in fact cannot do so. If a twentieth-century reader asks himself the question who he is and what he is, then he is relatively soon inclined to search for his true personality and to find it in something that is indeed truly personal, that which makes him as it were incomparable and an irreplaceable individual, an autonomous being who depends on nothing and nobody. The fact that all this is still pretty vague and poses as many problems as it solves does not matter at this moment. Reuben, Joseph, Eleazar, and so many others choose immediately as it were a different and opposite direction: when they wish to know who they are they turn to the past or to the traces that the past appears to have engraved in the present. In the double meaning of the word they direct themselves to the past: they look in that direction and receive from there their own direction because they adjust themselves to it. The past is for them a directive.

It is in any case certain that this interpretation does not go far enough or at least has left one especially important element out of consideration. A modern reader would probably be surprised to see that the relationship with reality has become a totally different one. For such a reader reality is not much different from that which exists and is present around him. The past, which by definition no longer exists and is neither there nor present, becomes unreal. According to some, it consists solely of words. None of this applies to the mythical characters who, according to Mann, are exemplary for the human being in general. In their case there manifests itself the opposite of what we are used to accepting as normal. For the so-called contrast between a reality that is present on the one hand and the past on the other has been substituted something that no longer comprises a contrast but has become a unity. The past permeates the present; there is even no difference between the two; and this unity can be integrated into reality. Here reality really signifies that this unity is active. In such a mythical world there is no passage of time, or at least there is a very different one from that which one seems to be experiencing; in such a world terms like past, present, future, beginning, and end do not exist. It is probably true that in a continuously progressing movement the same thing continuously occurs in a renewed way. And that is indeed what happens. The most remarkable proof of this is perhaps to be found in *Joseph* (but *Lotte* is also characteristic in this respect). It is to be found in the considerations that accompany in various places the word *einst* meaning at the same time "in days past" and "in days to come": "So it goes when the double meaning of 'einst' exercises its magic power; when the future has become past, when everything has long ago gone by and now again shall happen in precise present."[6] Perhaps the word *einst* is the mythical word par excellence: pointing to the past or to the future, according to the context, it seems to signify a continual and continuing present that repeats itself. When a fairy tale begins with the traditional words "Once upon a time," these words do not so much signify a past that can be recaptured in time as an ancient past that is still around and will remain so.

Several times attention has been called to the problem of time in the work of Thomas Mann.[7] To this general aspect of the art of the novel his "mythological" novels are no exception. One need only recall the impressive opening sentence of *Joseph:* "Deep is the fountain of the past. Should one not call it unfathomable?" But it is precisely the fact that a fountainhead is being discussed. Moreover, it is a fountainhead that cannot be fathomed, that perhaps does not have a solid ground, that leads to a consciousness of time that may be called specific. Its nature is entirely peculiar because the basis of this mythical world is not in the first place enclosed in time, in the way we experience it, but in a certain systematic pattern that is present everywhere and always. To be sure this pattern unfolds itself in time, but simultaneously it is abolished in it. From this one may derive two consequences. It is in the first place characteristic of Mann's art that Joseph is convinced that he understands "the intentions of God" and that he lives by them. There is no doubt in his mind that in the entire course of his life one may discover something *planmässig* (methodical, systematic). With this, moreover, another relationship has ensued between *Tun* (doing) and *Geschehen* (happening). Here again a separation into two parts must be made: precisely because a pattern must be the foundation of the mythical life, nothing happens that did not already happen. Moreover, the *Geschehen* consists in a "doing," or to put it in another way: the human-mythical "doing" unfolds in a *Geschehen*.

When Joseph is thrown by his brothers into the dry pit (again a pit, which is no coincidence) he has the following thought: "But what had happened had only been happening, not an active doing; one couldn't call it that. Although it happened through them, the brothers, they really didn't do it but it had happened to them."[8] There, one might say, is a basic pattern that in the course of time continually repeats itself and in which time is overcome. Human doing conforms to this pattern, which in this manner has also become a happening. One must emphasize, however, that the mythical man undergoes this voluntarily. If such were not the case, then he would merely be strongly predetermined in what he does or does not do. Now he is, so to say, fatally placed into a pattern, but he wants it to be so. He cannot do otherwise than to want to do what he has to do, so that it becomes a systematic happening. One is confronted, as has been correctly observed, by a sort of *amor fati*.[9] Since the name of Nietzsche presents itself in this connection, we may certainly not leave out Goethe either. It is no coincidence that in the novel about Goethe, *Lotte in Weimar*, a term such as *Prägemuster* (coined pattern) occurs.[10] One need only think of poems such as *Dauer im Wechsel* (Perpetuity within Change), *Im Gegenwärtigen Vergangnes* (Past in the Present), or of Goethe's famous saying, "Coined pattern which develops itself alive," in order to realize that Mann is continuing a very conscious Goethean tradition. In continuing it he adapts it to his own needs. A minor detail in *Lotte* is remarkable proof of what I have just said. Lotte's daughter, whose name was Clara, is here given the name Lotte. Why the author has consciously and voluntarily violated historical reality is easily ascertained. This daughter, who does not otherwise play a significant role in the novel, hereby joins the ranks of the Eleazars and the other characters in whom an arch-pattern unfolds and is always present.

We need no longer justify the opinion that Mann in his entire work, that is, in the novels *and* in his theoretical writings, repeatedly concerns himself with the precise meaning of *Vergegenwärtigung* (making present), *Wiederholung* (repetition), *Wiederkehr* (return), and imitation. In Joseph one regularly finds "theoretical" considerations, such as the following: "In this case we are concerned with a phenomenon which we should like to call an imitation or emulation, namely an approach to life which sees the task of the individual life in filling different forms, mythical patterns, which had been coined by the ancestors with presence, and to incarnate these forms again."[11] These words speak for themselves and do not need further explanation. Nor shall I dwell on the thought that as it were obsesses Joseph in Egypt: the theme *Nachsichziehen* (having as a consequence) and *Nachkommenlassen* (letting follow).[12] All this finds a natural setting in the all-embracing presence of an arch-pattern that fulfills itself, a well that never dries. There is, however, one extremely important point. In these mythical novels the characters not only cause the myth to recur, they live out the myth, they are the myth itself. Thus, as Mann himself said, their life, "the life within myth," is also "a quotation-like life." The terms are taken from a long essay entitled *Freud und die Zukunft* (Freud and the Future), an essay of great importance for the understanding of Mann's relationship to psychoanalysis and the relationship Mann–psychoanalysis–myth. Mann's formulation, "quotationlike life," may seem somewhat too modern; it may surely be called literary. But what does that mean? By saying "literary" can one deduce that mythical-typical life is only possible in literature? And in that case, what does one mean by "literature"? Before attempting to answer these questions even provisionally, it is necessary to point out that Thomas Mann never hesitated to make use of quotations in the usual sense of that word. One finds them all through his work and, in spite of lengthy research, they may not all have been detected.[13] Much more important is the fact that Mann saw in this repetition of a literary nature a derivation of mythical repetition in general. He believed that each repetition was a cause and a consequence of mythical consciousness. In this way one might say that mythical life becomes novel, so to speak, while "novels" by definition imply mythical life. Joseph and all the others are *history* and at the same time in a story. The *Zweideutigheit* (duplicity, ambiguity), a term Mann so often cherished, is fundamentally important here, as is the word *Geschichte* (history, or story), in which, for example, *Tun* (doing) and *Geschehen* (happening), past and present, flow into each other and are no longer distinguishable. One is reminded of the curious figure of Tamar, who wishes as it were to work herself into the *history* of Jacob's tribe. All this, taken together, is characteristic of *das Festliche* (the Solemn) with which Mann is so much concerned.[14]

Even if one does not delve further into the preceding problems, one cannot deny that a remarkable relationship between life, myth, and novel has come into being. The taking up again of the life of Joseph occurs in a text that takes its point of departure from another text and makes the latter live again. This reliving takes place in a way that is possible only in texts, that is, in literature. If the term *Zitathaft* (quotationlike) demonstrates anything, it is that the mythical-typical displays itself textually, that "life" is now text.[15] In fact, everything experienced is *prescribed*, in both the chronological as well as the imperative meaning of that term. The mythical, which is also the sacred, reveals itself according to Mann in literary texts. But is this still the case when texts are taken up again? One's first inclination is to answer this question positively; imitation and emulation are after all an essential element in the mythical. If one looks closer at the problem, however, a legitimate doubt arises, which slowly becomes certainty. "Imitation" and "emulation" contain in themselves other characteristics, which have not yet been mentioned here, and of which one must never lose sight in the case of Mann.

One gets the impression that Joseph, a typical descendant, is placed differently in the mythical history than Jacob. He seems to have a freer and more playful relationship to his own *Geschichte* (history and story). He is not less a believer than the others but he is less naive. Whereas Jacob and Rebecca live exclusively *in* their patterns, Joseph lives in his and surveys it at the same time. He carries out that which must happen, and he also knows that everything must happen thus and not otherwise. That which is valid in the case of Joseph is even more true in the case of Mann and, no doubt, in the case of every novelist who writes a history, that is, a story and also a history. In a certain sense with Joseph and absolutely with Mann, the mythical has changed its function. The imitation (or emulation) has taken on elements of a game that must indeed be played out as it is written, but of which in one way or another the rules have become common knowledge. It may well be that with this knowledge the holiness of the mythical has been contaminated and has even turned into something that in its final consequences would have to be designated as antimythical.

It may be assumed that the mythical takes on different contours in literature than in the original myth, which is a sacred story. Thomas Mann was not exclusively concerned with the mythical as such: he also had other intentions with this concept, giving it a specific function adequate to his purpose. For him myth and therefore the mythical were inseparably connected to a form of psychology. He also hoped to attain a use for myth that would not be troubled by Nazi "obscurantists." His efforts were directed to the transformation of the myth "ins Humane" (into the human and the humane).[16] How he succeeded in carrying this out in, for example, *Doktor Faustus* is of no concern here, nor is the significance that the myth takes on for concepts such as culture, education, and humanity. Here I am concerned with the *Umfunktionieren* (transformation) itself, and that, in the case of Mann, is nothing more or less than the secularization of the mythical: "What mainly . . . achieves fulfillment within me is a certain tendency toward 'secularization' of the religious concept in the direction of the psychological transformation into the profane into the ethical and into the psychological."[17] What takes place with the myth in Mann's work is in any case an apparently essential change within the mythical. This much is certain. Yet it is more difficult, perhaps even impossible, to ascertain whether hereby an enrichment of the mythical, or rather a contamination or even a falsification, has taken place.

This problem, however, can be clarified. We must remember that Mann's preoccupation appears to be both psychological and ethical. More important, however, is his critical attitude, which predominates everywhere and therefore also in his creative work. To put it even more strongly: there is really no distinction in his thought between "creation" and "criticism." As early as 1905 he reports about himself: "To some extent I certainly belong to the 'creative ones': but I have a weakness for everything which is called critical. . . . I think that no modern creative artist can perceive the critical as something which contradicts his own existence."[18] Whereas here the reference might still be to the traditional contrast between literature and criticism, there is no doubt whatsoever that Mann (along with many others since Poe and Baudelaire) is not sensitive to this contrast and, moreover, does not consider it generally acceptable. What has now been said in regard to myth? Is it possible that the mythical (which encompasses the antimythical and the secularizing) can stand or even accept criticism? The fact is that Mann handles the myth thus and not otherwise.

There is no doubt that the strongest attraction exercised by his work consists in his ability to compress elements that are perhaps irreconcilable, in any case difficult to unite, and to transform them in his own thinking into an admirable unity. It closely relates to his often-discussed and celebrated humor, irony, and psychological distancing.[19] The concept of theatrical role becomes important in this context. It seems as if the mythical, specifically in the case of Joseph, is a game of roles or parts, which *must* be played, but remains a game. Even if one were quickly inclined to point to extremely well-known notions such as *theatrum mundi,* still one can hardly perceive anything of this topos in these novels. They are what one might call too mythical for that. On the other hand, there is not for a moment a lack of playing *in* the myth and thus a playing *with* the myth. As soon as one speaks about a game, one is not willing to be serious these days. The contrast between the two has become too well known and the emphasis on seriousness too great. Nevertheless, specifically after Freud, one should know that the opposite of game should not be solely or primarily seriousness, but reality.[20] However vague in its turn the concept of reality may be, one may assume as a certainty that the mythical can achieve itself playfully and at the same time seriously. It is therefore no coincidence but, on the contrary, a conscious effect when it is stated that "Laban played his holy role with more or less consciousness and consent."[21] A sacred role? This sounds almost a blasphemy, but is nevertheless precisely the only thing that in Mann's opinion can be said about the mythical world. It seems to be not entirely serious and therefore deviates from the myth in the original form, but nevertheless remained serious in a peculiar or a particular way. "The unification of sympathy and reason into a kind of irony," said Mann himself, "was present in my mind, an irony which did not need to be unholy."[22] A game has been played *with* truth and *within* truth; it is indeed a holy game.

In order to be maintained, the concept of sacred-mythical must be lived through and *contaminated.* It is lived through or "gone through" particularly in "the Solemn" and in a "sacred cheerfulness" to which Mann repeatedly refers. But since every successful work or work of art and notably these novels is a sort of feast, the mythical reveals itself here also.[23] It does so, surely not to a lesser degree, but in another way and even by means of a contamination. The sacred must be desacralized by the critical and (overly) conscious contemplator in order to remain holy. In fact, what we have in Mann's work is a mythical-typical world, which, hollowed out, remains standing and in this new form has simultaneously lost and kept its mythical characteristics. It would be incorrect to see in this form something specifically modern. It seems tempting to discover in Mann someone who is himself a descendant (someone who comes after) par excellence, and who is thereby constrained to emulate. All the more so because he himself occasionally called attention to this and had good reason to describe Joseph, who is also, if not primarily, an "artistic temperament," as a descendant.[24] Without lessening this artistic effect in any way, other facts need to be considered here. In literature imitation is a long-familiar enterprise. To be sure, imitation, as we find it in the authors of antiquity and of the Renaissance, cannot be compared in all respects with the imitation, or rather emulation, in Mann. Nevertheless, one can also note conformity. A work such as Erasmus's *Ciceronianus*, which is one of the most important works devoted to the problem of imitation, could well be an example of this. Not only does it pose the question of who and what is to be imitated but especially how this is to take place. There is no need to demonstrate that there is no lack of multiple ironic remarks. They concern especially those who consider Cicero's work as a sacred text and do not want to write a single word that Cicero could not have used. However this may be, Erasmus never claims that imitation itself could or should be ironic. Thus he might have indirectly proven the modern, ironizing, even pastiche-making character of Mann's imitation.

The proof may be reinforced by a perusal of a theoretical work such as the *Deffence et illustration de la langue française*. In the seventh chapter Du Bellay, following so many others, speaks about imitation, and in particular, about emulation of Greek writers. According to him, if one wishes to succeed in this, then these Greek writers should be literally swallowed up. The imitator must "transform himself into them." They must become his flesh and blood. This procedure was (much later) correctly described as *innutrition*. Mann never went as far as Du Bellay; one could defend the point of view that the sixteenth-century work represents the ultimate consequence of Mann's *Sympathie*. In Du Bellay's manifesto, however, there is just as little trace of irony as in the work of any other sixteenth-century theoretician.

So is Mann modern after all? That becomes doubtful when one turns from the theoretical writings of the Renaissance to the literature itself. Whereas a Ronsard or a Du Bellay remains extremely serious in these imitations, such is not the case with Rabelais or Donne, to name two completely different types of authors. These two imitate with a certain playfulness and in many cases do not at all dissimulate their admiration of the imitated author on the one hand, but on the other hand do not hide the fact that their admiration is ironical or, if one prefers, distanced. The great difficulty of establishing these nuances is apparent moreover from the fact that Thomas Mann in his celebrated seventh chapter of *Lotte in Weimar* carries out imitation à la Ronsard, whereas elsewhere he proceeds à la Rabelais. (It is obvious that no historical influence is meant by this, but rather a systematic conformity.) However that may be, it would not be difficult to draw a line from Rabelais into the twentieth century by way of the burlesque literature of the seventeenth century, with works such as the *Enéide Travestie* by Paul Scarron, Laurence Sterne, Diderot, and many others. One is here dealing with literature that imitates other literature. According to Mann, emulation, repetition are in themselves a category of the mythical that reveals itself continuously in the fulfillment of given patterns. This filling up again is for him not merely ironical and thereby eventually unholy. It is also holy and signifies, to borrow a term from Goethe and the German Romanticists, critical *Steigerung* (climax). In the curious Hegelian sense of the word, the mythical in Mann's work is indeed *aufgehoben*, that is, simultaneously uplifted and canceled out, but only in this sense. The mythical-typical disappears in Mann's work in its sacred quality, which amounts to its being antimythical. Yet on another and higher level it reappears in its total richness. The antimythical, the ironizing and critical repetition of the given, is melted into the myths.

The critical repetition of given material, which reflects and contaminates the myth, can also present itself in an entirely different fashion. A starting point could for example be found not in a religious text such as we have in *Joseph* but in a relatively arbitrary (literary) text of which an adaptation is in the making. In that case, one might say, a parody of the original or even a pastiche or a falsification comes into being; in any case, some forms of imitative activity, as in works of epigones, inevitably appear. All this could also take place when the given text is of a mythical and sacred nature. In that distinction one cannot find the difference. The best proof of that has already been presented: in the works of Thomas Mann traces of irony, distancing, and playfulness can be found without any difficulty. One must look in another direction to indicate the differences, and one may come up with the fusion which is either realized or not. Instead, however, of a general exposition, which would necessarily have to be limited to generalities, it would be useful to approach the problem of the pastiche concretely in the work of a single writer.[25]

In the *pastiches* of Marcel Proust a form of repetition is always present and even fundamental. The problem is how and why that happens. In asking why I am not thinking so much about biographical facts that could lead to an explanation but rather about a "systematical" organization that is present in his work. It is well known that Proust, in his great work *A la recherche du temps perdu* but also even earlier, brought up the problem of time.[26] It has no less frequently been explained how the passage of time, as we know it, ultimately has no significance for him and is dissolved in a "putting outside of time." To put it briefly, what is taking place is a coinciding, literally a falling together, of an experience from the past and a present one, so that according to Proust both of them—which have become one—are put outside time. We are here dealing paradoxically with a moment of eternity, which presents itself in complete purity and ecstasy, which alone gives meaning to the life of man and can be reflected solely in art by human creation. With this surely no myth has been created or taken up again; nor is one dealing with myth in the sense of a pattern that must be filled up. What one is dealing with is a form of mysticism and just as much with an abolishment of time that leads to superhuman reality. The differences between this and what we find in Mann, for whom "worldly" and "supernaturally" are totally fused, are clear. Nevertheless, two aspects in Proust must not be forgotten even though they are usually much less sharply illuminated than the mystical elements in this "putting outside of time." First of all, one must certainly remind oneself that the putting outside of time always takes place via a physical perception, a sensation. It happens, in the most famous example, when the narrator eats a *madeleine*. When he dips the cake into the tea a distant past is actualized, even though at that moment he does not yet know what he is to do with it, and he in fact solely experiences moments of intense ecstasy. In order to continue these he keeps making efforts to repeat the first sensation: he continues nibbling at the cake, but the force of the experience diminishes precisely by his doing this. He has clearly chosen the wrong road to fathom what he is experiencing. And with this I have come to the second indispensable element. There exists a method not merely to live out the sensation but also to understand it. One must search for "l'équivalent profond" (the profound equivalent) of the experienced sensation,[27] and this searching cannot take place without the help of the intellect, without its complete commitment. Only in this way, that is to say, only through an extratemporal experience and the intellectual fathoming of it, will the essence of life and reality show itself in art. Only then will our deeper personality, our true "I," receive in total joy the *céleste nourriture* (celestial nourishment). Only then does one experience the strange moments that must be called "réels sans être actuels, idéaux sans être abstraits" (real without being actual, ideal without being abstract, 1:347ff.).

One can hardly attempt a comparison with Mann. All the same, I question whether these words of Proust do not describe fairly precisely what one should understand by a mythical *schema* (pattern). It seems to me that they point in that direction, even though they are functioning in a different system. The fact is that Proust is not concerned in his creative works with causing this pattern continually to relive but rather to continually represent and reproduce it in a form of reactualization. While in the work of Thomas Mann one may discover a biblical-figurative form of thought in which the temporal-later is a repetition, enrichment, and fulfillment of what appears always given, in the case of Proust we are rather dealing with Platonic ideas, which may be considered as patterns, and which are deciphered anew by each great artist. It is therefore no coincidence that words such as *déchiffrer* (decipher), *traduire* (translate), and *interpréter* (interpret) are quite often found in his works and actually always have the meaning that has here been outlined.[28] In this connection it is surely important to treat one of the passages that indicate the essence of a work of art. When instrumentalists play a melody, it seems as if they are carrying out the ritual acts that are necessary in order to bring down to earth the tones that exist elsewhere in total purity (1:347 ff.). Similarly, the work of art truly is elsewhere; it must be read (in the sense of deciphered) by the artist; and then it appears temporarily on earth.

May one not sense in this, in spite of many differences, some similarity with the function of the Platonic myth?

Let me, however, return to an aspect of the myth that is essential in Mann's work, to the typical. In the works of Proust it is also present right from the start. I am not even thinking in the first place of a form of *geminatio:* the mother and grandmother of the narrator fuse after the latter's death more and more into one; the daughter of Odette de Crécy looks more and more like her mother as the years go by; a battle takes on the pattern of an earlier one, and so on. There is more: Swann, of Jewish origin and frequenting the highest aristocratic circles of Paris, wants shortly before his death to introduce his wife to this closed circle. He meets the Duchess of Guermantes while his face is marked by death. What does this suggest? "The clownish nose of Swann, long absorbed in a pleasant face, suddenly seemed enormous, tumefied, crimson, quite that of an old Hebrew . . . Besides, perhaps in him during these last days the race made the physical type which characterizes it more noticeable . . ." (2:690). Another example: Robert de Saint-Loup, who belongs to the Guermantes but is very critical of his family circle, is killed at the front, "and this Guermantes dies more himself, or rather more of his race in which he fused, in which he was no more than a Guermantes." This is symbolically expressed at his funeral: no titles, no names, only "the G of Guermantes which he had become again through death" (3:851). In both cases it is clear that the individual for one reason or another returns to a type. It is thus certain that the typical exists, but it is just as certain that an individual diverges or diverged from it in order to come back to it again later. This Proustian concept differs from what Mann understands by mythical-typical, but is not entirely foreign to it. Here, to be sure, one is not dealing with a type that repeats itself in the course of time but rather with an individual who ultimately does integrate into the group, the category, the type to which he belongs, and in that "typical" rediscovers his true individuality. Although it would still be possible in this way to talk about the mythical in Proust's work, albeit with some difficulty, it is much easier to point to its antimythical tendencies. This is chiefly due to the fact that these tendencies are not to be found in the novels themselves but in separate works, and they can therefore be studied as separate entities. The antimythical irony and playfulness in which the mythical *Joseph* is drenched are here practiced for their own sake, and the way they function can thus be clearly delineated. First of all, however, one must avoid a misunderstanding in Proust's work also. Just as with Mann, it would actually be incorrect to make a radical distinction or perhaps any distinction at all between the (critical) *Pastiches* that he published and the creative, mythical work.

A strong argument against such distinctions is the mimetic talent that Proust had throughout his life and that has been pointed out by so many. Besides this biographical factor, to which perhaps no great literary significance need be attached, there are also the data. On the one hand there is for instance the above-mentioned phenomenon of "putting out of time," which is considered to be so characteristic of the *Recherche*. It was, however, present long before the writing of this work and can be easily found in the early novels and essays that were published after the death of the author. On the other hand critics like to speak of a *période des pastiches* (the most important parts of the pastiches were made public in 1908 and 1909), but in reality such a period only presents pastiche accumulation, which is, however, quite interesting. In various critical works[29] (reprinted and gathered posthumously in *Contre Sainte-Beuve* and also in other editions) one finds pastiches or an incomplete attempt at "take-offs" dating from different periods; there are still more in letters of 1921 and 1922. All this points to the fact that neither Proust nor Thomas Mann made a profound distinction between so-called creative and so-called critical activities. A last confirmation of this is contained in the first versions of pieces on Sainte-Beuve and his critical method that were integrated into the *Recherche*. In reality the author also intended this novel as a sort of proof of the extent of the great nineteenth-century critic's error.[30]

Conversely, the pastiches of Proust may be called creations. It is important to stress the point because in this way the relationship may be made clearer between the mythical and, on the other hand, the antimythical, which seems to be characteristic of pastiches. Why are they written and how do they come into being? Proust himself answered both questions, and I shall mainly if not exclusively keep to his statements. In a letter dated March 18, 1908, he expressed to Robert Dreyfus his relief that only one pastiche was left to do: "As far as the pastiches are concerned, thank God, there is only one left. It's because I was too lazy for literary criticism and wanted to enjoy myself by putting literary criticism 'into action.' "[31] What are we to make of that criticism "in action"? The question is all the more significant because these words have been repeatedly quoted by critics, but have led to no real explanation.[32] This is quite strange because Proust clearly did make a distinction in this simple phrase between two differing sorts of literary criticism. There is first of all the traditional form of criticism that usually deals in considerations about the work, the life, the ideas, and the style of an author. The critical procedure that Proust carried out in his pastiches, on the other hand, becomes completely—perhaps almost too completely—a taking up again of what the author achieved. As a critic Proust was so deeply penetrated by the author he was reading that he could do nothing but write as that author. We may literally speak of a certain madness that takes hold of him in a curious manner. Let me again choose as a starting point a letter to Robert Dreyfus, this one dated March 23, 1908. This time Proust let him know how easy it was for him to write à la Renan: "I had adjusted my interior metronome to his rhythm and I could have written ten volumes like that."[33] To be sure, there is probably an element of exaggeration here. We are concerned, however, with the fact that what counts is not the taking up again of words (meaning here images, and so on), but rather of a rhythm, an almost unseizable totality of a writer, which could nevertheless be imitated. With this we have indeed touched the essential element of the pastiche, at least in the case of Proust, as may be confirmed by another of his statements: "From the moment that I start to read an author I quickly recognize under the words the song's tune ... and while reading I unconsciously hum it ... I have a more delicate and sharper ear of that sort than many others, and that allows me to make pastiches because with writers when they have the tune the words come pretty quickly."[34] The pastiche rests first on that tune, on that "sing-song."

It is all the more important to call attention to this because one will no doubt be inclined to think that the *pasticheur* (which includes Proust) proceeds in a totally different fashion. It will be assumed that all who wish to write pastiches will search for characteristic tropes, words, and thoughts and will use these in their imitations. Even a scholar such as Milly who has rendered enormous service by his extremely careful investigation of Proust's pastiches perhaps still emphasizes this point too much. He is too easily led, in spite of his attention to the "song's tune," to speak of *décomposer* (decompose), *recomposer* (recompose), and even *pulvériser* (pulverize) the work that is subjected to the pastiche.[35] I don't claim that this is entirely incorrect, but it is surely not the element that must first and principally be considered. Nor are these aspects the ones that most impress readers of pastiches. In this literary genre they are probably quickly reminded of the parodizing character of the inevitable irony, which must also have been present in the pastiche-maker. A work "is singing" as it were in the critic, who takes up that song again, continues it, and performs it in his own way. The new-old manner will always encompass some exaggeration, as has repeatedly been pointed out.[36] To be sure, though it has been often claimed, the claim is not a proof. To put it differently: The question is whether the undeniable element of exaggeration does not depend in turn on something else. The style, to put it very simply, of a Michelet, which is his and belongs to him by nature, takes on a somewhat mechanical character in Proust's pastiche of Michelet. It becomes an automatism that functions continually and finally overwhelms the reader. The very same material that develops organically, in the original text, appears in the pastiche in extremely concentrated form. Through this mechanical concentration of effects (that is why I used the word "sing-song") the pastiche becomes to some extent a ridiculing of the original work. The pastiche-maker always seems to be parodizing, even when he does not want to, so that the reader can almost never avoid smiling.

We are, of course, talking about an experienced reader or at least a reader with a certain knowledge. As is well known, Proust took a legal case concerning the making of diamonds (the *Affaire Lemoine*) in 1908 as starting point for his pastiches of Balzac, Sainte-Beuve, etc. Let us now suppose for a moment that I have never read any works of Balzac. Nor am I concerned with anachronisms that often find their way into this genre but do not belong to its essence. What is *not* Balzac is a sentence such as this one: "Is genius not in fact a kind of crime against the routine of the past which our time punishes more severely than crime itself, since scholars die in the poor-house, a sadder place than the prison?" Here is another example: ". . . this enthusiasm of thinkers which seems ridiculous in the middle of the profound dissimulation of high society."[37] It would seem to me that Balzac could have written in this way (maybe the sentences are in fact quotations from his work?), so that there is really nothing enjoyable about such texts in themselves. The enjoyment only arises—and Proust no doubt counts on that—if the reader knows Balzac and recognizes him in the pastiches, though it be in a transformed or, if one prefers, deformed shape. The pastiche depends totally for its effect on its reference to another work; it is therefore always a text about a text. Were one not to take the word in a pejorative sense, one could speak without objection about the "parasitizing" character of this genre. Moreover, this literary parasite concentrates in itself, intentionally or not, vital elements of the work to which it has attached itself and with which it remains forever connected. In this genre, instead of style we have a technique with which any subject at all may be treated. The formal aspect has become detached from the content.

All the preceding discussion was needed to show one of the most curious forms of repetition, which is according to Mann the mythical and also the antimythical. In the *Joseph* novels and in other works one may perceive a fusion of both. One could speak in a certain sense of a pastiche, but with the restriction in Mann's case that the pastiche coincides with the original story. Nevertheless in that case also the ironizing and antimythical attitude are not absent. The novel of Thomas Mann takes up again a holy story that is being contaminated and still keeps its holiness. This distinguishes it from Proust's works in two ways: the work and the pastiche do not coincide, so that the latter can be more easily contemplated in its own nature, and second, there is nothing of a holy story. Let me express myself more cautiously: there is no biblical text as a basis for his pastiches. Perhaps with this all has not been said. It is after all no coincidence that Proust chose literary texts (for example, Saint-Simon) of which the great majority were very dear to him, and which in a way were holy to him and which he had completely absorbed. So even though Proust does not use a biblical text, one might nevertheless say that he used a text that was holy to him, of which he had become possessed and from which he had to liberate himself. That could only happen through a repetition and at the same time a (parodistic) transformation of the holiness and the mythical character. Precisely through this repetition one may demonstrate that the mythical character of a literary text, whether biblical or not, has persisted in and is confirmed by the transformation that it has undergone and that to a certain extent came into being through the application of antimythical procedures. If the mythical is to continue existing, then it can do so only in this way.

Why, in the case of pastiches, or in connection with *Joseph*, does one not simply speak of copies or even of falsifications? As regards the former there will be no hesitation: at first glance it is perfectly clear to anyone that a pastiche in whatever form is *not* a copy. To be sure, there is the fact that Proust, again in 1908, seemed to express the contrary in a letter to the Countess of Noailles. Dis-

cussing his pastiche of Michelet he says of the pastiche in general:
"It is an easy and vulgar exercise. Just the same though, I believe . . . that they are good 'copies,' as they say in the fine arts."[38]
Moreover one cannot deny that pastiches, novels like *Joseph*, and
copies all belong in one and the same category that one might
designate with the term reproduction. Within this category one
must, however, make the necessary distinctions. That is easier
said than done. Everyone knows that copies in the usual sense of
the word have an important function and also that they have something in common with pastiches. Both are dependent on another
work, which they imitate. This imitation, however, does not happen in the same manner nor with the same purpose. The copyist
repeats an existing work of which he (ideally) wishes to make a
duplicate, a copy that could no longer be distinguished from the
original. Such is the case in the fine arts, where the original work
exists only once. In literature we find countless copies of a single
poem, all of which are equally "original." In that sense, therefore,
copying has no literary significance. For painters, however, copying could fulfill an important didactic function, in which the making of pastiches and of copies are intertwined. Beginners in art
often emulate more than they themselves realize.[39] However that
may be, the literary pastiche-maker differs in this respect from the
painter in that although he does repeat a work, he does not copy it.
He alters it and concentrates on a different perspective. The result
of this is that what is created is not a duplicate but a so-called new
and therefore also unknown work of a known author.

If one prefers, he may consider this a falsification. Justifiably,
however, many will protest such a judgment. When discussing
literary forgers one most likely thinks in the first place—I am
restricting myself to the past—of a Lacurne de Sainte-Palaye and
his eighteenth-century troubadour poetry, or of Ossian with his
Celtic poems. Even were one not to consider the false success
and also the illegitimate commercial gain that they and many
others were after, forgers they remain, because they pretend to
be somebody they are not and hide behind someone else.
Though Mann and Proust no doubt hoped for success—I am not
discussing financial gain—this does not make them forgers. They
honestly and openly admit—actually what do they admit? One
tends to answer: their falsifications. With this the problem has
become more delicate than it appeared to be at first. All the more
so is this true, when one is once again reminded that the nature
of an artist is related to the *Hochstapler* (high society swindler)

Krull, or that Proust's narrator is and is not Proust, so that the reader can hardly make out with whom he is dealing. To be sure, pastiche-makers do not usually hide behind someone else, but who do they wish to be? What differentiates their "falsification" from the *Disciples at Emmaus?* I have purposely selected a celebrated pictorial falsification by Van Meegeren as an example because the problems we have discussed have presented themselves in it in the sharpest possible way and generally—for reasons that may easily be guessed—regularly present themselves in that context. To be sure, someone like Savage is precise in his definitions, which he provides immediately: "Forgeries are copies of works of art or craft for fraudulent purposes; fakes are genuine works which have been altered in character . . . reproductions are copies made for honest purposes . . . replicas are contemporary reproductions. The term [forgery] needs to be used with great care because the intention is all-important."[40]

In other writers one finds practically identical conceptions. If it were true that everything indeed depends on the intentions of the authors, which in this case means forgers, then one can easily make a distinction, that is, if those intentions could be easily perceived! Usually this is not the case. If one abandons the search for the intentions, then perhaps there is little to go by in order to come to a precise distinction between pastiche and forgery. It is no doubt best to establish that a forger "does as if," while a pastiche-maker does "as." Proust does "as" Saint-Simon. Mann does as the writer of the biblical Joseph story. The same is true of the forger. But in addition he does as if he *were* Saint-Simon or a biblical narrator. The difference between these two categories perhaps does not reside so much (and surely not primarily) in the fact that in one case the person does and in the other case the person does not declare what he is doing. The pastiche-maker has a different purpose in mind. His work shows the result of the recreation of a sacred story, which thereby and only thereby remains sacred. The forger intrudes as it were into the sacred, which he does not create. He merely adds to it and thus rather kills it than keeps it alive. In the case of the forger one may detect a simple direction; from himself to the work of another, which he wishes "to fill up" (without essentially enriching it), and in which he wishes to be absorbed. This last desire, besides a social-economic motivation, represents a supplementary reason to remain anonymous. The pastiche-maker is characterized, just like the good critic, by a double movement: from himself to the work and from the work to himself. Here we may speak of assimilation in the fullest sense of that word.[41]

Forgery seems therefore to be the antimythical par excellence. By wriggling himself into the holy story that is the myth and by acting as if it were the myth itself, the forger gives the forgery an aspect that can be characterized only as hypocritical ("apparently holy"). The forgery may be called literary hypocrisy, in which the appearance of holiness presents itself as if it were its essence. In other words: the imitation of the text functions as if it were the text. The myth does seem to be maintained in this manner, but is contaminated because "dead wood" has been added to it. One cannot conceive for a second that any kind of enrichment of the myth has taken place in this case. Totally different is the treatment of the mythical-typical in Mann's work and in the Proustian pastiches. Even though there may be similarities with a forgery, such similarities are canceled out by the differing aim. When Proust condenses and even mechanizes the style of an author in his pastiches, he does after all attain a better and more complete representation of the typical of that style. Perhaps he does this even better and more completely than the original author himself. In any case one may certainly recognize in this procedure an aspect of the "critic in action" and also of the ironic-playful distancing that appears to characterize these works. In addition we have now demonstrated that pastiche-making is a different process from and produces works of a different nature than forgery. Whereas in the latter holiness is only an appearance, in the *Joseph* novels, among others, it is precisely because of the emphasis on the critical appearance that the essence of the holiness and of the mythical-typical is not threatened. In this way we obtain a *Steigerung* (climax) that is completely absent in forgery. This critical perfecting can take place, not in spite of the change that the mythical undergoes, but precisely because of this change.

To remain alive the sacred myth must be re-created and therefore admit into its bosom the so-called antimythical of parody and criticism. Then it is safeguarded from forgery, which only appears to confirm the mythical but which in reality is a continuous menace to it.

Translated by Herman Salomon

48 SEM DRESDEN

Notes

1. From the countless studies that have dealt with these subjects I select only
those in which further bibliographical references may be found: Jean Pépin,
*Mythe et allégorie—Les origines grecques et les contestations
judéo-chrétiennes* (Paris, 1958); B.A. Sorensen, *Symbol und Symbolismus in
den ästhetischen Theorien des 18. Jahrhunderts und der deutschen Romantik*
(Copenhagen, 1963); P. Albouy, *Mythes et mythologies dans la littérature
française* (Paris, 1969); J. Strelka, "Psychoanalyse und Mythenforschung in der
Literaturwissenschaft," in V. Zmegac and Z. Skreb, eds., *Zur Kritik literatur-
wissenschaftlicher Methodologie* (Frankfurt am Main, 1973); G.S. Kirk, *Myth—
Its Meaning and Functions in Ancient and Other Cultures* (Berkeley and Los
Angeles, 1970), in which the ideas of Lévi-Strauss are extensively discussed.
2. Cf. for further data M. Dierks, *Studien zu Mythos und Psychologie bei Thomas Mann* (Bern and Munich, 1972); J. Finck, *Thomas Mann und die Psychoanalyse* (Paris, 1973).
3. K. Kerényi, *Romandichtung und Mythologie—Ein Briefwechsel mit Thomas
Mann* (Zürich, 1945), p. 19. Cf. Thomas Mann, *Autobiographisches* (Frankfurt
am Main, 1968), p. 55.
4. Whether we are dealing here with metempsychosis as Dierks (p. 20) claims is
at the very least problematic.
5. *Joseph und seine Brüder* (Stockholm, 1948), 1:556.
6. *Joseph* (Stockholm, 1948), 2:193. Cf. *Joseph der Ernährer* (Stockholm, 1943),
p. 332: " 'Einst' ist ein unumschränktes Wort und eines mit zwei Gesichtern;
es blickt zurück, weit zurück, in feierlich dämmernde Fernen, und es blickt
vorwärts, weit vorwärts, in Fernen nicht minder feierlich durch ihr Kommen-
sollen als jene anderen durch ihr Gewesenisein."
7. Cf. R. Thieberger, *Der Begriff der Zeit bei Thomas Mann* (Baden-Baden,
1952), and practically all studies of Mann, from which I select T.J. Reed, *The
Uses of Tradition* (Oxford, 1974); H. Wysling, *Mythos und Psychologie bei
Thomas Mann* (Zürich, 1969); H. Lehnert, *Thomas Mann—Fiktion, Mythos,
Religion* (Stuttgart, 1965); and finally works that investigate the problem of
time in the novel, for example, M. Church, *Time and Reality* (Chapel Hill,
1962), pp. 131 ff.
8. *Joseph*, 2:626. Cf. *Krull* (1954), p. 111, where the topic of discussion is "something sleepwalking—median, half way between doing and happening, acting
and suffering." It would be worthwhile to verify the nature and function of
the pattern in authors who differ as much among themselves as Nabokov and
Hesse in his *Magister Ludi* or Musil with his "collateral action" and the title
of the second part of book 1 of *The Man without Qualities*, "The Like of It
now Happens." Cf. especially, *Der Mann ohne Eigenschaften* (Hamburg,
1970), p. 591.
9. Cf. Dierks, pp. 103 ff.
10. (Stockholm, 1939), p. 250.
11. *Joseph*, 1:139. Cf. *Neue Studien* (Stockholm, 1948), pp. 166–67: "Because the
Tyrannical is indeed the mythical, in as far as it is the arch-norm and
arch-form of life, a timeless pattern and ancient formula into which life

flows . . ." or *Adel des Geistes* (Stockholm, 1945), p. 9: ". . . an 'arch-type' coined by our forefathers, in which posterity will recognize itself, in whose footsteps it will follow—in other words a myth, for the Typical is mythical and the essence of the myth is recurrence, timelessness and everlasting presence." In a certain sense the subject here is continuously what I wish to indicate by *geminatio*. Cf. P. Bauschinger, "Vollig exceptionelle Kinder," in W. Paulsen, ed., *Psychologie in der Literaturwissenschaft* (Heidelberg, 1971), pp. 191–99.

12. *Adel des Geistes*, p. 596. There can be no doubt that these conceptions show highly curious similarities with that which in biblical exegesis is understood by the term "figurative thought." Cf. R.P.C. Hansen, *Allegory and Event—A Study of the Sources and Significance of Origen's Interpretation of the Scripture* (London, 1959), passim, and E. Auerbach, *Gesammelte Aufsätze zur romanischen Philologie* (Bern and Munich, 1967), pp. 55 ff.

13. Cf. H. Meyer, *Das Zitat in der Erzählkunst* (Stuttgart, 1961), pp. 207 ff.; and for *Der Erwählte* especially H.J. Weigand, "Mann's Gregorius," in *The Germanic Review* 27 (1952):10–30 and 83–95 with a letter from Mann to Auerbach concerning this point.

14. Cf. Dierks, passim.

15. Concerning life that becomes text and particularly novel, one may find much in the works of the German Romanticists but also in the works of Gérard de Nerval.

16. Kerényi, p. 82.

17. Ibid., p. 57. Cf. *Neue Studien*, p. 170.

18. *Nachträge* (Frankfurt am Main, 1974), p. 246. Cf. p. 170.

19. Cf. especially R. Baumgart, *Das Ironische und die Ironie in den Werken Thomas Manns* (Munich, 1964); K. Hamburger, *Der Humor bei Thomas Mann* (Munich, 1965); E. Heller, *Thomas Mann der ironische Deutsche* (Frankfurt am Main, 1970).

20. *Der Dichter und das Phantasieren* in *Gesamelte Werke* (London, 1941), 7:214.

21. Joseph, 1:410.

22. *Nachträge*, p. 164.

23. In this connection a study must be mentioned that is unjustly neglected: Roger Caillois, *L'Homme et le sacré* (Paris, 1939), pp. 89 ff. Cf. also *Le mythe et l'homme* (Paris, 1938).

24. The relationship Joseph–artist–"swindler" is of course characteristic for Mann's work (and partly also for Nietzsche!). Data concerning this may be found in D.F. Nelson, *Portrait of the Artist as Hermes* (Chapel Hill, 1971), although incomplete.

25. Cf. W. Hempel, *Parodie, Travestie und Pastiche*, in *German.-Roman. Monatsschrift*, 46 (1965):150–76; R. Picard, "De l'aprocryphe comme genre littéraire," in *Revue des Sciences Humaines* (avril-juin 1963); W. Kazzer, *Parodie, Travestie, Pastiche* (Munich, 1977).

26. Cf. as an example among many others R. Arbour, *Henri Bergson et les lettres françaises* (Paris 1956), pp. 335 ff.

27. *Recherche* (Paris 1954), 1:375. References in the text are to this edition.

28. Cf. *Recherche*, 1:46, 85, 908, 948; 2:260, 431, 578, 971 ff.; 3:262, 878.

29. Cf. *Jean Santeuil* (Paris, 1971), pp. 194, 280, 332, 398 ff., 536; *Contre Sainte-Beuve* (Paris, 1971), pp. 76, 211, 374, 417 ff.

30. It remains to be seen whether he does justice to him in all respects. Cf. M.

50 SEM DRESDEN

Otten in the collection *Sainte-Beuve et la critique littéraire contemporaine* (Bibliothèque de la Faculté de Liège, 1972), pp. 95–100.

31. *Correspondance générale* (Paris 1933), 4:227.
32. For instance, hardly at all in W. Pabst and L. Schrader, eds., *L'affaire Lemoine von Marcel Proust* (Berlin 1972).
33. *Correspondance générale*, 4:230.
34. *Centre Sainte-Beuve*, p. 303. Cf. p. 140: "There is no better way of becoming conscious of what one feels oneself than to try to recreate within oneself what a Master has felt. In this profound effort we uncover our own thought along with his."
35. Jean Milly, *Les Pastiches de Proust* in *Le Français Moderne* (1967) 35:33–52, 125–41. Cf. his excellent edition *Les Pastiches de Proust* (Paris, 1970).
36. Pabst and Schrader, passim.
37. *Contre Sainte-Beuve*, pp. 8 and 9.
38. *Correspondance générale* (Paris, 1931), 2:181.
39. Cf. André Malraux, *Les Voix du Silence* (Paris, 1951), p. 310: "Every artist starts with pastiche."
40. George Savage, *Forgeries, Fakes and Reproductions* (London, 1963), p. 1. Cf. Sonia Cole, *Counterfeit* (London, 1955), p. 3; H. van de Waal et al., *Aspects of Art Forgery* (The Hague, 1962).
41. It is perhaps useful in connection with this assimilation to quote more completely the passage of Du Bellay to which I have alluded earlier. He says in *Deffence* (Paris: H. Chamard, 1948), p. 42: "Imitating the best Greek authors, transforming themselves into them, devouring them and after having digested them well, converting them into blood and food . . ." In these words the double movement here referred to is sharply delineated. On the one hand the imitator must transform himself into the imitated writer. On the other hand he must make the latter his flesh and blood. The relationship between text and commentary, which is closely connected to the one between critical pastiche and text, is also traditionally characterized by the term *ruminatio*, which I have discussed at length elsewhere (cf. S. Dresden: *Het herkauwen van teksten* in *Forum der Lettern*, 3/4, 1971). This image is also still used in modern literature, among others by Valéry. Furthermore, it is important to investigate the extent to which the repeating imitation is indeed literally physical and related to what Freud says (for example, *Gesammelte Werke*, 10:231) about "devouring" and "incorporate."

Lillian Feder

MYTH, POETRY, AND CRITICAL THEORY

In the last three decades, critical approaches to the function of myth in poetry have generally been influenced and sometimes determined by nonliterary findings, a development natural enough, since myth is by no means a purely literary structure. Anyone who has investigated recent studies of the role of myth in literature must surely react with some conflict—an appreciation of the perspective and insight provided by such fields as anthropology and psychology, and a certain bewilderment and perhaps resentment at the contradictory definitions and conclusions that seem to emerge from the use of such sources. The situation is, of course, complicated by the intellectual and psychological predispositions of critics. A less obvious but more serious problem is that many commentators either avoid or oversimplify the implications of the very backgrounds of myth that they acknowledge: its primordial beginnings, its relation to ritual, its roots in both the psychic and the social structures it originally reflected and served. The critic who writes on myth in literature must first decide—at least to his own satisfaction—what myth is, and this he cannot do by merely accepting a handy scheme of archetypes and forcing every literary work as well as every mythical allusion or symbol to fit its grand patterns.

Myth is both more complicated and less sophisticated than such schemes would allow. Its aesthetic functions can best be determined by acknowledging its unique characteristics, for these persist not only in literature but in all the arts. I have elsewhere defined myth in some detail;[1] here I only briefly outline what I consider its essential features, which appear in an enormous variety of adaptations.

Myths must be regarded as both historical and perennial structures. Emerging no doubt from dream and fantasy, myths express in symbolic form unconscious mental processes that characterized the stages of human phylogenetic development in which they were created. That the drives and impulses of such stages persist, even as human beings have further developed individually and collectively in relation to environmental and social changes, need, I think, no longer be proven. Each human being's dreams and myths are his own evidence. Myth, not only in its early stages but continually, has also had a social function. Although I do not believe that the ultimate qualification of a myth is its identifiable ritual origin, there is little doubt that the connection of myth with ritual is often inextricable. Such rituals remind us of the earliest functions of religion in binding together individuals in a social unit.

The narrative structure of myth depicts an inner compulsion to control through symbolic means what is fearful and challenging within the self and the universe. The conflict between the human desire for omnipotence and the recognition of limitation is portrayed in endless tales of the involvement of heroes with gods and goddesses. In violating social prohibitions through incest, parricide, infanticide, and cannibalism, mythical figures symbolically express the efforts of human beings to test and come to terms with their own nature and the conditions of human life. Essentially the distortions of mythical narrative convey a perennial struggle between inner demand and external necessity, and in this respect myth is heuristic. Its action is ritualistic, ceremonial, or compulsive. The characters of myth, their action, and motives are inseparable; as one, they are the symbolic means by which unconscious drives are at once expressed, acknowledged, and thus controlled in relation to environmental limitations and social demands.

In its evolution as a literary device, myth has never totally lost its connection with its primordial and ancient roots, except in conventional allusions to "the tuneful Nine" or Phoebus or in other such circumlocutions, which serve a purely literary function. The literary scholar, however, must acknowledge that even in their earliest appearance in extant poetry and drama mythical figures and narratives have already been adapted to new social and aesthetic purposes. The gods of Homer may retain primitive attributes, but Zeus at least often behaves like a Mycenaean overlord. Certainly both Greek and Roman myths concerned with the origins of tribes and cities reflect conscious efforts to adapt primitive materials to later religious and political ends. Myth in literature is thus encrusted with centuries of accumulated adaptations. Nietzsche, for example, in nineteenth-century Germany still rages against Euripides' fifth-century B.C. interpretation of a primordial deity. In so doing, Nietzsche not only reflects his own time and place but resurrects something of the primitive nature of Dionysos.

Although one cannot follow the historical course of every myth one encounters in literature, nor is such a procedure always necessary, one must surely be aware that if, for example, a poem such as Allen Tate's "Aeneas at Washington" is based on a Roman foundation myth, the twentieth-century American poet is imitating in literature a process of constructing a national identity on a mythical and legendary basis that served important political functions in Rome of the second century B.C.[2] The approach to myth in literature is thus complicated by the history of myth itself, and by the special capacity of this structure to retain something of its fundamental character through centuries of adaptation to both general and individual expression. Myths are used in literature in three major ways: mythical narratives and figures are the overt base on which plot and character are created; or they are submerged beneath the surface of realistic characters and action; or new mythical structures are invented that have a remarkable resemblance to traditional ones.

I have no wish to add to the already excessive number of evaluations of Northrop Frye's contribution to archetypal criticism, but since it still seems necessary to estimate the validity of such an approach to poetry, certain central issues in his work must be considered. Whereas Frye's *Anatomy of Criticism* and other works on archetypes have greatly influenced those critics of English literature who know little about classical, Oriental, or other mythologies, they have had practically no effect on scholars and critics who have investigated the origins and functions of myth in ancient societies in relation to their literary adaptations. Yet few critics have revealed more precisely the particular function of actual myths in poetry than Frye has—in the work of Blake, Spenser, and others. Furthermore, while rejecting Frye's equation of literary art with myth, one can certainly accept his sensitive adaptation of Freud's work on the relation of myth to dream and of both to the origins of poetry.

But Frye, of course, is chiefly known for his monomyth concocted out of Jungian archetypes and the ritual theory of myth of the Cambridge anthropologists, which became popular in the 1940s. In speculating on the function of myth and ritual in ancient and primi-

tive societies, Frye goes no further than do Frazer and his literary
followers. In abstracting a single all-encompassing myth out of the
rich and varied body of actual myths, moreover, Frye ignores
mythical narratives and ritual practices that do not serve his hypothetical scheme. Furthermore, as W.K. Wimsatt has pointed out,
there are basic errors, such as the hypothetical "four seasons," in
the foundation and "coordinating principle"[3] of Frye's structure,
and there are contradictions within the critical scheme itself.[4]

None of this would matter very much if Frye's archetypal
scheme could accomplish what he intends: "To show how all literary genres are derived from the quest-myth," a "derivation" that
is "logical . . . within the science of criticism," and if it could elucidate the structure and contents of literature on the basis of what
Frye calls "the central myth of art" that "must be the vision of the
end of social effort, the innocent world of fulfilled desires, the free
human society."[5] But much of literature, even that based on actual
myths, eludes or adjusts only peripherally to this neat pattern.

The fact is that the most fruitful aspects of Frye's scheme are
those that grow out of the familiar attributes of the gods and heroic
figures and the narrative contents of traditional myths. His discussion of Venus in Spenser's *The Faerie Queene*, for example, as a
representative of "the whole order of nature, in its higher human
as well as its lower physical aspect,"[6] strikes us immediately as
valid because it calls to mind functions of Aphrodite or Venus
adapted from ancient myths by writers as different from each other
as Homer, Virgil, and Lucretius. When Frye applies his archetypes of the scapegoat, the dying god, or the leviathan to literary
works in which their myths are latent or overt, his insights are
often profound. When, however, one tries to categorize actual literature within the four mythoi of comedy, romance, tragedy, and
irony as "four aspects of a central unifying myth,"[7] one must finally reject this scheme on the basis of one's own experience of
myth and the very genres and modes that Frye abstracts from it.
Frye's work has served an important function in revealing some of
the complicated ways in which actual or latent myths and rituals
exist within literature, but his hypothetical monomyth has sometimes obscured the very territory he has been instrumental in opening to exploration.

The essential limitation of the monomyth results from the fact
that it is a critical construct that, in imitating a mythical one, sim-
plifies it, imposing anachronistic literary determinants ostensibly
for the purpose of releasing "primitive" ways of thinking and feel-

ing. This Frye freely admits, yet he seems also to insist that the roots of his system lie deep in myth itself. Thus Frye both disclaims the "historical" validity of his scheme and continually demands a response to the remnants of the "primitive" elements of myth, indeed to the revitalization of these within his own hypothetical construction. Discussing *The Golden Bough* "from the point of view of literary criticism," Frye insists: "It does not matter two pins to the literary critic whether such a ritual had any historical existence or not." He goes on to say, however: "It is very probable that Frazer's hypothetical ritual would have many and striking analogies to actual rituals, and collecting such analogies is part of his argument."[8] One can hardly object to such use of analogies in the effort to discover the origins and early nature of a structure so ancient and continuous as myth, especially when they are tested in relation to whatever more precise evidence is available. The question that arises for the critic who believes that evidence of origins is important is: what purpose will such analogies serve? When such analogies are adapted to suit the requirements of a critical scheme employed as an imaginary source of all mythical prototypes and all literary genres, they serve not to elucidate the evolving functions of myth in art but to create an alternate pseudomyth, the distortions of which do not, as in actual myths, function as vehicles of disclosure.

In an essay on Wallace Stevens, generally brilliant in its penetration of what Frye calls "the processes of poetic thought at work,"[9] he at times seems to force the body of Stevens's poetry to the requirements of his own scheme. "In the poems of the winter vision," he says, "the solar hero and the green queen become increasingly identified with the father and mother of a Freudian imago."[10] A parenthetical reference to page 439 of *The Collected Poems of Wallace Stevens* (1954) at the end of this sentence refers to the poem "Imago." Of course, Frye has been discussing Stevens's later poetry in this section of his essay, and "Imago" is but one example, but it seems to me that this poem, like others to which he refers, resists Frye's neat categorization.

As the editors of the *Standard Edition* of Freud's works point out, "The term 'imago' was not often used by Freud, especially in his later writing."[11] Freud uses the term once as a parenthetical explanation in a consideration of "new objects," which are "chosen on the model (imago) of the infantile ones" (11:181). Elsewhere, referring to the "father-imago" as one of the "prototypes" within a patient's mind, he says that he is using "the apt term introduced by Jung" (12:100). Freud is here discussing the nature of transference in psychoanalysis, and a bit later in the same essay he deals with the "regressive course" of this process, which "has revived the subject's infantile imagos" (12:102). Stevens admired Freud for having "given the irrational a legitimacy that it never had before,"[12] and certainly the awareness of the ever-recurrent, ever-vital past that permeates his poetry is related to Freud's discoveries of the multilayered territories of the archaic and the personal past in the unconscious mind, portions of which are disclosed obliquely in dream, fantasy, myth, and art. Furthermore, as Frye and other critics have indicated,[13] certain mythical structures in Stevens's poetry reveal the influence of Jung's work on archetypes, particularly his concept of the anima. But it is not the "Freudian imago" or the Jungian either that Stevens describes in "Imago"; it is his own conception of the imagination's capacity, *"in a leaden time and in a world that does not move for the weight of its own heaviness,"*[14] to disclose the essence of reality by means of its unique processes of transformation:

> Who can pick up the weight of Britain,
> Who can move the German load
> Or say to the French here is France again?
> Imago. Imago. Imago.[15]

The solidity of the earth's very presence and the heaviness of its long history challenge the unsubstantial imagination, whose very limits are its instruments of conquest. For "Medium man" or man as "medium" between the inner and external worlds, without magic but only through the "motions in the mind and heart," forms new territories within created out of both realms. It is the "motions" of the mind that assure the continuity of history, that move the "weight" of the actual earth with

> Something returning from a deeper quarter,
> A glacier running through delirium,

lifting "this heavy rock," and forming not a "father-imago" but a conception of a "land" that can *"Move lightly through the air again,"* more extensive than any actual one and containing all lands and the buried histories of those who inhabited them. The imago contains and reveals what Stevens elsewhere says is the nature of poetry itself: "the movement of a self in the rock."[16]

Although the "imago" Stevens creates in this poem is not a myth, the very process of its formation, which he here explores, enters into the creation of myth, and it is the mythical process rather than myth itself with which Stevens is mainly concerned. Whereas one can only agree with Frye's view that "the father and mother" of Stevens's later poems "in turn expand into a continuous life throughout time of which we form our unitary realizations,"[17] there is no justification for regarding these as myths. They are archetypes, which "the sense of the archaic"[18] that exists within continually recreates out of the material of daily reality. The mere fact that a poet "sees individual and class as metaphorically identical" does not result in his working "with *myths,*" as Frye suggests.[19] Stevens's creation and use of archetypal presences and scenes are extremely important elements of his poetry, but not as a pervasive mythical structure. Moreover, when Stevens occasionally employs traditional myths or alludes to them, and even when he creates his own, his purpose is essentially to discover their unique revelations of what he calls the "human" or the "real."

Like many modern poets, Stevens explores the nature of myth in the very process of adapting or creating it. In two apparently contradictory passages about the muse in one of the essays of *The Necessary Angel,* a collection that he describes as his "contributions to the theory of poetry," he provides an essential clue to the philosophical and psychological basis of many of the myths he uses in his poems. Considering "poetic truth" as rooted in factual reality, he declares:

> *No longer do I believe that there is a mystic muse, sister of the Minotaur. This is another of the monsters I had for nurse, whom I have wasted. I am myself a part of what is real, and it is my own speech and the strength of it, this only that I hear or ever shall.* (p. 60)

Although he never entirely abandons this position, and it can be said that his critical stance is rooted in it, he does modify it as he goes on to recognize that fact is "as extensible as it is ambiguous." His observation that "absolute fact includes everything that the imagination includes" leaves no place for "the false conception of the imagination as some incalculable *vates* within us" (pp. 60–61), but it opens the way for an acceptance of the very muse he has ostensibly rejected. For if, as he says, "Poetry is the imagination of life," depicting a world within of our "own thoughts" and our "own feelings," which are our only connection with perceived reality, the myth that portrays our imaginative synthesis of the "geography" of actuality with our own being—a synthesis achieved only symbolically—is our riddle and our persona, our vehicle of truth:

> *Inexplicable sister of the Minotaur, enigma and mask, although I am part of what is real, hear me and recognize me as part of the unreal. I am the truth but the truth of that imagination of life in which with unfamiliar motion and manner you guide me in those exchanges of speech in which your words are mine, mine yours.* (pp. 65–67)

In his poetry, Stevens seldom uses traditional myth. "The death of one god is the death of all," he says in the first poem of "Notes Toward a Supreme Fiction," and he goes on to declare: "Phoebus is dead." Yet in this poem, as in many others, Stevens probes for the origin of myth itself:

> There was a muddy centre before we breathed.
> There was a myth before the myth began,
> Venerable and articulate and complete. (p. 383)

In the poems of "Notes Toward a Supreme Fiction," Stevens is chiefly concerned with the "abstract" or conceptual basis of myth. The Fiction, as R.P. Blackmur says, "must be an abstract idea of *being*, which when fleshed or blooded in nature or in thought, will absorb all the meanings we discover. That is to say, it must be archetypal, and a source, an initiator of myth and sense, and also a reference or judgment for myth and sense."[20] The "Supreme Fiction" is thus not a myth but an archetype, a symbolic construct of the essential materials of reality—places, presences, relationships—which both incorporates and objectifies human perception and response and can therefore adapt to changing "geographies" and various inner transformations. Such fictions are intrinsic to the myths Stevens evokes and invents in his poems as he seeks the "muddy centre" out of which life springs and to which it returns; for this he has said is ultimately the source of myth itself.

The myths that Stevens invents in *Owl's Clover* have been discussed with great subtlety by Helen Vendler, who points out that even his "mythical satire on myth" in this work ends in lines "too close to approving passages in Stevens ... to be dismissed as a continuing satire on the angels"[21] of "The Greenest Continent."[22] This is Africa, which, he says, "No god rules" (*OP*, p. 55). What Vendler sees, however, as an expression of Stevens's "divided feelings" toward the angels who are powerless against the menace of Africa and yet return to "their tabernacles" to

... contemplate time's golden paladin
And purpose, to hear the wild bee drone, to feel
The ecstasy of sense in a sensuous air (*OP*, p. 56)

is a revelation of the ambiguous qualities of myth itself. Incapable
of combating the realities of violence and death undisguised in
the greenest continent, myth nevertheless, even in the figures of
these powerless angels, exerts a form of control—a primitive insistence on the heroic and the purposeful in the very face of the
severest limits.

All the myths of *Owl's Clover* incorporate its last one, Ananke or
Necessity, which Stevens calls "the common god" (*OP*, p. 59). He
is their qualification and by him they are finally defined. Stevens's
Ananke seems to have been influenced by Freud's several references to this ancient concept, always capitalized either in Greek
or transliterated, and sometimes a personification or a mythicized
being. In one place Freud defines Ananke as "the reality of the
universe" (16:430), and in another as "the exigencies of reality"
(21:139). In his best-known adaptation of this concept Ananke is
one of the parents—Eros being the other—"of human civilization"
(21:101).

Ananke in *Owl's Clover* is also a principle of reality; his mythicized form as "the common god" or "the final god" only exposes
the nature of godhood:

> He sees but not by sight.
> He does not hear by sound. His spirit knows
> Each look and each necessitous cry, as a god
> Knows, knowing that he does not care, and knows,
> Knowing and meaning that he cannot care. (*OP*, p. 59)

Ananke, as the hidden forces within external nature, which includes man, emerges from the human mind in devious forms that
would seem to deny his unseeing, uncaring essence. In that mind
Ananke sees "the angel" and the other myths that enact the human struggle with his limits, but Ananke himself is incorporated
into the very wish for omnipotence that ultimately contains and
reveals its origin in human mortality: he is

> Lord without any deviation, lord
> And origin and resplendent end of law,
> Sultan of African sultans, starless crown. (*OP*, p. 60)

In ceremony and ritual honoring lords and gods, it is Ananke who
is finally paid tribute.

Ananke named or unnamed is the motivating force behind most of the myths Stevens invents in his poetry. One feels its presence especially in "The Owl in the Sarcophagus," in which Stevens consciously creates what he calls "the mythology of modern death." It is a poem that itself portrays and exposes the process of myth-making. Here Stevens's mythical figures and narrative enact an acceptance of mortality by a mind that has abandoned belief in eternity or any life after death. But death, the ultimate reality, can be apprehended only indirectly, through myths whose very distortions indicate the process of their creation. Thus death takes "two forms of thought," which are "high sleep" and "high peace," mythical "brothers" who attend the dying. These are accompanied by "a third form, she that says / Goodby in the darkness."

Stevens goes on to describe these forms, which "are visible to the eye that needs, / Needs out of the whole necessity of sight." Ananke motivates the creation of these forms and lies within the very contradictions of their nature and conduct. Sleep as "ultimate intellect" is the elemental existence of mind, which includes its end. Peace is both "brilliant" and "hollow"; he has been "formed / Out of our lives to keep us in our death." Both sleep and peace are gentle and destructive, ultimate goals and "nothingness." As mediator between them and the dying, the third figure "is the mother of us all." As "earthly mother and the mother of / The dead," she embodies the contradictory forces of creation and destruction, life and death, which dwell within us and define our being, and therefore "she was a self that knew, an inner thing." This essential inner self holds "men closely with discovery." As "speed discovers," as "invisible change discovers what is changed," the mind of man, without conscious awareness, discovers the reality of his own extinction through the myths he creates out of his own being, out of a "desire that is the will" to confront the conditions of his existence. The very power of creation within him produces "beings of the mind," which, ironically, are his one means of acknowledging the inevitability— indeed the necessity—of death.

In his essays and poetry, Stevens's essential concern with both archetype and myth is not their illustration of the patterns or contents of seasonal ritual. To him they are constructs that both portray and disclose processes of mind, especially those that unite the inner world of the imagination with the demands and limits of reality. Critical theory regarding the use of myth in twentieth-century poetry must include poets' own explorations of the nature of myth even as they employ it, for Stevens is by no means the only modern poet who is continually preoccupied with the conflicts and discoveries revealed in its symbolic structure. After further consideration of critical approaches to myth, I shall return briefly to other investigations within poetry itself, since these, I believe, provide a standard for evaluating any theory of the function of myth in poetry.

One critic, Elizabeth Sewell, illustrates her conviction that it is in poetry that the structure of myth is most evident by including in her theoretical study *The Orphic Voice* a series of what she calls her "Working Poems," which convey through myth some of her major ideas on its nature and functions. Actually the poems repeat in brief the theory that the rest of her book develops: "For the last 400 years, with the coming of what one might call the modern age, poetry has been struggling to evolve and perfect the inclusive mythology on which language works and all thought in words is carried on, and . . . this type of thinking is the only adequate instrument for thinking about change, process, organisms, and life." Orpheus, she explains, "is poetry thinking about itself."[23]

Sewell's theory of myth is even more inclusive than Frye's. If she limits her literary field to poetry, she extends the province of myth in other respects, suggesting that "language and mind, poetry and biology meet and bear on one another in the figure of Orpheus" (p. 5). Logic, mathematics, and biology, like poetry, fall within her conception of discovery as "a mythological situation in which the mind unites with a figure of its own devising as a means toward understanding the world" (p. 20). Essentially her aim is to reunite poetry and science by revealing that both result from similar thought processes that can be defined as mythical. Sewell's view of myth as an "activity" of mind expressed by language encompasses an enormous area of thought and expression: "All striving and learning is mythologizing; and language is the mythology of thought and action, a system of working figures made manifest" (p. 28). It seems fair to say that she regards all conceptual thought and its products as mythical.

Paradoxically, this apparent broadening of the province of myth results in severe limitations in her interpretations of the actual functions of mythical narrative. Thus, while she regrets the failure of contemporary investigations "in the natural history of thinking" to employ the fields of "biology, poetry, psychology, and anthropology" in "a common front" (p. 334), she herself underestimates the importance of both psychology and anthropology in the study of myth. She objects to the extensive use of Freudian and Jungian psychology in contemporary literary discussion of myths and to the influence of Frazer's *The Golden Bough*. While one could hardly approve of the simplistic distortions of Freudian psychology in certain approaches to mythical figures as real persons—not to say patients—it is shortsighted to ignore the extremely important contributions of Freud, Jung, and Frazer to modern investigations of myth as a clue to individual and social expression.

Sewell praises Freud as "a true mythological thinker who had to work at inventing his myths of interpretation for his subject matter," but concludes that he "was hampered by not recognizing that this was the nature of his task, myth and poetry being unacceptable in this era as scientific method" (p. 334). She obviously has not read Freud very carefully. Although by no standards except her own can Freud be considered a "mythological thinker," Freud was probably the first conscious explorer of myth as a self-revealing scientific instrument. In fact, Freud refers to his own use of "scientific myth" (18:135) and to "our mythological theory of instincts" (22:212). "Instincts," he says, "are mythical entities, magnificent in their indefiniteness" (22:95). It was Freud's interpretation, use, and invention of myths as clues to the unconscious mind that opened the way not only to a broader critical understanding of the role of myth in poetry but to poets' own explorations of the ancient figures and narratives they evoked and revitalized.

Sewell's evaluation of Frazer's *The Golden Bough* as a work that "insulates itself from poetry" (p. 335) is surprisingly insensitive. Actually, Frazer's approach to myth and rite is often more literary than scientific. Certainly his capacity to recreate the emotional intensity of the participants in ritual observance and to reveal the importance of myth and rite as keys to social behavior have had an enormous effect on modern poets. John Vickery's comment on *The Golden Bough*, "In literature alone it touches nearly everything, from the most significant to the most ephemeral works,"[24] can hardly be questioned by the reader of twentieth-century poetry and fiction. Sewell's underestimation of the contributions of Freud and Frazer to the study of myth results essentially from her unwillingness to view myth as separable from poetry or poetry as separable in any respect from the processes of conceptual thought.

Perhaps the chief limitation of Sewell's method is that, in rejecting psychoanalytic findings of the unconscious roots of myth, she oversimplifies the many levels of "the activity of mind and language" (p. 57) that enter into the process of creation or discovery.

Her salutary effort to reveal the inextricable connection between imaginative and scientific discovery is impeded by her failure to acknowledge that, while both imaginative and rational conception can make use of mythical constructions, they do not themselves necessarily emerge from either mythical or mythopoeic processes. In distinguishing between these last two modes of thought and discourse, Toshihiko Izutsu offers definitions of both that are valuable to those engaged in the study of myth. "The mythical or mythological level of discourse," he says, is one in which

> words are used in such a way that they disclose all the prehistoric memories and associations that lie dormant in them. Fantastic images are thereby called forth out of the deepest recesses of the mind. The primordial images thus evoked from the forgotten past of humanity tend to conglomerate into a more or less coherent narrative form and bring into being the various myths.

Izutsu describes the shaman as "the man who is endowed with a special ability to conjure up primordial images of this sort out of the semantic storehouse of language." The difference between the mythical level of discourse described above and the mythopoeic is that, whereas the former involves merely an "imaginary transcendence" of empirical reality, the latter expresses actual transcendence—as recorded in the poetry of the shamans Izutsu discusses, the immediate experience of "an ecstatic oblivion of ego in the midst of a primordial purity of Being."[25] In the light of these definitions, it seems clear that although myth, as scientific, philosophical, or literary construct, can portray attitudes and evoke feelings that emerge from a mythopoeic level of consciousness, one can hardly assume that scientific discovery and aesthetic creation must depend upon the use of such unconscious experience.

In objecting to the obvious fallacy that logical and imaginative thinking are sharply separated, Sewell oversimplifies the whole problem, making no differentiation between conscious and unconscious processes, and thus insisting that "all thinking is of the same kind" (pp. 19–20). Surely one cannot believe that the mental processes involved in solving a mathematical problem are exactly the same as those which produce the "atemporal and aspatial dimension" of the mythopoeic level of consciousness.[26] Yeats's description of the "one moment of creation" as "the moment when we are both asleep and awake" and his revelations of his use of his unconscious mind in states of self-induced trance[27] elucidate his own creative processes, but they do not necessarily disclose those of all poets or even the "one" way in which his own mind operated. One of the most remarkable functions of myth in Yeats and other poets is its very capacity to mediate between and thus convey various levels of consciousness and thought.

Although Sewell's "inclusive mythology" is unconvincing, her demonstration of the significance of Orpheus in Renaissance and later literature is often illuminating, as is her perception of the method of approaching reality that the mythical figure and narrative themselves provide. On occasion, however, one wishes she had not ignored the "historical" Orpheus, especially when, as she herself admits, the poet she is considering (in this case Erasmus Darwin) refers to the "founder of a cult" (p. 174). Still, in tracing the poetic adaptations of Orpheus or Orphism as expressions of man's engagement with the world, she elucidates both the mythical evocations and the literary works in which they appear. In her discussion of Goethe's "Urworte: Orphisch," for example, she indicates the means by which the myth is used to reveal "a mind passionately interested in the dynamics of life, in the individual organism, in nature at large, in human beings and in his own thinking and feeling and acting self" (p. 274).

Orpheus has been studied extensively by contemporary critics of poetry as representative of the mind and feelings of the poet himself. "He is the figure, the myth entrusted with the burden of poetry and myth," says Walter A. Strauss in *Descent and Return: the Orphic Theme in Modern Literature.* Concentrating primarily on Continental writers from 1900 to 1925, Strauss examines many adaptations of the myth that depict the "poet-as-thinker." As such, Orpheus "journeys down to the depths of the pysche," to death itself, and finally emerges as a "reconciler of opposites," who creates a poetic fusion of the Dionysian and the Apollonian.[28]

In his brief but suggestive conclusion, Strauss indicates the chief changes in attitudes toward the Orpheus myth in the years since 1925. He points out that even in the "quest . . . for a total integration of all the contraries," which is the theme of Nikos Kazantzakis's *The Odyssey: A Modern Sequel,* Orpheus "is reduced" to a rather trivial follower of the hero Odysseus.[29] If the "harmonizing" Orpheus does persist among some writers, there is also a widespread rejection of the Orphic ideal, a disbelief in reconciliation, in fact, an insistence on discontinuity.[30]

Since the 1920s, Odysseus has been a more prevalent and more challenging mythical presence in literature than Orpheus. Of course, Odysseus or Ulysses appears in every century of Western

literature in a variety of interpretations. But it is in the twentieth
century and increasingly in fairly recent poetry that this figure,
whose resourcefulness, enormous desire for knowledge, and vast
experience no doubt reflect his multiple origins in myth, folk tale,
and history, has been employed to represent essential qualities of
the mythical symbol itself.[31] In many modern and contemporary
poems, Odysseus, like the Orpheus of earlier periods, is depicted
as a thinker, but he applies his knowledge and his fabled resourcefulness not to convey the nature of the poet or of poetry, but
to explore his own myth as he probes the many meanings of his
voyages and adventures.

The development of an increasingly analytic approach to the
Odysseus myth within poetry itself is not, of course, unbroken.
Still, it can be said that poetic adaptations of this myth in the
twentieth century illustrate a general tendency that has already
been mentioned in connection with the poetry of Wallace Stevens: the effort by the poet to abstract the mythical process from
myth itself, to follow its distortions of reality to the hidden levels
of consciousness and experience of the self in relation to natural
and social phenomena that they ultimately disclose.

As early as 1911, the Greek poet C.P. Cavafy, in his poem
"Ithaca," interprets the journey of Odysseus, "full of adventures,
full of things to learn," as taking place in a generalized mind.[32]
The quality of the journey is determined by those who undertake
it. The savagery that the traditional Odysseus encounters can be
avoided: "The Laestrygonians and the Cyclopes and fierce Poseidon you will not meet, unless you carry them in your heart, unless
your heart sets them in your path." The poet, as instructor, interprets the myth as a guide to the delights and the "stores of knowledge" to be gathered in a lifetime. But these are to be obtained
only at the cost of ultimate disillusion. Ithaca, the goal, has motivated the journey, but "she has nothing more to offer." The "wisdom" and "experience" acquired in encountering reality inevitably destroy the idealized fantasy: "You will have already realized
what these Ithacas mean."

Cavafy's interpretation of the myth pits the real experience of
life against its imagined goal. Twenty years later, George Seferis,
beginning with a glance at Joachim du Bellay's sonnet on Ulysses
and echoing his first line, "Fortunate he who's made the voyage of
Odysseus," sees the journey as a paradigm for the pain and loss
that life exacts.[33] Yet these are redeemed by "the shade of Odysseus" whom the poet summons as a companion to make the voy-

age and his sense of exile more acceptable. Odysseus provides comfort by his effort to free the modern voyager from the superhuman challenges of his myth:

> It's as if he wants to expel from among us the superhuman
>   one-eyed Cyclops, the Sirens who make you forget
>   with their song, Scylla and Charybdis:
> so many complex monsters that prevent us from remembering
>   that he too was a man struggling in the world with
>   soul and body.

and by remaining an example of a heroic encounter with memories and loneliness. Within the mind of the poet, the mythical Odysseus, "as though he were my father / or certain old sailors of my childhood," symbolizes the resourcefulness and endurance demanded by any conquest of reality in the face of "the waveless blue sea in the heart of winter."

The most explicit analysis in poetry of Odysseus as the symbolic interpreter of experience is, not unexpectedly, Wallace Stevens's "The Sail of Ulysses."[34] Introducing him as *"symbol of the seeker,"* who *"read his own mind,"* Stevens records Ulysses' soliloquy as he proceeds on his journey, the goal of which is "knowledge." Ulysses, as symbol, his voyage, and all that he learns are one, for his myth depicts "the thinker / Thinking gold thoughts in a golden mind." His voyage is a quest for the meaning of symbol itself:

>   Each man
> Is an approach to the vigilance
> In which the litter of truths becomes
> A whole, the day on which the last star
> Has been counted, the genealogy
> Of gods and men destroyed, the right
> To know established as the right to be.
> The ancient symbols will be nothing then.
> We shall have gone beyond the symbols
> To that which they symbolized, away
> From the rumors of the speech-full domes,
> To the chatter that is then the true legend,
> Like glitter ascended into fire.

Going "beyond the symbols," Ulysses asks: "What is the shape of the sibyl?" Answering his own question, he rejects the traditional image of holiness and power, the "gorgeous symbol," and seeks instead "the sibyl of the self," the creature of "poverty" and "need." Within the self, the sibyl is "a blind thing fumbling for its form." It is a "dream too poor, too destitute / To be remembered." Returning the myth of the sibyl to its origins in the dream's distorted expression of deprival and wish, Ulysses, like all of Stevens's mythical figures, confronts Ananke: "Need names on its breath / Categories of bleak necessity," which, once named, produce "another plane" of knowledge, releasing the symbol from its origins within us, freeing the mind to recognize its own creations: the sibyl is "an inhuman of our features," as is Ulysses himself.

Many modern poets interpret Odysseus' encounters with supernatural beings as a confrontation with the self. W.D. Snodgrass's "$\mu\eta\tau\iota\varsigma$ . . . $o\dot{\upsilon}$ $\tau\iota\varsigma$"[35] suggests the syncretic elements of his myth, as the cunning that distinguishes him as a hero is contrasted with the implications of the name Noman that he assumes to trick the Cyclops. Unable to "silence" his "defiant / Mind," Odysseus carries away with him the guilt of blinding the Cyclops: "I had escaped, by trickery, as no man." Ithaca, when he returns, is "No Man's land," where "all seem stone blind." Finally, it is the "dead blind guide," the Cyclops, the shepherd who had tended his flock, who leads Odysseus to

> Still waters that will never wash my hand,
> To kneel by my old face and know my name.

In a phrase that reminds one of the biblical psalmist, the Cyclops is described as the blinded victim who guides the hero to self-knowledge. The punishment that Odysseus received from Poseidon as a result of proudly shouting his identity to the Cyclops, as he sailed away from his island, is here internalized. Disguised in Ithaca, unknown to others, Odysseus has learned how he won his well-known epithet, and thus he resumes his name. This reestablishment of his sense of self has none of the proud assertiveness of the Odysseus persona of Ezra Pound's *Pisan Cantos*, who, in despair, also sees himself as "OΫ TIΣ / OΫ TIΣ / I am noman, my name is noman," but whose identity as the omnipotent Odysseus is soon resumed, apparently unqualified by temporary dissociations.[36] "Odysseus / the name of my family," replies this persona in answer to his own question: "OΫ TIΣ: OΫ TIΣ?" whereas the heroic name Odysseus never appears in Snodgrass's poem, perhaps because its speaker knows that his identity will forever include his role as Noman and his remembrance of the victim who became his guide.

W.S. Merwin's poem "Odysseus" is also concerned with self-knowledge; this is acquired throughout his many voyages to "the islands / Each with its woman," which he recognizes as always "the same."[37] "The knowledge of all that he betrayed" does not bring an end to his quest, for the very betrayal of his myth of varied and fabulous encounters defines his real experience. In recent poems by Yannis Ritsos and Joseph Brodsky, Odysseus is a myth to be exposed within the minds of Penelope and Telemachus. Ritsos's "Penelope's Despair" describes the disparity between the idealized figure in the mind of the woman "waiting and dreaming" and the "wretched stranger / soaked in blood" who returns.[38] Penelope recognizes her husband easily, for the traditional "signs" are "clear," but her voice saying "welcome" seems to be "someone else's." It is the voice of a woman who realizes that she must relinquish a self defined by the dreams and fantasies she now abandons in "her final endurance" of the limitations of her husband's nature and her own.

In Brodsky's "Odysseus to Telemachus," it is Odysseus who expresses weariness and confusion, recalling his years at Troy and his many voyages.[39] Writing to Telemachus, whom he hardly remembers, about a war that is only a vague memory and journeys filled with tedium, of his disgust and his suffering, he finds consolation in the fact that, separated from him for so long, Telemachus is "quite safe from Oedipal passions," and thus can have "dreams" that "are blameless." His address to his son suggests an effort to free him from any influence of the mythicized father and from a mythical concept of heroism that the hero's experience has revealed as a painful illusion.

One of the most striking features of modern poetic explorations of the myths of Odysseus, Dionysos, Agamemnon, and other mythical figures is that, in interpreting them, and the legendary materials they have gathered, as symbolic expressions of psychological need, conflict, and discovery, the poet, in Stevens's terms, reveals the movement of the ancient world in which myth and rite served essential social functions to a realm within the mind of twentieth-century man. This inner territory is depicted by Radcliffe Squires in his recent "A Sequence of Poems" as a series of gardens tended by Medusa, Hecate, Ariadne, and Maia.[40] Juxtaposed with these symbolic sites of inner choices is external reality, "The Garden of the World." The "you" addressed in these poems is suspended, in the garden of Medusa, between the desire to behold Medusa "in the dark mirror you will find / Has grown in the palm of your hand" and the option "to forget the mirror and / See what the face really looks like." Within the garden of Hecate, the observer recognizes imagined lovers as "dead and brittle vines"; in the garden of Ariadne, he finds that

> the priapus at the gate
> Has lost aspect and seems no more
> Than a milestone; . . .

Even those who have lived long under the sway of these mythical realms discover within them the evidence of their dissolution. As the quester, "cold and wet," moves toward the cave of Maia, the nymph herself bars his admission:

> "You cannot enter," she says. "It has been
> Too long. I am nothing now, though I am back
> Of everything. I am not here, though I
> Am behind what is here. Go now and forget
> Me. Or, if you think of me at all, think
> Of me as the white violet crushed beneath
> Your instep. Its will gathers to lift you."

Ejected from the mythical gardens, consigned to the garden of the world, where "the botanist" has replaced the goddesses, "you" must accept your aloneness in and alienation from a natural world without purpose or concern with human affairs. The myths have revealed idealized love and friendship for the "glacial" fantasies they are; the keepers of the mythical gardens have disclosed the frailty beneath their promises of omnipotence. If one still feels their power, it is in "a lust that will almost / Kill you," in the sound of an ancient "laughter" within, exulting in savagery.

> Here, at this point, where the gate dissolves,
> And you are neither within nor without,

the mythical realms, with their threats and comforts, recur as stages of the self, as of mankind, never quite recoverable and never entirely lost. In their explorations of these ambiguous territories, Squires and the other poets I have discussed provide the surest clues to the nature and function of myth in modern poetry.

Notes

1. *Ancient Myth in Modern Poetry* (Princeton, 1971).
2. For a brief and excellent discussion of this process, see Walter Donlan, "The

Foundation Legends of Rome: An Example of Dynamic Process," *The Classical World* 64, no. 4 (December 1970):109–14.

3. Northrop Frye, *Fables of Identity: Studies in Poetic Mythology* (New York, 1963), p. 9.

4. W.K. Wimsatt, "Northrop Frye: Criticism as Myth," *Northrop Frye in Modern Criticism: Selected Papers from the English Institute*, ed. Murray Krieger (New York, 1966).

5. *Fables of Identity*, pp. 17–18.

6. Ibid., p. 80.

7. Frye, *Anatomy of Criticism* (Princeton, 1957), p. 192.

8. Ibid., p. 109.

9. "The Realistic Oriole: A Study of Wallace Stevens," *Fables of Identity*, p. 239.

10. Ibid., p. 246.

11. *The Standard Edition of the Complete Psychological Works of Sigmund Freud*, trans. from the German under the general editorship of James Strachey in collaboration with Anna Freud (London, 1966–74), 19:168. References to Freud's work are to this edition.

12. Wallace Stevens, *Opus Posthumous*, ed. Samuel French Morse (New York, 1966), p. 219.

13. See Frank Doggett, *Stevens' Poetry of Thought* (Baltimore, 1966), esp. p. 39.

14. Wallace Stevens, *The Necessary Angel: Essays on Reality and the Imagination* (New York, 1951), p. 63.

15. Unless otherwise indicated, all quotations from Stevens's poetry are from the *The Collected Poems of Wallace Stevens* (New York, 1954). Page numbers are given for passages quoted from longer poems.

16. *The Necessary Angel*, p. viii.

17. "The Realistic Oriole," p. 246.

18. Wallace Stevens, "Things of August," *Collected Poems*.

19. "The Realistic Oriole," p. 249.

20. "Wallace Stevens: An Abstraction Blooded," *Form and Value in Modern Poetry* (New York, 1957), p. 214.

21. *On Extended Wings: Wallace Stevens' Longer Poems* (Cambridge, Mass., 1969), pp. 79–97 and 95–96.

22. *Owl's Clover*, in *Opus Posthumous*, hereafter referred to in the text as *OP*.

23. *The Orphic Voice: Poetry and Natural History* (New Haven, 1960), p. 47.

24. *The Literary Impact of The Golden Bough* (Princeton, 1973), p. 3.

25. "The Archetypal Image of Chaos in Chuang Tzŭ: The Problem of the Mythopoeic Level of Discourse," *Yearbook of Comparative Criticism*, vol. 4, *Anagogic Qualities of Literature*, ed. Joseph Strelka (University Park, Pa., 1971), pp. 271–76.

26. Ibid., p. 270.

27. "The Symbolism of Poetry," *Essays and Introductions* (New York, 1961), pp. 159–60; and *Per Amica Silentia Lunae* (London, 1918), pp. 47–49.

28. Cambridge, Mass., 1971, pp. 17–18.

29. Ibid., pp. 248–49.

30. Ibid., pp. 269–71.

31. See Denys Page, *The Homeric Odyssey* (London, 1955); and W.B. Stanford, *The Ulysses Theme*, 2d ed. (New York, 1968), pp. 8–11.

32. Trans. Constantine A. Trypanis, *The Penguin Book of Greek Verse* (Harmondsworth, Middlesex, 1971).

33. "Upon a Foreign Verse," *George Seferis, Collected Poems, 1924–1955,* trans. Edmund Keeley (Princeton, 1967).
34. "The Sail of Ulysses," *Opus Posthumous.*
35. *Heart's Needle* (New York, 1972).
36. *The Cantos (1–95)* (New York, 1956), Canto 74.
37. *The Drunk in the Furnace* (New York, 1960).
38. *Gestures and Other Poems, 1968–70,* trans. from the Greek by Nikos Stangos (London, 1971).
39. Trans. from the Russian by George L. Kline, *New York Review of Books,* 5 April 1973.
40. *Sewanee Review* 80, no. 3 (Summer 1975).

John J. White

MYTHOLOGICAL FICTION AND THE READING PROCESS

Myth criticism often finds itself in a state of fundamental disarray on matters of first principle. Most critical discussions of myth in modern fiction, for example, have tended to involve at least three distinct, yet complexly related conceptions of myth, and many of the protracted debates that have surrounded specific novels have stemmed from disagreements and uncertainties about their interrelationship. These aspects can be summarized as: the notion of *myth as a structure* (of time, space, character, and fable, a view substantially complicated by the sectarian differences concerning etiology and exegetical emphasis to be found among diverse schools of myth interpretation); that of *myth as received mythological material,* a literary element consciously derived from previous cultures (involving specific allusions and motifs, symbolic figures, and inherited plots); and finally that of the *mythical status* attributed to certain modern works.[1] The question frequently arises as to whether such a status, often expressed in the idea of a "new myth" (which, as Frank Kermode points out, is "the kind critics talk of when they wish to confer upon fiction some of the prestige of . . . regular myths"[2]), necessarily involves the qualities found in older myths. To read some commentaries on such creators of new myths as Melville and Kafka, one might well assume that it inevitably did. Indeed it has even been claimed that "all art worth discussing achieves myth";[3] yet Philip Rahv has rightly sounded a caveat here, emphasizing a need to distinguish more rigorously than some scholars are disposed to do between mythically and poetically effective elements, and charging that "by confusing these different powers the inflaters of myth are able to credit it with properties that really belong to art."[4]

As for the relationship between received mythological material and myth as mana, many nowadays would be inclined to agree with the view that "the creation of 'new myth' is frustrated . . . by the return to traditional myth-material."[5] And yet, notwithstanding such largely pragmatic conclusions, it is almost invariably assumed that mythological material, when it occurs in modern fiction, is necessarily being misguidedly used in order to exploit some putative mythopoeic residue. John Barth offers a recent example of this widespread assumption:

> I always felt that it was a bad idea on the face of it, though there are beautiful counter-examples, to write a more or less realistic piece of fiction, one dimension of which keeps pointing to the classical myths—like John Updike's *Centaur*, or Joyce's *Ulysses*, or Malamud's *The Natural*. Much as one may admire these novels in other respects, their authors have hold of the wrong end of the mythopoeic stick. The myths themselves are produced by the collective narrative imagination (or whatever), partly to point down at our daily reality; and so to write about our daily experience in order to point up to the myths seems to me mythopoeically retrograde. I think it is a more interesting thing to do, if you find yourself preoccupied with mythic archetypes or what have you, to address them directly.

Barth cites his own ingenious tale "Echo" (from *Lost in the Funhouse*) as an experiment in this direction, seeing it as "a story about the myth of Narcissus and Echo, instead of a realistic story that echoes narcissism";[6] and as long as Barth's skeptical argument is confined to particular novels, rather than working from premises that are assumed to be axiomatic, it makes good sense. But to decide from the outset that there is but one reason for fiction's resorting to counterpointing modernity with old myths (namely, being "preoccupied with mythic archetypes") and a single "mythopoeic stick," which can be grasped in only one way, seems methodologically less prudent than to retain a certain caution about the relationship between mythological material and myth and to avoid any a priori assumptions about function. Actually, if the kind of fiction Barth has in mind is "pointing up" to anything, then Joyce's *Ulysses* is the literary model it would be prestigious to emulate, rather than directly the figures in some classical pantheon.[7]

Myth criticism has been bedeviled by oversimplified generalizations ascribing single monolithic functions to the myth element. Often enough these derive from attitudes to myth in general that either underestimate the *literary* context or have been elevated from the individual instance to the status of axiom. Hence some have argued that myths used in literature automatically "ennoble contemporary life," while others have held that recourse to mythological analogies constitutes an "effort to claim for your book a depth of meaning it does not possess." We have been told that, in the case of mythological novels, "not only does myth represent a means of making sense of reality, it also points to the collective nature of the problems facing each of us as individuals." It has been equally forcefully argued that "mythical order reduces existential complexity." As for the feasibility of creating new myths in novels based on old ones, there is the sweeping claim that "once so much is known *about* myths and archetypes," as our present age knows,

> they can no longer be used innocently. Even their connection to the unconscious finally becomes attenuated as the mythic materials are used more consciously. All symbols become allegorical to the extent that we understand them [and] a writer, aware of the nature of categories, is not likely to believe that his own mythic lenses really capture the truth. Thus his use of myth will inevitably partake of the comic.

On the other hand, the view has also been expressed, with equal conviction, that "some of the effect that we experience in the face of genuine myth can be experienced in the face of contemporary 'comic' fictions using mythic materials." While they are not all mutually exclusive of one another, these reasonable-sounding generalizations reveal both the dividedness of attitudes to the mythical aspect of much modern fiction and also the extent to which particular findings are held to be matters of generic principle.[8]

What I wish to demonstrate in this essay is that there is a stage in our experience of the kind of mythological fiction that John Barth mistrusts that must precede any of the interpretations and perspectives indicated so far (be they a priori or inductive). This stage concerns the nature of our initial reading response. To quote Stanley Fish: "Most literary quarrels are not disagreements about response, but about a response to a response."[9] Whatever conclusions we may reach in the case of individual novels in respect of the role and value of myths in them, and whatever general views may be held about mythological fiction as a genre, it should be possible to discover a measure of common ground in considering the way in which such fiction is read and in clarifying our initial responses to it. For one basic and largely underestimated feature of this kind of literature, whose plot is in some way anticipated by the myth(s) to which it alludes, is that we must read it in a different way from works for which no such classical analogy has been offered. To focus critical attention on this feature of mythological fiction does not entail an *alternative* approach to the ones so far cited, but an additional and, it can be argued, more immediate consideration of the characteristics of a certain literary form.

Various critics have recently sought to shed more light on the act of novel-reading as a complex conjectural process, rather than as the means to one specific, unequivocal, retrospective interpretation. It is the analysis of this underestimated aspect of fiction in general that can do much to illuminate the peculiarities of mythological novels. In Robert Scholes's words:

> We read any story by engaging in what Poe called ratiocination. As we start to read we build up expectations in the form of cloudy tentative structures, into which we try to fit the details of character and event as they are presented to us. We modify these tentative structures as we are forced to by elements that do not fit, and we seek to perfect them as we move towards the end of the story.[10]

The process is one which Scholes illustrates in some detail in the case of the opening paragraph of Iris Murdoch's *The Unicorn*. Here he shows a "local inferential activity" to be in progress, as "the reader is still half-consciously commencing some vague blue-prints for the entire structure"; in this particular instance "a 'Gothic' structure of expectations" is seen to be gradually built up.[11]

A more detailed exposition of such an analytical approach to the reading process has been made by Fish, who seeks to convince us of the need for "*an analysis of the developing responses of the reader in relation to the words as they succeed one another in time.*"[12] "Essentially," Fish argues, "what the method does is *slow down* the reading experience, so that 'events' one does not notice in normal time, but which do occur, are brought before our analytical attentions."[13] But the model of slowing down reading time may be less accurate than the idea of simply analyzing more closely our initial responses to elements of a piece of fiction as part of the ongoing reading process. Of course, once one gets to the end of a book, many of the enigmas and suppositions that were part of the actual reading have been superseded; hence Fish can say that to "read the *Phaedrus* . . . is to use it up. . . . It is . . . a *self-consuming* artifact,"[14] for the patterns of conjecture and prognosis become redundant once the work is looked at in retrospect.

In the case of mythological fiction, this process of reading is in some respects complicated by the presence of a prior pattern: that of the myth (or myths) alluded to. Scholes's point that while the "local inferential activity is in progress, the reader is still half-consciously commencing some vague blue-prints for the entire structure" has to be modified for our present purposes, because the reader has already been offered some general potential blue-print for the structure (by an explicitly symbolic title, say, in the case of Joyce's *Ulysses*, or by means of the author's introduction and "Mythological Index" in the case of John Updike's *The Centaur*). As a result, the reader's concern is more with the relationship of the "blue-print" to the modern work unfolding before him. The "structure of expectations" has now become to some degree mythological (rather than "Gothic"), and the local inferential activity is bound to be controlled in some way by our knowledge of the signaled myth.

In another context, I have sought to explore some of the ways in which a "myth introduced by a modern novelist into his work can prefigure and hence anticipate the plot" of his work.[15] This prefiguration model is a way of relating the distinctive features of recent mythological fiction to the older tradition of typological exegesis:

> In the original religious context of prefiguration, the earlier event was subordinate to the latter, since it merely prophesied the greater thing to come. This sense of subordination—making the earlier less important than the later phenomenon, be it work of literature or coming of a Messiah—can be transferred to the secularized connotation of prefiguration.[16]

Such figural techniques have of course been a popular way of giving an added religiously symbolic dimension to much literature from the Middle Ages to recent times.[17] In a discussion of the way in which the German Baroque dramatist Andreas Gryphius uses the Crucifixion as a prefiguration for his depiction of the execution of Charles I of England, Albrecht Schöne has analyzed some of the salient features of literary prefigurative techniques. While Gryphius is still operating within a religious sphere of symbolism, many of the points made about his Christian prefigurative techniques could also be applied to those of the mythological novel. They have now become, Schöne argues, a matter of literary *creation* (not a method of figural *interpretation*, as they were in patristic thinking); the literary work follows, rather than precedes, the New Testament *veritas* to which it corresponds; and the application is now to secular events, rather than more strictly religious contexts. On the basis of this analysis, Schöne proceeds to the suggestion that one can best consider Gryphius's *Carolus Stuardus* to be a poetic "postfiguration" of the Crucifixion.[18] And the term postfiguration has gained a certain amount of currency in criticism of recent novels working in such a way.[19]

However, I wish to argue that in a consideration of the reading process necessitated by the mythological novel the use of the term postfiguration may be too constricting a perspective: mythology *prefigures* the events of mythological novels, in the specific sense that it creates a horizon of expectation in the reader, but this does not mean that there are many cases where the modern action that results can be satisfactorily or with much precision described as a postfiguration of the relevant myths, for the concept postfiguration suggests a congruence of myth and modernity comparable to the concordance with the religious model of the *imitatio Christi*, and this seldom proves to obtain in mythological novels worth their salt. Obviously there is more spiritual need on the writer's and readers' parts to see a concordance of prefiguration and postfiguration in the Christian context than there would be in a mythological novel. When the hero of Michel Butor's *L'emploi du temps* (Passing Time) says of the Theseus-prefiguration we shall be considering later, "The pattern is complete and I am left out of it,"[20] we do not experience a sense of failure. Although even with postfigurations where the pattern *is* completed, our interest is more likely to be in the way in which this happens, not in the simple fact that it does occur.

A work of fiction prefigured by a myth is read in such a way that our reactions to character and plot are transformed by an awareness of the mythological precedent; it is a relation whose importance lies primarily in what it brings to bear on the act of reading and interpreting, not in any determining function it may have in respect of the actual plot. Prefigurations arouse expectations in the reader which may or may not be fulfilled, and in any case will probably be satisfied in unexpected ways.

In the fourth chapter of Joyce's *Ulysses*, my first illustration of how a prefigurative component can affect the way we read a novel, the hold of retrospective conclusions over our views about it is very marked. An obvious indicator of the mainly hindsight attitude about how *Ulysses* relates to the *Odyssey* lies in the fact that this chapter is usually considered to correspond to the Calypso episode of Odysseus' adventures. Yet this view underestimates the complexities of the reading process. Since Joyce excised the headings for the individual chapters from the final version of his novel, only someone approaching this chapter either with extraneous genetic information (such as that supplied by the Gilbert, Gorman, or Linati plans[21]) or bringing to bear information available only later in the chapter would know in advance that this section relates to book 5 of the *Odyssey*. But let us for a moment try to reinstate the dynamics of the reading process and picture the detection and "ratiocination" undertaken by someone not approaching the novel with anything more than his reading so far has supplied, whose knowledge at this point in the work and whose prognostications about what is to come are conditioned only by what he has hitherto accumulated. For this is surely the essence of the reading experience of any work; it is merely complicated by the use of prefigurative material.

Assuming that by the time we are introduced to Leopold Bloom we have recognized that the first three chapters of Joyce's novel relate to the initial part of Homer's epic known as the Telemachiad (a likely conclusion, in the light of the novel's overall title and the various son motifs in the first part), it would be reasonable to infer that the pronounced division between chapters 3 and 4 of *Ulysses* marks the equivalent to that between books 4 and 5 of the *Odyssey*. (If one has not arrived at this conclusion and noticed the way in which the Telemachiad prefiguration from the *Odyssey* has been compressed to three sections and structured triadically, perhaps according to the complex principles outlined by Richard Ellmann in *Ulysses on the Liffey*, then it is possible that one could still be expecting further Telemachus material; but with the appearance of a major new figure, in the person of Bloom, and with the emergence of a distinctly different configuration of characters, this expectation would not be upheld for long.) On the basis of the general parallels established between Joyce's novel and the *Odyssey* in the first three chapters, it would seem logical to assume that *Ulysses* is adhering to the narrative order of the *Odyssey*. Only later, when this pattern is substantially interrupted,[22] will it become necessary to operate with more complex sets of expectations, but at this point in the reading it would appear rational to deduce that we have left the Telemachus correspondences behind and are now, *probably*, entering upon the Calypso episode's modern counterpart. And these are in all probability the only two inferences the reader will have justifiably made as he embarks upon the first paragraph of the fourth chapter.

Critical commentaries dealing with the relationship of this part of the novel to the *Odyssey* have tended to locate a considerable number of symbolic correspondences, but by presenting them out of sequence, statically, they have not only displayed little regard for the actual process of reading the novel, they have even misinterpreted their findings.

Stuart Gilbert's detailed exposition of Victor Bérard's theories about Calypso's home leads to the positing of certain geographical connections between Marion Bloom's former home of Gibraltar ("Calpe's rocky mount," as it is subsequently called in the Cyclops chapter[23]) and the possible location of Calypso's cave in that part of the Mediterranean. Yet such a quasi-euhemeristic approach to the novel[24] shows scant respect for the fact that Marion Bloom's connections with Gibraltar are only once mentioned and by no means specifically stressed in the Calypso chapter.[25] Only a cumulative, and from the point of view of this particular chapter premature, image of Molly would see her Gibraltar origins as the most striking link between her and Homer's Calypso.

Other symbolic correspondences between the Calypso chapter of *Ulysses* and book 5 of the *Odyssey* have been misrepresented by ignoring the way in which they are presented to the reader. The "great cavern"[26] where Calypso held Odysseus captive has been seen to be reflected in the "dark caves of carpet shops" Bloom imagines in the Orient,[27] and various further images of darkness and enclosure have been related to this complex. But in fact the cave motif is attached to the East, that is, the goal of Bloom's longing, and not his present predicament, which is less a correspondence than a transposition of the imprisonment idea. Bloom's preparing of breakfast for Molly has been seen as a reversal[28] of the corresponding preparation of food for Odysseus by the nymph Calypso: "the Nymph laid at his side the various kinds of food and drink that mortal men consume," in the words of the *Odyssey*.[29] And Bloom's expedition to the shops to buy something for his and Molly's breakfast and his encounter with the Jewish butcher Dlugacz ("a reminder of racial affinities" and the spur for some of his thoughts about his oriental origins) have been taken to symbolize "the Recall of Odysseus from the far island of Calypso eastwards to his own country,"[30] though again narrative sequence needs attention, for Bloom has in fact been thinking of the East even before this encounter. That Molly each day receives a ration of cream has been taken as the equivalent of the ambrosia that the legendary Calypso partook of as an immortal.[31] And a further parallel has been found in the fact that Homer depicts Calypso as being secretive, in not telling Odysseus that she has received a message from the gods via Hermes. Joyce's narrative, it is argued, "imitates Homer by a series of secret messages . . . the most obvious one [being] Boylan's letter," which Molly keeps secret from her husband.[32]

The complaint that too often Joyce criticism has treated every Homeric parallel and analogical detail as of equal symbolic importance represents a major objection to the indiscriminate accumulation of correspondences.[33] Some, like the cream-ambrosia parallel, are at most peripheral conceits, at worst overinventive fantasies on the critic's part. Others, like the motif of imprisonment, are so complexly displaced that the mere location of a "correspondence" ought to be the starting point for critical activity, not the goal that it so often is. One might combat this compulsive allusion-hunting by making a distinction between major and minor correspondences, which is what various critics have strongly urged.[34] An alternative solution would be to concentrate more on how these items affect the reading as an ongoing process. It might, for instance, seem of small significance that the symbolic parallel between Molly and Calypso is at one point clinched by means of a picture that the Blooms have hanging over their bed, *Bath of the Nymph,* an illustration used by Bloom in his explanation of how "metempsychosis" should be understood. The nymph bathing here is not specifically referred to as Calypso, but the reader should ideally approach this passage with the prefigurative knowledge that in the *Odyssey* Calypso is continually described as a nymph. Hence there is an appropriateness, mythologically, to Bloom's feeling that the picture is "not unlike [Molly] with her hair down."[35]

Considered from the viewpoint of the reading process, this episode is significant as the first unequivocal reference to the Calypso prefiguration, the other motifs and potential correspondences (Bloom's incarceration, his yearning for the East, the food motif, and the element of deception) being not so much simply covert up to this point as remote enough from the prefiguration to be read at first simply on the realistic level. It may be all very well in retrospect to see in Bloom's getting Molly's breakfast an inversion of the way in which Calypso waits upon Odysseus, but an inversion may be so distant as to be implausible until some form of explicit relationship has been established with the general prefiguration.

Hugh Kenner has argued that the fundamental parallels between the *Odyssey* and *Ulysses* are "not between incident and incident, but between situation and situation."[36] One could go even further and apply this point to the reading process by assuming that a reader of *Ulysses* is scarcely likely to expect an equivalent for each incident in the Homeric epic, but merely situational parallels (perhaps supported and reinforced by covert motifs and the occasional conceit). When the general outlines of the Odysseus-Calypso relationship are not easily fulfilled by the early part of this chapter (Bloom is serving Molly rather than she him, he is able to leave the house and come back, and no messenger comes to secure his release, although he does experience certain longings for the East), the reader may well wonder whether Joyce's novel has not already departed from the Homeric sequence. Only when the prefiguration has been emphasized, about two-thirds of the way through the chapter, is its effect really felt, and then retroactively. Here it is important to note that the parallel is presented through Bloom's eyes: it is for him alone that Molly resembles Calypso the enchanting nymph, hence the subjectivizing of the epic. This discrepancy explains some of the major differences between the reader's expectations, as he approaches the first few pages of this chapter, and what in fact happens in it. Bloom's "release" is a case in point.

The first part of the Calypso book of the *Odyssey* is concerned with Athene's distress at the imprisonment of Odysseus in Calypso's home and the subsequent dispatch of Hermes, the messenger of the gods, to bring about his release. It would of course be a naive reader indeed who began the fourth chapter of *Ulysses* (after what has happened so far in the novel) expecting some close parallel to the gods to appear. Conceit hunters may see equivalents to Hermes, in his role as divine messenger, in the fact that Bloom's awakened interest in the Orient is largely triggered by a piece of newspaper in which his provisions come wrapped, for it bears an evocative advertisement: "Agendath Netaim: planter's company. To purchase vast sandy tracts from Turkish government and plant with eucalyptus trees. . . . Orangegroves and immense melonfields north of Jaffa."[37] It would be no less ironically appropriate for the modern equivalent of the messenger of the gods to be a scrap of newspaper than for the palace of Aeolus, the King of the Winds, to have been transformed into a newspaper office. But if one reads the Calypso chapter with the details of its Homeric prefiguration in mind, one is more likely to be struck by the *absence* of any clear-cut or significant parallel to what happens at the beginning of Homer's book 5. From an interpretive point of view, the lack of some parallel to the prefiguration, the failure of the modern narrative to complete the pattern, can lead to conclusions that are as important as those encouraged by the actual presence of symbolic correspondences.

The reason for the lack of any modern divine messenger—to correspond to the reader's recollections of the *Odyssey*—is revealed in this chapter: Molly is only a nymphlike Calypso in Bloom's eyes; she is not holding him prisoner in the way her counterpart was Odysseus, and so there is no need for some messenger to be sent to persuade *her* to release him. Instead, and at most, the message (not the messenger) comes to Bloom.

Approaching the end of this chapter with the Homeric prefiguration in mind, one might expect Bloom's departure into the Dublin world to be some form of emancipation in a physical sense from Molly. Those critics who see Molly as both Calypso and Penelope—Gilbert refers to her as "Calypso, the veiled nymph, to him, but Penelope as she sees herself,"[38] and Ellmann asks in what sense Molly might "be both the immortal nymph Calypso and the mortal Penelope"[39]—may again be reading this part of the novel with an overreliance on later information. That Molly is Bloom's wife might make her automatically a candidate for consideration as a Penelope figure; but the fact that he appears to be leaving her to "voyage" out into the city seems a more convincing indication of her role as Calypso within the confines of this particular chapter. Symbolically, and in Bloom's eyes, this is the Calypso episode of their relationship. It is a view of their marriage reinforced by such leitmotifs as the song about *"Those lovely seaside girls,"*[40] whereas Penelope-correspondences are relatively understated at this stage.

For all we know at this juncture, Bloom may never return that evening; possibly, though rather improbably, knowing Bloom, he might even set out on a literal, rather than figurative journey. It is only later in the novel that the emphasis on Molly as Penelope is pronounced, and then most clearly in the last chapter of all. At this point the Calypso prefiguration, read without the hindsight of later information, lends Bloom's relationship to Molly much more precariousness than it later acquires. To view the Calypso chapter only from the vantage point of the novel's end weakens some aspects of the initial reading perspective and betrays the openness of the work-in-progress.

What emerges from even this brief consideration of one chapter of *Ulysses* is the way prefigurations affect the reading process and can lead to a different set of findings from those eventually arrived at when considering novel and prefiguration from the vantage point of hindsight. Clearly what is needed is some theoretical model within which such an exploration can be accommodated. However, little work has so far been carried out on the mythological novel in this respect.

In a recent discussion of the relationship between *Ulysses* and the *Odyssey*, "Der Archetyp als Leerform: Erzählschablonen und Kommunikation in Joyces *Ulysses*,"[41] Wolfgang Iser examined the effect of prefigurations on the novel's style largely on the basis of a model borrowed from Gestalt psychology. Rather than seeing the technique of mythological prefiguration as either an archetypal scheme to which modern events were reduced or as a yardstick against which they are to be measured, Iser worked with a figure-and-background model, showing the way in which the Homeric material "has the character of an explanatory hypothesis," one that "continually encourages the reader to project meanings" and hence functions as a kind of "Erwartungsinstruktion" (a channeler of expectations). This model is only a tentative system of "preorientation," which may often fail to coincide with the depiction of the modern world.[42] In stressing the use of a prefigurative myth as part of Joyce's "narrative strategy,"[43] and in particular in seeing this strategy as a matter of giving "signals"[44] to the reader that do no more than create expectations, Iser's Gestalt approach is the nearest myth criticism has come to exploring the process of ratiocination. Iser is mainly concerned with the stylistic repercussions of the *Odyssey* prefiguration in the individual chapters of Joyce's novel. But in suggesting that such a mythological background offers an interpretive *possibility*, Iser shows one way in which the reading process can be treated. As was pointed out in the resultant discussion of his paper, he "could have gone further and said that during the course of the story the potential changes."[45] This is what our brief look at the Calypso chapter of *Ulysses* reveals, and it is also true of our next example. But in order to pursue the implications of this further, it may be necessary to abandon the Gestalt model in favor of another one.

The most elaborate model for exploring the impact of prefigurations upon the reading process to date is supplied by Roland Barthes in *S/Z*, his analysis of the reading of Balzac's *Sarrasine*. Prefigurative myths in modern novels function as part of what Barthes would term the "cultural codes" of the works: they are part of the body of knowledge that we must bring to bear in order to understand the works.[46] Moreover, the kind of expectation-channeling function we found in the Calypso prefiguration is very close to the description Barthes gives in S/Z of the "hermeneutic code": a code that embraces "all the units whose function it is to articulate in various ways a question, its response, and the variety of chance events which can either formulate the question or delay its answer; or even, constitute an enigma and lead to its solution."[47] In Barthes's sense, the role of the *Odyssey* prefiguration in *Ulysses* is largely hermeneutic. However, the value of S/Z for the consideration of how we read the mythological novel lies less in its specific taxonomy of codes (some of which have already been criticized as oversimplifications[48]) than in the way in which Barthes's study takes the reader sequentially through *Sarrasine*, weighing up the amount of information received so far and at any given point considering what processes of ratiocination are likely to be being engaged in. This has the virtue of showing that en route we have a far more complex set of expectations about the novel than the picture arrived at when we reach the end. To quote Barthes: "The *step-by-step* method . . . is . . . the *decomposition* (in the cinematographic sense) of the work of reading . . . a way of observing the reversibility of the structures from which the text is woven . . . a renewal of the entrances to the text, it avoids structuring the text *excessively*."[49]

The various mechanisms of complication to be found in the hermeneutic code (for which Barthes invents such terms as "snare," "false reply," and "jamming")[50] have obvious equivalents in the mythological novel. Often the relationship between myth and modernity is overstated or misrepresented at an early point in the novel (as a matter of simple mythical "identity"—or a result of "metempsychosis," in the case of *Ulysses*); analogies can quite often have the function of red herrings, and the final view of the novel may differ considerably from the tentative images and conjectures entertained at earlier points. As a result, the reader of the mythological novel assumes the role of a detective for whom a trail of allusions—signals or clues—has been laid. It is not by chance that in recent years mythological prefigurations have often appeared in conjunction with the most pronounced embodiment of the hermeneutic code in fiction: the detective novel. Like mythological fiction, the detective novel both brings into relief certain features of the reading process in general and in other ways modifies them. Not surprisingly, therefore, certain French *nouveaux romanciers*, who have been particularly concerned with the role of ratiocination in the reading process, have used the detective novel and mythological prefigurations as reciprocally illuminating paradigms. Alain Robbe-Grillet's *The Erasers* (Les gommes) and Michel Butor's *Passing Time* (L'emploi du temps) are the two best-known examples of this hybrid genre.

"The New Novel," it has been argued, "is the detective story taken seriously."[51] Just how this process of detection then becomes part of the reading process is something I should like to consider in the case of my second illustration: Butor's *Passing Time*.

When the hero of *Passing Time*, Jacques Revel, comes to the fictive English city of Bleston to spend a year there as a clerk, he soon finds himself struggling to survive in a basically hostile environment. He gradually becomes caught up in various intrigues and emotional attachments, which he later tries to sort out on paper. For almost everything that happens to him during his stay prefigurations are offered: basically he is compared to Theseus in the labyrinth, although Theseus' other exploits are also used to illuminate various aspects of his adventures, and we are offered further comparisons between Revel and Oedipus and Cain. To quote one critic: "The parallels are on the whole obvious to anyone with a reasonable knowledge of mythology and the Bible, especially as both Butor and Revel take pains to make them so."[52] This is certainly true, and it would seem as if those critics who have spelled out the novel's scheme of correspondences[53] are merely reminding the reader of what is patently obvious from a first reading, since the narrator-hero makes specific reference to all the prefigurations involved.

Butor's prefigurative scheme here is complex, for all its explicitness, however, and it would require a lengthy exposition to do justice to the subtle ways in which the Theseus and Oedipus myths are interwoven and Biblical and Greek mythological images are blended. But as in the instance of *Ulysses*, no retrospective assignation of mythological roles to the modern characters will adequately show the way in which such a prefigurative novel works. As the hero himself says, in his capacity as commentator on his own narrative: "The labyrinth of my days in Bleston [is] incomparably more bewildering than that of the Cretan palace, since it grows and alters even while I explore it" (p. 183).

Let us start with the traditional retrospective method of presenting mythological correspondences—almost in the form of equations—and then consider what new insights a consideration of the reading process will bring. The relationship between Revel and his Theseus prefiguration would be (and has been) described in the following terms:

> Jacques Revel is Theseus. For just as the Greek hero fought the Minotaur in the Labyrinth, so Revel battles with the labyrinthine city of Bleston and its inhabitants. Just as Theseus is helped in his endeavor by Ariadne, Revel is offered guidance by Ann who saves him from losing his way in Bleston: both literally, by selling him a map, and symbolically through her friendship. And just as Theseus abandons Ariadne for her younger sister Phaedra, so Revel's affections are later transferred to Ann's sister Rose.[54]

Bearing in mind the reading process, we can observe that such an account of the novel's symbolic correspondences is a simplification. It is the equivalent of the one offered at that stage in the narrative, where Revel declares: "The whole pattern had fallen into shape" (p. 154), for it is here that he thinks he can see these various parallels most clearly. Slightly later, taking a friend along to the local museum to see the Theseus tapestries that have become the main focus of his mythological introspection, Revel reinforces the image of a complete pattern with the remark: "I carefully avoided telling him that for me, hence-forwards, Ariadne represented Ann Bailey, Phaedra was Rose and I myself Theseus, while he was the young prince [Peirithous]" (pp. 168ff.). After some considerable time, as we have already noted, Revel is to come to the recognition that this assumed pattern was a false construction as far as he personally was concerned: "The pattern is complete, and I am left out" (p. 250), although even this insight comes some way from the end of the book and has to be treated with caution. In the light of this shifting set of perspectives, what I should now like to offer, as just one illustration from Butor's novel of how attention to the reading process will offer a more differentiated view of mythological fiction, is a short account of the way the motif of Theseus in the Labyrinth is handled.

The primary interpretation of this motif is a physical one: that of the city of Bleston itself as a labyrinth. But since Butor's novel is not called *Theseus* or *In the Labyrinth*, and since all modern cities are to some extent labyrinthine, the question arises of how and when the reader is made aware of the prefigurative analogy. In the early part of the novel the word "labyrinth" and its cognate adjective are specifically avoided; they do not appear in Revel's narrative until after he has been to Bleston Museum and become aware of the Theseus analogy. (Thus, although Revel narrates his experiences from a later vantage point, he withholds some of his conclusions until later.) In the early descriptions of Bleston there is much that, *in retrospect*—or on a second reading—appears to be covertly alluding to the Labyrinth prefiguration. It is "unfamiliar ground" (p. 9); Revel refers to his "wanderings" (p. 10) through Bleston on the night of his arrival; the city is "leading him astray" (p. 29); there are "narrow streets, blind alleys" (p. 33); the "town had begun to wear me down with its wiles" (p. 34), he confesses; he is "lost amidst its filaments" (p. 42); there are whole "zones into which I have never penetrated" (p. 43); and we are told that "Bleston was an unfriendly power" (p. 51). There is certainly enough in Bleston to make it the modern equivalent of a labyrinth: confusing "doubles" (an old and a new cathedral, various similar stations and similarly named restaurants, which add to Revel's disorientation), and a general maze of streets, bus routes, and warrenlike districts. But it is important that we are not presented with the mythological prefiguration for all this straightaway. Apart from the fact that Butor avoids explicitly applying the cliché of the labyrinth to its modern physical equivalent, there are good psychological grounds for the delayed signaling of this Theseus myth. For during the course of the novel, Revel's perspective begins to widen, from interpreting his private experiences merely as individual events to generalizing about their typicality. At first, Bleston is simply a rather unappetizing northern industrial city; then it is depicted anthropomorphically as some kind of hostile, bewitching power, a kind of Minotaur surrogate. Gradually it becomes the archetypal evil city: Revel refers to "such gigantic insidious crawling towns as Bleston" (p. 222) at one point and later, largely as a result of various culture films and travelogues he sees at the local cinema, he ranks Bleston alongside Rome, Timgad, Baalbek, and Bombay as centers of evil (p. 259), a sense of loathing ultimately to be rendered in the image of Bleston as the Hydra (pp. 225, 237). Accordingly, the prefigurations are only gradually introduced into the narrative and then begin to acquire an increasingly obsessive hold over the hero's analysis of his situation. Michael Spencer's observation that if Revel "had spent a little less time acting out some kind of mythical or biblical role, his sentimental life would have been less catastrophic" has much truth in it;[55] and it is a truth that is reflected in the delayed introduction of the Theseus prefiguration. The reader thus shares Revel's early perspective, at the beginning agreeing with his sense of the individuality of events and slowly becoming preoccupied with the typicality, even "archetypicality," of what is happening.

The use of the Labyrinth prefiguration in *Passing Time* soon becomes multilayered. Just as the most straightforward physical interpretation of it is beginning to emerge unambiguously as a mythological analogy, the narrative gives it a further and far more crucial meaning. The reader is now presented with a series of striking images that give the prefiguration a spiritual significance in two senses: the act of remembering, understanding, and ordering reality is presented as a variant on finding one's way through a labyrinth (the path through "the labyrinth of time and memory" (p. 282), as it is put at one point); more specifically, Revel's attempts at reconstructing his experiences through writing about them gradually becomes the second dominant figurative meaning the prefiguration receives in the modern context. Revel's writing is a form of "crawling towards remembrance, line by line, page by page, tunneling my way to light" (p. 115). He speaks of "the rope of words that uncoils down through the sheaf of papers and connects me directly with that moment on the first of May when I began to plait it, that rope of words is like Ariadne's thread, because I am in a labyrinth" (pp. 182f.).

As the more spiritual aspects of the labyrinth situation are unfolded, more and more complications are added to the prefigurations, in particular through affiliations with the Oedipus and Cain motifs. Hence the image the reader has until this point of Revel as a kind of twentieth-century Theseus in a labyrinth—in the labyrinth of Bleston and fighting the Minotaur of Bleston—has to be modified. One of Revel's acquaintances, on first hearing that he is writing something, remarks: "A detective story, I bet." Revel replies: "Much simpler than that: I'm writing down what has happend to me here" (p. 82). Yet this is only a half-truth, for in doing this he does manage to write a sort of detective novel, and he becomes his own Sherlock Holmes and Oedipus at the same time.

R.-M. Albérès has observed that there are two labyrinths in the novel: one of time and the other of space.[56] The spatial one Revel explores throughout his sojourn in Bleston. As a writer he is later shown to be more concerned with the temporal one, though the two are often intertwined. The more the temporal one begins to dominate the story, the more insistently the reader is presented with the Oedipus prefiguration. The positive Theseus prefiguration gives way to a much more ambiguous Oedipus image. It is for this same reason that the Cain prefiguration, which, as I have argued elsewhere,[57] is a far more negative interpretation of Revel's predicament than that of Theseus in the Labyrinth, is only introduced and dwelt on at a later stage. To underestimate the role sequence plays in all this and to present the novel's prefigurations as a series of symbolic correspondences retained simultaneously in the reader's mind is a substantial simplification of what happens in *Passing Time*.

At one point in his essay on Joyce, Butor says of *Ulysses:* "In the middle of the strangeness of contemporary life the ancient myths are reincarnated and the relationships that they express remain universal and eternal" (p. 206). Whether this statement could be equally appropriately applied to Butor's own *Passing Time* is a leading question about the significance of mythological material in the novel. I would venture to suggest that it cannot be answered unequivocally by the kind of closer concern with the reading process that I have been advocating. There are clearly those who believe that the mythological motifs in *Passing Time* are operating in the same generalizing and archetypal way as Butor believes them to be in *Ulysses*,[58] yet it would be just as possible to concede that Revel's quirky obsession with prefigurations and his own failure to complete the mythological pattern delineated at one point could lead one to the opposite conclusion. A concern with the reading process will not necessarily make such problems of interpretation any easier, but it can and ought to lead to a deeper appreciation of the peculiarities of one particular way in which myths have been used to great effect in modern fiction.

Notes

1. For two excellent recent surveys of the status of myth in literature, see Bernard Ostendorf, *Der Mythos in der Neuen Welt. Eine Untersuchung zum amerikanischen Myth Criticism* (Frankfurt am Main, 1971), a far more extensive work than its title would suggest, and William Righter, *Myth and Literature* (London and Boston, 1975).
2. "The Myth-Kitty," *Puzzles and Epiphanies: Essays and Reviews (1958–1961)* (London, 1962), p. 35.
3. Barbara Hardy, "Golding's First Phase," *Daily Telegraph*, 20 April 1967, p. 22.

4. *The Myth and the Powerhouse* (New York, 1965), pp. 9f.
5. E. Herd, "Myth Criticism: Limitations and Possibilities," *Mosaic* 11 (1969):74f.
6. Joe David Bellamy, ed., *The New Fiction: Interviews with Innovative American Writers* (Urbana, Chicago, and London, 1974), pp. 8f.
7. Significantly, Michel Butor, who has written a number of mythological novels and whose *L'emploi du temps* (1957) will be considered below, produced in 1948 a critical account of the role of myth in Joyce's work; see his "Petite croisière préliminaire à une reconnaissance de l'archipel Joyce," reprinted in *Répertoire 1* (Paris, 1960), pp. 195–218.
8. These theoretical positions have been culled, respectively, from: Gilbert Highet, *The Classical Tradition: Greek and Roman Influences on Western Literature* (Oxford, 1949), p. 512; Margaret Dalziel, "Myth in Modern English Literature," *Myth and the Modern Imagination*, ed. Margaret Dalziel (Dunedin, 1967), p. 45; John Sturrock, *The New French Novel* (London, 1963), pp. 156f.; Frank Kermode, *Continuities* (London, 1968), p. 40; Robert Scholes, *The Fabulators* (New York, 1967), p. 171; and Bellamy, op. cit., p. 12.
9. "Literature in the Reader: Affective Stylistics," *New Literary History* 11 (1967):147.
10. *The Fabulators*, pp. 107f.
11. Ibid., pp. 110f.
12. "Literature in the Reader," pp. 126f. The italics are Fish's.
13. Ibid., p. 128.
14. Ibid., p. 137.
15. John J. White, *Mythology in the Modern Novel. A Study of Prefigurative Techniques* (Princeton, 1971), p. 11.
16. Ibid., p. 22.
17. For the medieval context, see Erich Auerbach, "Figura," *Neue Dantestudien* (Istanbul, 1944), pp. 11–71 and *Scenes from the Drama of European Literature* (New York, 1959). For more recent discussions, see J.A. Galdon, *Typology and Seventeenth-Century Literature* (The Hague and Paris, 1975) and Theodore Ziolkowski, "Typologie und 'Einfache Form' in *Gruppenbild mit Dame*," *Die subversive Madonna*, ed. Renate Matthaei (Cologne, 1975), pp. 123–40.
18. "Ermordete Majestät. Oder Carolus Stuardus König von Gross Britannien," in *Die Dramen des Andreas Gryphius. Eine Sammlung von Einzelinterpretationen*, ed. Gerhard Kaiser (Stuttgart, 1968), pp. 167f.
19. In the essay by Ziolkowski cited above and in his book *Fictional Transfigurations of Jesus* (Princeton, 1972), esp. chapter 1.
20. *Passing Time*, trans. Jean Stewart (London, 1961), p. 250. Subsequent references, cited by page number in the text, are to this edition.
21. See Richard Ellmann's detailed comparison of these various schemes in the Appendix to his *Ulysses on the Liffey* (London, 1972), pp. 187ff.
22. For details, see the discussion of narrative order in David Wykes's "*The Odyssey* in *Ulysses*," *Texas Studies in Literature and Language* 10 (1968): 301–16. Wykes charts "the extent to which the plot development of *Ulysses* is independent of *The Odyssey*" (p. 306), although the patterning of expectations may be more bound up with the *Odyssey*'s structure than this conclusion would suggest, and even departure from the Homeric sequence (like the inversion of certain symbolic correspondences) can become part of an elaborate playing with expectations.

23. Joyce, *Ulysses* (Harmondsworth, 1968), p. 318.
24. Gilbert, *James Joyce's "Ulysses": A Study* (New York, 1962), pp. 140ff.
25. We are simply told that Bloom's wife comes "all the way from Gibraltar," *Ulysses*, p. 58.
26. Homer, *The Odyssey*, trans. E.V. Rieu (Harmondsworth, 1961), p. 89.
27. *Ulysses*, p. 59. For an elaboration of this motif, see Gilbert, pp. 144f.
28. Adaline Glasheen, "Calypso," *James Joyce's "Ulysses": Critical Essays*, eds. Clive Hart and David Hayman (Berkeley, Los Angeles, and London, 1974), p. 51.
29. P. 93.
30. Gilbert, p. 144.
31. Ibid., p. 65.
32. Ellmann, pp. 35ff.
33. This criticism is well set out at the beginning of chapter 5 of S.L. Goldberg's *The Classical Temper: A Study of James Joyce's "Ulysses"* (London, 1961), pp. 145ff.
34. One method has been to attempt a distinction between those correspondences which are critically useful to the reader and the others which (following Ezra Pound) are assumed to have been chiefly of use to Joyce (cf. Wykes, p. 305, and Harry Levin, *James Joyce. A Critical Introduction* (Norfolk, Conn., 1941), p. 53); however, to assume that the correspondences which are indefensible from the reader's point of view must have had genetic value involves a bold measure of speculation.
35. *Ulysses*, p. 67.
36. *Dublin's Joyce* (London, 1956), p. 181.
37. *Ulysses*, p. 62.
38. *James Joyce's "Ulysses,"* p. 145. Gilbert's attempt at suggesting that her maiden name "Tweedy" "may be a suggestion of Mrs Bloom's Penelope aspect as a weaver of webs" (p. 143) ignores the more obvious parallel at this point to Calypso "as she wove at the loom and moved her golden shuttle to and fro" (*Odyssey*, p. 89).
39. *Ulysses on the Liffey*, p. 33.
40. *Ulysses*, p. 69.
41. *Terror und Spiel. Probleme der Mythenrezeption*, ed. Manfred Fuhrmann. *Poetik und Hermeneutik*, 4 (Munich, 1971), pp. 369–408. Further material on the subject is offered in the record of the discussion following Iser's paper on "Mythen im 20. Jahrhundert: Depotenzierung und Usurpation" (pp. 687–719).
42. These quotations are from pp. 372, 377, 385, and 405, respectively. The useful term "Erwartungsinstruktion" is borrowed from Harald Weinrich's *Linguistik der Lüge* (Heidelberg, 1966), p. 46.
43. "Mythen im 20. Jahrhundert," p. 689: this is Eberhard Lämmert's apt description of Iser's contribution (in the discussion that followed it).
44. Iser, p. 384.
45. The point is made by Lämmert, "Mythen im 20. Jahrhundert," p. 690.
46. *S/Z*, trans. Richard Miller (London, 1975), p. 20.
47. Ibid., p. 17.
48. Cf. the strictures in Jonathan Culler's *Structuralist Poetics: Structuralism, Linguistics and the Study of Literature* (London, 1975), pp. 203 ff.
49. *S/Z*, pp. 12f.

50. Cf. *S/Z*, pp. 42 and 47.
51. Ludovic Janvier, quoted in Sturrock, p. 160.
52. Michael Spencer, *Michel Butor* (New York, 1974), p. 56.
53. The most useful account is the section "Myth" in Marian A. Grant's *Butor: "L'Emploi du Temps"* (London, 1973), pp. 56–60. See also Jean Roudaut, *Michel Butor ou le livre futur* (Paris, 1964), pp. 127f. and R.-M. Albérès, *Michel Butor* (Paris, 1964), pp. 33ff.
54. Grant, pp. 56–57.
55. *Michel Butor*, p. 56.
56. *Michel Butor*, pp. 33f.
57. *Mythology in the Modern Novel*, pp. 211–18.
58. See, for example, Gerda Zeltner-Neukomm, *Das Wagnis des französischen Gegenwartromans* (Hamburg, 1962), p. 113, and Sturrock, p. 157.

SPECIAL PRACTICAL EXAMPLES

Helen Adolf

RILKE—TRANSCENDED OR TRANSCENDING?

Rilke's way led from an initial delight in words and images through arduous self-discipline to an encounter with myth. What is myth? We may adopt, and adapt for our purpose, the definition given by Alan Watts in *Ritual in Christianity* (1954) and *The Two Hands of God* (1963): a numinous story or image that both reveals and conceals an important inner truth. Can Rilke's most personal "myth of concern" (Northrop Frye) ever become ours and help us to "organize our experiences" (Mark Schorer)? An analysis of some poems by Rilke and of some comparable poems by modern authors will serve to answer this question; the aesthetic or phenomenological approach will lead us to an existential evaluation.

On December 4 of 1975, we celebrated the centenary of Rilke's birth; on December 29 of 1976, the half centenary of his death. The question to be asked is: does Rilke the centenarian still surpass all other lyrical poets, or is he perhaps already surpassed by some modern trends? As far as Rilke scholarship is concerned, he has just come into his own in America; let me mention the excellent investigations by Schoolfield, Bradley, Rolleston, and Webb. But there is also an icy blast blowing over the campuses. Professor Egon Schwarz reports that for the young generation Rilke has become "ein grossartiges poetisches Taj Mahal, das total funktionslos in der Gegend herumsteht."[1] I suppose these young activists prefer to read Brecht. How did this about-face happen? For one thing, it has been a reaction against too much spirituality. There is little of red blood in Rilke's verse; in his own veins he must have carried ichor, like the Olympian gods—in fact, he died of leukemia. The guts of common people rebelled against his refinement. I could quote from Brecht, or from Peter Weiss, to make

my point; but I rather choose their French comrade, Jacques Prevert, who is blasphemous without being sacrilegious:

> Our Father who art in heaven—
> Stay there!. . . . .
> And we'll stay on earth—
> Earth with its seasons and years. . . . .
> Its pretty virgins and old tarts. . . . [2]

But impudence can very well coexist with beauty, just as the Carmina Burana coexisted with troubadour idealism. The real danger
came from elsewhere.

Rilke himself had been deeply affected, almost muted, by World
War I. That was only the beginning. The collapse of France, the
horrors of the concentration camps and of Hiroshima, and the threat
of total extinction brought about a world revolution in poetry—a
revolution, to be sure, that had already started with Rimbaud and
Mallarmé after 1870. Corresponding to a universe that seemed to
be without rhyme and reason, verse had to give up its rhyme, and
syntax was shattered:[3] nothing remained but metaphors spawned
by the unconscious and ejected lavalike by a human volcano:[4]

> Schwarze Milch der Frühe wir trinken sie abends,
> wir trinken sie mittags und morgens, wir trinken sie nachts,
> wir trinken und trinken. . . .
> > Der Tod ist ein Meister aus
> > Deutschland . . .
> . . . dein goldenes Haar, Margarete, dein aschenes Haar,
> Sulamith.

These few bars from Celan's *Todesfuge* demonstrate the incompatibility between the new and the old idiom.

And yet, within limits, a comparison is possible. I shall choose
three poems by Rilke and oppose them to poems of the same title,
or dealing with the same theme, by a representative of the new
trend. As our first example, let us take "The Panther," that famous
Dinggedicht from the *Neue Gedichte*. Its chief constitutive element
is the heart-stricken empathy for a victim of fate, for a prisoner (in
the *Neue Gedichte* it is preceded by two poems on "Der Gefan-
gene"). The line of the first strophe, "Ihm ist, als ob es tausend
Stäbe gäbe," can very well be interpreted as a personal utterance of
the, alas, tongue-tied cat and thereby connect this poem with the
"Voices" 1905–1906, in the *Buch der Bilder*, where nine victims of
fate voice their despair in the first person singular. If this empathy
were raised to the highest degree of contemplation ("Wesens-
schau"), then we would obtain an intuition into the very heart of

animaldom (see "ein grosser Wille" in the second strophe), as in the crowning conclusion of Rilke's poem "Die Aschanti" in the *Buch der Bilder*:[5]

> O wie sind die Tiere so viel treuer,
> die in Gittern auf und nieder gehn . . .
> teilnahmslos dem neuen Abenteuer
> und mit ihrem grossen Blut allein.

Instead of this, Rilke followed the advice of Rodin *(travailler, rien que travailler)*, and he studied his panther. What he saw was the struggle between restless motion and growing paralysis (müdbetäubt, hört auf zu sein); he went closer and closer to his object (der Vorhang der Pupille) and thus obtained a perfect portrait of the panther in a special situation.

Kafka's Panther is different. I am referring to "The Hunger Artist," not a poem but a tale, written and published during Rilke's lifetime, in 1923. The scene is an amusement park, where people crowd to watch the performance of a hunger artist, a man who has broken all records in fasting so that he has become unable to ingest any food at all; he shrivels and shrinks to the point of inanition. (This is not a Kafkaesque extravagance but a condition called anorexia. Young people, especially young girls, may be affected by it: Simone Weil, the revolutionary philosopher sometimes considered a saint, died of anorexia in 1943.) "I would eat," says the hunger artist, "if there were any earthly food which I can stand." There is none, so he expires.

> "Nun macht aber Ordnung!" sagte der Aufseher, und man begrub den Hungerkünstler samt dem Stroh. In den Käfig aber gab man einen jungen Panther. . . . Ihm fehlte nichts. . . . Nicht einmal die Freiheit schien er zu vermissen; dieser edle, mit allem Nötigen bis knapp zum Zerreissen ausgestattete Körper schien auch die Freiheit mit sich herumzutragen; irgendwo im Gebiss schien sie zu stecken; und die Freude am Leben kam mit derart starker Glut aus seinem Rachen, dass es für die Zuschauer nicht leicht war, ihr standzuhalten.[6]

By what alchemy did Kafka manage to distill these two formidable essences, the hunger artist and the panther? One might say that they represent, according to Freud's later theory of the instincts, the instincts of Death and that of Life. But they were certainly not invented to illustrate these forces; rather Kafka himself had become the battlefield between them, while still aware, like the prophets of old, that a higher truth existed beyond them, the very counterpart of the absurdity around us. At any rate, com-

pared with Rilke's exquisite piece of craftsmanship, his panther is
overlifesize. "Ihm fehlte nichts"—because he had devoured the
situation and now ruled supreme.

In our second example, we shall abandon the depths while trying to probe the heights; Rilke's poem "Den Schwan" will have to
face "Der Schwan" by Nelly Sachs.

Rilke's "Schwan," in itself a thing of great beauty, raises a question: does the swan serve to stimulate certain transcendental
speculations, or are these speculations but the means to make us
visualize the swan? In other words: do we have here a parable
(Gleichnis) rather than a Dinggedicht,[7] or did Rilke attain here the
perfect fusion between "Beschreibung" and "Deutung"? The
poem itself, strangely enough, starts with the Deutung (interpretation), which fills the first two tercets of this shortened sonnet: this
toilsome life of ours equals the waddling of the swan, while upon
entering into death we shall glide, like the swan—and there follows, in the concluding sextet, the description: of the receding
waters and of the swan's glorious process into eternity. "Unendlich," in line 10, is not just an expletive; although I felt tempted,
against all manuscript evidence, to read "nun endlich still und
sicher," that is, "at last no longer 'ängstlich.'" But "unendlich," of
which I found some thirty instances from *Buch der Bilder* to *Sonnets* and *Elegies,* is a Rilkean key word, denoting, not without
vagueness, our shifting reaction to the "open"—as we tend toward
it and as it tends toward us.[8] If we dare break the enchanted circle
of this quasi-sonnet, we shall get the answer to our question. For
in the *Elegies,* which give so much room to the dead, the young
and the not so young ones, the dead inhabit a mountainous country and not a watery expanse, while in the "Hymnen an die
Nacht"[9] the swan is promoted to a symbol for the gods—

> Schön wie ein Schwan
> Auf seiner Ewigkeit grundloser Fläche!
> So zieht der Gott und taucht und schont sein Weiss...

—the gods, those doubtful entities, blessed and aloof, of remote
Epicurean ancestry. Our conclusion therefore is: the Swan is the
thing, as Rodin and Rilke watched those handsome creatures in
Meudon,[10] and as His Majesty the Swan deigns to glide ("zu ziehn
geruht") over a page of the *Neue Gedichte.* Bathed in an unearthly
light, it is an impressionist's enraptured painting.

It may be a coincidence that in Nelly Sachs's volume of poetry
Die Fahrt ins Staublose (1961) there is a poem entitled "Der

Schwan."[11] That her work invites a comparison with Rilke is not a coincidence. Her early neoromantic poetry had lacked any Rilkean overtones; but when her world broke apart, when she was left alone with language, the dead, and the constellations, then she could continue Rilke's quest into the unknown. Cabalistic readings had opened to her the Gates of Beginning:[12] thus Rilke's swan-inspired quasi-sonnet was turned by her into a kind of haiku:

> Nichts
> über den wassern
> und schon hängt am Augenschlag
> Schwanenhafte Geometrie
> wasserbewurzelt
> aufrankend
> und wieder geneigt
> staub schluckend
> und wieder geneigt
> Staub schluckend
> und mit der Luft Massnehmend
> am weltall—

The one happening essential to the haiku is our sudden perception, which reiterates the moment of creation, of something she calls "schwanenhafte Geometrie."[13] What does this mean? The idea, the form, the shape, the luminous design? Luminous, because the three remaining elements are enshrined in the ensuing characterization (wasserbewurzelt-Staub schluckend . . . mit der Luft), in which swanlike grace accounts for the two lines only: "aufrankend und wieder geneigt." What an economy of means! And yet the water-fowl, emerging from Divine Nothingness, rises to participation in the universe (Weltall).

Impressionism has been left far behind: instead of it, we are facing a hieroglyph, something reminding us of an abstract painting by Kandinsky: a luminous phenomenon set against a cosmic background.[14] It seems then that in both dimensions, in depth as well as in height, modernistic poetry, although spare in its use of stylistic devices, tends to surpass in scope the consummate art of Rilke. One might argue that we should have chosen models from his later, not from his middle period, since he transcended himself writing the *Elegies* and the *Sonnets*. Nevertheless, for a third example of his poetry, we shall go back to the winter of 1901/1902, when he wrote "Der Schauende." In order to explain our choice, a quick survey of Rilke's literary career is indicated.

This career started with a miracle, when his indifferently neo-

romantic lyrical idiom was suddenly transformed into something
new and authentic. At this time, his mind was amazingly open to
all kinds of influences—he not only wrote plays and novels in
naturalistic style, he also broached philosophical and religious
problems, in a skeptical mood and eager for new solutions.[15] From
this viewpoint his two Russian journeys with Lou Andreas-Salomé
(around 1899) were so particularly helpful because the vast soli-
tudes of that un- or underdeveloped country freed him from the
intellectual carnival to which he had been exposed in Munich.
Worpswede with its plains and its reverently contemplating
painters served the same purpose. His inner riches were now
channeled into the mystical songs of the *Stundenbuch.* But a further pruning of his poems was needed; to ensure further growth
he had to cut back the branches of his luxuriously spreading
imagination. His passionate desire for such a growth animated
three poems in the *Buch der Bilder:* "Musik," "So wurden wir
verträumte Geiger," and "Der Schauende."[16] The date is now
1901.

By this time he had reached the halfway mark in the life span
allotted to him by fate, and it became a turning point in his career,
for soon afterward he decided to sacrifice everything to his work
as an artist: he gave up his marriage and went to Paris, to Rodin
whom he idolized as if he were God or God's angel. Learning
from him, he "pruned" his poems until they became "Dingge-
dichte," that is, more objective than subjective, while at the same
time he exposed himself mercilessly to the depressive sights of
the metropolis; for according to Nietzsche's gospel the true Son of
Earth has to accept earth unconditionally.[17] And yet he still kept
longing for transcendence. The war interfered. Not until 1922 was
he granted the second miracle of his life as a poet: its fruit was the
termination of the ten *Duino Elegies,* accompanied by the fifty-
five *Sonnets to Orpheus.* In the former, the poet scaled the
heights of essence and existence; in the latter, the music of his
violin was amplified by the organ and flute sounds of a vaster
consciousness: in both, his mission as a poet was explained and
justified. How far do they have universal validity?

Instead of embarking on an analysis of these two works—as if
the breath of inspiration could be analyzed that had swelled "the
little rust-colored sail of the Sonnets and the gigantic white canvas
of the Elegies,"[18]—let us concentrate on the turning point of 1901
and the poem it engendered. Its theme is the wrestling with the
angel.[19] This is the story told in Genesis 32:24–32, how Jacob

fought a fight at the ford of the Yabbok—a confusing story about a river demon who could not stand the light of day but who also was Jehovah, or Jehovah's angel, from whom Jacob exacted and received a blessing, a new name Israel and a "wound" (the laming of the hip), whereupon he was granted a vision at dawn. Higher Bible criticism sees here the conflation of three different sources. Interpretations abound, from Philo of Alexandria to Jacob Böhme, Carl Jung, and Thomas Mann. Painters too have wrestled with the subject. They all felt that this unique fight, in which victory was defeat and defeat victory, represented an archetype of human experience: man's encounter with the supernatural.

Do we still want this encounter? or are we afraid, or is God unwilling? Our enfant terrible, Jacques Prévert, dissuades us from accepting the fight:[20]

> It's no good
> The match is rigged
> in advance
> you will be down for the count
> and he will strike you below the belt
> and you will fall again
> . . . .
> never be able to get up and make love again.

(Not so abstruse an assertion, since Philo had stated that the instincts must be curbed to make room for the supernatural.)[21] Prévert wrote this in 1946, as a child of modern mass society. It had been different around 1900. Genius felt attracted by the great individual that dared accept the challenge. "Jacob charges like a bull," says Lord Kenneth Clark,[22] describing Delacroix's towering altarpiece of St. Sulpice in Paris; and August Strindberg, who went through his own personal inferno in 1897, was helped in his spiritual struggle by watching the spirited fight of Delacroix's Jacob.[23]

As to Rilke, we may safely assume that during his stay in Berlin (1899) he visited the former Kaiser Friedrich Museum and saw Rembrandt's painting *Jacob Wrestles with the Angel* there. Later on, in 1902, in the preface to *Worpswede*, he commented on the absence of landscape in Rembrandt's biblical works and concluded: "liegt nicht vielleicht darin das Geheimnis und die Hoheit Rembrandts, dass er Menschen wie Landschaften malte?" Although these words do not refer to the Jacob painting in Berlin, they fit it to a T; for there is no jungle of trees there to symbolize the instincts, as in St. Sulpice; nothing but the two contestants,

and it is the face of the Angel—impassive, mysterious, even smiling—that captivates the imagination.[24] Rilke lived at Berlin-
Schmargendorf at that time (winter of 1900/1901). From his window, he could watch the storms shaking the trees in the woods
outside, and he was riddled by fears of future ordeals. The poem
he wrote in the middle of January 1901 was entitled "Sturm." It
was sent, with a string of eight sentimental lines, to Clara West-
hoff. Its much improved final version, composed in October 1901,
was called "Der Schauende" and found a niche in the last section
of the *Buch der Bilder*. Chronologically it belonged to the first two
parts of the *Stundenbuch*, while thematically it foreshadowed the
Duino Elegies; existentially, it seemed to have more substance
than either of those earlier or later ecstasies. Its thirty-four lines,
unbridled by any numerical pattern, but melodiously swelling,
receding, and advancing, form a whole as strong as a charm and as
effective as a cordial; one wonders why the poet, in his inner
struggles later on, failed to use it.

In true "Zauberspruch" fashion the poem starts with a brief
narrative statement:

> Ich sehe den Bäumen die Stürme an,
> die aus laugewordenen Tagen
> an meine ängstlichen Fenster schlagen,
> und höre die Fernen Dinge sagen,
> die ich nicht ohne Freund ertragen,
> nicht ohne Schwester lieben kann.

But time and place dissolve into timelessness, and Wisdom, the
very voice of Eternity, urges him twice to yield to the storm:

> "Wie ist das klein, womit wir ringen,
> was mit uns ringt, wie ist das gross; ...
> Was wir besiegen, ist das Kleine,
> und der Erfolg selbst macht uns klein."

The scene is prepared for the Angel:

> Das ist der Engel, der den Ringern
> des Alten Testaments erschien.

As in Rembrandt's painting, "der Schauende" (the gazing eye)
empathizes with him:

> wenn seines Widersachers Sehnen
> im Kampfe sich metallen dehnen
> fühlt er sie unter seinen Fingern
> wie Saiten tiefer Melodien.

As to the human opponent, he will emerge from this almost lethal fight nameless, upright, and great:

> Wen dieser Engel überwand,
> welcher so oft auf Kampf verzichtet,
> der geht gerecht und aufgerichtet
> und gross aus jener harten Hand,
> die sich, wie formend, an ihn schmiegte. . . .

What is this? The perfect image of an existential test?[25]

> Sein Wachstum ist: der Tiefbesiegte
> von immer Grösserem zu sein.

But why, so we wonder, had Rilke later on to borrow from R. Kassner another formula: "Der Weg von der Innigkeit zur Grösse geht durch das Opfer"?[26] What exactly does the title "Der Schauende" mean? Most important, why was the biblical theme so thoroughly altered? Perhaps these three questions can be reduced to one: what happened to the archetype?

In modern criticism the term "archetype" has acquired a more general meaning. It denotes "a communicable symbol" (Frye), or any "persistent pattern of human thought and experience" (Wheelwright).[27] But for our purpose an approximation to C. G. Jung's definition will do best,[28] because it will account for the numinosity of the archetype: there are in our unconscious (inherited or not, here lies the crux of the matter) memories or prefigurations of experience that far surpass, in depth as well as in height, any ordinary experience; their numinosity may be due either to a power outside (the Creator's), or to a power inside, that of the individual's own creative imagination.

Let us now watch the growth of the archetype in Rilke's imagination. At Worpswede, he had lived a second, happier childhood, "ohne Verzicht und Ziel"; all roads were still open to him. Moving among the "Worpswede" painters and paintresses, he learned from them how to "see" (schauen) in preparation for the second phase of the mystical life, the vita contemplative. Then, at Schmargendorf, when winter and anxiety closed in on him, the panes of his window protected him from the storm outside; "der Schauende" (the gazing one) had become one not yet called to action. But as the *Buch der Bilder* reveals to us, he deeply felt, in spite of his fears, the need for a new initiation; the seed of the archetype was stirring in him. At this time, Gerhart Hauptmann's play *Michael Kramer* gave him hope and trust; as the father who lost his wayward son tells us: "Da wird man aus Leiden gross." In Rilke's imagination, Hauptmann's Angel of Death was replaced by the Old Testament angel, and an encounter with him was anticipated. However, Rilke's attitude toward this Angel was ambivalent. He had longed for this encounter (in fact, he never ceased doing so), but he also wished to identify with him, whom he regarded as a patron saint of artists, and not with his human opponent. So the encounter never took place in reality; for Rilke had already made his choice. His road, that had seemed open to all possibilities, had led to the turning point where Rilke chose art: Paris, Rodin, greatness—the heroic adventure, not the spiritual quest. Did Rilke ever realize that the anticipated spiritual encounter he extolled in 1901 was a modification of the biblical theme? To be sure, the mythological bottom layer or the three-story archetype, the fight with the demon, and the religious layer at the top, the epiphany at dawn, were preserved, and blended together, producing the extraordinary lure and uplift,[29] the cordial-like quality we mentioned before; but it was a quality more akin to Tao than to Ya'u (an ancient name of Jahve), for indeed the entire middle, Jahvistic part of the archetype was omitted: Gone was "wound" (laming of the hip); gone the blessing attached to a new name (he who fought with God, or he who saw God).[30] No doubt this was a serious curtailment, since Jahve (or the Dark Fire of God, as Böhme called him) is the Ruler of History and of personality as well. In this respect Rilke's poem bears the imprint not only of the poet's predominant devotion to art but also of the times that engendered it, the halcyon days around 1900.

It took the catastrophes of World War II to inspire a poet for a renewed "wrestling with the Angel."

The poet who did so was a delicate little woman. A photograph from the days of her youth shows her with the dark tender eyes of a little fawn.[31] It is, of course, Nelly Sachs. Suffering with the sufferers, writing in order to survive,[32] the little fawn became a seeress, a sibyl, and incidentally, for such are the ironies of life, a Nobel Prize winner.

The second of her great verse volumes, *Sternverdunkelung* (1961), was dedicated to the memory of her father and contained poems on the Old Testament heroes: Abraham, Jacob, Job, Daniel, and again: Israel. Contemporary events have turned the Old Testament story into a nightmare:

> O Israel,
> Erstling im Morgengrauenkampf

wo alle Geburt mit Blut
auf der Dämmerung geschrieben steht.
O das spitze Messer des Hahnenschreis
der Menschheit ins Herz gestochen,
o die Wunde zwischen Nacht und Tag
die unser Wohnort ist!

And addressing Jacob's descendants, she says:

vom schweren Engel über uns
zu Gott verrenkt
wie du![33]

There is the horror of pain, but also an insensate hope, as in the utterances of the prophets. We have entered a new dimension. The beauty, the *fascinosum* of Rilke's vision, has been shattered, but a new and old truth, the *tremendum*, has been regained.

To be sure, Rilke too had sought, had courted the *tremendum*. Ever since the *Stundenbuch*, he was aware of a dual obligation: "Lass dir alles geschehen, Schönheit and Schrecken." At last the awesome presence materialized in the *Duino Elegies*: "ein jeder Engel ist schrecklich." But the Angel, whoever he was, denied his blessing.

Rilke's religion, as it broke forth in 1922, can truly be called Orphic. Like the *symbolon* on some of the Orphic gold tablets of South Italy, his motto could read: "I am a child of earth and the starry Heaven,"[34] and the storm of enthusiasm that lifted him far beyond the level of his everyday experience might be described by the quaint metaphor used on the Orphic gold tablets: "A kid I have fallen in the milk."[35] What had actually happened? Having opened up unreservedly, like the anemone, to sun and rain, to delight and horror, to life and to death, the poet was rewarded by a wave of superreality, which he identified with Orpheus, that legendary figure whom the Orphics claimed as their founder. He did not turn into Orpheus; rather, it was Orpheus who went through him. He was not given the name of Orpheus; rather he became nameless (namenlos)—Niemand (No-body), the ever-present, ever-absent cause of his songs, as his epitaph intimates: "Niemandes Schlaf unter soviel Li (e) dern." Instead of the Angel's blessing, he received the blessing of earth, and his task was to sing the things for the Angels, to sing suffering, love, and death for the humans. What does that mean for us?

All those, be they male or female, in whose minds the masculine element prevails—whether we call it the father principle, or the philosophy of the Stoics[36]—will conclude that Rilke did not attain the blessing of the spirit; among these critics are Elsie Butler, Eudo Mason, and also Hugo Kuhn.[37] On the contrary, those who live entirely through the heart, and mostly they are women, will find him entirely (why not say "unendlich") satisfying.

The strangest case is that of Lieselott Delfiner. She never met Rilke in the flesh. But in 1928, two years after his demise, "he came to her and stayed"; or, as she wrote in her native French:

Tu si profondement en moi . . . Tu es presque moi-meme . . .
Tu es en moi,
Et tu le seras
Tu seras en d'autres,
vivant a jamais. . . . [38]

To be sure, this mystical or poetical indwelling of the poet in the reader can just as well be explained as a gentle reader's indwelling in the word palace prepared for him, or her, by the poet. Then why not call this palace a Taj Mahal—something commemorating feminine grace and beauty? Its function, in this dehumanized world of ours, is to keep alive the supremely feminine gifts of sensitivity, delicacy, and intensity of feeling.

Meanwhile a new architectural style is in the making. Resting on deeper foundations, new spires will be piercing the skies.

We cannot foresee the future. Some poets may abandon the use of words in order to leap into action; others may end in utter abstruseness or devote their talents to the cultivation of vocabulary and syntax of the new poetical idiom; others again—who knows?

It all depends on the inclination of the numen, and on the quality of the hearts and minds that are going to receive the numinous. But this we know: so far, no cathedral equaling Rilke's Taj Mahal has been erected.

Let this be the answer to the question that we raised in the title.

Notes

1. Egon Schwarz, *Das verschluckte Schluchzen: Poesie und Politik bei Rainer Maria Rilke* (Frankfurt am Main, 1972), p. 1.

2. *Prévert II.* English adaption by Teo Savory (Santa Barbara, 1976), p. 15 ("Paternoster").

3. Cf. Hugo Friedrich, *Die Struktur der modernen Lyrik von Baudelaire bis zur Gegenwart* (Hamburg, 1956).

4. Cf. Wilhelm Jacobs, *Moderne Dichtung. Zugang und Deutung* (Gütersloh, 1962), pp. 170f.

5. R.M. Rilke, *Sämtliche Werke* (Frankfurt am Main, 1955–1966), 1:461. Both "Der Panther" and "Die Aschanti" *(SW,* 1:394f.) date from the same period (Paris, 1902/3).

6. Franz Kafka, "Ein Hungerkünstler," in *Das Urteil und andere Erzählungen* (Frankfurt am Main, 1967), pp. 187ff.

7. B. Blume, "Ding und Ich in Rilke's Neuen Gedichten," *MLN* 67 (1951):222; cf. also K. Oppert, "Das Dinggedicht. Eine Kunstform bei Mörike Meyer und Rilke," *Deutsche Vierteljahrsschrift für Literaturwissenschaft und Geistesgeschichte,* 4 (1926):755.

8. Cf. the *varia lectio* to the Incomplete Elegy, *SW,* 2:460: "am unendlichen Gegenüber beinah unendlich." I thank Professor Otto Springer and Dr. Diane Blumenthal for their helpful criticism of my hypothesis.

9. *SW,* 2:52f. (Paris, end of February 1913).

10. Brigitte Bradley, *R.M. Rilkes Neue Gedichte: Ihr zyklisches Gefüge* (Bern and Munich, 1967), p. 185, fn. 5 (Briefe 1902–1906, p. 262).

11. Cf. *Das Buch der Nelly Sachs,* ed. Bengt Holmqvist (Frankfurt am Main, 1968), p. 269; also Olof Lagercrantz, *Versuch über die Lyrik der Nelly Sachs* (Frankfurt am Main, 1967), p. 83 (with a short commentary on the poem).

12. Her knowledge derived from the book by G. Scholem, *Die Geheimnisse der Schöpfung: Ein Kapitel aus dem Sohar* (Berlin, 1935), which is a rendering of the *Sifra di-Zeniutha* (Buch der Verborgenheit), a six-page commentary on Genesis 1:6, which forms part of the *Zohar.* See G. Scholem, *Die jüdische Mystik in ihren Hauptströmungen* (Frankfurt am Main 1957), pp. 175 and 463 (p. 430 deals with the possible connection between the Jewish theosophy of Mme. Blavatsky). On Nelly Sachs, see Holmquist, pp. 43ff., 50f.; Lagercrantz, pp. 75ff; and P. Kersten, *Die Metaphorik in der Lyrik von Nelly Sachs, Mit einer Wort-Konkordanz und einer Nelly-Sachs-Bibliographie* (Hamburg, 1970), pp. 370ff.

13. Kersten, p. 383ff., lists nine cases of the term "Geometrie" in the work of the poetess.

14. Cf. Cornelius Doelman, *Wassily Kandinsky* (New York, 1964), p. 18: "To discuss mysteries by means of the mysterious—is not that the meaning."

15. Rilke, *Visions of Christ: A Posthumous Cycle of Poems,* ed., with an introduction, by Siegfried Mandel; poems translated by Aaron Kramer (Boulder, Colo., 1967).

16. See K. E. Webb, *"Das Buch der Bilder:* A Study of Rilke's Changing Attitudes & Artistry." Diss., University of Pennsylvania, 1969, pp. 36–41.

17. Cf. E. Heller, *The Disinherited Mind: Essays in Modern German Literature and Thought* (Philadelphia, 1952, p. 105. Rilke is seen as the St. Francis of the Will to Power).

18. Rilke in a letter to Witold Hulewicz, November 13, 1925; see *Selected Letters, 1902–26,* trans. R.F.C. Hull (London 1946), p. 396.

19. Cf. H. Adolf, "Wrestling with the Angel: Rilke's 'Gazing Eye' (Der Schauende) and the Archetype," in *Perspectives in Literary Symbolism,* vol. 1,

Yearbook of Comparative Criticism, ed. J. Strelka (University Park, Pa., 1968), pp. 29–39. In this article, I failed to mention the paintings by Rembrandt and by Delacroix. As to Odilon Redon, he transposed Delacroix's nocturnal scene into the glow of the dawn, whereas Gauguin had fallen prey to "Japonism," that great wave that swept over France in the second half of the nineteenth century.

20. "Battling with the Angel," *Prevert II*, p. 40.

21. *De somniis*, 1:127–32. Cf. J. G. Kahn. "Connais-toi toi-même a la manière de Philon," *Revue d'histoire et de philosophie religieuses* 53 (1973).

22. *Civilisation* (London, 1969), p. 315, fig. 216.

23. August Strindberg, "Jakob brottas," in "Inferno och Legender," *Samlade Skrifter*, 38:325–98. Cf. also Nils Erdmann, *August Strindberg en kämpande och lidande sjaels historia*, 2 (Stockholm, 1920), pp. 321f.

24. Cf. W. Bode, Catalogue of the Kaiser Friedrich-Museum (now State Museum Berlin-Dahlem), No. 828. Best color reproduction is in L. Muenz, *Rembrandt* (New York, 1967), p. 132. Cf. also Rilke's 'Einleitung' zu Worpswede (*SW*, 5:17).

25. A term used by M. Buber. See A. Hodes, *Martin Buber: An Intimate Portrait* (New York, 1971), p. 33.

26. See G. Mayer, *Rilke und Kassner. Eine geistige Begegnung* (Marburg, 1951), p. 41.

27. Northrop Frye, *Anatomy of Criticism* (Princeton, 1957), pp. 118, 365. Philip Wheelwright, *The Burning Fountain: A Study in the Language of Symbolism* rev. ed. (Bloomington, 1968), p. 55.

28. On C.J. Jung, see this author in *Perspectives in Literary Symbolism*, p. 31 and fn. 5.

29. Ibid., p. 34.

30. "Der Gebogene wird selber Bieger," as Rilke says in "Imaginärer Lebenslauf," *SW* (1923), 2:142f.

31. *Nelly Sachs zu Ehren* (Frankfurt am Main, 1962), p. 95 (Jugendbildnis).

32. *Nelly Sachs zu Ehren zum 75. Geburtstag am 10. Dezember 1966.* (Frankfurt am Main, 1966), p. 123: "Hätte ich nicht schreiben können, so hätte ich nicht überlebt," in a letter to Gisela Dischmer, 12 July 1966.

33. N. Sachs, *Das Leiden Israels* (Eli; In den Wohnungen des Todes; Sternverdunkelung) (Frankfurt am Main, 1965), pp. 122f. See also Lagercrantz, p. 53; Kersten, pp. 90, 112, 214, 302.

34. On the gold tablets, see O. Kern, *Orphicorum Fragmenta* (Berlin, 1922), no. 32, pp. 104–9; Gilbert Murray, "Critical Appendix on the Orphic Tablets," in Jane E. Harrison, *Prolegomena to the Study of Greek Religion*, 3d ed. (Cambridge, Eng., 1922), pp. 659–73; Jane Harrison, ibid., pp. 572–99; W.K.C. Guthrie, *Orpheus and Greek Religion* (London, 1935), pp. 171–93 (on the kid and the milk: "to attain in abundance that which one had always desired," p. 178).

35. Cf. also the cosmic-astronomic interpretation by R. Eisler, *Orpheus—the Fisher* (London, 1921), pp. 59ff., and in *Orphisch—dionysische Mysterien-Gedanken* (Leipzig, 1925; 1966), pp. 357ff.

36. Goethe called it "Geist": "das Vorwaltende des oberen Leitenden," *Noten und Abhandlungen zum West-östlichen Divan*, Allgemeinstes).

37. Hugo Kuhn, *Kleine Schriften* (Texte und Theorie) (Stuttgart, 1969), 2:96ff., in an interpretation of Rilke's late poem "Der Magier."

38. Lieselott Delfiner, *Rilke Cet Incompris* (Paris, 1960), pp. 294ff.

Heinrich Dörrie

THE MEANING AND FUNCTION
OF MYTH
IN GREEK AND ROMAN
LITERATURE

I

During the classical period, myth and literature had a close mutual relationship. Objects of myth could only be properly expressed in high poetry—in the epic, in hymns, in tragedy. Handbooks of mythology could only have a supplementary function, perhaps to aid recollection. Such handbooks were widely available beginning in the Hellenistic period, circa 331–300 B.C. They were written on different levels and served various purposes (See section VI below.)

The Greek mind made a careful distinction between mythology and myth—the distance between them is the same as that between history and the writing of history. The term mythology was used by the Greeks exclusively to designate factual recounting of mythological events. But myth goes further; it touches its reader or hearer closely; it has an effect, for it contains a piece of advice or more frequently a warning. Aristotle describes this effect as a "cleansing of the emotions" *(pathematon katharsis,* Poetics 1449 b 27). He ascribes this effect to tragedy, in his day the only form of literature that expressed myth. To have an effect of this sort was both the responsibility and the right of the poet. That is why the entire classical world was convinced that all myths had originally been announced by poets. This applies also in the historical sense. Most of the myths that continued to be effective were treated in the epic poems of the Homeric and post-Homeric period. There was no room for the idea that perhaps compilers of prosaic handbooks might have had any part in the important task of mythic creation—*mythopoeia*.

A modern analyst of the problematic nature of "myth" will do well, therefore, to remember at all times that the approach—*accessus*—to myth through handbooks is illegitimate. Such an approach has led to many erroneous concepts. Handbooks cannot help us reconstruct a definition of myth; it must be learned through the experience of poetry. It is difficult to regain this immediate experience.

The following example may enlighten us about the close relationship between high poetry and myth. With one famous exception, classical tragedy always drew on myth for its materials.[1] The poet was allowed all possible freedom to make the myth useful for contemporary questions and to apply it to them—if necessary by changing traditional details. The poet, committed to this rule for his theme, was in no way obliged to keep his distance from actuality. On the contrary, it was an aspect of his art to find and effectively apply the mirror suitable to the questions he wanted to treat.

We may imagine an analogy in the modern frame. How would it be if there had been a poetic law to the effect that a particular genre—let us say the novel—could and would only deal with materials taken from the chivalrous world surrounding King Arthur? Such a law would have established the "literary initial situation" for the shrewd knight, Don Quixote, for whom there was no other literature than that which drew its inspiration from the "myths" of the Middle Ages. The analogy we have just belabored becomes even more striking when we realize that Don Quixote allows these "myths" to determine his behavior. He sets out to realize the ideals of Christian knighthood.

This parallel is intended to clarify the following. As far as the form and content of life are concerned, the waning Middle Ages were reduced to absurdity by Miguel de Cervantes. By contrast, the validity of classical myth was much more deeply rooted. It remained unshaken by frequent, drastic alterations in social conditions. Some things changed; new demands were taken into account. But on the whole, once a period of trenchant criticism had been overcome (see section V), myth took on a lasting stature from about 400 B.C. What we have just called stature is determined only in part by the content of myth. More important, there was a consensus, never shaken, concerning the function of myth. Myth was charged with enabling statements about what is human, and especially about the deformation of what is human through longings and passion. Such a statement, supported by myth, obtains particular force and credibility because, removed from the everyday trivialities, it is raised to the sphere of what is generally accepted.

In this sense myth was universally applicable. It is true that originally it mirrored the aristocracy ethic of the Homeric period; but it had long since made itself free of this constricting connection. It must be designated as one of the great achievements of the fifth century B.C. that it brought about this universal applicability of myth. It was inevitable, though deplored by contemporaries, that this development was tied to deheroization. (The critical comparison between Aeschylus and Euripides, drawn by Aristophanes in *The Frogs*, emphasizes this difference. The fact that Euripides took steps toward deheroization was noted and judged adversely.) The heroes of the myths do not serve as ethical prototypes, to be praised or condemned. Their fate becomes exemplary less because of their actions than because of their sufferings; they serve to depict the destructive power of passion. After these radical changes, myth simply could not (and here ends the analogy introduced for clarification above) be carried *ad absurdum* to the extent that Cervantes reduced the ethic of the period preceding his to absurdity.

For myth was no longer a piece of the past; the myth was quite genuinely timeless. For centuries it did not run the risk of becoming old-fashioned; myth has never been accused of expressing yesterday's values. Myth simply could not become obsolete.

These two characteristics—universal applicability and permanent timelessness—brought about the transformation of myth to the function of a mirror. Comedy aside, we cannot name a single writer who did not make use of this mirror.[2] The impact of a work depended on the artfulness with which this mirror was employed. The cultural, intellectual, and aesthetic development that occurred in Greece can be gathered from the degree that myth was made fruitful for literature and philosophy.

If myth ever had undergone a phase when it was completely and unequivocally the expression of conscious or unconscious material, this phase was transcended in Greece. More, it is no longer evident in the period when literary tradition became established—that is, at the time of the Homeric poets. As is true for all subsequent writers, it is true for these poets that the myth does not contain its own purpose; it contains an argument, and it is told in order to bring this argument to bear. No trace leads back to a myth narrative "in itself," and it is a presumption, unsupported by any evidence, to claim what certain myths "really" mean for a time at such a distance from ours and a culture so different from ours as ancient Greece. We should quite firmly turn from the kind of interpretation of myth that was practiced until recently to the point of philistine abuse. My next few remarks may serve to illuminate the process that led to an unfortunately deeply rooted misinterpretation of the meaning of myth.

II

It would be worth special study to determine why Christianity, in spite of its frequently incisive criticism of Greek myth, was not able to shake its validity. Myth in its original rights was reestablished long before the high Italian Renaissance, with its return to ancient art forms; it was already firm during the much earlier return to Ovid (around 1300). Ovid furnished a collection of examples that were in every way on a par with those of the Old Testament. The two traditions served to confirm one another. While this connection was abandoned in Michelangelo's century—from then on the writer was forced to choose one or the other—the serious attempts to treat Biblical materials in the creation of a literature intended to demolish the domination of pagan myth failed.[3]

The literature that now clearly emerged from the clerical-sacral connection committed itself all the more firmly to myth, especially in the form given it by Ovid. A quite unusual achievement of the Renaissance and the subsequent classical period in France and Germany—one that has not been much acknowledged so far—consisted in the fact that the function of myth in the ancient sense was repeated. It was never questioned that myth contained a rich store of eternally valid experiences, safe against relativizing and not subject to the "happening." Goethe's Iphigenia no less than Euripides' use this form to express something universal, above the quotidian. Because classicism throughout Europe claimed to be the realization of the absolute and permanently valid, it could not afford to omit myth—not because of the themes it offered, but because of the immutable validity of the truths it mirrored. This unanimity in understanding myth—a common assumption among all people of culture, seldom discussed until that time—was permanently destroyed by Romanticism. It was at that time that the dissention emerged which has lasted to this day.

In 1835 Jacob Grimm published his work on German mythology. His choice of title stressed the fact that, in the author's view, German literature and usage had been built on the basis of myths just as much as were classical literature, classical art, and classical ethics. At the same time the choice of title emphasized the claim, still under dispute at the time, of German philology of being on a level with classical philology, since in both areas myth seemed to be the point of departure for all developments in art and literature. With this stress, it was completely overlooked that the Old High German stories of gods and heroes—from now on called myths—exercised a quite different function, which simply was not comparable. Thus the first step leading to today's confusion of concepts was unfortunately taken. The rich tradition of tales and legends of the early Germanic period was, sadly, not provided with an adequate catchall name (though use could have been made of derivatives of *Märe, Sage,* and *Kunde).* On the contrary, the word "myth" was applied as a collective name, although "myth" applied to something quite different. (Jacob Grimm's lack of understanding went so far that he spoke of certain parts of the legends as *die Mythe*—feminine singular—a linguistic deformation that was continued for some time.)

Since scholarship was now dealing with a "German mythology" (and soon thereafter with an "Indian" and a "Finnish" one, based on the Kalevala), the concept of myth was narrowed in the sense that applied the word primarily to the archetypes of the events narrated in mythology. Examples are tales of the Great Flood, fratricide, the sacrifice of a son or daughter, a woman's leading many heroes to their death. The Brothers Grimm seem to have departed from the assumption, surely erroneous, that myth reveals native lore—more immediately understood as popular lore, the primitive, original onset of human thinking and feeling, existing before any culture. This assumption, not justified by any evidence, attained quite uncontested domination.

Instead of refining the tools used in the exploration of myth or of many myths, further blunting ensued. First, any nonhistorical tradition from any literature became designated as myth. Second, it became customary to evaluate the general validity of the "myth" in question on the basis of the facts reported in such "myths," as if the story reflected a so-called original event. We must realize that such a procedure appeared to open a road leading back to a primal period. Now it seemed to become possible to work out a kind of primal history or prehistory of human experiences, or at least of their bases—an expectation that fascinated many researchers who were more critical in other areas. Unfortunately, perhaps out of fear of jeopardizing the result that was longed for, often enough the scholars were content with insufficient analysis of superficially determined "myths." It must be remembered how readily, even frivolously, concepts of "totem" and "taboo" were identified among many cultures—and yet in the last ten years it has become highly doubtful whether the customs and concepts of North American Indians have ever been properly interpreted. It is probably that a premature joy of discovery allowed scholars to impose mistaken or at least insufficiently warranted results, on quite unrelated findings among very disparate peoples. Unfortunately, in this field premature associations and identifications prevailed. A further example will serve to illustrate these.

Around 1895 Sigmund Freud was tracing the problem of father-son conflicts. In 1896, shortly before he made his pioneering discovery, he attended a performance of Sophocles' *Oedipus Rex* in Paris. He was very much moved by the performance, as he himself noted in letters. It was his belief that the problem he was researching had been covered by a classical author who was aware of this "archetype." On the basis of his own experience, from then on Freud called the object of his investigation the "Oedipus complex." Perhaps it is a gain that this designation, which has become a label, serves to name adequately, and for many satisfactorily, this conflict of the son between father and mother. In this sense we may consider the phrase a neologism without which a new science cannot get along. But a further conclusion is entirely unwarranted—that not only the label but also the persistently postulated universal validity of the phenomenon are supported by the depth-psychological statements of classical poets. Neither Sophocles nor Seneca so much as touched upon Freud's concern in their tragedies. For the Oedipus of classical drama acts in total ignorance. He does not know that it was his father whom he killed, and he does not know that it was his mother whom he wed. Rather the myth deals with the heart-rending fate of a single individual. It never voices the idea that all sons are threatened by such a snare—that is, that all are prone to such a "complex." The classical value varies radically from Freud's. The fact that, in a mixture of guilt and innocence, Oedipus commits two terrible crimes represents such an affront to the gods that many years later they disclose and punish Oedipus' guilt. The classical writings ask only how Oedipus acts in this final phase. His efforts to resist the discovery are in vain, for the gods will exact their punishment.

It would be even more idle to refer to earlier versions of the legend, surviving only in fragments.[4] None of them ever served as an example of the "Oedipus complex." Rather they were illustrations of the fact that a human being can become unwittingly guilty; and they served to illustrate the fact that the gods meted out their punishments not according to the transgressor's intention but according to the objective severity of the guilt as pollution. Precisely because this legendary tale has a clearly visible function as exemplum, it can be stated with absolute certainty that it does not have the function Freud assigned to it. But the fact that a thoroughly modern discovery became accepted through the term Oedipus complex, as if classical myth had already contained such depth-psychological declarations—that is characteristic of the often very frivolous manner of associations indulged in all too readily by contemporary myth scholars.

It may well be that the widespread legend of the Great Flood refers back to a primal fear of flood catastrophes. It may even be that the legends of fratricide—such as Cain and Abel, Etyocles and Polynices, Romulus and Remus—and of incest among siblings testify to an original repulsion against actions that destroyed the family. (Even this statement, however, is not universally applicable. We need only recall the ancient Egyptian custom of intermarriage between brother and sister.) Legends about a father willing to sacrifice a son or daughter—Isaac, Iphigenia—are often backed by historical reminders that human sacrifice has been abolished: the gods do not want it. With every possible caution we may interpret myths as cultural-historical (but surely not psychological) documents.

The traits of Greek myth are quite different. Its essence is not at all marked by what more recent scholars understand by the word myth. For only minimally is that which makes up myth grounded in the appearance and course of the narration. Myth, after all, is much more than legend. Each myth teaches something; each myth faces its hearer with the task of making fruitful for his own situation whatever the myth demonstrates on an extraquotidian object. Myth is exemplum. And for every exemplum we must ask what purpose is served.

Though it is a step in the right direction to ask, with

Lévi-Strauss, about "structures," we must not rest there. For the structures, which are extraordinarily capable of transformation, are in the service of the function assigned to a myth. As an inviolable rule this assignment of a function happened consciously and deliberately. It makes clear the intention of a narrator, an author. This author aims at achieving a multiple purpose. Of course he wants to communicate the sequence of events, the course of the action; he may even want to use it to entertain.[5] Almost always he aims to go further, to teach, warn, admonish, advise for or against. And it is obvious that precisely this intention underlies the often cautious, often deeply radical changes the narrator or poet makes in the material. That is why from the outset myth is a cultural factor. It is a tool—for a long time even a very outstanding tool—of *paideia*. It is manipulated quite consciously, even artfully. It is very far from the unconscious.

III

The myths of the Greeks cannot be derived from a single source, either historically or functionally. It is probable that Greek myth was so rich in phenomena and variations because it mingled Hittite, Cretan, and autochthonous traditions. Though myth is maintained as a universally constant force by a tradition of secular validity, this tradition has always been able to adopt new, previously unknown elements.[6]

At the same time myth has never exerted one function only. As we shall discuss in detail below, it was an almost universal tool to explain the incomprehensible or to document a claim. That is why previous attempts to define exhaustively even only the extent of myth have remained thoroughly unsatisfactory.[7] Myths were related to the gods only in part; the relationship between myths and cults was often very slight, and often nonexistent.[8] Only for a very small number of myths—these are the myths of the *adventus* of a god—was it true that they were copied in a ritual. The principal one is the arrival of Dionysius-Bacchus, which culminated in a ritual in many places, including Athens. But the major portion by far of all myths had nothing to do with ritual.

The current but frequently insufficiently grounded concepts that tend to identify myth with the religious or sacral sphere must be thoroughly modified. Undoubtedly there are many connections between myth and religion. But it is an oversimplification to derive myth from cult or ritual or to see myth as something with religious origins, as a form that has lost the concept of faith.[9] All these attempts to define myth exhaustively, or even to justify it, have missed their mark.

Instead myth must be defined as a rich store of knowledge and experience, available to all. This store of experiences was available, as a matter of course, to answer small everyday questions and large questions, such as those concerning the world and its creation. Later the question was raised whether the mythic tales could be seen as authenticated history—a question which, after some vacillation, was answered in the negative. In the early period, which can be said to end roughly in mid-fifth century B.C., with Pindar and Aeschylus, the question of verifying the narrative presumably never arose. Only the critical thought of the waning fifth century shook the absolute certainty ("faith") that the myth encompassed valid reminiscences.[10] Subsequently, though the world of myth was not considered actual, it was still perceived as a quasi-historical area. The experiences myths contained were at a distance from everyday life, especially its trivial aspects.[11] That was why, after all, they were generally accepted in a higher sense and all the better able to be applied to questions of the present.

This continuum of mythic tradition is made clear through the literature; and ultimately we can only describe and interpret it in the light of literary evidence. But we must not forget that classical man was everywhere surrounded by visual expressions of myth. We need only recall the black- and red-figured vases, primarily of Attic origin, as well as the wall painting of Pompeii and the late-classical sarcophagi that were amply decorated with scenes from myth—not to mention the figurative decorations of the temples, most especially their tympana.

As mentioned above, myth had more than sacral aspects. Its applicability reached deep into the profane. Apparently there were no boundaries that myth could not transcend on pain of becoming blasphemous; Christianity was the first to set such limits. The objects of myth were never considered holy in a transcendental sense, so that they could only be intruded into the confusions of this world with pious awe. On the contrary, myth encompassed the full extent of the experiences in this world, often especially in harsh, in tragic situations. That is why myth was allowed to infiltrate daily life—it served as ornament and entertainment, as advice and admonition, as an aid to the imagination in difficult questions. Complicated matters could be elucidated by a mythic example; simplicities could be differentiated by mythic encoding. To this extent the presence of the mythic, not only in classical literature, but especially in the quotidian, in the rooms one lived in and the objects one used, was much more universal than, for example, the presence of the sacral in the Christianity of the high Middle Ages. Only a fraction of it was deposited in the literary realm.

IV

Frequently the Homeric poets comment on the course of actions they are narrating (the struggle for Troy, Odysseus' return) by citing examples from other myth groups. Almost regularly such examples lead to advice on the proper response to a given situation. Niobe came close to turning to stone out of grief for the death of her children; but after fasting for nine days, she began to take nourishment again (Omega 602 and 612). Therefore, Achilles advises, Priam should also partake of the meal. This may be seen as the absolute paradigm of mythic exemplum. (Schiller duplicated this theme at the end of his poem "Das Siegesfest.") The entire content of this mythological tale is not reproduced; in particular, the lesson this myth in its actual sense intends to teach is not replicated by the Homeric poet. Niobe was punished because her pride as a mother seduced her into a position of *hybris*. The tale of the cruel revenge the offended gods took is surely to be assigned to the Apollonian myths, which warned against disparaging the *maiestas* of Apollo, his sister Artemis, and their common mother, Leto. The Homeric poet, however, mentioned none of this in Omega 602–17. Only a marginal aspect is brought to bear on his subject: even Niobe, so harshly punished, finds her way back into human, commonplace life.

Here we find the point of departure of the figure of speech varied innumerable times in classical and modern literature: the mythic exemplum.

If the Homeric poems allude to extra-Trojan myths, then such knowledge is always presented as alive in the memories of preceding generations. Phoenix lived to see the dire consequences when Meleager angrily withdrew from battle, so that the city Calydon was threatened with capture and destruction (I 526–99). In his youth Nestor (A 262–72) saw the Lapithae and witnessed their ruin. Glaukus (Z 155–97) knew how his grandfather Bellerophon was driven out of Ephyra/Corinth, how he slew the chimera and thereafter found a new home in Lycia; this is given as the motive for his grandsons Sarpedon and Glaucus fighting on the side of the Trojans.

Clearly the Homeric poets are far from a systematic ordering of mythic elements. However, since later on everything was taken as authoritative if it was found in "Homer," so the subsequent literary usage of mythic elements was very strongly marked by what has just been described: the figure of speech of the mythic exemplum, and the myth as stored experience of an older and wiser generation.

V

In the seventh and eighth centuries B.C. the element of the mythic gained several additional dimensions, previously not present.

It became indispensable to the legitimation of the ruling aristocracies of the day to derive their descent from one of the dynasties named by Homer and, through these dynasties, to one of the gods or goddesses. Now genealogical myths in great number were created—surely because it was politically significant to support the right to rule by proof of divine descent.

Hesiod's didactic poem *Theogonia* was intended to do more than demonstrate the origin of the gods; rather it flowed into long catalogues of those who had had relations with gods or goddesses and thus became progenitors of famous dynasties. Others also undertook to collect such genealogical material, for its part authenticated as established memories. The poet of the *Lambda* of the *Odyssey*, the *Nekyia*, inserted into his poem a catalogue of the women who had enjoyed the affection of a god and borne him children. It had clearly become an important task of the *aoidos*, the singer, to include in his poem testimony of the divine origins of the family in whose castle he sang and from whom he received his wages. Hesiod ultimately arranged and shaped this material, which previously had surely been disordered and proliferated wildly. Only then did it become obvious how many families claimed descent from Zeus. The correctness of such a tradition was never called into question; such seemingly historical facts were received seriously and continued in the tradition. Criticism touched upon a quite different issue, which could not have been foreseen. If Zeus was the father of so many heroes—a claim, as noted, that was never doubted—then he must have seduced an

equal number of women. Here we find the point of departure of
the endlessly and variously used jibes that made Zeus appear as
the permanent lover, the resourceful seducer. Subsequent writers
never tired of inventing ever-new concurrences and ruses by
which Zeus approached his love objects—as bull, as golden rain,
as swan, and finally even in the guise of the husband Amphitryon.

Before this time the invention of genealogical myths had a
clearly demarcated political purpose: they gave support to an aristocracy rooted in the situations described by Homer and intent on
preserving it. But soon thereafter such constructions lost their purpose. However, they were by no means abandoned; rather they
were elaborated on with downright relish in order to please the
hearers with the amatory prowess of the father of the gods and of
men.

The conservative stance adopted by Hesiod was contrasted by
an awakening movement that was customarily designated by the
name of Orpheus. This movement had as its aim to lead men to
"salvation"—soteria—that is, to a blissful life after death. While
Homeric religiosity is pronouncedly poor in eschatological motives, the question of what occurs after death takes the foreground
in the Orphic movement. This leads to a different interpretation of
the mythic as well. It was believed that a penalty for bad behavior
and a promise of bliss for proper behavior could be read in them.[12]
Accordingly, particular myths have two levels of meaning. We
may disregard the profane, all too accessible, level: only the disciples of Orpheus have access to the real level, the one relevant to
human salvation. Surreptitiously the comprehension of symbols
becomes occult lore. The mystery of Eleusis, while not originating
in Orphism in the proper sense, grew out of a comparable attitude.
A single myth was made the basis of the cult through a secretly
handed-down symbolic relationship. Orphism made two changes
in myth: the events narrated in the myths are not located in the
past but are ever present—even now the Titanic element struggles
with the divine authority in each human being. Second, correct
interpretation of particular myths is essential to salvation. But
these two changes hardly came to expression in the literary realm.
Much later, however, in the second to fifth centuries A.D., Orpheus was regarded as a key figure, as someone who had announced all theological truth and wisdom in the dawn of history,
before Homer.

Now it seems at first glance as if those who wanted to view
myth as the symbolic expression of basic verities or, more re-

cently, primal experiences would find support for their conception in Orphism. There, after all, the attempt was made to penetrate through the interpretation of universally familiar mythical tales to the basic and primal truths that represent a basis common to all mankind. To document this, bold associations were often required. Because the traced analogues seemed immediately reasonable, particularly striking or accessible coincidences were taken to have been definitively proven.[13]

But the view of myth taken and understood by generalizing theology at the beginning of the twentieth century was hardly the way the classical period viewed and understood it, aside from minimal variations. Orphism offered this understanding to later generations. But the offer was refused; aside from the frequently mentioned exception of the Eleusinian mysteries, myth did not become the vehicle of a redemption lore or a religion directed to the winning of salvation.

To a much greater degree the relationship of the Greeks to myth was formed by two controversies with long-lasting consequences, which were waged in the sixth and fifth centuries B.C.

1. In an earlier phase of myth criticism, moral displeasure was dominant. It seemed unbearable that Homer and Hesiod told of gods who lied, stole, committed adultery. Homer and Hesiod could only have invented such stories because they wished to blaspheme against the gods. It seemed necessary to suppress such a tradition because it threatened the youth.[14] Subsequently Plato quite seriously adopted this line of reasoning.

2. A later phase was marked by rationalistic criticism. Now the miracles often enough reported in myths seemed factually incredible. In this phase attention was called to the absence of documentary evidence. (In defense, an argument somewhat as follows was cited. Homer and Hesiod did not really care about the surface narration. In reality the gods of myth are nature forces. All epics represent steps in the creation of the world, cosmogony, which does indeed apply to the beginnings of Hesiod's and Orpheus' theogony. Therefore the passion of Ares and Aphrodite must not be seen as a scandalous story of adultery, the poet's didactic purpose having gone far more deeply.) Because the events reported by the myths were not historical, they had to be untrue. (The defense against this argument was basically weak. It limited itself to interpreting away the miraculous elements, thus enervating the objection of incredulity.) This view of myth can be traced from the

waning fifth century B.C. to deep into Hellenism. It was subsequently given sustained support by the novellike work of Euhemerus of Messina.[15]

It is clear, then, that discussions about myth stretched very far. None of the vying tendencies gained the ascendancy: neither the tendency that called for rejecting the myths for their moral offensiveness, nor the tendency that was offended by the improbable elements. Both critical trends applied quite other criteria to myth than during the archaic period. Both together brought it about that myth was retained as an important vessel of the Greek intellect. The individual questions, even accusations, directed at the mythic tradition never seriously touched its substance. But they stimulated the search for new interpretations and new justifications.

It had, we must recall, been a long time since Greece had grown beyond the Homeric world, which was drawn in all its details in myth. The culture of the cities had long since replaced the aristocracy of the Homeric and post-Homeric world. But the new society that arose could not do without the old didactic concepts. To be sure, a very few, who were to remain outsiders, demanded that the traditional myths be abandoned. But in spite of all attacks, the mythic tradition was very firm, and what this tradition achieved could not be replaced by anything else.

Thus a downright paradoxical situation resulted which, as far as I can see, has no analogy in any other literature. Precisely in the century when myth radically fought for survival—the fifth century B.C.—the concept of myth became so rooted that it grew into a dominant continuum. This is true not only for all phases of Greek literature until the victory of Christianity, but also, and to a much greater degree, for Roman literature. Precisely in this area the Romans, who—a few tribal legends aside—had no mythological tradition of their own, adopted the Greek model in the broadest measure, with alterations and without subtractions. It was especially the adoption of mythic elements that closely connected Roman literature with Greek literature.

VI

Plato rejected the myths insofar as they were immoral, and to Aristotle *mythodes* stood for whatever was unproven and unscientific. With these two notable exceptions, from about 400 B.C. to the threshold of the Middle Ages, the following concept of the nature of myth prevailed. What was voiced in myth was not history but was supratemporal; myth encompassed a world of examples. Looked at in this way, mythology was only in small part the myths of the gods. Though everyone knew the facts that have been reported from time immemorial, they hardly mattered in the literary treatment. For interest turned decidedly on the human beings who acted and suffered in the myths. This recognition decisively abandoned a path delineated by Pindar and Aeschylus: the human beings of mythology were by no means heroes of moral decision; rather the figures of mythology were subjected to a lasting deheroization. All the actors were subject to instinct, even impulsiveness. For the passions were seen as irresistible forces.[16] Eros especially was such a despotic ruler that all humans—those of the myth and those of the present day—were subject to his rule. Thus, from Euripides to Ovid, mythology grew into an abundant collection of examples of "human nature."

But this human nature was not seen in the sense of modern humanity; only rarely did heroic decision triumph over instinct and passion. Stimulating examples of this dynamic were furnished by history rather than myth, such as Leonidas' heroic decision at Thermopylae or the assassination of the tyrant by Harmodius and Aristogiton. The conflict between duty and inclination was, characteristically, not a theme in classical literature to the extent that it was devoted to mythology.[17] Rather, the proper subject was the deformation of a personality that was originally great, unable to release himself from the web of its passion—this was as true for Hippolytus as it was for Phaedra, for Medea as well as for Oedipus; it was true not only for familiar figures from tragedy, but also for the characters of the Hellenistic epyllion as well as the passion-plagued figures in Ovid.

The deceptive term "tragedy of inevitability" applied only in the following clearly demarcated sense: myth teaches us the ineluctability of the affects, most particularly love. Hellenistic and Roman literature were to compete in mirroring ever-new variations of erotic *furor* in mythic events. What was fateful was the inescapability of the entanglement, because it expressed a condition that applied to all men.

The literary form of mythology since Euripides was not exemplary in the sense that heroic actors behaved properly, thus offering models.[18] Rather literature oriented to myth depicted and taught through faulty behavior, through the inevitable entanglements. The one exception to this rule was Hercules, who opted for

the narrow, steep road and was frequently praised as an example
of the philosophically correct decision. This attitude was held by
Prodicus of Ceos and subsequently by the Cynics.

This variation introduced by Euripides allowed mythology to
place a contemporary image of man in the mythic frame. It is not,
therefore, saying too much to claim that mythic tale (in epic) and
the unfolding plot in the mythic frame (in tragedy) properly became the means of representing mankind. In this area we encounter important statements about classical humanity.

An example may serve to prove the point. Quite intentionally
Apollonius of Rhodes (circa 250 B.C.) does not depict the protagonist of his epic, Jason, as a cheerful go-getter; he is shown as a
basic loner, who lives for a great task. He does not command
superhuman powers but is aware of his responsibility to use the
means at his disposal—especially the ship *Argo* and his twelve
companions—meaningfully and without running unnecessary
risks. This awareness brings him into conflict with his companions
at times.[19] This depiction by no means established a model.
Rather it served to prove that the uncommon dangers of a long
journey to a foreign land can only be mastered when a nature such
as Jason is shown as possessing guides the journey of the *Argo*.

Earlier it might have seemed that the epic had been condemned
to die out. The fact that mythology overcame the fifth-century
crisis that threatened its existence had serious significance for the
survival of the epic. The very same mythology, filled with new
meaning, once more furnished the material for epic poetry. Although already pronounced dead by Callimachus, it gained new
life, for the old reciprocal relation between myth and epic was
reestablished. It was precisely for this reason that Virgil, in an
epic, was able to express what he wished to make vivid to the
Romans of his time: *arma virumque*. In order to present the humanity of Aeneas, he frequently referred back to the model supplied by Apollonius of Rhodes.

Along with the total material of mythology, Rome also adopted
the concept just defined. Many epics and many more tragedies
were composed in Rome.[20] One thing, however, mythology was
not able to achieve; ideal figures, compelling models were not
within its vocabulary. In this regard Rome kept strictly to the
rules; the historical exemplum was created. The history of Rome
was turned into a kind of hall of fame, where such figures as
Regulus, Cincinnatus, and Cato were worshiped. The Greek
myths had little of this; the great poets no more than the nonliter-

ary or semiliterary tradition ever praised their heroes or raised them to the rank of the exemplary—with the exception of Hercules, cited above. The Homeric Achilles may have been the strongest man in Troy, but he was anything but a model retainer. His wrath endangered the common enterprise. That is why the hero of the Iliad cannot be compared with Virgil's hero, with Aeneas. In reality Aeneas stepped outside the myth; he initiated the line of the great historical exempla. To this extent Virgil suspended the separation between myth and history, which was usually thoroughly observed, in the service of his hero.

When shaping mythic themes, the poets, like all creative artists, were only loosely limited by the framework of the action. Of course the principal facts could not be ignored; but in the actual elaboration, the poet was generally free. Most particularly, the poet was granted the liberty of stressing the motives of the protagonists in such a way as to make them correspond to his poetic intention. Additions and alterations were in large measure seen as permissible. In one of the most telling examples of such alterations, Jason's infidelity to Medea and Medea's revenge on her rival are traditional elements; but Medea's killing of her own children in order to hurt Jason is Euripides' addition.

To the same extent the poet was not obligated to adopt rigidly the versions of a legend as they were offered by an authority, such as Homer. In this area there was ample room for partial myth criticism—that is, for correcting details which in the new version become inessential. A considerable number of presumptions could be altered, with the undisputed claim of presenting them properly—that is, tailored to the inherent purpose of the myth. The often-cited principle of "nothing without proof"—*amartyron ouden*—applies only to names and events,[21] not to the interpretation of a myth.

In this sense, a poet eager and able to make use of them had almost unrestricted access to the nearly inexhaustible supply of traditional materials. In the Hellenic period a number of handbooks came into being that furnished this material. Some of them were designed to offer their subjects to future poets; others were dedicated to ordering the whole area, preferably along genealogical lines; still others furnished collections on a particular theme, such as tales of metamorphosis. Finally, there were books that correspond to our tales of the great operas, meant to educate their readers about mythic materials they might encounter in reading or in the theater—such as the *fabulae* of Hyginus.

Certainly attempts were made to raise control over this material to a technical skill, turning mythology to an end in itself, used for its own sake; but such attempts were soon abandoned.[22] A poet—we may point to Ovid as an example—had to be able to estimate how much of the detail of the myth and how much subtlety he could expect his readers to absorb. But these are reflections that must be weighed before employing any genre; excess and banality must always be avoided.

VII

Classical literature has always claimed to transcend its own day. Homer, who held undisputed sway for more than a millennium, is the chief example. Many authors hoped for a similar secular fame, especially should they succeed in outdoing Homer; commitment to mythology also meant competition with Homer. The modern postulate that a poet must work within his own day—that is, observe the laws of realism—would in the classical period have been considered valid for only a few genres, such as satire or *mimus*.[23] For the condition, actually considered to have priority, that the poet must have an ulterior, moral purpose was, in the classical view, more easily met if the poet was not restricted to the everyday and trivial. The inexhaustible means that allowed him to preserve distance and still remain factual were the matter of mythology.

The high poetry of the Greeks and Romans, of the Middle Ages, and of all contemporary classical revivals avoids two devices as being quite simply antipoetic: reference to the present, and approximations of the trivial. In this respect classical literature and the material considered to be literature today were diametrically opposed. Nevertheless, the central theme of classical literature was man.

The irreconcilable condition thus created could be resolved only with the help of mythology. And because the incompatibility had to be reconciled, myth was indispensable.

The listening and reading audience was disposed along the same lines. Each poet could assume that the basic lines of mythological action were well known; anyone rash enough to confuse the wooden horse outside the gates of Troy with the wooden bull of Daedalus marked himself as boorish—like Trimalchio in Petronius' Satyricon (52:2). It is quite certain that the universal applicability of mythology was a given only so long as familiarity with mythology was an unshakable part of the education of the reading public. This was precisely the reason why an extensive mythological-mythographical literature arose and became current. Anyone who feared that, like Trimalchio, he would leave himself open to embarrassment could make use of it to increase his knowledgeability. But this familiarity was never in question during the classical period.[24]

The poet who dealt with the material offered by mythology did not, like a modern writer, worry about suspense. In isolated episodes he might be eager to supply suspenseful narration, a task that in tragedy was often assigned to the messenger's report. With this technique the poet not only related what could not be shown on the stage but also introduced suspense. Yet on the whole the poet was not interested in suspense and was free to concentrate on the essentials. He could and should emend the tradition, the course of events known to all, transform them so that the specifically human quality of the protagonists was fully stressed. For an educated public felt sufficient suspense in following, not the course of the action, but the modifications introduced by the individual poet.

For all these reasons myth is an element indispensable to classical poetry. The tie to mythology granted a great deal of freedom to the classical poet—the freedom of removing himself from the present,[25] the freedom to depict mankind far from triviality and a workaday existence. These freedoms, it was felt, assured him of penetrating to the essentials. The frame offered by myth was elastic enough not to cramp the freedom of the chosen material. We recall the richness of the mythic material treated by Ovid.

For these reasons classical poetry and classical myth determine each other. This reciprocal relationship raises both to cultural factors of high intensity and binding force. There is no doubt that, as a consequence, classical poetry was something unique and became the model for contemporary literature during significant epochs because new literature was always able to base itself on myth as something ever present. Such a premise applies to no modern literatures.

Only classical poetry was able always to look up to the world of mythology. Above we have shown why this reference did not contain within itself either the risk of falling prey to schematization nor the danger of becoming unrealistic. Such perils existed only for those poets who were not up to their poetic task.

Mythology was a world in which simple laws,[26] and especially simple human relations in hate and love, fear and bewilderment,[27] reigned. The world of mythology was neither a counterworld nor was it the ideal world. But for the classical poets it was, to a high degree, the *proper* world, because it allowed the presentation and interpretation of man in his proper shape. We could even designate the world of mythology as the properly epic and tragic world.

Translated by Ruth Hein

Notes

1. The exception was *The Persians* by Aeschylus, which deals with an event from the recent past—the defeat of Xerxes in 480 B.C. This was seen as an event of such consequence that it was equated in worth with myth. Thus even Xerxes gains something of the stature of the defeated hero of tragedy, for all the glory of Athens is set in opposition.

   In Rome, Naevius created a dramatic category, the so-called *praetexta*, in which the action was carried by outstanding Romans. The label "historical tragedy" is a modern one; in the classical view, such a play simply was not a tragedy.

2. Even comedy was, at the outset, a comedy of folk tales or a travesty of myth. At all times it was capable of returning to this origin, as often happened as late as the midfourth century. We need only recall the theme of Amphitryon, which entered world literature.

3. The *Heroides Sacrae* are an instructive example. These tales competed with Ovid, who had allowed heroines, in their distress, to write to the faithless lover. This overly pagan insertion was in part corrected, in part surpassed. Heroines of the Old Testament or of pagan legend are accountable for their confession of faith, which generally leads to martyrdom.

4. One such version is recounted in a brief summary in the *Nekyia*, gamma 271–80. According to it, the gods immediately made the desecration known. Epikaste, Oedipus' mother and wife, cursed her son and hung herself. By adding the circumstance that the discovery occurs only much later, Sophocles altered the legend. According to Homer and others, the mother's curse is the cause of pain and disaster; Oedipus nevertheless continues to rule over Thebes for many years. The curse punishes but does not destroy him.

5. This is indeed a primal function of the telling of myths, as is evidenced by the song of Demodocus (Theta 266–368). The guest, who is still not recognized, should be entertained; the singer is prepared even for such a function; he sings the cheerfully frivolous song of Ares and Aphrodite.

6. One example is Pygmalion. I have researched the manifold variations of the influence through time of this myth in *Pygmalion. Ein Impuls Ovids und*

seine Wirkungen bis in die Gegenwart, Rheinisch-Westfälische Akademie der Wissenschaften, Lectures G 195 (with summaries in English and French), (1974).

7. In a sense of irony, G.S. Kirk *(Myth: Its Meaning and Functions in Ancient and Other Cultures*, Cambridge, Eng., and Berkeley, 1970, pp. 242–43) cites the attempt at a definition by H. J. Rose in *A Handbook of Greek Mythology*, 5th ed. (London, 1953), p. 14. Even though Rose's formulation—"Greek myths . . . reflect the national character"—is open to attack, on the whole Rose is more correct than Kirk in stressing the peculiarity of Greek myths as compared to all other pseudomyths. For it is Greek myth that became a cultural factor.

8. Only one myth represents an exception to this statement—the Eleusinian myth of the disappearance of Persephone, her reappearance, and the spread of agriculture. In this case a symbolic relationship such as was postulated for all myths was applied to the search, the discovery, and the mission. For further discussion, see my essay "Philosophie und Mysterium. Zur Legitimation des Sprechens auf zwei Ebenen durch Platon," in *Verbum et Signum:* Festschrift für F. Ohly (Munich, 1975), no. 2, pp. 9–24.

9. This is the formulation considered fundamentally valid by U. von Wilamowitz *(Der Glaube der Hellenen*, Berlin, 1932, 1:1–5).

10. Not only von Wilamowitz but also the majority of his contemporaries had great difficulty in forming abstractions from the concept of "religious certainty." It had been felt so intensely—its converse being doubt—that it was considered as an absolute, applicable also to pre-Christian religiosity.

11. Of course it was quite possible, for a joke, to translate mythic themes into the trivial environment. Examples of this are frequently offered by the Old Comedy in Syracuse and Athens and later the mockery of the Cynics, adopted more than once by Lucian but also by Seneca in the *apocolocynthosis*. It was possible; but it remained peripheral.

12. Most particularly, the punishment of the forty-nine Danaides who slaughtered their husbands during their wedding night was seen as a warning example for all who missed the purpose—*telos*—of their life; they were condemned to purposeless activity for the rest of their lives. Just as these young women culpably missed their *telos* in marriage, so anyone becomes culpable who misses the dedication of Orphism.

13. A favorite device was to combine linguistic associations—so-called etymologies—with the associations furnished by the myth. The standard contemporary interpretation of myth, which proceeds almost entirely by association, has much in common with Orphic interpretation. I assume the missing link to be the religious speculations of the late Romantic period—especially those of F. Creuzer, J. Görres, and J.J. Bachofens, which claimed to be able to show evidence of a mystical-mythic religious primal awareness among the people of antiquity. More narrowly specialized scholars were soon in a position to overcome this attitude, especially thanks to A. Lobeck, *Aglaophamus* (Königsberg, 1829), even though Nietzsche and H. Usener had affinities with the trend just described. While criticism of late Romantic interpretations was extremely severe among specialized scholars, to this day such criticism has not sufficiently prevailed in those areas in which more than one area of scholarship connect (ethnology, religious studies, psychology). In these fields it is still the rule that whatever pleases is allowed.

14. Conversely, the tradition was excepted insofar as it covered interpretation of the names of the gods. There was a wealth of speculation concerning the etymology of the divine nomenclature—that is, attempts were made to penetrate to the proper and true meaning of the names of the gods by linguistic associations. Precisely in the case of a god, pure nature must be reflected in the name. This was an aspect of ancient theology that was long seriously studied.

15. Euhemerus of Messina was employed from 311 to 298 by King Cassadrus, one of Alexander's successors. He gave a kind of historical foundation to the cult of the ruler that was newly emerging: even Uranus, Cronos, and Zeus had been humans, though they had understood how to become recognized as gods.

16. Here there is a close connection between tragedy, which presents the passions, and the Stoic teaching of the affects. Chrysippus made a point of collecting statements by Euripides that pertained to the topic central to his doctrine; ultimately he included all of *Medea* by Euripides in his collection of examples. Diogenes Lartius, 7, 180.

17. This conflict is embedded in book 4 of Virgil's *Aenead*. Aeneas' attraction to Dido is in conflict with the mission *fate* has set for him. Without putting up much of a fight, Aeneas obeys the command of the *fatum*. This is not a dramatic conflict in the nineteenth-century sense.

18. Herein lies the reason why nineteenth-century classicism could not form a relationship to Euripides and his many successors. To the extent that they were seen from the viewpoint of the classicists, Aeschylus and Sophocles were also understood unilaterally, at heart. Classicism, with its didactic orientation, was prevented from gaining a broader basis.

19. Conclusive arguments for this view are given in Hermann Fränkel, "Ein Don Quijote unter den Argonauten des Apollonios," *Museum Helveticum* 17 (1960): 1–20.

20. One single epic had a historical subject, unlike all the others, which treated mythical ones. This was Lucan's epic treatment of the civil war. The actors in this epic, then, are not mythic heroes. It was long considered a scholarly crux why Lucan had forsworn the opportunity of allowing the gods to have some effect on the actions he describes, as was done in epics before and after his time. For this is an element in the mythic frame: in suprahistorical times the gods are present in men. These coordinates of myth could not be applied to an action occuring in real time, such as the civil war. Surely the barely twenty-five-year-old Lucan understood this impossibility.

21. Callimachus, 612 Pfeiffer.

22. On the one hand it was tempting to search out far-fetched tales and to be the first to give them poetic treatment; this was the area in which Callimachus became pre-eminent. On the other hand, the temptation existed to confront the readers with riddles by offering mythological material in artful encoding. One example of this is Lycophron's Alexandra (the name is intended for Cassandra; her brother is Paris, who is also called Alexander). Aside from a few efforts along this line, it never happened that mythology degenerated into a kind of virtuosity, thus becoming an end in itself.

23. Even comedy does not apply in this case. Though in Aristophanes' time it was directed solely to reality, Menander and his period turned it toward universal validity. The center of the action is occupied, not by mythic figures, but by

clearly characterized personalities: the miser, the misanthrope—*dyskolos*—the boastful soldier, the cunning slave, the deceived deceiver.

24. It would have been unthinkable to represent a plot taken from current events under a title borrowed from mythology, as is done in George Bernard Shaw's *Pygmalion*, Jean Anouilh's *Antigone*, or the film *Orfeo Negro*. During the nineteenth century it became customary to indicate the distance from the classics by the adjective "new"; thus Karl Immermann's *Der Neue Pygmalion*—a form of the title that can without a doubt be traced back to Jean-Jacques Rousseau's *La nouvelle Héloïse*. Our contemporary custom shows that the awareness of myth is waning among both authors and their audience. What remains is a generally inappropriate ceremonial use—for example, the Oedipus complex, discussed in section II.

25. The Augustan poets almost literally fought for this freedom. For Augustus urged them to treat his achievements in epic form. Had this come about, all of the freedoms defined above would have been abrogated.

26. Basically, these were still the conventions of Homeric poetry, in which gods acted out of human motives. The discussion on this point has ceased to exist since the third century B.C. The acceptance of myth brought with it its special conditions and laws.

27. I use the term "bewilderment" to translate the highly controversial concept of *eleos*.

Georges Dumézil

FURY AND MADNESS, "MENOS" AND "LUSSA" IN THE *ILIAD*

At the beginning of my work in comparative studies in 1942, I published a small book which, understandably, I now find lacking; the truth that we glimpse rarely leaves the well unstained. *Horace and the Curiatii (Horace et les Curiaces)* shed light on the well-known Roman tale by the equally celebrated Irish tale of Cuchulainn's first battle fought against three brothers. In particular, the final episodes were shown to parallel one another. Cuchulainn, returning to his city, finds himself in such a state of excitement on account of his exploits that he must be literally paralyzed by the sight of a naked woman (and a woman no less than the queen) in order that, with the aid of several tubs of water, a damper might be put on his "fever," and that once detoxified, he might return to his normal place in society. By comparison we find Horace returning to Rome, greeted at the gates of the city by his own sister who, transported by grief, reproaches him for having killed one of the Curiatii, her fiancé. Horace, beside himself, kills her, and before he can recover his place in society, the requirement of religious atonement, which is in reality a rite of passage, must be satisfied.

This comparison brings together two species that belong, in effect, to the same genus, though they are only distantly related. In both cases the matter involves a risk of excess implicit in any victorious struggle, though in each case the dynamic is different. In Cuchulainn's case it is the combat itself that has engendered in the hero a second state, which reveals itself in corporeal terms by means of monstrous, frightening transformations, a state in which his will and his reason have no place. The cure that he must undergo is intended to bring him back to "normal," the normal world of civilian life that will follow his victory, while saving, in the event of future need, the key to this second state with its bizarre, even hideous, side intact. We see nothing comparable in the case of Horace. During battle he keeps his head, conceives and employs the plan that wears down his adversaries, and one by one delivers them into his hands. After the struggle, it is not under the influence of a second state that he kills his sister: with Roman sternness, he finds the sorrow that greets his success insulting to him and criminal in the larger context of the fatherland, and thus he does not restrain himself from punishing the offender. His action is simply a sin, completely human, which calls not for medication but sanction or expiation.

It is in this corrected perspective, in 1956, that I re-examined the tale of the third Horace in *Aspects of the Warrior Function among the Indo-Europeans (Aspects de la fonction guerrière chez les Indo-Européens)*, shedding light on it by another parallel.[1] The "first sin" of Indra, eventually of the hero who acts on his own, Trita, "the third," namely the killing of the Tricephalous, is no less essential to the welfare of the gods than the murder of the three Curiatii, by the third of the three Horaces, is to the welfare of Rome. But the Tricephalous has the rank of brahmin, and thus his murder is brahminicide, whence the necessity of an expiation. In both the Indian and Roman tales the dynamic is psychological: Indra calculates, measures, and accepts the risk involved. Put another way, it is in the context of the "sins of the warrior," studied at length in the first part of *Myth and Epic* II, (1971) (*Mythe et epopée* II), that I place the case of the young Horace: it does not belong to the theoretical discussion of warrior fury (*furor guerrier*) or of the Irish *ferg*, nor to the Scandinavian *berserksgangr* in which the combatant "becomes" a wolf or a bear.[2]

Do we conclude that the oldest Indo-European warriors of Italy did not dare to overstep the bounds of their human nature, a license that, in battle, increased their strength by tenfold, and that, once the battle was finished, was not without its drawbacks? Certainly not: literary and plastic representations of warriors capped with wolf's heads abound, notably in Italy, which signifies that the character thus equipped pictured himself at least as strong and as feared as a wolf. Even in the midst of the historical era, in Livy's descriptions of warfare, it is not rare that the Roman army sees victory as the result, not only of arms, but of its *ire*—an ire usually justified by the wrongdoings of the enemy—and everyone knows that anger must sometimes replace composure in the conquest of the impossible. We are still, however, far from the Celtic and German representations, for donning a wolf's head is not becoming a wolf, and ire, in spite of etymology,[3] is no more than a normal passion of the soul, at least in Rome.

I would add that what one glimpses of warrior cults in the environs of Rome, the sacred legion of the Samnites, for instance, leads in another direction: the resplendent brightness of their arms and the coercion of resounding oaths brought the warriors closer to the gods than to wild beasts. I would also add that those groups of classic Italians who, we are sure, called themselves wolves, the Hirpi Sorani brigands, for example, were not warrior societies. Is not this noble animal equally if not more well-known as a thief than as a combatant?[4] As for the Romans themselves, the *milites* who grouped themselves under the standards of the eagle, the wolf, and the wild boar did not, as a consequence of this, cease being ordinary men.

Thus I fear having in 1942 unfairly exploited the ambiguity of the Latin word *furor* by lending it the same inhuman provinces and the same transforming effects that the belief and practice of northern Europe attached to the *ferg* and to the *môdhr*. This insight applies also to Greece. But in Greece we have the privilege of observing, throughout the songs, the hidden springs that feed the conquests in the *Iliad*. They are neither those of the *berserkir*, nor those of the legionaries.

At the height of their powers, the Homeric heroes do not undergo a transfiguration. The poet compares them time and again, in magnificent and precise frescoes, to aggressive or intractable lions, to wild boars, to wolves, to other wild beasts, to the eagle even; but these are only comparisons that imply no more transformation, even interior, than when it is said that Patroclus, fighting next to the corpse of Kebriones after having bounded "like a lion" (16. 752), is "Ares' rival, . . . equal to a *daimôn*" (784, 786); or that Diomedes fights "like an overflowing river" (5. 87); or that Hector assaults the long boats of the Greeks "like the baneful fire which furiously clambers up the hills and across the underbrush of the deep forest" (15. 605–6). We also see warriors who don panther or wolf skins, but so might Paris, not much more than an "honorable" officer (3. 17) or even the ill-fated Dolon, the opposite of a mighty leader (10. 335). Clearly, this attire should have transformed them, even morally, into wolves or panthers on the battlefield no more than the Nemean hide transformed the vanquisher of the lion into a lion himself.

That which carries both the Achaians and the Trojans into action is the *menos,* akin to the *thumos,* a fury tightly wound in all of the muscles of the body, which renders it efficacious in action to a maximum, but not a supernatural, degree.[5] The gods know this well, they who watch over, inflate, augment the *menos* (a "great *menos,*" a "powerful *menos*") in the heroes that they favor, just as they diminish the *thumos* among those they wish to destroy. The substantive *menos* reappears time and again in the stories, with its family of verbs, *memaōs, emmemaōs, meneainein;* and the fiercest battles are those in which the two armies "entangle," each fortified by its *menos* (21. 370), "share between themselves the *menos* of Ares" (18. 264). A few examples among many follow.

Athena and Apollo agree on substituting a man-to-man combat for the general massacre. "How shall we provoke it?" asks the goddess. The god answers: "Let us stir up the mighty fury *(orsō-men krateron menos)* of Hector, breaker of horses, and see if he doesn't go out alone and defy one of the Danaans to stand up to him in combat in the midst of the bitter slaughter" (7. 38).

At Diomedes' request Athena intercedes on his behalf in three evidently complementary ways: she takes the stiffness and fatigue from his limbs; she puts the "fury of his father" *(menos patrōion)* into his breast; she gives his eyes the capability of distinguishing the human from the godly combatants (5. 121–32).

The prudent Ulysses foresees that the decisive meeting will not be short-lived, once the battalions lock arms "and a god breathes the *menos* into the two armies *(en de theos pneusēi menos ampho-teroisin,* 19. 159)."

The generals also know that they must stir up the *menos* of their troops, and both Greeks and Trojans do not wait to do so. They also know that, whether natural or inspired, the *menos* cannot maintain itself at its maximum degree unaided. While Ulysses proposes that the Greeks eat before engaging the enemy, for, he holds, bread and wine contain the *menos* and the *alkē* (fury and warcraft) (19. 161), Achilles, burning to avenge Patroclus, shuns this vulgar device. He would rather see it put off until there is a lull in the fighting and until he feels a weakening in his own *menos,* "when there isn't as much fury in his heart" (202–3).

This fury does not exclude lucidity. At the height of his ravaging, Hector, equal to storms, wild boars, and lions, listens to and follows sound advice, abandons impossible schemes, and methodically organizes an assault (12. 80–81). Fury is not even incompatible with discipline: "Which other Achaian, says one charioteer to another, can vie with your ability to maintain both the reins and the fury *(dmēsin te kai menos)* of Achilles' immortal horses?" (17. 476).

Reasonable fear, the result of checking possible gains against necessary risks, might brake, even decimate, both *menos* and *alkē*. Achilles cries out to Hector that he knows the hour fixed by destiny for Hector's death and that the hour has come, and with this he throws his javelin and misses: "You're just a braggart, a trickster, answers the Trojan, and you hoped that, seized by fear *(hupoddeisas)* I would forget my *menos* and my *alkē (fury and warcraft)* (22. 281–82)!"

This then is the *menos,* at once both more ample and more specific than Bruno Snell's definition: *"die Kraft, die man in seinen Gliedern spürt, wenn es einen juckt, auf irgendetwas loszugehen."* In the Iliad at least this *"losgehen"* must end in a hostile act, the adversary must really be the enemy, and one must wish to destroy him. It is worthy of note that this word does not appear in the various contests that, in book 23, ornament the funeral rites of Patroclus: like good sportsmen, those who enter the contest spiritedly have no more recourse to *menos* than they can expect of the anger they feel, except in the case of Ajax, son of Oileus, and Idomeneus, who let themselves be taken in, and whom Achilles must calm.

Nothing in all this changes the soul, even less the body, of the warrior; we see neither transformation nor "defiguration." In particular, the calculated monstrosities attested to and favored by the heroic prowess of Cuchulainn, or the animalizations and ferocious grimaces of the Berserkir, are as foreign as can be to the Homeric imagination, which always remains sensitive to the beauty of man, of the robust young man, even to the beauty of his fallen corpse (22. 70–75). The only corporeal manifestation that resembles one of the "forms" of Cuchulainn is not part of a battle scene. It is when Achilles, coming back into the battle, joins the Greeks, passes the rampart, and stops before the ditch unarmed (18. 202–16). Athena "kindled a flame which sprang from his body," and "from his forehead the brightness scaled the heavens." The sign of divine protection does not alter the man's face nor transform him; it does not increase his powers. The flame, the brightness are not spontaneous products of the body and forehead of Achilles, like the "battle moon" and the other projections Cuchulainn is capable of, but rather they are lights added by the handiwork or the will of the goddess.

Just recently an important discovery was thought to have been made, a discovery that found, besides the *menos*, the equivalent of the transfiguring fury of the Celtic and Germanic heroes in the *Iliad*. The word *lussa* was said to signify the transmutation, at least internal, of man into animal. I am afraid that this is but a mirage, an etymological mistake.

Certainly *lussa* is very probably a derivative of *lukos*,[6] but whatever the semantic evolution imagined, this derivative has a very specific meaning from which the wolf has long been chased, and no one has the right to let him in again. *Lussa* is rabies and, as today, the rabid animal first and foremost in the eyes of the Greeks was the dog.[7] In book 8 Agamemnon incites Teucer to attack Hector. Teucer answers:

> Most lordly Atreus, I am eager to fight, why push me? As long as I have an ounce of strength in me, I fight . . . I've already let fly eight long-flanged arrows, and each now rests in the flesh of a valiant young man. But this mad dog (*touton . . . kuna lussētēra*, 299), I can't topple him!

Hector, during this episode, simply has his *menos* in him, the protection of Apollo, with the provisionary favor of Zeus. He is "drunk with power," and he pursues the Greeks all the way to their ramparts like a hunting hound—hardly rabid—takes to the scent of wild boar or lion (338–42). Having arrived at the palisade and the ditch, he wheels about the edge of the enemy's fortifications with his horses, "in his eyes the stark stare of the Gorgon, or of murderous Ares" (349). Here we see the highest level of *menos* and nothing more: from the beginning of the *Iliad*—and in the first mention of *menos*—in more civil surroundings, the poet showed Agamemnon in a furious state with the same flaming eyes: "His gut filled with a terrible, black fury (*menos*) while his eyes blazed fire (*osse de hoi puri lampetoōnti eïktēn*) . . . " (1. 103–4).

In book 8, the Gorgon and Ares replace the fire because the character is engaged in a battle, but the symptoms and causes are the same. If Teucer calls Hector a "rabid dog," this is no more than an insult, which "dog" makes common enough, and to which specific circumstances have been added in *lussētēr*. In fact, throughout this fight Hector is humanly *memaōs*, "full of fury (118)," and along with him so are the Trojans to whom he cries, "These ramparts won't contain our fury *(ta d' ou menos hamon eruxei)*."

The *lussa* is a disease. Anyone afflicted with it certainly becomes more dangerous to his enemies, but he himself will die of it, and he is, unlike the simple *emmaōs*, uncontrollable and unable to change his destiny. The word appears four times in the *Iliad*, once in the form of the epithet *lussōdēs*. It is applied to the two condemned to death in the siege of Ilion, three times to Hector, once to Achilles; and three times, like *lussētēr* in book 8. 299, it is used by enemies to express their hate. Three times also it implies, in the heart of the hero penetrated by *lussa*, the fatal blindness we know as *hybris*.

In book 9, when the Greek fathers come to stir Achilles from retirement and inactivity, Ulysses appeals to his mind, his heart, and his pride all at the same time. He describes for him the distress of the Greeks before the flood of Trojans that Hector carries in his wake:

> Zeus, son of Cronos, like lightning, shows the Trojans the way to victory, while Hector rages intoxicated by his power, the irresistible, relying on Zeus, giving way to no one, neither man nor god: a brutal rage possesses him *(oūd ti tiei / anera oude theous, kraterē de he lussa deduken)*. (236–43)

This is the substance of Ulysses' argument, the bait hooked onto the end of his discourse: by this *lussa* Hector will surely commit the fatal mistake that he has thus far avoided: he will attack Achilles:

> Oh! what glory you may win among the Greeks! For now you might undo Hector, who now will come close to you, sick with his rage *(lussan ekhōn oloēn)*, for he believes he is without rival, without match among the rest of the Danaans that our ships have brought here! (303–6)

So the *lussa* will do what the *menos* could not: it will lead Hector into the trap of destiny. But Achilles is not beguiled by Ulysses' argument, though he does confirm its foundation in fact:

> When I was fighting among the Achaians Hector refused to lead his attack beyond the walls. He went only as far as the Skaian gates and the oak tree. There, once, he waited for me. I

was alone and he was spared no pain in his escape. But now it
is I who refuse to fight the brilliant Hector . . .

In book 13, with the Greeks pressing all around, Apollo, who
has taken the face of Calchas, says to the two Ainte: "I fear there's
one weak spot in our defenses, were something to happen, it's the
spot where they have the rabid Hector leading them, that firelike
one *(lussōdēs phlogi eikelos)*, who calls himself the son of Mighty
Zeus . . . " (52–54). Apollo is no doubt lying, but had Hector really
dared to call himself the son *(païs)* of Zeus while being, eight
generations removed, no more than one of his distant and innumerable descendants, this would have been a show of *hybris,* the
very *hybris* that, as we have seen, accompanies *lussa* even in 9.
238–39.

The last time we come across the word, it is in reference to Achilles. In book 21 he has returned to the fight and is occupied in
killing anything Trojan, heavy-shod horses and men alike (521).
The Trojans flee in the direction of the city's tall gates, which Priam
has had opened: "Achilles pursues relentlessly, lance in hand; a
brutal rage grips his heart *(lussa de hoi kēr / aien ekhe kraterē),* he
burned to taste victory *(meneaine de kudos aresthai)* . . . . (542–43).
Thus Achilles is animated by warrior fury *(meneaine),* which
makes him long for glory, and possessed by the madness (rage)
that obscures the play of the *menos.* The rest of the episode shows
this clearly, as does Apollo's banter at the beginning of book 22.
Apollo has boasted the audacity of the Trojan Agenor, who in
order to give the Trojans time to get through the city's gates and to
safety, waits before Ilion to tempt Achilles into battle and divert
his attention. Apollo wraps the imperiled Agenor in a mist, assumes his likeness, and sprints off, with the Greek in wild pursuit
at his heels. When they are far from the battle the god reveals
himself:

> Why, son of Peleus, do you pursue me so ardently? You are
> but a man; I, an immortal god. You haven't yet recognized me
> as such, so obstinate are you, so wound in your fury *(oude nu
> pō me / egnōs hos theos eimi, su d'asperkhes meneaineis)?* (8–
> 10)

No doubt, had it not been the *lussa* that held sway over his heart,
Achilles would have governed his *menos* with more lucidity.

To these five mentions of *lussa,* one should oppose, from the most violent of scenes, the innumerable examples of *menos, thumos,* and their quasi-synonyms in order to see clearly that, among Homeric heroes, it is not the malady called *lussa* that permits great feats; nor does it confer the state of *berserkr,* nor does it have anything to do with wolves.

Translated by Thomas Eckerle

Notes

1. Taken up in the first part of *Heur et malheur du guerrier,* 1969; English translation, *The Destiny of the Warrior* (Chicago, 1970).
2. *Horace and the Curiatii (Horace et les Curiaces),* chapter 1, "Fury" *(Furor).*
3. Cf. Sanskrit *ishira,* Icelandic *eiskra,* technical terms of the warrior function. On the evolution of Indo-European vocabulary for the second function in Rome, see *La religion romaine archaïque,* 2d ed., 1974, pp. 221–22; English translation, *The Archaic Roman Religion* (Chicago, 1970), pp. 211–12.
4. See the discussion—to be reoriented as a result of the present article—in "L'homme: **ner-* and **uiro-,*" *Idées romaines* (Paris, 1969), pp. 225–41. The Luperci, who at least carry the name of the wolf in their name, are no more a warrior society than the others mentioned.
5. On the *menos,* see Bruno Snell, *Die Entdeckung des Geistes: Studien zur Entstehung des europäischen Denkens bei den Griechen* (Hamburg, 1946), pp. 34–36; Rüdiger Schmitt, *Dichtung und Dichtersprache in indogermanischer Zeit* (Wiesbaden, 1967), pp. 104–21 (pp. 109–13 on *hieron menos* compared to Vedic *ishiram . . . manas;* bibliography in the notes, pp. 667–80).
6. Pierre Chantraine, *Dictionnaire étymologique de la langue grecque* (Paris, 1974), 3:651. See *lussa.* Book 8. 299 is sufficient proof that the sense of "rabid" (as a dog) is definitely behind the Homeric use of *lussa.*
7. By extension in book 8. 623, Menelaus calls the Trojans *kakai kunes* (dirty dogs); in book 21. 481, Hera calls Artemis a *kuon addees* (shameless dog).

Kurt Weinberg

LANGUAGE AS MYTHOPOESIS: MALLARMÉ'S SELF-REFERENTIAL SONNET

MYTH, EDENIC LANGUAGE, AND POETRY[1]

The concept of *mythos* as a prescientific form of inquiry into the nature of the universe, the etiological "answer to a question"[2] through poetry, by far preceded the technical term "myth," which for France (*mythe*) is first documented in 1818 (*Petit Robert*), and for England as late as 1830 (*OED*). Chronologically less precise, Grimm quotes from Uhland's *Gedichte*, which would situate German *die Mythe* in the neighborhood of 1815.[3]

From the beginning, the creative and reflective powers of human discourse occupied the center of discussions on *mythos*, regardless of whether it was seen as interchangeable with *logos* (in Homeric Greek both terms signifying "word," "speech," "narrative," and so on, indifferently as to their truth or falsehood), or opposed to *logos* (since Herodotus [2.45] "facts," as interpreted by an individual speaker). Theories of *mythos* (fabled accounts) as distinct from *logos* (logical discourse) reach back to Plato's ambiguous attitude toward the poet/*mythologos* (cf. *Laws* 941b; *Rep.* 392d, 398b; *Phaid.* 616) as the inventor of past, present, and future events. Plato speaks pejoratively of Homer, because he narrates untrue tales for their own sake and not, like the philosopher, to reveal moral truths through the veil of parables—on the order of Plato's myths of the cave and of Er.

Rather than pursuing the long history of semantic shifts, I shall leap into the eighteenth century, where Vico adds a new dimension to *mythos* by claiming that mythopoesis was the first but not necessarily primitive pursuit of the human imagination in the earliest of the three recurrent cycles (*corsi e ricorsi*) he perceives in his speculations on history. In Vico's "age of the gods," *mythos* represents the attempts of "theologian poets" to comprehend man's fate and the recurrence of natural phenomena through the metaphors hidden in onomastics and etymologies. Although little read, and much misread, Vico set both mood and modes for nineteenth century discussions of myth and mythology. He saw myth as *vera narratio*,[4] the power of archaic poetry; that is, the mystical discourse of irrational truths, speaking through metaphors, metonymies, and fables, most of them latent in and emanating from the names of gods and heroes. One of the earliest thinkers to oppose the growing rationalism of eighteenth-century philosophy, Vico unwittingly prepared the way for Romanticism in literature, philology, mythography, and dialectical idealism.[5] With Vico, the Aristotelian concept of *mythos* (*Poetics* 6, 9) as the "poetic mimesis of a (real, historical, mythological) action"[6] is narrowed down to *significant* fiction, the parabolic arcana of mysteries concealed not merely in the accounts of mythical events but in the very essence of language. Vico contrasted *mythos* with *logos* (the "fact"-finding word of logic, and the verbal signifier for things). He likened *mythos* to Plato's and Jamblichus's idea of an ideal, "natural" speech (*parlar naturale*) and to the Edenic language of Adam before the fall, which was believed to have created truth through the mere act of naming objects.[7] Vico speculates that, applied to the names of the ancient gods and heroes, the *parlar naturale* is the language of imagination, speaking in terms of "animated substances," most of which are fancied to be divine ("un *parlare fantastico per sostanze animate*, la maggiore parte divine," *La Scienza nuova*, 1:162). In Jupiter, Cibele, and Neptune he sees personified metonymies, standing for their functional domain (heaven, earth, and sea). Heroes he regards as metaphors for attributes—Achilles allegorizing the idea of valor common to all strongmen, and Ulysses incarnating the prudence common to all sages. Vico's theologian poets, as the instruments of truths reflected in myths, anticipate on the level of Schiller's literary theory (or mystique) the concept of *naive Dichtung*: the assumedly naive, that is, innate, native (in the sense of *natural*) poetry (*un parlar naturale!*) of the bard, that theogonic myth-maker par excellence, whose art was believed to incarnate the tribal imagination and the nature of the collective unconscious.

Unlike Vico, Mallarmé regards the perfection of verse as man's most mature achievement, the *supernatural* triumph of art over nature. In a striking oxymoron, he acclaims verse as "ce civilisé édennique,"[8] the civilized type of Edenic perfection—an artifact so esoteric and delicate that, in its highest form, it can only be wrought at an apex of human civilization. Verse thus mythically personifies man's recovery of his lost Edenic language, not in a blessed state of ignorant innocence but through conscious labor and lucidity, without the intercession of any grace other than human art, sensitivity, intuition, and craftsmanship. Myth, then, is poetic discourse per se, evoking a fluid universe through metamorphoses of visions, sounds, and rhythms, which man projects against nature, as his own *meta*-physical creation.

POETRY AS THE POET'S "SUICIDE"

The analogy between Vico and Mallarmé proves fruitful for the establishment of *distinguos* rather than affinities. No direct influence exists, although Mallarmé may have gleaned insights from Michelet. Be this as it may, Mallarmé's verse, this "civilisé édennique," fulfills no epistemological function: verses are written to produce evocative effects. In this, Mallarmé follows the lead of his idol, Poe:[9] the poet depicts "not things, but the effect they produce."[10]

In Mallarmé's theoretical vocabulary (elaborated in 1869), language stands for the idiom of poetry. It expresses essence, the ideal. *Le verbe* is seen as the polar opposite of *le langage*. It is Mallarmé's term for expository prose and the idiom of the marketplace. The poet's task is not to create the illusion of beauty through the use of language, but to show language's inherent virtue of tending toward its own perfection, and its poetic design of becoming beautiful.[11] The poet's voice must transform an object into its musical essence, which absorbs the particular in the universal. His quest proceeds from the Platonic copies of things to the discovery of their Platonic Ideas or archetypes: "I say: a flower! and, out of the oblivion where my voice relegates every contour, something else than the known calyxes musically rises, an identical and suave idea, the one that is absent from all bouquets."[12]

In its highest accomplishments, literary art scorns narrative, public confessions, didacticism. Vaticination is singled out as something ridiculous both in the eyes of the poet and in those of the cultivated audience. To underscore his dislike for the poet as

self-appointed latter-day prophet, he chose *vaticiner* as the last
and most contemptible word, the note of mocking irony on which
to end *La Musique et les lettres* (654). The poet is neither *vates*
sacer nor *hieros*, though his poetry is hieroglyphic and imbued
with the mystery of timelessness negating the present. A hieratic
act, a solemnity, it banishes from its performance everyday reality
and the poet himself in the visible rôle of officiating priest: "Ex-
clus-en (de tes vers) si tu commences / Le réel parce que vil" (73).
The tone of this poem ("Toute l'âme résumée") is reminiscent of
Verlaine's "Art poétique," published thirteen years earlier, in
1882; but its aesthetics is exclusively Mallarméan. It shuts the
poet himself out of his poetry: his exploits are seen as committed
not by him but by and in his imagination ("Exploits, il les commet
dans le rêve, pour ne gêner personne," 370). He must not stand in
its way, nor interpose his own emotions between his work and his
reader. Like the blue rings of his cigar smoke, which evoke the
ideal (*l'azur*), his verses will efface each other's traces, leaving
mysteries intact in their vaporous imprecision: "Le sens trop
précis rature / Ta vague littérature" (73). The poet is but the impersonal instrument that "resounds at the touch of various sensa-
tions," elected by "the instinct of rhythms" (383). Literature
worthy of this name must efface its author, suppress all remnants
of the "gentleman who is writing" ("La littérature, d'accord avec
la faim, consiste à supprimer le Monsieur qui reste en écrivant,"
657). The text should speak by itself, of itself, for itself, without an
author's voice (663).
    Suicide is the proper metaphor for the act of writing, which
must eliminate the present and the poet's presence, prevent his
intrusion into a text that enters the nontemporal space of myth and
leaves behind the "quotidien Néant" (372). Transcending his personal feelings, preoccupations, and enthusiasms, the poet will
achieve the transposition of a natural phenomenon into a pure
notion.[13] The perfect work of art demands the "elocutory disappearance of the poet, who yields the initiative to words mobilized
by the shock of their disparity" (366). Words in unusual syntactic
arrangements spark mutual reflections, which are "like the virtual
trail of lights on precious stones, replacing the perceptible respira-
tion of the antiquated lyrical 'inspiration' (*souffle*), or the personal,
enthusiastic direction of the phrase/sentence" (366). The poet's
action is limited to pursuing his chimera, his dream, and to forcing
it to manifest itself in the shadowy lines of his writing, veiled in
obscurity, myth, mystery, and mystification. For "one does not

write luminously on a dark field. . . ; man pursues black on white" ("On n'écrit pas, lumineusement sur champ obscur. . . ; l'homme poursuit noir sur blanc," 370). What sings here is language, not the poet; the poem, not its maker, issues from labyrinthine depths and acts through the dark Ariadne thread of script (*l'écriture*).

MYTH AND LINGUISTICS

Myth and linguistics are closely linked in Mallarmé's *Les dieux antiques* (1880), a reworking of George W. Cox's *Manual of Mythology* for children. Archetypal myths of gods and heroes are seen as arising from onomastics and etymology. In their migrations from one language/culture to another, they are metamorphosed in accordance with semantic changes, which are the inevitable by-products of linguistic and cultural transfers. What remains intact is the meaning to which they can all be reduced: in Mallarmé's and Cox's view,[14] Nordic, Eastern, and classical Greek myths indifferently enact variations on one and the same theme: the cosmic drama of the rise and setting of the sun—which Gardner Davies sees as central to Mallarmé's poetry.[15] But more important than Mallarmé's concept of mythology—a conventional one, in keeping with his times—is his experimentation with language as myth, in the spirit of Vico but without Vico's mystical approach. In this, he anticipated and in some ways outstripped *avant la lettre* Freud, Otto, and Jung. In *Les mots anglais*, he insists on the importance of playful punning as a serious guide to riddles posed by myth and philology, suggesting that in puzzling rapprochements of English words and the French models from which they derive, "il se cache toujours quelque jeu heureux!" (997). These "lucky games" can be narrowed down to certain rhetorical devices, which whimsically act through the medium of translation. They engender mystifying verbal myths through the unpredictable fortunes of associations and fertile misunderstandings. Mythology and philology work through analogous processes.[16]

For Mallarmé, verse is the timeless link between the dim past and a future potential. It has the power to unite all stages in the evolution of its words, and all cumulative layers of meanings at once. It can simultaneously dismantle and reassemble its verbal elements into homophonous multivalence, anagrams, homonyms, and paronomasia, to form a new and total word out of several words, which in the process of phonemic regroupings reveal un-

derneath their surface identity semantic substructures that double
their meaning, or are palimpsests of a more schizophrenic nature:

> The verse which remakes out of several vocables a total
> word,—new, alien to language and quasi-incantatory,—
> achieves this isolation of speech: in its sovereign wake negat-
> ing whatever random element remains in the terms, despite the
> artifice of their alternating immersion in meaning and sound; it
> causes one the surprise of never having heard certain ordinary
> fragments of elocution, together with the simultaneous remi-
> niscence of the object named, bathed in a new atmosphere.[17]

In short, verse is that sophisticated end product of a civilization,
"ce civilisé édennique," that immerses literature again in the beginnings of language.

LITERATURE = LITTERAE = (LES) LETTRES

Literature quite literally springs from the alphabet's "twenty-four
signs" (850). They allow the summary identification of literature
with *litterae/belles lettres*. Less programmatic (and more pro
grammatic) than Jacques Derrida,[18] Mallarmé links the esoteric
suggestiveness of the letter (*gramma*) in script and typography
with the arabesques of words, phrases, and sentences that, strewn
on the page, create their frozen myths and ballets. The creative
process must be able to reverse its ordinary course, moving from
synthesis to analysis, and proceeding by regression. Arriving at
the letter by starting from the sentence, it will use the sign (or
script) that binds the word to its meaning ("Arriver de la *phrase* à
la *lettre;* en nous servant du *signe* ou de l'écriture, qui relie le mot
à son sens," 852). Grammar, *la Grammaire*, broadens to embrace
functions of Greek *grammatiké*, which reach beyond mere grammatical rules into criticism, linguistics, magic scrawls (Mallarmé's
grimoires), the exoteric/esoteric study of script, hieroglyphics, emblematic figures, and all uses of letters (*grammata*), the signs that
build words, sound patterns, phrases, and verse—to interlace in
rhetoric, the formal flow (*rhea*) of metaphors and metonymies into
the mythologizing language of poetry. In short, *gramma* / letter—
"thát which is drawn; a line, a picture, a figure,"—the visual configuration of consonants, vowels, and diphthongs, enters into the
grammatic fabric as much as do morphological and syntactic structures. Independent of the diachronic / synchronic dichotomy, the
individual letter, by its very figurative nature, is pregnant with

emblematic and symbolic significance, which adds a mythic dimension of universality to its purely functional existence as a sign:

> S, dis-je, est la lettre analytique; dissolvante et disséminante, par excellence: je demande pardon de mettre à nu les vieux ressorts sacrés . . . . j'y trouve l'occasion d'affirmer l'existence, en dehors de la valeur verbale, autant que celle purement hiéroglyphique, de la parole ou du grimoire, d'une secrète direction confusément indiquée par l'orthographe et qui concourt mystérieusement au signe pur général qui doit marquer le vers (855).[19]

Would it be idle to assume that Mallarmé's admiration for the hieroglyphic universality he saw in the letter s—so clearly a symbol for his own dissolving and disseminating poetry—may have caused him to change the title of his initial sonnet for *Poésies* (posthumous, 1899) from the original "Toast"[20] to "Salut," thereby significantly opening his book with the visual sign that best emblematizes his aesthetic aspirations?

It would be fastidious to multiply examples of letters transcending their orthographic function to become pure signs (or hieroglyphs). I draw on "Salut" to show the point to which the central image, the *coupe* of champagne, is graphically multiplied by the recurrent letter/sign v: "Vierge Vers" (line 1); "à l'enVers" (line 4); "naViguons . . . diVers" (line 5); "Vous l'aVant" (line 7); d'hiVers" (line 8); "iVresse" (line 9—here distinctly evoking the effect of the beverage in this *coupe*); "Valut" (line 13). Associations too multiply; thus in "mainte à l'enVers," the v graphically underscores the erotically fertile image of the drowning sirens' upturned fish-tails, evoking the unspoken paronomasia *croupe/coupe*, and lending new connotations to the Vierge Vers/Vert, rising from *écume* on the transparent *(rien) coupe/*shell, like Aphrodite from the sea (the "Verte Vénus" of "Plainte d'automne," 270).

ANAGRAM, HOMONYM, HOMOPHONE, PARONOMASIA

Implicit anagram has the virtue of dialectically doubling a negative meaning, which again may be revoked by a return to the etymological root-word that overshadows the term it animates. Thus the first word of "Salut"—*Rien*—is resonant with its anagrammatic correlative *nier*, which strengthens the negation it denotes, while at the same time pointing back to its Latin etymon. In "Rien, cette écume, vierge vers," both *rien* and the anagrammatic *nier* (implicit in *rien*) extend to the substantiality (if not to the essence) of the whole ternary unit, amounting to the magic formula of a triple assertion / eradication: *écume* (foam), asserting *and* negating itself in the very blankness of air bubbles that constitute it, and the *vierge vers*—yet unsung, inviolate in its virginity—affirming its haunting presence through its blankness, its rhythmic phantom existence, still awaiting the impulse that will cause it to well up from its unknown source ("Le chant jaillit de source innée: anterieur à un concept," 872). Its mythical essence is tacitly confirmed by the distant etymological source of *rien*, Latin *rem*, a "thing," "object," "something."

In *Igitur,* the *explicit* anagram ("La FIOLE vide, FOLIE, tout ce qui reste du château?," 443), while referring back to the Tristan myth, puns on a container (*fiole*), itself contained in a larger receptacle (*château*), both as void as the volatile metonymy (*folie*) of its contents (the unnamed potion), which abstractly lingers, emptied and questioned like the imaginary castle, now purified, that is, deprived of its substance, by the departed Nothingness ("Le Néant parti, reste le château de la pureté," 443), and bracketed out of existence in a parenthesis that, nonetheless, guarantees its surreal survival within the flowing and floating confines of script (*l'écriture*) and in the true realm of Mallarméan poetry, *le rêve*—dream superseding reality.

Homonyms multiply levels of meaning.[21] In this sense, the second line of "Salut," "A ne désigner que la coupe," supports the literal image of the poet toasting his confrères of *La Plume,* at a banquet in his honor, "cette écume" signifying the champagne in his elevated flute (*la coupe*), which renders its transparent substance visible. But on the aesthetic level of the still-embryonic poem, this line serves to underscore the identity of the series "*Rien=cette écume=vierge vers*" as the haunting rhythm of the as-yet-unwritten and hence mythical line of poetry, dormant in the poet's mind, but in its preverbal rumblings already designating its caesura (*coupe*).[22]

But ultimately it is the spoken word, *la parole,* that presents the ear with words hidden within words, released through homonyms and homophones that dissect and rearrange phonemic structures, building mythical alternatives out of identical sound patterns, which they free from orthographic bondage and syllabic fetters. It is the spoken word, quite literally reverting to its mythologizing powers, as they flow from its etymology in *la parole < parabola /* parable. This process is alluded to in Mallarmé's concise appositional phrase, as "les mythes, mêlés intimement à la parole" (1170). Homonyms like *la coupe* (champagne glass / caesura) provide ambiguity, the very stuff of which, according to T.S. Eliot, poetry is made. Homophony opens up perspectives on multiple readings, while archaic phonemes (for example, old French *oè, è* for modern French *wa* in the pronunciation of *oi*) may reveal an archaic word underlying a modern term. In the distich: "TELLE lOIn se nOIe une troupe / De sirènes mainte à l'envers" ("Salut," lines 3–4), the graphic neighborhood of two *visual* (if phonemically distinct) *oi* configurations (lOIn and nOIe) points to a potentially concealed *oi* in *telle,*" which here conspicuously functions as an indefinite adjective. And *telle* indeed is an old French form of *tOI*le, which adds to the distich a palempsestic boutade at the expense of inferior rhymsters, eclipsed by the present banqueteers. For what is seen drowning on a far-off canvas (*telle loin = toile loi(n)* are facile and meretricious sirens, vanquished in their competition with the archetypal poet reincarnate, as they were once before driven to self-destruction by Orpheus during the Argonauts' travails. The implied paronomasia *se noie = se nie (nec-are/negare)* suggests the sirens' tacit consent, their cooperation, their obliging suicide, which confirms their defeat.[23] Mallarmé's sirens are not birds with women's faces and rooster claws as they are depicted by Hyginus (*Fabellae* 141), Ovid (*Metamorphoses* 5:557): their "impatientes squames ultimes bifurquées" ("Un Coup de dés," 470 f.) indicate that he follows Littré who, quoting Brunetto Latini, describes them as "moitié femme(s), moitié poisson(s)." Half woman/half fish, they evoke an abbreviated version of Horace's grotesque, combining two features of its incongruence: "Desinat in piscem mulier formosa superne" (*Ars poetica,* 4)—Horace's pejorative metaphor for the work of a bad poet, who distorts human nature. Here again, Mallarmé's intention may be anti-Horatian, or at least ambiguous, since his own poetics calls for metaphysical boldness in the poet's transcendence of reality.[24] The truth about Mallarmé's sirens may well lie concealed in hidden homophones: *sirènes = scies reines* (regal = dominant or prevailing "saws") *mainte à l'envers = mainte à l'en vers* (many a one WITHIN THE VERSE) or even *mainte à l'en verre* (in the champagne cup, and ready to be downed/drowned in the present "Toast"), but also, possibly: *allant vers/Nous* (enjambment of lines 4–5), "moving toward us," but fortunately swallowed by the *blanc,* silent space intervening between "their" presence in the first quatrain and "ours" in the second. *Telle/toile* (line 3) would then anticipate the multiple reflections darkly flickering in the sonnet's last word, which is *toile*, first on the most literal level, the tablecloth on the banquet table, and second, on the metaphorical level of the sea voyage, the sails set by these banqueteers / poets / Argonauts in their navigation toward poetry's uncertain future—a golden fleece, not yet the parchment, the *toile*, the white page on which the *vierge vers* might display its abstract and still negative figures. In the end, "Le blanc souci de notre toile" (*telle*) (line 14) turns out to be the very *telos* of this purely imaginary navigation. It is a *navigation sur place*, marking time at the weaving of the assembled body on the waves of its communal inebriation. Its pseudonautical pitch reduces the fancied ocean voyage and its implicit vehicle, the *navire*, to the diminutive proportions of a weaver's shuttle (*navette*). The "Nous naviguons" (line 5) has semantically shrunk to "nous faisons la navette." Movement and instrument of the metaphorical weaving revert to their literal state. They evoke shuttle and loom, *le métier*, prompting new associations relating the act of weaving to the poet's professional craftsmanship, his *métier*, from which the *toile* / textile / text (all derived from Latin *texere*, "to weave") will emerge as the object of their joint aspirations, the *telos*, the future of poetry. This *toile* / *telle* / *texte* is as yet a blank canvas and preoccupation (*blanc souci*), a disquieting motion toward action (*souci*, from Latin *sollicitus*, "violently moved"), a shuttling as white and blank and immaterial as the "Rien, cette écume, vierge vers." The sonnet has come full circle, shuttling to and fro, on its stationary voyage in the pitch of metaphors of inebriation (or *furor poeticus*), with its imagery emerging from Nothingness (*Rien*) and returning to Nothingness: to the blank solicitation of a text still on the *métier* (loom) of (presumably) the best qualified *hommes de métier*, gathered here to honor the Master, Mallarmé, while holding out a promise few will fulfill.[25]

FREUDIAN DREAM WORK IN REVERSE

We can now see more clearly why Mallarmé insists on *le rêve* as the proper domain of the lyric. Evidently he is not referring to a vague type of *rêverie*, nor to dream as a mere metaphor for the creative imagination. These are remnants of Romanticism he has long overcome. Rather, like Poe, he aims at the lucid and almost algebraic manipulation of those linguistic mechanisms which characterize the subconscious processes of association, distortion, and symbolic abbreviation that take place in the surrealist world of dreams. His poems are experiments, which anticipate the analytical work undertaken decades later by Freud; but he goes the road inverse to that of synthesis: his poetic labors *consciously* imitate what Freud, in *The Interpretation of Dreams* (*Die Traumdeutung*, 1900), will call *Traumarbeit* (dream work), the *subconscious* displacement (*Verschiebung*) and *Verdichtung* (poorly translated as "condensation," for it also means the myth-making activity of *poetization*). Since Freud's theories are well-known, there is no need to detail his views regarding the dependence of dream work on the mechanisms of puns, etymological figures, and the full repertoire of rhetorical devices, which have become quasi-automatisms in European literature. These are sources from which Mallarmé's poetics derives so many of its dreamlike effects. They dictate the use of an allusive language, which evokes but never directly names objects. Intentionally obscure, its incantatory spell must be reduced to virtual silence.[26]

Unlike Freudian dream work, the poet's "dream" is not passively experienced. It is skillfully *constructed* with plays on words, rapid sequences of Protean metaphors, the full range of acoustic experimentation with assonance, alliteration, striking alternations of vowel patterns, rare rhyme schemes, syntactical inversion, and the alienating use of unusual juxtapositions of words. The poet's "dream work," like its Freudian counterpart, structures through regression from thought content to symbolic imagery. It is *antimimetic*. It scorns the imitative representation of reality in favor of hallucinatory effects, for "Nature takes place; one cannot add anything to it but cities, railroads," and so on ("La Nature a lieu, on n'y ajoutera pas que des cités, les voies ferrées et plusieurs inventions formant notre matériel," 647). While Mallarmé praises Zola's "evocative art," he rejects Zola's work, together with all Naturalism, since "there is something more intellectual to literature than that: things exist, we do not have to create them; we must only seize their interrelations; and the thread of these interrelations forms verses and orchestras" (871). "The Orphic explication of the Earth" is seen as the poet's task par excellence and his "sole duty."[27] Friedrich Creuzer seems to provide the key for the meaning of "Orphic": he defines poetry about persons and events as Homeric, poetry about elemental forces and mixtures as Orphic.[28] This definition essentially conforms to Mallarmé's most striking formula for poetry as "the expression of the mysterious meaning of existential aspects, by means of the human language recalled to its essential rhythm: in this manner it endows our sojourn with authenticity and constitutes the only spiritual task."[29] It is this thorough rejection of mimetic poetry, with its bombastic dramatizations of legendary events, and *Heldenkitsch* on stage, which explains Mallarmé's discreet objections to the *Musikdrama,* despite his admiration for Wagnerian music—a taste acquired late in life: "If the French mentality, *strictly imaginative and abstract, hence poetic,* brilliantly excels, it will not be in this way: *it feels loathing for legend,* and in this it is attuned to Art in its integrity, which is inventive" (544). The attribute *inventeur* (inventive) directs creativity to its own resources, far from all Wagnerian noise and mass appeal. It is significant that Mallarmé never made the pilgrimage to Bayreuth; nor had he ever attended the performance of any Wagnerian opera, although he had fervently defended their right to be produced in a Paris seething with anti-German chauvinism after the Franco-Prussian war.[30] There is faint praise in Mallarmé's characterization of Wagner's work, where "everything is revivified in the primitive stream: (but) not as far back as its source" ("Tout se retrempe au ruisseau primitif: pas jusqu'à la source," 544). Poetry must be freed from its Wagnerian subservience to music and histrionic rodomontades. It must be restored to the silent stage of the book, where its own harmonies, fugal structure, melodic lines, and leitmotif can unfold their splendor without the extrinsic noise and vulgarity attendant on Bayreuthian pomp and circumstance. Rather than imitate music, the poet must reconquer everything that nineteenth-century poetry has surrendered to music, "in this righteous act of restitution which must be ours," Mallarmé writes to René Ghil, "of taking back from music its rhythms which are only those of reason, and its colorations which are those of our passions evoked by rêverie . . . "[31]

ETYMOLOGICAL FIGURES, MYTH, AND POETIC CREATION

The latest fad is not necessarily the last word. With this axiom in mind, and Gérard Genette notwithstanding (*Mimologues,* 257 ff.), I side with Claudel, Valéry, and Robert Greer Cohn, who consider *Les mots anglais* as a major key to the understanding of Mallarmé's poetics, and to his keenly associative imagination.[32] In this study thematic variations and the practical dream work of displacement and condensation play an eminent rôle. Here paronomasia, the god-mother to assimilation, creates dreamlike effects. It demonstrates the creativity of bilingual misunderstandings that produce unex-pected results, for example, grotesquely transforming *buffetier* into *beef-eater,* the inn signboard from the days of the Norman con-quest, *Chat Fidèle,* into *The Cat and the Fiddle* (997). I shall limit myself to one example to illustrate how Mallarmé's conscious and intuitive imitation of dream work knows how to incorporate "philo-logical" findings into the myth-making processes of his creative work, by showing variations on an etymological play on words, as it displays its fireworks in *Les mots anglais,* in a sentence in *Igitur,* and, fugally unfolding, in the sonnet "Ses purs ongles."

In the first of these instances, "LANTHORN (HORN), la *corne* servant de verre à cette LANTERNE" (997), bilingual assonances allude to semantic similitudes, which have a sound foundation in etymology: in ancient Rome, lanterns were fashioned from lami-nated horn; witness Martial, Plautus, Lucretius, and Pliny.[33] My second example is a cryptic sentence in tableau IV of *Igitur* ("Un coup de dés"): *"Le Cornet est la Corne de licorne—d'unicorne"* (441, Mallarmé's italics). Here the triple meaning of cornet (musi-cal instrument/turbinate bone/dice-cup) releases associations with the hunting horn sounded in the pursuit of an elusively legendary beast, while suggesting that the short sequence of rapidly meta-morphosing images is evoked by a chance configuration of etymo-logical figures, a verbal cast of the dice. The images *cornet/corne/licorne/unicorne* appear in linear succession, like the associative clusters of images in Freudian dream work; but *they are born simultaneously* and blend into a polyphonic chord: the horn of the unicorn and the implied (but silent) blast from the hunting horn are conascent and identical with the cup from which are rolled the dice that determine by their chance constellation the poetic imme-diacy of their elusive conception, an evocative, dreamlike pres-ence without real existence in any given present. They *re*-present myth in the purity of its abstraction from both reality and the univocity of description and narrative, while illustrating at once Mallarmé's principle of "dispersing verses like arrows" (*des vers par flèches*), "less in succession than almost simultaneously (rep-resenting) the idea," so that they reduce duration "to an intellec-tual/spiritual division appropriate to the subject" (654). The trajec-tory of the series *"Le Cornet est la Corne de licorne—d'unicorne"* exemplifies Mallarmé's mastery in laconically exploding a word into the pyrotechnics of simultaneous strata of allusions, which then rebound by a sudden reversal, effacing the multiple traces left by this word. Together with the title of tableau IV of *Igitur*, "Un coup de dés," the unicorn's constellation (Monoceros, in the Southern Hemisphere), discreetly evoked in this verbal sequence, could serve as a shorthand notation announcing the symphonic structure (in the form of a score) of Mallarmé's stellar poem par excellence, "Un coup de dés jamais n'abolira le hasard." But it also points to the circularity of this postulation, which lies concealed in the etymology of *hasard*, Arabic *al assahar*, contracted into *assar*, Littré's (and consequently, no doubt, Mallarmé's) option, meaning *dé*, the die. The poet's cast of the dice may achieve harmony and timelessness in the perpetuation of a pure concept. It may eternalize a chance moment into the necessity of an indestructible verbal artifact. Yet his apparent success is fraught with failure: no matter how often repeated, his gesture will forever fall short of abolishing chance and its agents, the dice, perpetually surviving in the dice game (= *assar* = *hasard*). The arrows of his verses may well attack and "resolve" the brute natural fact (and its random existence in linear time), and supersede nature with dreamlike constructs. But these mythical monsters, emerging from the poet's *fiat* and existing only through his *parole*, do not eliminate their potential supersedure by future *coups de dés*. Nor can they assume existence without the concurrence of the solitary reader, who alone through his receptivity can breathe life into their unfolding fabric of verbal blocks, surrounded by the eloquent silence of white interspaces and margins.

MALLARMÉ'S NEGATIVE MYTHS

The *licorne*/unicorn belongs in the ménagerie of what I am tempted to call Mallarmé's negative myths, that is, myths that are nipped in the bud; myths that deny or exorcize reality; myths that transform the human figure in motion into the abstraction of lace- and scriptlike arabesques. Its supra- and unnatural companions are the Wagnerian *Musikdrama, le-Monstre-Qui-ne-peut-être* (541), a somewhat singular bliss, "new and Barbarian" (544); the chimera (*chimère*), omnipresent in Mallarmé's prose; the drowning or briefly surfacing and self-eclipsing Siren, abbreviated version of the Horatian grotesque—a seductive image of meretricious perversions of poetry, temporarily threatening its future with shipwreck, but ultimately remaining speechless as "le flanc *enfant* d'une sirène" (70);[34] Hamlet, *le seigneur latent qui ne peut devenir*, who in Ophelia destroys the myth of his past (his unrecoverable childhood), and in Polonius slays the specter of a frightening future (senility)—thus committing two symbolic suicides (300 ff.). One might add the three witches of *Macbeth*, whose first appearance and vanishing constitute a *fausse entrée*, taking place *before* the play begins, as though the curtain had risen "one minute early, baring intrigues of the Fates" (350). Choreography, dance, and ballet too are part of these negative myths, which consume themselves while happening (or even before they can happen). Their ornamental script is effaced and renascent in the very movement of its unfolding, as, for example, the living arabesque of the dancer Loïe Fuller, abolishing herself in the tornado of her floating draperies and blending into one with the fluid essence of her dance. "Inexhaustible source [or fountain] of herself" (311), she could well be likened to the "dark lace" of script, which retains in its folds the infinite ("ce pli de sombre dentelle qui retient l'infini," 370). All could stand as hieroglyphs for poetry's passage through the Gates of Horn, images for a labor giving birth to visions on presignificant mysteries of script and acoustics, on *la Figure que Nul est* (545), the figure that Naught (0) represents and that quite literally is Naught (0), a geometric ellipsis, symbolizing the rhetorical ellipses, which the poet achieves through his dream work of displacement and condensation/poetization (*Verdichtung*).

THE SONNET AS MYTH AT DECREE ZERO: "SES PURS ONGLES"

La Figure que Nul est finds its poetic realization in my last example, Mallarmé's "sonnet nul, se réfléchissant de toutes façons."[35] The early version (1868) was given the title "Sonnet allégorique de lui-même," which underscored its self-referential nature. Its final form indirectly poeticizes etymological variations on the now-familiar theme of *corne/cornet/licorne/lanthorn*—although its main characteristic goes far beyond these thematic banalities: it is a sonnet stripped bare of the presence of man and nature, and as such a prime example *avant la lettre* for Ortega y Gasset's thesis on the dehumanization of modern art (1925). I reproduce both versions for the convenience of the reader who may want to deduce for himself the process of regression and condensation that, analogous to Freudian dream work, adds opaqueness and mystery to "Ses purs

ongles" (1887), largely by replacing the mere phenomenon of night
("La Nuit approbatrice") by anguish ("L'Angoisse"), night's disquieting effect on the here-absent human psyche.

(1868)

Sonnet allégorique de lui-même

La nuit approbatrice allume les onyx
De ses ongles au pur Crime lampadophore,
Du Soir aboli par le vespéral Phœnix
De qui la cendre n'a de cinéraire amphore

Sur des consoles, en le noir Salon : nul ptyx,
Insolite vaisseau d'inanité sonore,
Car le Maître est allé puiser l'eau du Styx
Avec tous ses objets dont le rêve s'honore.

Et selon la croisée au nord vacante, un or
Néfaste incite pour son beau cadre une rixe
Faite d'un dieu que croit emporter une nixe

En l'obscurcissement de la glace, Décor
De l'absence, sinon que sur la glace encor
De scintillation le septuor se fixe.

(1887)

Ses purs ongles très haut dédiant leur onyx,
L'Angoisse, ce minuit, soutient, lampadophore,
Maint rêve vespéral brûlé par le Phénix
Que ne recueille pas de cinéraire amphore

Sur les crédences, au salon vide : nul ptyx,
Aboli bibelot d'inanité sonore,
(Car le Maître est allé puiser des pleurs au Styx
Avec ce seul objet dont le Néant s'honore.)

Mais proche la croisée au nord vacante, un or
Agonise selon peut-être le décor
Des licornes ruant du feu contre une nixe,

Elle, défunte nue en le miroir, encor
Que, dans l'oubli fermé par le cadre, se fixe
De scintillations sitôt le septuor.

The early version was sent to Henri Cazalis in answer to a request
for a sonnet that was to be, but never became, part of a volume,
Sonnets et eaux-fortes, edited by Philippe Burty and published by
Lemerre. In his accompanying letter, Mallarmé had described his
sonnet in terms strangely anticipatory of Freud's definition of
dream work: "It is inverse; in other terms, the meaning, if there is

one . . . , is evoked by an internal mirage of the words them-selves."[36] His sonnet, he admits, is lacking in plasticity. Yet its "black and white" texture would lend itself to an aquafortis "full of Dream and Void":

> For instance, an open nocturnal window, with its two shutters fastened; a room with no one in it, despite the air of stability provided by the fastened shutters, and in a night made of absence and interrogation [crossed out: *oubli*], without furni-ture, except for the plausible ghost of vague consoles, the bel-licose [crossed out: *monstrueux*] and tarnished frame of a mir-ror attached to the background, with the stellar and incompre-hensible reflection of the Great Bear, which unites to the sky alone this lodging abandoned by the world.[37]

Where myth is inextricably bound up with and in language, the poetic process of form engendering itself becomes an integral part of the sonnet's contents. Mallarmé had said as much when he sug-gested to Cazalis that his "Sonnet allégorique de lui-même" evokes its elusive meaning "by a mirage of the words themselves."

1 Ses purs ongles très haut dédiant leur onyx,

It is this verbal mirage, where individual letters can assume seman-tic autonomy, and where words, or their fragments, are refracted in often multilingual associations, which condenses the unwanted imagery of "Ses purs ongles" into a hallucinatory sequence of mythical allusions and figures. They arise from the womblike (*noir*) *salon vide* in line 5. R.G. Cohn and others have rightly noted the etymological reflection of *ongles* in *onyx*. But by failing to pursue their research beyond *ungula* to *unguis,* the Latin synonym directly derived from Greek *onyx;* they overlooked a melodic modulation that bridges the acoustic gap between (*ongles*)/*onyx* and *Angoisse.* By way of metonymy, the privative attribute *purs*, qualifying *ongles,* and by refraction *onyx,* accentuates the negative existence of *l'Angoisse,* the hauntingly shadowy protagonist of the sonnet's first quatrain. For *pur,* we are reminded by Hugo Friedrich, is a privative term.[38] Horace's "(carmen) decies non castigavit un-guem" (*Ars poetica,* 240) would seem to lend coherence to the enigmatic enhancement of *ongles/onyx* and their relationship to *l'Angoisse,* allowing the latter to be identified with the poet's never-ending *anguish* concerning the satisfactory completion of his artifact: this preoccupation is evoked by the metaphor of the sculp-tors of ancient Rome, whose *fingernails* gave the final polish to their statuary. The identification of the affective term *Angoisse* with the powers of darkness—direct in "La Nuit approbatrice"—is here discreetly concealed in a charade implicit in *onyx*: the invocation *O Nyx*, addressed to the Greek goddess of Night,[39] *nyx*/night as a metaphor for Death in Sophocles (*Ajax*, 660), and the phenomenon of night as such.[40] Cohn has aptly seen the etymological connections suggested by the aural effects of *dédiant* (*dé/datum*), associated with *digit/nombre* and *digitum/doigt*.[41] To this etymological series I should add the implied etymon *corne/cornu/*horn: the material substance of fingernails, dice, and a number of objects named or suggested in this sonnet—but also evocations of musical instruments, as we shall see.

> 2 L'Angoisse, ce minuit, soutient, lampadophore,
> 3 Maint rêve vespéral brûlé par le Phénix
> 4 Que ne recueille pas de cinéraire amphore

The breathless staccato of line 2 is suggestive of the brevity, distress, narrowness, the "straits" implied by the etymology of *Angoisse* (Latin *angustia[e]*). The dual hyperbaton (*ce minuit, lampadophore*) points to metaphorical and literal straits, a narrow opening like the entrance to the Styx (line 7). *L'Angoisse/*Anguish, the allegorical torchbearer (*lampadophore*) sustaining the extinguished torch (attribute of Death / *Thanatos* / *Mors*), serves two purposes: first, on the level of the solar myth, she represents distress over the quelled light (*lampas*) of the sun, for which *lampas* is a metaphor in Parmenides and Sophocles.[42] Second, grief over the solar Phoenix's nocturnal "death" is paralleled by *anguish* over "many a vesperal dream" (*maint rêve vespéral*), cremated by the setting sun (line 3). With her lantern (*lampas*) of *laminated horn* (see note 44), where the evening's dreams were burned, Anguish / *l'Angoisse* / *lampadophore* stands here as a disquieting symbol for the Homeric and Virgilian Gates of Horn, through which pass the true figures of dreams.[43] These gates open on Sleep / *Hypnos* / *Somnus,* a mere semblance of death, which, leaving no ashes, leads to a rebirth prefigured in the cycles of self-consumption and renascence of the Sun/Phoenix during the four stages of the day. They correspond to the seasonal stages of the year and find a rhythmic echo in the tetrameter of line 2. The poet's unactualized dreams, burned out by "le vierge, le vivace et le bel aujourd'hui" in its final *Götterdämmerung* state, are cyclically haunting memories, now returned to their presignificant limbo, where they hover on the threshold of a new day (*ce minuit*), at that unreal point of transition where today blends into tomorrow. Their absent ashes fill no funerary urn (*cinéraire amphore*), no well-proportioned receptacle; that is, no white page has as yet received their volatile imprint. But like the charades of Freudian dream work, the dying Phoenix, who will rise again, prefigures their potential rebirth. Its very name enigmatically prophesies legendary dream figures that will emerge in this sonnet's tercets: the erotic imagery of unicorns hurling their fire (*feu*) against a nixie (*nixe*) lies dormant in the French pronunciation of the Latin for *Phénix, Phoenix = feu/nix(e)*.

> 5 *Sur les crédences, au salon vide: nul ptyx,*
> 6 *Aboli bibelot d'inanité sonore,*

The absence of punctuation between the quatrains produces the effect of sentences and stanzas flowing into one another in enjambments that efface all boundaries. It is an effect resembling that of oneiric images and scenes overlapping in a logic of their own, alien to the conscious mind. The nonexistent *cinéraire amphore* (line 4) now projects its negative image onto the buffets (*crédences*), which are promptly negated by the *empty salon*. As a remnant of the preceding quatrain—where *l'Angoisse* performed its dark rites in a vaporous, undefined space—the empty funerary urn is now admitted as a purely negative form into the clearly defined, but equally void *salon*. But like the absent *ptyx*, this negative *cinéraire amphore* has gained admission only *on credence* (the archaic sixteenth-century meaning of *crédence*). That we are in the presence of a dubious act of faith seems to be further confirmed by the fact that *crédence*/credence (substituted in 1887 for *consoles*) denoted a liturgical object: the console table where, in the Roman Catholic mass, consecrated bread and the cruet with wine rest before the sacrament of the Eucharist is offered. To the agnostic Mallarmé,[44] this prerequisite for the ritual enactment of the Last Supper is as meaningless as the sacrament itself, though its solemn mixture of grief and anticipated triumph could be made to represent on the aesthetic level an "intrusion into future festivities" (392) of a secular nature, for example, the solitary communion with the "Book" as the "spiritual instrument" par excellence (378 ff.) and the very end for the production of which the "world is made" ("le monde est fait pour aboutir à un beau livre," 872). The Catholic mass is a "mystery other than representative; . . . Greek, Play, Service" (393). In the "fastidious aesthetics of the Church," this liturgical re-enactment of the Passion, "with the revolving fires of hymns," is equivalent to the ancient sacramental tragedies, which were based on the legends of Prometheus and Orestes, and like these, the mass is a "human assimilation of the tetralogy of the year" (393). In an age of syncretism that tolerates both disbelief and belief in all faiths, (hence the plural, *sur les crédences*), and dominated by secular rather than religious *Angst/Angoisse*, the Eucharist is likely to be self-referential, erasing its meaning in its mere gestures. What then remains is a theatrical performance. The communion it procures is an almost secular mystery, comparable to that festive bond which unites a theater audience, vibrating in unison under the spell of a solemnity they collectively experience. The litany, "incomprehensible" to the singers, "but exulting," participates in the "sublimity reverberating toward the (architectural) choir: for here we have the miracle of singing: one projects himself as high as the strident voice goes" (396).

We may now venture to place a less tentative interpretation on those mysterious "pure fingernails," which, raised "very high," are "dedicating/celebrating their onyx" *in excelsis* (*très haut*). They abstractly crown equally abstract hands, cupped and extended on high, like jewels on the elevated chalice of the Eucharist (and like the Latin hymn stridently but ineffectively soaring into lofty heights). In the phantom chalice, sustained by a phantom priest or priestess (*l'Angoisse*), no wine is transubstantiated into a god's life blood, and the transept remains silent with the absent congregation's unsung Latin hymn, incomprehensible in this secularized temple, the *salon vide*, where the rites of poetry are momentarily not celebrated by the absent Master.[45] Not the Master but Anguish officiates here, both in a negative mass and as torchbearer (*lampadophore*) of archetypal myths. Phantoms of Christian and pagan myths in the modern silence of belief, their shadows are haunting the depths of dream and of the poetic imagination. Their symbols are simultaneous and interchangeable. Anguish, the torch-bearer of the dying and resurrecting solar gods of Mediterranean and Nordic antiquity; Anguish *lampadophore*—linguistically clad in Greek, like the vestments of the Roman Catholic celebrant—holds up a dual symbol: the empty chalice and the burned-out torch, both paraphernalia used in the enactment of myths of death and rebirth. On the level of the Catholic mass, the absent amphora may additionally stand for the insubstantiality of the "cruet," a ritual instrument (missing from the equally ghostly "credences") without which the wine cannot be conveyed to the here-nonexistent faithful.

Much ink has been spilled over the mysterious *ptyx*. Some

critics have interpreted it as a sonorous conch, without giving any philological evidence for their bold surmise. Others have correctly read it in its main Greek meaning, as "fold" (*pli*), properly relating it to one of Mallarmé's favorite metaphors. Mallarmé's coquettish claim of ignorance as to the exact meaning of *ptyx*[46] may be regarded as mere reticence, *captatio benevolentiae*, and a kind of mischievous mystification, perpetrated with the intent of intensifying the enigma. It would be unthinkable that the lexicophile Mallarmé could have been unaware of the use made by Aeschylus (*Supplices*, 947) of the plural *ptychais biblon* and by Euripides (*Iphigenia Aulidensis*, 98), *grammaton ptychas*, as "writing tablets." It is equally unlikely that Pindar's metaphor for "sinuous hymns," *hymnon ptychai* (*Ode* 1:105), would have escaped his attention. Both writing tablets[47] and sinuous hymn seem as worthy of the critic's interest as the equally well-documented fold/*pli*, and certainly more so than the far-fetched conch. With these probabilities in mind, I suggest that *nul ptyx* may signify, first, the absence of any writing tablet, with its never-recorded dreams of the eve. Those vesperal dreams were burned out with the setting sun, leaving no trace (or scriptorial "folds," Euripides' *grammaton ptychas*) of a poem left uncomposed. Second, here no "sinuous hymn," no "incomprehensible but exulting" litany is accepted on anyone's faith (*sur les crédences*). In this *salon vide*, the secular temple reserved for festive occasions, and now emptied of singers and celebrant, no hymn—be it pagan or Christian—could rise toward the god it exalts "as high as the strident voice goes" (396) Here the liturgy remains silent in anguish's mimicry of a communion without sacrament and congregation. The sinuous hymn is reduced to a purely aesthetic phenomenon, hermetic, seemingly meaningless, and exhausting its virtues in the theatricality of its performance. It can be presented, in an onomatopoetic imitation of its hymnal sinuosities, as an *aboli bibelot d'inanité sonore*, the glistening reverberations of its multiple phonemic echoes hardening into a metaphor for the individual verse itself. In the same year that saw the completion of "Ses purs ongles," Mallarmé had defined the ideal verse as a "significant gem to be handled by the eye and weighing in the hand."[48] In this connection it seems pertinent that the reflexiveness of verse is mirrored in its etymology: *versus* < *vertere*, "to turn around," originally a furrow made by the plow, *folding* the upturned earth. By the very quality of folding, which it implies in both its agricultural and literary meanings, *versus* conforms to the primary import of *ptyx*, "a fold," revealing the latter to be a charadelike metaphor for "verse." Like verse and *ptyx*—the ancient Greek phantom word, absent from modern French, as is *lampadophore*—and like the poet's vesperal, now-abolished dreams, the phantom hymns (*hymnon ptychai*) are emptied of their outlived significance. But the beauty of their errant ghosts continues to haunt with the *danse macabre* of its arabesques this dark witching hour (*ce minuit*). In the void of their archaic meaninglessness, they retain their nocturnal charm (*carmina*) as self-referential trinkets without market value (*bibelot*[*s*]), that are consumed in the act of reading (*aboli*[*s*]), or recitation, but whose obsessive mystery and beauty remain intact by the purely aesthetic effect of their sonorous emptiness (*inanité sonore*).

> 7 *(Car le Maître est allé puiser des pleurs au Styx*
> 8 *Avec le seul objet dont le Néant s'honore.)*

In his mystifying anonymity, *le Maître* conceals at least three major figures. On the level of the solar myths, he unmistakably represents Phoebus Apollo, god of light and poetry, and his vesperal plunge into the waters of Oceanus,[49] of which the Styx constitutes the tenth part.[50] He has taken with him the mysterious *ptyx*, now recognizable as first, an attribute of poetry in general, second, a hieroglyph for verse in particular, third, the lyrical poet's blank writing tablet, and fourth, as a plural, a metaphor for sinuous hymns to gods and heroes, Pindar's *hymnon ptychai,* which have lost none of their beauty but most likely all of their incantatory efficacy. They may resound anew when the god's rays rise again to strike Memnon's column at Thebes, and in their northern form they may re-emerge when the sun thunderously rises again beyond Scandinavia from ocean waters as frigid as the Styx.[51]

The second figure evoked by *le Maître* is the dying and resurrected god/man of Christianity. A symbol of his ritual paraphernalia had been brandished by Anguish, but his *crédences* have been shown to be as questionable and void of liturgical mysteries (*pas de cinéraire amphore*/cruet and *nul ptyx*) as his "credentials," which are no longer widely accepted on credence, on blind faith. We are told that he descended *ad inferos,* "to draw tears from the Styx." Will he immerse his ceremonial *hymnon ptychai* in its inky black waters to guarantee their survival, in imitation of the gesture by which Thetis once tried, not quite successfully, to render Achilles invulnerable?

Above all, however, the Master's journey represents the poet's Orphic descent into a subliminal underworld, his quest for the potential of future poetry, his temporarily lost dreams, now vanished from consciousness, but haunting its empty *salon* with their muffled rhythms emanating from the tearful waters of the Styx. Their disappearance is allegorized by the extinguished flame of the setting sun/consumed Phoenix—symbol of a *Götterdämmerung* foreboding rebirth in perpetual cycles of death and renascence. What was burned out here by the now-extinct flame holds the promise of being reborn in the rekindled torch of dream personified. For though traditionally held by Thanatos/Death, the burned-out torch of Anguish/*lampadophore*, is here denied its complementary attribute, the evoked but absent funerary urn (*pas de cinéraire amphore*). The Master is shown as he stops short of crossing the Styx into Hades. All indications are that the flame will be relit in dream's *Gates of Horn*, the torch's lampshade made of laminated horn.[52] And indeed we are made to perceive the Master literally bracketed by parenthesis marks (), signs in the shape of *horns*, emblematizing first the *cornua*, the two horns giving resonance to the poet's Orphic and Apollonian lyre,[53] and second, those *Gates of Horn* through which pass true figures of dreams, and which Virgil locates near the exit of Hades.[54] The importance of *horn* as the substance that gives coherence to the poem's imagery is driven home once again by the Master's act of purification: it was believed in classical antiquity that only objects made of horn could hold Stygean water without being instantly destroyed by its corrosive acidity. According to tradition, water from the Styx could be transported in a horse's, a donkey's, or a mule's hoof, or in the horn of a species of horned ass said to be found in Scythia, which becomes confused with "fleet-footed Indian asses," reported by Ctesias to have on their foreheads "a horn a cubit and a half long, colored white, red and black," which reputedly had the virtue of purifying water.[55] All these fabulous animals are eventually combined with Aelian's one-horned Indian horse[56] to produce in the end the legendary *unicorn* that we have already encountered, accompanied by etymological figures, in a line from *Igitur:* "(*Le Cornet est la Corne de licorne—d'unicorne,*" 441). The unicorn's "unique horn" seems to provide the basic material for this sonnet's (only seemingly) disparate images. We see them range all over this poem, from *ongles*, *onyx*, *lampadophore*, over the unnamed object, now identified, with which the Master is intent upon drawing water/tears from the Styx, to *déCOR*, *liCORNES*, *enCOR;* not to mention *Somni*/Sleep's implicit attribute, the *horn* (of plenty) from which he indifferently scatters dreams (false and true) that issue through the Gates of Ivory and those of Horn, and which, regardless of their truth or falsehood, will eventually strike the *cornea* of the poet's and his reader's inner eye. Altogether, the Master's journey to the Styx signifies that symbolic act of self-immolation, the poet's ritual suicide, by which he excludes his personal life from lyrics, whose intentional impersonality, further hardened by their immersion in the Styx, increase their chances of immortality.

The quatrains mark a vertical descent from an anguished outreach for inaccessible heights ("très haut dédiant leur onyx,/ L'Angoisse") to the Master's presence on the banks of the Styx, near the edge of *le Néant*. But this movement proceeds "down and under"; for the immateriality of *Nothingness*—in the first version clearly identified with *le rêve*—is the very arsenal of poetry, filled with insubstantial but substantive figures: arabesques, unicorns, nixies, reflected stellar images. In short, it is teeming with Mallarméan chimerae, which shun plasticity, naturalism, realism, mimesis. The tercets are the turning point, after which the sonnet is reoriented upward and out of the nether region of personal and personified Anguish. This sudden reversal is heralded by the abrupt *Mais* at their beginning.

9 *Mais proche la croisée au nord vacante, un or*
10 *Agonise selon peut-être le décor*
11 *Des licornes ruant du feu contre une nixe,*

The all too human *Angoisse* of the quatrains seems exorcised. Her death struggle is faintly echoed by the imperfect anagram *Agonise* (line 10), which in the first tercet occupies a position that symmetrically corresponds to that of *l'Angoisse:* like the latter, it is the first word in the second verse of its stanza. Its core *oni(s)* acoustically evokes an oneiric (*ONIrique*) ambiance, but also, combined with "un or" (line 9), the translucid *ongles/onyx* cupped to form the transparent lampshade of horn, where another gold had expired, but unlike this "or," without leaving any visible trace. Clearly, at the crossroads (*croisée*) where quatrains and tercets intersect, the sonnet takes the decisive step into impersonality. The chaotic metamorphoses of essentially abstract and psychological imagery, which haunts the *salon vide* of the quatrains, gives way to a sequence of more distinct images, decorative first, but eventually reaching the cosmic proportions of a mystery marked by the absence of human Anguish, and by the silence of nature and gods. In the tercets, the *now totally impersonal,* fully dehumanized sonnet finds its bearings, its north *(au nord).* It keeps steering on this course right to its last word, *septuor.*

Visual and auditive impressions now combine. The vacant "croisée au nord vacante" elaborates into a concrete image of emptiness the purely abstract and aural void of *inanité sonorelle Néant s'honore.* Simultaneously it extends into spatial dimensions first the sonnet's own "crossroads" *(croisée),* where the vertical descent of the quatrains (to the Styx) intersects with the diagonally upward thrust of the tercets (toward the reflection of a celestial constellation). Second, the vacant rise of aesthetically enchanting—but as incantations inefficacious—*hymnon ptychai* toward lofty architectural heights. For, in terms of ecclesiastical architecture, the *croisée vacante* is strongly suggestive of the empty TRANSEPT (= *croisée*) of a northern *(au nord),* that is, most likely, a Gothic cathedral. The etymological components of both *croisée (croix/*cross) and transept *(transversus + septum)* release further associations with the transversal/crosswise orientation of the tercets VERSES (TRANS/VERSUS), and their perpendicular relation to the quatrains' semantic verticality, within the sonnet's lofty but structurally narrow form, its enclosure (= SEPTUM). In the end, the *croisée* emblematizes its correlative, the difficult rhyme in *-ixe(e)/-yx(e),* which in itself is a sonorous hieroglyph, a sound pattern identical to the French pronunciation of the consonant *x,* the transversal sign and cross figure par excellence. The entire rhyme scheme doubles its crosswise structure; the *rimes croisées* of the quatrains in *-ix* and *-ore* become transsexual when they cross over into the tercets, the feminine *-ore* changing to masculine *-or,* and the masculine *-ix* to feminine *-ixe.* Most exegetes have duly noted the "alchemical" transmutation into gold *(or, -or),* without recognizing the rather obvious bilingual play on words,[57] which here performs this service quite naturally (and without recourse to alchemy), by extracting the tercets' (French) *or* from the quatrains' rhymes in (English) *ore.* If there is an allusion to alchemy, it should be sought in the act of purification, which is implied in the *quintuple* use of *or* in the tercets. It suggests *quintessential,* that is, supranatural, ethereal gold, refined from the quadruple *ore,* from the impure raw material found in the lowest of nature's *four* elements, that is, earth. It needs the concurrence of the other elements (fire and air for the smelting process, water for cooling and hardening the melted gold). The act of purification transposes natural elements into the quintessential precious metal of dream, art, and poetry. It takes place in the sonnet's *sonorities*. We have heard them dormant in the bilingual ultrarich rhyme *sonore/s'honore* (French *son*/English *ore*), and its vague echo in line 9 (*au nord/honore*).

We now clearly perceive that "internal mirage of the words themselves," which will produce a "rather cabalistic sensation," if one "lets oneself go to murmuring (this sonnet) several times."[58] This internal mirage is sonorous as much as visual. It extends to syllables and unsyllabic groups of letters. In line 9, for example, homophonous imperatives, consonant with the words they atomize and recombine, *sotto voce* substitute for "Mais proche la croisée au nord vacante, un or" their own underlying message, which undermines the integrity of the verse's syntax, verbal structure, punctuation: "Mais proche la croisée, HONORE, VA! C(H)ANTE un or." This gold, until the tercets neither seen nor sung, lies expiring (*Agonise*) in the *décor*. It vaguely flickers in the gold leaf of a mirror's frame, the stage set (*décor*) gilding a tarnished golden legend of unicorns hurling their fire against a nixie. Latent *en cor* (*encor*), in the golden sound of the horn (*cor*), it lies ready to emanate from the *dé/cor*—the prefix *dé* denoting separation, but also absence and privation. Its potential is multiplied by the *liCORNES*, while its acoustic and spectacular possibilities are dramatized in the scintillations and dormant polyphony of the *septuor*, the harmonious metaphor for Ursa Major, reflected *en abyme* through the window frame (*croisée*) into the empty drawing room's mirror, framed in turn by the tarnished gilt frame with its legendary dream and stellar figures.

Creation *ex nihilo*, springing from the *décor*, the setting where these figures are perceptible in a climate of uncertainty: "selon PEUT-ETRE LE DECOR / Des licornes ruant du FEU contre UNE NIXE." This violent and hallucinatory scene, animated by a herd of unicorns in hot pursuit of a defunct nixie, is, with all due respect to Camille Soula,[59] a myth unknown to mythology. Suspended in Nothingness, it agonizes (together with *un or*) in that reified state of being which, in a Sartrian sense is devoid of existence. These seemingly dynamic figures lie petrified in the gold-leafed but tarnished moldings of a mirror's frame in the empty *salon*, opposite the *croisée*: they are the very antithesis to nature, which remains outside the framework of this window with northern exposure.

As legendary creatures that migrated from Oriental and Mediterranean myths into Nordic lore, these unicorns add their phantom weight to the sonnet's northern orientation. The nixie, a water sprite created by the northern imagination (and corresponding to the nymph of classical antiquity) further underscores the sonnet's northern "course." It is now *fixed* in the tercets (*au nord*), but it was tacitly present in the quatrains, despite their wealth of Hellenic and Hellenistic allusions. For while south designates high noon (*le midi*), north marks the nocturnal separation of East and West, *ce minuit* (line 2), that *croisée* where, in a moment of timelessness, today imperceptibly crosses over into tomorrow and lapses into yesterday. The sonnet's northern course is implied in stellar evocations—first arrested in the mirror's frame, then nocturnally "fixed" in the mirror's reflection of Ursa Major: the unicorn's constellation (*Monoceros*), located in the *southern* sky, is shown hurling its fire in multiple refractions (*DES licornes*) against a former nymph, now, as the constellation Ursa Major, forever set in the northern sky. Callisto (defunct but transposed into a northern stellar configuration) is now shown naturalized into her northern counterpart, the nixie, defunct but immortalized as Ursa Major:

> 12 *Elle défunte nue en le miroir, encor*
> 13 *Que, dans l'oubli fermé par le cadre, se fixe*
> 14 *De scintillations sitôt le septuor.*

Or are we invited to read *feu* (line 11) as an adjective substantivized, derived from popular Latin **fatutus,* "who has accomplished his fate," as the equivalent of *défunt*? Then the unicorns would be hurling their "fated past" against the similarly outlived former incarnation of this nude (*nue*) nixie that may have borrowed her semblance from the instantly eclipsing reflection of a passing cloud (*nue*) on the mirror's gilt frame. Both readings are admissible, not as alternates but as simultaneous impressions, the uncertain and fragmentary return of "maint rêve vespéral." The unicorns "hurling their fire" (or bygone significance), as well as their target, the defunct (or nebulous) nixie, are arrested in midair on the tarnished gilt surface of the mirror's frame. They remain marginal, like the frame itself, evoking legends that remain unexplored: first, the unicorn's horn, praised by Aelian as purifying water and offering protection against poisons,[60] does not penetrate the liquid element, symbolized by the nixie. The potential act of purification remains a dream halted, before it can take place—like the Master's arrested gesture of drawing water/tears from the Styx. Similarly, the immobile southern constellation of Monoceros fails to break through the mirror's frame to join the image of the northern Ursa Major, the transfigured nymph Callisto, quadruply exiled (*a*) as a nixie (*b*) from her Mediterranean (high noon) climate (*le midi*) (*c*) into the northern (midnight) sky (*ce minuit*), and now (*d*) merely reflected in the empty *salon*'s mirror. Nor can the hallucinatory unicorns and their fire (or defunct legend) find refuge *in gremio virginis*—symbol for the mystery of the Word's Incarnation.[61]

The charade of the *Phénix* = *feu/nix(e)* (see above), burned without leaving ashes, now proves to duplicate the symbolism of these unicorns: their spiraling tricolor horns are like the arrows of Apollo's rays hurling themselves at sunset toward the Stygean waters of Oceanus. Their meaning coincides with that of the crimson (Greek: *phoinix*) radiance of the burning Phoenix, an Egyptian hieroglyph for the setting sun.[62] The symbolical concordance of unicorn/Phoenix does not stop there. Phoenix and unicorn alike are used in Patristic literature as topoi symbolizing Christ's death and his resurrection, and like the unicorn *in sino virginis*, the Phoenix exemplifies the immaculate conception.[63] In short, the Phoenix *duplicates* in every way the functions of the *feu/nixe* it evokes, and those of the figures (unicorn and nixie) that so vaguely incarnate them. Altogether, unicorns, nixie, Phoenix—like the *Angoisse lampadophore*, the empty *amphore, ptyx*, and the absent Master intent upon drawing tears from the Styx—are so many metamorphoses of *la Figure que Nul est*, the ZERO emblematized and multiplied by the very shape (oval and upright) of Anguish's translucent *ongles/onyx*. In the oblivion closed by the frame— "dans l'oubli fermé par le cadre," which itself is framed by enjambments, these images are rapidly evoked and obliterated (*oubliées*), literally erased by the vertiginous succession of letters forming negative frames for the intangible residue of "maint rêve vespéral."

In the *salon vide*, which is the imaginary space and the spatial image of this sonnet, all semblance of life is frozen in rigid gestures that are staggered *en abyme* before lapsing into oblivion. It is a *Walpurgisnacht* of absurd and empty mock-rituals, loosely mirroring arcane similitudes, evanescent and yet pervasive. They are ultimately dispersed by a powerful "although" (*encor/Que*), which, like a magic wand, puts an end to the flux of images growing out of each other, by sublimating the defunct nymph Kallisto into the unchangeable essence of beauty. It is distilled by her (absent, that is, unpronounced) name, "The Fairest," very much as the sonnet itself grew *sua sponte*, and without naming itself, out of a procession of intertwined visual and sonorous evocations—all negative myths and self-negating mysteries, filling with their phantom appearances and obliterations the vacant space of this poem made of absences, which now, however, give way to the reflections of a presence: the sublimation of Kallisto out of a cloud (*nue*) seems almost to follow Leonardo's precept for painters, that they should look for dormant landscapes, *figure strane* and *diverse battaglie* (like the unicorns hurling their fire against a nixie) in stains on walls or *pietri di varij misti* (for example, the *onyx* of "Ses purs ongles").[64] The transfiguration of the nymph Kallisto into a cosmic *coup de dés*, the casting of the number *seven* (as composed by the *three* stars of Ursa Major descending toward the polar North Star from their four trapezoid companions) is witnessed by us through its reflection in the sonnet's intimate looking glass. On the level of poetic creation, it congeals in a cast of the dice that brings into being this sonnet out of its own *décor* (*COR-net à DEs*), that is, out of the tonalities and artifices produced by the verbal mirage that constitutes it. This *coup de dés* becomes dually manifest in the stellar configuration itself (Ursa Major, the *late* nymph/nixie, *FEUe* Kallisto) and in its reflected image within the sonnet's mirror, which, in turn, is situated within its larger framework of the *salon vide*, opposite the vacant window frame (*la croisée vacante*), which allows the sonnet at last to take its bearings (*au nord*).

The mythical *coup de dés*, which the poet discovers in Ursa Major, and whose eternal beauty he fixes from memory "dans l'oubli fermé par le cadre" (that is, in the mirror of his sonnet) is that ambivalent cast of the dice, the SEVEN, which either takes or loses all, depending on whether it occurs in the beginning or in the further course of the game. Its double occurrence here (in the northern sky and on the sonnet's nocturnal mirror) marks the ambiguity of beauty appearing through myth in a glass darkly, and valid per se, independent of any literal truth. Ursa Major and its inherent myth, the metamorphosis of Kallisto, "The Fairest," into the eternal beauty of seven stars fixed in their northern configuration,[65] find their double in the sonnet's *fourteen* (twice seven) lines, forever glorifying poetic ambiguity, as it is allegorized in the *dual seven*, cast by the dice of fate in a constellation and its intimate reflection in the sonnet's looking glass. After many a tormenting transformation and many a polishing touch given by Anguish's *ungues*,[66] the quiet splendors of Ursa Major's *septuor* are reflected in the sonnet's mirror, while its celestial harmonies vibrate in the *salon vide*, which—freed from Anguish's disquieting rites—has recovered vesperal dreams of a constellation now fixed in its space. Within the narrow frames of mirror (image of the text) and *salon vide* (the silent blankness of margins and interspaces), the sonnet's two *septets* ring forth in the muted tones of a fugal *chamber music.*

These sonorous scintillations recall the *correspondances* of the sonnet's intimately polyphonic "mirage of words" with the Pythagorean harmony of the spheres in the vacuum that is outer space, while the golden strains of the *septuOR's CORs* point back to the *ongles/onyx/licornes,* which solidified into those dreamlike phantom objects that passed through etymological figures to form imperceptible Gates of Horn, from which issued, in the final analysis, the sonnet's self-referential constellation. Its complex *chamber* music, so close to the Mallarméan dream and myth of a music of silence, and gemlike enclosed in a minor but infinitely precious *genre,* discreetly "takes away from music" what rightly belongs to poetry, in a climate light years remote from the brassy vulgarities of the Wagnerian *Musikdrama,* and where the "verse that out of several vocables refashions a *total word* ("un mot total," 368) subtly triumphs over the pseudoprimeval chaos of *das totale Kunstwerk.*

CONCLUSION

I have attempted to show, by way of "Ses purs ongles," how Mallarmé distills private myths from language itself and from the syncretic use of traditional mythology, by essentially leaving the initiative to words themselves. Their Ariadne thread leads to etymological discoveries and acoustic experiments, which provide musical paraphrases for (or underSCORE) verbal ambiguities—inherent less in objects than in intangible analogies and interrelationships. They are transmitted and coded in an idiom of absence and privation, as it behooves Mallarmé's intention of restoring the original luster of words by an act of purification, that empties them of that commonplace degradation, dullness, and inelegance which they daily acquire on the marketplace. Their multifaceted splendor is made to reflect and refract their own beauty—not in the ignorant innocence of Edenic language, but by recapturing, in their civilized state of ambiguity, complexity, and sophistication, the Edenic gift of creating through the very act of naming.

An undertaking of this nature calls for a thorough housecleaning, the destruction of idols; in short, for a *tabula rasa,* a basis of negative myths. And indeed, "Ses purs ongles" is such a Cartesian enterprise. It radically delivers the sonnet from all extrinsic ballast. Verbally mirroring a void of its own creation, the sonnet fills this void with that portentous silence which, in a bold etymological leap, Vico had related to myth, by deriving (Latin) *mutus* from (Greek) *mythos*.[67] Against the silence inflicted upon ancient myths by nineteenth-century positivism, and against their Romantic distortions, "Ses purs ongles" projects its own negative myth, a modern myth steeped in silence, which, like all myths, begins where the physical world ends: in the psychological and reflective reverberations of language as an absolute, creating its own object. As language's subjective agent, this sonnet denies the reality of objective existence by reducing all objects to their very absence, whence emerges a phantasmagoria of specters. They are metaphors celebrating the autonomy of mythopoesis and the poet's purifying labor on his ancestral language, degraded by everyday usage[68]—a purification that empties words of their stereotyped triteness.

Immolating in its lines the objective world, and stripped of all mimetic intent, the definitive version of Mallarmé's "Sonnet allégorique de lui-même" represents (to paraphrase Roland Barthes) the *sonnet at degree zero*. It creates *ex nihilo*, or *sponte sua*, a text opening onto a turbulent vision of void encompassing void. The mythical figures in the tercets, arising from the decaying gilt frame and blending with the enigmatic stellar reflection in the tarnished mirror, in their disembodied ghostliness and paralyzed frenzy intensify the stillness and inner void of the *noir Salon/salon vide*—in the quatrains, the true vessel of emptiness and Anguish—reflecting in turn the cosmic vacuum and its terrifying, eternal Pascalian silence of infinite spaces. The "tribal words" are purified not by a rejection of their inherent banality, but by the dissolution of their all-too-solid flesh into *carmina*, incantatory sound patterns, into arabesques and vaporous figures of dreamlike insubstantiality. They are made to merge, as the simultaneous imagery they suggest gradually emerges from aural and scriptorial impressions, which playfully transcend the framework of verbal structures and the inhibiting spell of spelling.

As the reader was guided inward, to resonances deflected from words fragmented in the ghost-ridden echo chamber of the *salon vide*, the scene of the sonnet's solemnities, his eye was deceptively led to the *croisée au nord vacante,* but not there to take its bearings (its north) from nature and life outside. His glance was made to reverse its course, was *folded* back (*ptyx*-like) to the artificial void and lifelessness of the interior stage. Here—in the total absence of man, nature, events—ear and eye participated in the phantom act of the sonnet's self-referential introversion. On an uncertain stage set (*selon peut-être le DECOR*), reminiscent of Plato's cave and of the theater of the mind, the sonnet acts out the anguish and agonies of its own hallucinatory engenderment *ex nihilo*—much like that "ancient Dream," which Mallarmé had once described to Catulle Mendès as having "installed in (him) something like a marine grotto, where it performed curious shows for itself . . . ."[69] It is the spectacle of the sonnet coming into being in the process of its *performance:* it literally creates itself *per formam*, through its form, which is the splendid, translucent, and disquieting spectacle of a void it shares with most of the objects it evokes. From the *ongles/onyx,* cupped to form the *lampadophore*'s lampshade, to *amphore, salon vide, croisée, miroir,* tarnished mirror frame, they reflect *en abyme*—like so many "aboli(s) bibelot(s) d'inanité sonore"—forms/sounds refracting forms/sounds for form's/sound's sake. Where contents equals the evanescent scintillations flickering on the surface of form, and where polyphony is evoked in a silence pregnant with golden sonorities, there myth celebrates its ultimate triumph—the multifaceted splendor of language creating *sua sponte* an oxymoronic fullness of void, the anguishing Being of Nothingness attendant on the sonnet's creation *ex nihilo*.

Notes

1. Arabic numerals in parentheses refer to pages in *Œuvres complètes de Stéphane Mallarmé,* ed. and annotated by Henri Mondor and G. Jean Aubry (Paris, 1951). *C.,* followed by Roman numeral, refers to Mallarmé's *Correspondance,* ed. and annotated by Henri Mondor and Lloyd James Austin (Paris, 1959). *Propos* is *Propos sur la poésie,* ed. Henri Mondor (Monaco, 1946).

    I gratefully acknowledge my debt to critics from Thibaudet, Mondor, and Noulet to Cohn, Richard, Genette, and Derrida, to whose monumental contributions I modestly add my own eclectic findings, in a never-ending task of interpretation, which can best be described in Joycean terms as a collective "work in progress."
2. André Jolles, *Einfache Formen* (Darmstadt, 1958), p. 96.
3. For inexplicable reasons, Kluge (*Etymologisches Wörterbuch der deutschen*

Sprache), even in its eighteenth revised edition, by Walther Mitzka (Berlin, 1960), mentions neither *Mythe*, nor *Mythus*, nor *mythisch*.

4. Giambattista Vico, *La scienza nuova seconda*, giusta l'edizione del 1744 . . . a cura di Fausto Nicolini (Bari, 1953), 1:162.

5. It is generally acknowledged that, directly or indirectly, Vico's speculations on the cyclical nature of history affected Herder's folkloric philology, Hegel's phenomenology, and Michelet's historiography. His ideas on the symbolic truth of myths and mythology had a noticeable impact upon the semantics of the nineteenth-century neologism "myth." Unmistakably they left their mark on its codification by syncretizers like Friedrich Creuzer, Max Müller, George W. Cox, and others. They contributed to the oversimplifications of its cultural and linguistic aspects by anthopologists as dissimilar as Lévy-Brühl and Lévi-Strauss; to the identification of myth with poetry by critics from Matthew Arnold to Northrop Frye; and to the recognition of the mythologizing tendencies of the language in which we think, by theologian-philologists like Walter F. Otto and by psychoanalysts from Freud to Jung.

6. Heinrich Lausberg, *Handbuch der literarischen Rhetorik* (Munich, 1960), 1:566, para. 1180.

7. *La scienza nuova*, 1:162. "La divina *onomathesia*, ovvero imposizione de' nomi alle cose secondo la natura di esse cose . . . , " ibid.

8. "Transfiguration en le terme surnaturel, qu'est le vers . . . ce civilisé édennique" (646).

9. "I prefer commencing with the consideration of an *effect*," "The Philosophy of Composition," *The Works of E. A. Poe* (Philadelphia, 1908), 5:181.

10. "Peindre non la chose, mais l'effet qu'elle produit," *Propos*, p. 43. In a similar vein, Stendhal in *La vie de Henri Brulard:* "Je ne prétends pas peindre les choses, en elles-mêmes, mais seulement leur effet sur moi" (*Œuvres intimes*, Paris, 1955, p. 126), with this difference: that Mallarmé wanted to calculate (as Poe pretended to do) the effect of his work on his audience. Mallarmé could not have known Stendhal's *Brulard* when he enunciated his principle in a letter to Henri Cazalis, dated October, 1864, twenty-six years before Casimir Stryienski published Stendhal's posthumous manuscript.

11. "Dans le Langage poétique—ne montrer que la visée du Langage à devenir beau, et non à exprimer mieux que tout, le Beau—et non du Verbe à exprimer le Beau ce qui est réservé au Traité. / Ne jamais confondre le *Langage* avec le *Verbe*" (853).

12. "Je dis: une fleur! et, hors de l'oubli où ma voix relègue aucun contour, en tant que quelque chose d'autre que les calices sus, musicalement se lève, idée même et suave, l'absente de tous les bouquets" (368, 857).

13. "A quoi bon la merveille de transposer un fait de nature en sa propre disparition vibratoire selon le jeu de la parole, cependant, si ce n'est pour qu'en émane, sans la gêne d'un proche ou concret rappel, la notion pure?" (857).

14. Expounded at length in Cox's major work, *Mythology of the Aryan Nations*, 2 vols. (London, 1870).

15. Gardner Davies, *Mallarmé et le drame solaire. Essai d'exégèse raisonnée* (Paris, 1959). Richard Wagner thought along the same lines, but in euhemerist terms, seeing natural phenomena as first transformed into anthropomorphic gods, then into human heroes: "Wir sehen hier (Siegfried saga) *natürliche Erscheinungen, wie die des Tages und der Nacht, des Auf- und Unterganges der Sonne,* durch die Phantasie zu handelnden und um ihrer Thaten willen

verehrten oder gefürchteten Persönlichkeiten verdichtet, die aus menschlich gedachten Göttern endlich zu wirklich vermenschlichten Helden umgeschaffen wurden . . . ," *Gesammelte Schriften und Dichtungen* (Nuremberg, n.d.), Auswahlband 3: 38.

16. "Mythologie, autant que Philologie . . . c'est par un procédé analogue que, dans le cours des siècles, se sont amassées et propagées partout les Légendes" (997).

17. "Le vers qui de plusieurs vocables refait un mot total, neuf, étranger à la langue et comme incantatoire achève cet isolement de la parole: niant, d'un trait souverain, le hasard demeuré aux termes malgré l'artifice de leur retrempe alternée en le sens et la sonorité, et vous cause cette surprise de n'avoir ouï jamais tel fragment ordinaire, en même temps que la réminiscence de l'objet nommé baigne dans une neuve atmosphère" (858).

18. *De la grammotologie* (Paris, 1967).

19. Written in 1895, three years before Mallarmé's death, this powerful sentence became central to Jacques Derrida's discussion of Mallarmé in *La dissemination* (Paris, 1972). Derrida thought this digression on the letter S important enough to derive from it the title of his monograph.

20. "Toast" in *La Plume*, no. 92, of February 15, 1893.

21. Quintilian, *De Institutione oratoria* 8. 2. 12: "Obscuritas fit verbis iam ab usu remotis."

22. Pointed out by Kurt Wais, but staunchly denied by Gardner Davies, in " 'Salut,' Essai d'exégèse raisonnée," *Les Lettres*, numéro spécial (1948), p. 190, n.2.

23. On the sirens' defeat by Orpheus, see Apollonius Rhodius, *Argonautica* 4. 904. On the sirens as *meretrices*, see *Serviarium Commentarium in Verg. Aen.* 5. 864: "SIRENUM, Sirenes . . . tres . . . secundum veritatem meretrices fuerunt . . . ."

24. On Mallarmé's Orphism, see his autobiographical sketch: "L'explication orphique de la Terre, qui est le seul devoir du poëte et le jeu littéraire par excellence" (663).

25. For a fuller exegesis of this sonnet see *New York Literary Forum*, vol. 2, pp. 219–35.

26. "Évoquer, dans une ombre exprès, l'objet tu, par des motifs allusifs, jamais directs, se réduisant à du silence égal, comporte tentative de créer . . . " (400).

27. *C.* II: 301; to Paul Verlaine, November 16, 1885.

28. "Von Kräften und Mischungen zu singen war *orphisch*, von Personen und Handlungen, *homerisch*," *Symbolik und Mythologie der alten Völker* (Leipzig and Darmstadt, 1836), 1:27. Creuzer's views were introduced to France as early as 1843 by J.D. Guigniaut. They found an avid public. For details, cf. Henri Peyre, *Bibliographie critique de l'Hellénisme en France de 1843 à 1870* (New Haven, 1932).

29. "La Poésie est l'expression, par le langage humain ramené à son rythme essentiel, du sens mystérieux des aspects de l'existence: elle doue ainsi d'authenticité notre séjour et constitue la seule tâche spirituelle" (*C.* II: 266; to Léo Orfer, June 27, 1884).

30. On Mallarmé's ambiguous attitude towards Wagner, cf. Suzanne Bernard's brilliant monograph, *Mallarmé et la musique* (Paris, 1959).

31. *C.* II: 286; to René Ghil, March 7, 1885.

32. *Tel Quel* 69 (Spring 1977): 55ff.

33. Cf. Martial, *Epigr.* 16. 61, "Lanterna cornea"; Plautus' Mercurius uses the periphrase "Vulcanus in cornu conclusus" (*Amphytrion*, 341) to designate a lantern. Lucretius speaks of "praeterea lumen per cornum transit" (*De Rerum Natura* 2. 388). Pliny relates about *cornu*/horn: "Apud nos in laminas secta translucent, atque etiam lumen inclusum latius fundunt" (that is, cornu laternam translucido) (*Historia naturalis* 11. 45).

34. *enfant* < *infans* = "without speech," as pointed out by R.G. Cohn in *Toward The Poems Of Mallarmé* (Berkeley, 1965), p. 235.

35. *C.* I: 279; to Henri Cazalis, July 1868.

36. *C.* I: 278.

37. *C.* I: 279.

38. *Die moderne französische Lyrik von Baudelaire bis zur Gegenwart* (Hamburg, 1956), 103. The oval shape of *ongles*, which is reflected in the material that at once symbolizes and incarnates them (*onyx*), is underscored by their initial vowel, *O*—which is echoed by the acoustic closed *o* of *haut*, prominently placed at the end of the very first hemistich. As an autonomous numeral, *0* signifies zero, naught, and as such intensifies the ghostly evocation of *l'Angoisse*, whose abstract nonbeing now extends to those parts of her "body" (*ongles*) which had been hardened into stonelike imagery through the analogy with onyx.

39. *Iliad* 14. 259; Hesiod, *Works and Days* 17.

40. In its Latin homophone, *nix* (and related *niteo, nitidus*, and so on), it would evoke whiteness, blankness, snow, the frigid splendor of the inviolate white page.

41. Cohn, p. 139.

42. For Parmenides, cf. Diels, *Poetarum philosophorum fragmenta* (Berlin, 1901), pp. 10, 3; Sophocles, *Antigone* 879.

43. *Odyssey* 19. 562–67; *Aeneid* 6. 893; cf. infra, note 54.

44. In a letter to H. Cazalis, dated May 14, 1867, Mallarmé speaks of his victory "dans ma lutte terrible avec ce vieux et méchant plumage, terrassé, heureusement, Dieu" (*C.* I: 241).

45. And one might add, for the 1868 version, the still-unfulfilled dream of presiding over a literary salon; for the 1887 version, the absent disciples who, one suspects, will commune on Tuesday evenings in this unnamed chapel, located (it is easy to assume) in the rue de Rome, and which Mallarmé, scornful of literary *cénacles* and schools, refuses to call a *chapelle*. ("J'abomine les écoles . . . et tout ce qui y ressemble," 896).

46. Cf. in particular his letter to Eugène Lefébure, of May 3, 1868; *C.* I: 274.

47. Seen by Gretchen Kromer, "The redoubtable PTYX," *MLN* 86/4 (May 1971): 83.

48. *C.* III: 95; to René Ghil, March 13, 1887.

49. Jean-Pierre Richard, *L'Univers imaginaire de Mallarmé* (Paris 1961), pp. 215f. is distinctly aware of this.

50. Cf. W.H. Roscher, *Ausführliches Lexikon der griechischen und römischen Mythologie*, 4, 1570 (Leipzig, 1909–15).

51. Cf. Strabo, *Chrestomathiae* 17.1.46; and Tacitus, *Germania* 45: "Sonum (Solis) insuper emergentis audiri, formasque deorum, et raios capitis aspici persuasio adjicit." See also Goethe, *Faust*, the "Prologue in Heaven," ll. 243 f.: "Die Sonne tönt in alter Weise / In Brudersphären Wettgesang."

52. The narrowness (*angustia*/*Angoisse*) of these gates of true dreams points to

their syncretic fusion with the Christian metaphor of the "strait" gate (*Luke* 13:24).

53. Cicero, *De deorum natura* 2. 57. 144.
54. "Sunt geminae Somni portae: quarum altera fertur / Cornea, qua veris facilis datur exitus umbris: / Altera, candenti perfecta nitens elephanto; / Sed falsa ad coelum mittunt insomnia manes" (*Aeneid* 6. 893ff.; cf. *Odyssey* 19. 562ff., where these two gates are related to Sleep only, without reference to Hades).
55. Cf. Roscher, 4:1574; Aelian, *De natura animalium* 10. 40; Ctesias, *Indica opera*, ed. Baehr, 264.
56. *De natura animalium*, 2.1.
57. A pseudoetymological game on the order of the *lanthorn/horn/corne* variety in *Les Mots anglais* (997).
58. The already quoted letter to Cazalis, dated July 18, 1868; *C.* I:278.
59. Camille Soula, in *Gloses sur Mallarmé* (Paris, 1946), p. 139, has launched an apparent *canard* that has been accepted by most critics. He suggests that this image "(lui) paraît puisée dans une lecture de Heine car on trouve dans '*De l'Allemagne*' relatés des combats entre les licornes et les nixes non loin d'une page relative aux Cygnes." I have no recollection of any such combat being related anywhere in Heine's works.
60. *De natura animalium*, 4. 52.
61. Based on a mistranslation in *Psalm* 26:6 (Vulgate): "Dilectus quemadmodum FILIUS UNICORNIUM." This verse is interpreted as symbolizing Christ's incarnation, in the *Physiologus Latinus* (ed. Carmody, Paris, 1939, 16).
62. Cf. Horapollo, *Hieroglyphica* 2. 34, where the Phoenix is shown to be *symbolon tou heliou*—symbol of the sun.
63. For example, Tertullian, *De resurrectione* 58. 27; Rufinus, *Comm. in symbol. apost.*, 11.
64. Leonardo da Vinci, *Trattato della pittura*, ed. H. Ludwig (Vienna, 1882), 1, no. 66, p. 124.
65. Ovid, *Metamorphoses* 2. 401–530.
66. Horace, *Ars poetica* 340.
67. "(e la favola de' Greci di disse anco *mythos*, onde vien a' Latini *mutus*)," Vico, *La scienza nuova*, 1:162.
68. "*Donner un sens plus pur aux mots de la tribu*," line 6 of "Le Tombeau d'Edgar Poe" (70).
69. Letter of May 22, 1870; *C.* I: 324.

COMPARATIVE THEORETICAL TRENDS

Patricia Carden

FAIRY TALE, MYTH, AND LITERATURE: RUSSIAN STRUCTURALIST APPROACHES

Any student of literature and myth who decides to acquaint himself with the thinking of structuralist critics will soon find that he is repeatedly stumbling over the same obstacle in his path to the subject, for in discussing myth and literature, the structuralist turns to the fairy tale. If the student wants to look into the narrative structure of myth, he will find that the model for discussion is taken from the fairy tale (Greimas). If he wants to look into the question of the development of literary genres from myth, the fairy tale comes up (Lévi-Strauss). If he decides to explore the relationship between mythical and literary modes of language, again he will come against the fairy tale (Jakobson and Bogatyrev). If he wants to look into the underlying structure of narrative itself, the fairy tale turns out to be the model (Bremond). Indeed the study of the structure of the fairy tale, of its relationship to myth on the one hand and to later prose genres on the other, constitutes an important subfield of structuralist studies. Russian criticism is responsible for the great importance that study of the fairy tale has assumed, and the Russians continue to be among the most active and inventive contributors to the discussion.

Why has the fairy tale become the pivot of the structuralist discussion of myth? It is to some extent an accident of choice, for when Vladimir Propp embarked upon the project that was to become his seminal study, *Morphology of the Folktale,* his primary concern, as we shall see, was not to distinguish folktale from myth but to found a methodology that would lead to a scientific basis for the study of folklore. His choice of the fairy tale (*volshebnaia skazka,* or magic tale) as the object of his demonstrations was a happy accident that had far-reaching consequences. The study of the fairy tale is particularly significant for any discussion of myth and literature because it marks the point where the idea of *litera-ture* originates, as narrative detaches itself from sacred ritual and begins to live its own life. With the coming into being of the classical fairy tale, fiction is born. The loss of the ethnocentric concreteness that characterizes myth leads to the creation of a clearly fictional reality. In contrast to myths and tales of origin, "tale beginnings usually emphasize an undefined time and place of action, and their endings (often of the order of the impossible) suggest that the tale is in fact a fiction."[1] Propp understood the process of development from myth to fairy tale to be historical, but even if one accepts Lévi-Strauss's model of a system in equilibrium, with the tale a satellite of the more powerful myth, the tale continues to serve the "literary" function within the system. As Lévi-Strauss distinguishes them, in contrast to the myth the tale has more possibilities for play and for free permutation and progressively acquires an arbitrary quality. The reduction of the strength of the cosmic oppositions that impose a rigid structure upon myth opens the way for free invention and facilitates the passage into literature proper.[2] Thus at this primary plane the distinction between literature and myth can most profitably be discussed, and the issues concerning their intricate relationships with each other can be raised with greatest precision. Any discussion of the way contemporary criticism came to concern itself with fairy tale and myth has to begin with Propp.

Propp envisioned his *Morphology of the Folktale* as the cornerstone of a grand project that would found a new methodology of folklore study leading to discussion of the broadest range of questions. Propp's intention was to begin by founding a scientifically accurate system of classification comparable to Linnaeus's work in biology. He meant to proceed by distinguishing the variables from the nonvariables, thus to arrive at the minimum number of necessary attributes that will characterize a genre. To demonstrate his method he selected a single class of works, the *volshebnye skazki*—"magical" or "fairy" tales. At the level of greatest abstraction his model is general typological classification, but his more immediate model is grammar, hence the term "morphology." The fairy tales are to be described by their constituent parts taken in relationship to one another and to the whole, just as a study of morphology of a language begins by determining the classes of components and the mutual relationships that constitute the grammatical system of that particular language.

For Propp the primacy of classification in any scientific work is self-evident, since other work can only rest soundly on an accurate description of the thing dealt with:

> We insist that until an accurate morphology is established, there can be no correct historical scholarship. If we cannot dissect the fairy tale into its constituent parts, then we cannot make correct comparisons. And if we cannot compare, then how can we shed light on, for example, the relations of Indian to Egyptian folklore, or on the relations of the Greek fable to the Indian, etc.? If we cannot compare one folktale with another, then how can we investigate the connection between the fairy tale and religion, how can we compare folktales with myths? Finally, just as all rivers flow into the sea, all questions of folktale study taken together must lead to the resolution of the most important and still unresolved problem—the problem of the spread of folktales around the whole earthly sphere.[3]

Propp's choice of the fairy tale as his case for demonstration has made it the center of the methodological inquiry and led to a somewhat exaggerated emphasis on this one genre in subsequent studies.[4] As Propp makes clear, the morphological method can be applied to any folklore genre. Yet the choice of the fairy tale has given a second life to his work through the strong interest of contemporary criticism in structure of narrative. But before pursuing these more general implications of Propp's work, we will first turn to the details of his structural description of the fairy tale.

Propp focuses on the single attribute that he finds to be invariable in the fairy tale—function. While the personages and their attributes are subject to wide variations, the functions served by the personages' actions are few and constant. Propp lists thirty-one irreducible functions that determine the structure of the tale. The functions are defined not only according to the nature of the action but also according to position and significance in the course of the narrative, since similar actions have different significances in distinct contexts. Propp gives an excellent definition of function in his essay "Fairy Tale Transformations."

1. The king sends Ivan after the princess; Ivan departs.
2. The king sends Ivan after some marvel; Ivan departs.
3. The sister sends her brother for medicine; he departs.
4. The stepmother sends her stepdaughter for fire; she departs.
5. The smith sends his apprentice for a cow; he departs.

The dispatch and the departure on a quest are constants. The dispatching and departing actors, the motivations behind the dispatch and so on are variables.[5]

The stunning and unexpected result of Propp's examination of function was the complete and accurate characterization of a literary genre. The fairy tale was revealed to have a monolithic structure such that every tale would embody the same functions arranged in the same strict sequence. On the abstract level that monolithic structure can be described thus:

> The tale begins with the inflicting of some sort of loss or harm (abduction, expulsion, etc.) or with the desire to have something (the tsar sends his son for the firebird) and develops through the hero's setting forth from home and his meeting with a donor who gives him a magic object or helper by whose aid the object of the quest will be found. In the further development of the story there occur a duel with the antagonist (its most important form is a fight with a dragon), the hero's setting out to return and the chase.[6]

Propp had anticipated that the fairy tales would group themselves around several structural "pivots" or "cores."[7] He discovered that the thirty-one functions form a strict sequence from first to last. Not every tale contains every one of the functions, but the functions that do occur always occupy the same position relative to the total sequence, so that one tale may have the structure $A, B, D, F \ldots$ and another $A, C, D, F \ldots$, but no tale will ever have the structure A, D, B, F. Propp had discovered the single metastructure that encompassed all examples of the fairy tale.

The demonstration of the monolithic structure of the fairy tale was the realization par excellence of the underlying enterprise of Russian Formalist criticism—a wholly precise description of the necessary invariables that define an individual genre—and though it was found by accident due to Propp's choice of the fairy tale as a subject of investigation, and though it was never duplicated for another genre, the impact of the demonstration has given Propp's morphological method an authority that the equally exact, but more complicated description of a complex genre could not have.

Propp's *Morphology* leads in two directions that are of fundamental significance for literary criticism. The first of these is toward the differentiation on historical grounds of the classical fairy tale from myth, the description of how fairy tale evolves out of myth and what ties it preserves with it, in short, the description of the evolution of the concept of fiction. The second is the extension of Propp's structure of the tale with suitable modifications back-

ward toward myth and forward toward later genres in such a way
as to achieve a metastructure encompassing the whole of narrative. The realization of the second of these possibilities has been
primarily a project of French criticism and we will not discuss it
here.[8] Suffice it to say that Propp saw such applications as a viola-
tion of the spirit of his work, which aimed at the distinguishing of
genres rather than their unification.[9] It is testimony to the seductive power of the monolithic form discovered by Propp that it has
tempted later critics to use it as a single key to the nature of
narrative itself. The fruitful misunderstanding of Propp's work is
one example of the dialogue between Russian and French stuctur-
alism that has enriched both national criticisms.

Propp's suggestion in the *Morphology* that the class of tales he
had analyzed could, from the historical point of view, be designated "mythical tales" opened the way for a new stage of investigation, which Propp himself promptly pursued. His *Historical
Roots of the Fairy Tale*, published only in 1946, is concerned with
the origins of fairy tale structure in ritual and myth. Propp accepts
the theories of the Cambridge school of anthropology concerning
the ritual origins of myth.[10] His proposal that the primal narratives
originated to accompany and explain rituals is, of course, not new
with him. What is original in Propp's work is his careful demonstration of the preservation of the structure of rite in the structure
of the fairy tale. The body of the work is devoted to a step-by-step
examination of the elements of fairy tale structure as proposed in
Morphology of the Folktale. Propp concludes that the great majority of motifs of the fairy tale are derived from two sources: the rite
of initiation and primitive conceptions of death and the other
world. Beyond that, the sequence of events in these rites corresponds to the structure of the tale: if we narrate the rite of initiation in sequence, we get the fundamental structure of the fairy
tale. If we narrate what is supposed to happen to the dying, we get
the same core composition, but with the addition of the elements
that were lacking in the rite.[11] *Historical Roots of the Fairy Tale*
can be added to the substantial body of literature that develops
the theory of the ritual origin of myth through its application to
specific literary genres.[12]

The strong evolutionary bias of the ritual theory, with its dynamic
view of the transformation of myths as rites die out and culture
changes, coincides with the Marxist-influenced model of change
favored by Propp, as does the theory's emphasis on the relationship
of myth to specific social situations. In Propp's scheme the most

archaic form is a myth that is an inseparable part of the ritual and thus connected with the very existence of the tribe. As the hunting culture dies out, the rite of passage, which is inseparably connected with it, dies out too. The conceptions and practices associated with dying persist longer and continue to exert influence upon the narrative form. But with the loss of the social organization that supports the myth, the necessary tie between myth and society is lost and the form becomes aestheticized. This tale told for pleasure rather than out of the necessity to preserve the life of the tribe becomes in time the classical fairy tale. Its structure is a relic of earlier times, but its new relationship to society frees it to assume new forms and express new ideas.[13]

In 1946, when *The Historical Roots of the Fairy Tale* was published, the ritual theory was already undergoing significant revision in the light of the rich accumulation by anthropologists of ethnographic materials on myths and rituals.[14] Propp's ethnographic materials are drawn heavily from nineteenth- and early twentieth-century classics such as Frazer, Frobenius, and Kroeber. Though he does refer to later materials from such collectors as Boas, the work gives an impression of lagging behind contemporary ethnographic research, not surprising considering that it was very likely written during the thirties. The relationship between myth and ritual as it appears to us today and as was already apparent in the forties is considerably more varied and complex than had originally been supposed. Neither myth nor ritual can claim universal priority, as Kluckhohn shows. Myths are sometimes recited during ritual performances, but in other cases, even though they may be recited in a "ritual attitude," they do not enter into any ceremonial. There are exoteric (open to the tribe) and esoteric (reserved for the initiated) forms of the same myth. Some cultures have a rich mythology and a meager system of rites; others get along without mythology. Nevertheless, the assumption that myth does have a connection with ritual remains a valid one, accepted by the majority of anthropologists, and Propp's scheme is not disproven in its fundamental aspects by the qualifications of the ritual theory.

A more telling attack was mounted by Lévi-Strauss in his influential review of Propp's *Morphology*, which brings into direct confrontation the two distinct approaches of structuralism, the paradigmatic and the syntagmatic, as the folklorist Alan Dundes has called them.[15] The Proppian or syntagmatic approach works from the linear sequence of the narrative, showing how a "syntax" of the tale is created that defines the genre. The paradigmatic approach works from underlying patterns or schemes based on binary oppositions that show forth in the tale the model of the underlying cultural context. In criticism that applies mythical patterns to literary works, Northrop Frye's analyses with their reliance on archetypal schemes are paradigmatic in spirit. The analyses that came out of the ritual theory of myth are at least potentially syntagmatic, since the rite follows a prescribed order, and this order is taken to be the hidden or incipient form of the later work.

The division between syntagmatic and paradigmatic does not take into account one important feature of Propp's position that is shared by his school, the insistent historicism from which all explanations are drawn. Russian formalism was already integrating historical criticism into its method at the time of the writing of *Morphology of the Folktale,* and though Propp's approach in this work has more in common with such early work of Victor Shklovsky as "The Connection between Devices of Plot-formation and General Devices of Style" and "The Structure of the Story and the Novel,"[16] in its outline of future work it anticipates the movement toward historical background that is realized in *Historical Roots of the Fairy Tale.*

It is precisely in this combining of formalism and historicism that Lévi-Strauss sees the weak point of Propp's argument and mounts his strongest attack on Propp's position. This argument must be of particular interest to literary criticism. One can raise the fundamental objection to many of the applications of mythical pattern to literature that they seem arbitrary and subjective, attempting to validate their juxtapositions by reference to concepts like Jung's collective unconscious, which have not achieved general acceptance. Both structuralist approaches intend to base their work on more solid foundations than these. The dialogue within structuralism about what the bases of a sound study of myth would be is of direct relevance to mythological criticism.

To understand Propp's foundation we must consider his tie to Russian Formalism. In its later stages Russian Formalism turned from the study of the devices that characterize given genres to a study of the historical relationships between different literary epochs. This turn, which was already implicit in some early Formalist work such as Eikhenbaum's study *Young Tolstoi,* grew out of the necessity to create a larger framework that would have explanatory value. The Formalist rejection of the dichotomy between form and content, with its corollary that the form *is* the content (with the understanding of form greatly expanded to encompass a much larger area of the work's internal relationships), dispenses with the explanation that works of literature exist to express certain contents. The Formalists provide a new answer: literature is one semiautonomous area of human culture and hence is subject to historical evolution. New literary epochs develop out of past epochs according to certain rules. It is the literary critic's task to find these rules. Since literature is one cultural system within the larger sphere of culture, the relationships between literature and other systems within the web can be discussed, but this discussion can only proceed on the basis of a clear definition and analysis of literature itself as a system. The Formalists applied themselves to this analysis as the primary problem.

Propp's procedure follows this logic exactly, beginning with a close analysis of the structure of one genre and then proceeding to establish the historical context in which the genre has its being. Lévi-Strauss's comment that Propp wavers between the formalist vision and an obsession with historical explanations is thus a distortion, implying as it does that the harnessing of the two is arbitrary. The specific objection that he raises to Propp's historical interpretation of the fairy tale's origins must carry more weight. As he observes, any attempt to study the history embodied in the tales is futile, since we know too little about the prehistoric civilizations in which they were born.[17] Indeed Propp's opportunistic and unsystematic use of ethnographic materials in *Historical Roots of the Fairy Tale* does not inspire confidence. Assuming along with the ritual school of mythology that all of mankind undergoes one common evolution from primitive to civilized, with existing cultures representing various stages in the evolution, Propp used any ethnographic data that came to hand from surviving mythologies of past cultures to contemporary anthropologists' observations of primitive societies. One cannot say that Propp has constructed a convincing historical context that would demonstrate conclusively how tales rose from myths. As Lévi-Strauss sees it, the lack of reconstructible context accounts for the fact that Propp can so easily dismiss the content of the tales to concentrate on their form: "The formalist dichotomy which opposes form and content and which defines them according to antithetical traits, is not imposed on him by the nature of things, but by the accidental choice that he made of a domain where only the form survives while the content is destroyed."[18]

Lévi-Strauss offers as a substitute for Propp's historicism the examination of myth and tale in contemporary primitive societies in which the ethnographer can reconstruct the relationships between the two on the basis of observable facts. From his own experience as an ethnographer, he proposes the following model: the tale does not succeed the myth in time but is part of a total system of oral literature. In this system the tale is related to the myth as a complementary satellite. The tales deal with the same substance as myth but in a different fashion, being constructed on weaker oppositions of a local, social, or moral character, while the myth is constructed on cosmic oppositions. Because the tale is not subject to the strong pressures of religious orthodoxy and logical coherence that is characteristic of the myth's cosmic oppositions, it has more possibilities for free permutations. This very weakening opens the tale up to influences from outside and makes it difficult to secure pure examples of the form uninfluenced by civilization.[19]

This substitution of the ethnographer's task for the historian's does provide us with a reconstructible context, while the theory of the tale's freedom to permute explains its artistic or fictional character. The solution cannot be wholly satisfactory for the literary critic, however, for it appears to consign all archaic mythic materials to oblivion.

This is a matter of some concern to the literary critic, for the Western tradition is separated by many centuries from its own mythic culture. Even the classical fairy tales, which formed a still-living tradition in recent times and are our closest link with the mythic past, survived in a culture that was characterized by superstition rather than by an intact system of mythology. The attempt to establish the ties between literature and myth on historical grounds thus becomes tenuous. The dialogue between Lévi-Strauss and Propp does not provide a solution to this problem, but it does lead directly to later Russian structuralist work, as we shall see.

The definition of the tale as a satellite of the myth reveals Lévi-Strauss's bias toward cosmological explanations over social ones. This bias was not shared by Propp, who wrote:

> The tale, once freed of its religious function, is not in itself in any way inferior in comparison with the myth from which it came. On the contrary, once freed from its religious conventions, the tale breaks into the free air of artistic creation, moved now by other social factors, and begins to live its own full-blooded life.[20]

On this note of affirmation of the value of literature in itself we can leave Propp and turn to later work.

The publication of the American translation of *Morphology of the Folktale* in 1958 had a decided impact on folklorists in English-speaking countries and led to a new wave of studies that applied Propp's syntagmatic analysis to folktale and myth. Lévi-Strauss's review of the *Morphology* brought it to the attention of French critics who were influenced by Lévi-Strauss's structuralism. Thus Propp's work became the vehicle for the reintroduction of many ideas of Russian Formalist criticism into the mainstream of contemporary criticism. The earlier influence on structuralist criticism of structuralist linguistics, which had been closely allied with Russian Formalism in its early stages, was reinforced. The ritual theory of myth had in its day created an alliance between the ethnographers and the literary critics. Now structural analysis created an alliance between the folklorists and the critics.

In the Soviet Union a younger generation of scholars had developed for whom Propp's *Morphology* was the methodological key. These scholars were also influenced by the work of Mikhail Bakhtin, who had devoted himself to the study of the relationship between literary genres and culture. In his brilliant studies of Dostoevsky and Rabelais, Bakhtin had traced large cultural configurations (the Mennippean satire and the carnival) through centuries, showing how they took embodiment in new artistic forms, constantly undergoing changes that revitalized them in new social and cultural contexts. Bakhtin's work was in its turn translated and came to have its own impact on Western criticism. While the French critics were reading Propp and Bakhtin, the Soviet scholars were reading Lévi-Strauss and submitting their assumptions to reexamination in the light of his theories. So the Russian-English-French dialogue was initiated.

The Russian structuralists who study folklore and myth divide into two groups according to the emphasis of their work. Directly proceeding with Propp's project of syntagmatic analysis of tales are Eleazar Meletinsky and his collaborators, who form what might be called the school of Propp. The second group, led by V.V. Ivanov and V. Toporov, is engaged in developing a basis for the typological study of myth through the application of modern formal logic. Each group is influenced by the other's work (they often publish in the same collections of articles) and by the work of Lévi-Strauss, though Meletinsky focuses more on the implications of Lévi-Strauss's theories for the structure of genres, while Ivanov and Toporov are interested in his methods of analysis.

Meletinsky holds to Propp's evolutionary model, while revising it considerably to take account of new ethnographic materials as well as Lévi-Strauss's logical objections. He has particularly examined the question of the differentiation of myth and fairy tale on a number of levels, historical, structural, and thematic.

The revised structural model of the fairy tale offered by Meletinsky (and this is considered his most significant contribution to folkloristics, for which he won the Pitré Prize) reduces larger syntagmatic units of Propp's analysis to three tests. The test is a formulation of the binary principle at work in the tales that had already been noted by Propp. The tests fall into three categories that are hierarchically related to each other. Every tale must begin with a preliminary test. The significance of the preliminary test lies in its revelation of the characteristics of the hero that will lead to his success. These may be traits of character (kindness, modesty, intelligence) or, more interestingly, an awareness of elementary norms of behavior, what Meletinsky defines as "the rules of the game." For passing the initial test, the hero receives some marvelous instrument that will aid him in the tasks he must accomplish. The preliminary test is set apart from any other test that the hero may undergo in the tale because its function is not related to success in a struggle, but to manifestation of the hero's character. It is followed by any number of basic tests in which the emphasis is on the achieved result—liquidation of loss, avoidance of misfortune, and successful search. The distinction between the preliminary test and the basic test is means versus aim, validation of correct behavior versus the main deed or achievement. The basic test may be followed, though this is not an obligatory part of the tale's form, by additional tests for the identification of the hero (having done the deed, he must prove it and show up the false hero). The point of the additional test is the distribution of the acquired values (kingdom, money, bride).[21]

The significance of Meletinsky's structure is its overcoming of the dichotomy between form and content of Propp's analysis. The tests are not only the fundamental unit of form, they also point to the underlying unity of theme that accounts for the monolithic form of the tale. The theme of the fairy tale is social conflict, particularly as it arises within the family. The action begins, as Propp noted, with a lack or misfortune and ends with salvation from the misfortune, but the cause of the misfortune is a social conflict and is resolved by an elevation in the hero's social status produced by his success and symbolized by his marriage to the princess.[22] We will turn presently to Meletinsky's very interesting theories on the role of marriage in the tale. Here we will just note that Lévi-Strauss's objection to Propp's "formalism" has been successfully answered. (Meletinsky made a further rejoinder by pointing out that the seeming formalism of Propp's analysis was related to the formalism of the tale itself with its emphasis on "the rules of the game.")

The analysis of structure and theme leads to Meletinsky's distinctions between myth and tale. The myth differs from the tale significantly in its absence of hierarchic structure. The various mythical and narrative components in the search and struggle of the heroes stand by themselves and have an absolute value, rather than serving as a means to arrive at other goals. The finding of a *structural* difference between myth and tale is a significant departure from Propp, who had assumed that myth and fairy tale were distinguished not by form, but by social function.[23]

Meletinsky's revision of Propp's historical scheme begins from this structural difference. Recall that Lévi-Strauss had proposed that historical study of the relationship between tale and myth was impossible and had substituted for it the study of contemporary primitive cultures in which oral traditions are still intact. Meletinsky now incorporates into his historical framework Lévi-Strauss's characterization of the whole oral tradition, in which the tale and myth are not clearly differentiated. He proposes that archaic narrative folklore is indeed incompletely dissociated from myth and is distinguished from myth by its concentration on the acquisition of "individual values" (personal wealth and success) in contrast to myth's concentration on the acquisition of "collective values" (the group's harmony with the cosmos). But in the later stage of evolution represented by the classical fairy tale, myth and tale have become completely differentiated. The mythological world view is transformed into one of fantastic dramatis personae and objects, which compensate for the loss of mythic heroes (the initial test is precisely the basis for the transformation of the commonplace hero into a hero of extraordinary powers through the acquisition of the magical objects). The rules of behavior are not determined by magic, but by abstract sociomoralistic ideals.[24]

Meletinsky's theory is a tour de force that incorporates the more complex model of oral narrative constructed by contemporary ethnography, while preserving the essential feature of Propp's historical interpretation, the evolution of the fairy tale from myth due to the changing structure of society. In working out this new synthesis Meletinsky was forced to think through a number of fundamental questions about the differences in the narrative structure of myth and tale, questions that bear directly on our own central inquiry into the fictional nature of the tale. For example, Meletinsky shows how the necessity to demonstrate the sources of the hero's powers arises from the disappearance in the folktale of the supernatural power associated with the cosmic theme of the myth. As the attempt to differentiate myth and tale continues in subsequent work, the discussion leads more and more toward specific ways in which myth becomes embodied in narrative. The gap between myth and fiction begins to fill in.

A particularly interesting example is found in the folklorist Susan Reid's testing of Meletinsky's distinction upon some North American Indian myths. By moving to a level of greater generality she demonstrates that the tale's hierarchical structure can be extended to myth, since both follow the same underlying ritual logic. It is according to the law of ritual—that is, for an extraliterary reason that cannot be traced in the fairy tale—that the weaker always wins. Meletinsky, following his social interpretation that the fairy tale is about the individual's acquisition of values, had proposed that the underlying binary opposition of fairy tale structure was "own"– "foreign." Reid sees this as comparable to the opposition natural world (village)–supernatural world (forest, mountain, sea) in myth. This distinction carries the connotation of poor versus rich or powerless versus powerful. The hero who leaves the natural world for the supernatural is always weaker in the encounter, but this very weakness and passivity are the conditions of his gaining power from supernatural beings. In the fairy tale the villain is powerful and dominant, while the hero is passive and yet thereby gains his supremacy.[25] Reid's reaction to Meletinsky extends our understanding of the precise ways in which ritual comes to be translated into forms of narrative, of great importance for any understanding of how archetypes arise in literature.

Meletinsky's discussion of the role of marriage in folktale and myth is even more useful, considering the key role that marriage plays as denouement in fictional narrative of all kinds. Noting that marriage has extraordinary importance in the fairy tale, in contrast to myth, in which it plays a subsidiary or even minor role, Meletinsky attributes the difference to the rearrangement of values and its consequent reflections in the "syntax" of the tale, which he believes occurred during the transition from the "mythological" folktale of primeval society to the classical fairy tale. "Mythological heroism (where the hero does not obtain magic items for himself but for the father, king or community) changes over to novelistic complications ·and 'subtleties' where the hero uses a relatively easily procured magical object as a means of marrying the princess."[26] As Meletinsky writes, marriage "assumes a new meaning: it offers to the individual a peculiar, 'miraculous' escape from social and family conflicts."[27] In the novel marriage commonly serves the same function, but a further complication has taken place, for the social conflicts are embodied in the process of courtship itself. Oftener than not, marriage is not merely the formulaic reward but the very ground of the novel's action. In the fairy tale, the mediating role of marriage in resolving (or as Meletinsky modifies Lévi-Strauss, circumventing) the basic oppositions that arise out of social conflict is purely symbolic. The novel subjects the mediation to analysis and makes the analysis the subject of the narrative. It would seem likely that the novel may also include uses of marriage that approximate its use in myth, in which it is not a supreme value but only incidental to the acquisition of mythical (cosmic and ritual) objects or the acquisition of the guardian-spirit.[28] This might be especially true in certain novels (Dostoevsky's *The Idiot* comes to mind) in which the hero's drama is concerned not with his own success and self-realization, but with the collective welfare.

By using Meletinsky's insights to illuminate specific literary problems in which I see the possibility for juxtaposition, I am following the general practice of mythological criticism, which has tended to be opportunistic in its use of the ethnographer's materials. It is precisely this opportunism which often makes mythological criticism seem shaky. Structuralists of both persuasions insist upon the importance of a different kind of procedure, which deals with wholes and produces an internally consistent analysis of the entire phenomenon. We are obliged, then, to ask if Meletinsky's system as a whole answers the chief critical questions about the relationship between literature and myth. Alas, it must be said that his proposal, though fascinating and illuminating when taken in its separate parts, is not entirely persuasive as an explanation of the historical evolution of the concept of fiction. Meletinsky still makes a forced link between an "archaic" folklore, which is in fact recorded in modern primitive societies, and the classical fairy tale, which exists in a different tradition. There is no proof at all that the early twentieth-century myths of North American Indians are in any way connected historically to the myths from which the classical fairy tale sprang. The Indian myths can be related to the archaic myths of European civilization only by an ahistorical concept like the "pensée sauvage," which proposes a uniform logic in primitive thought. It would seem that Lévi-Strauss was correct when he said that Propp's project of establishing the historical origins of fairy tale in myth is futile and unrealizable.

If we surrender our search for a connection in history, does that remove us forever from any hope of understanding the evolution of our own narrative tradition from its most primitive origins? This very problem has been taken up by the distinguished historian Peter Munz, who, showing the inadequacy of structuralism to deal with problems of a historical nature, proposes the use of a typological classification built upon the initial analysis of structures.

> Granting the possibility of structural analysis, one should still not blind oneself to the fact that myths have historical dimensions; that in their historical dimensions they appear as typological series proceeding, as time goes by, towards higher degrees of specification. The real crux of the matter, then, is not whether myth should be interpreted structurally or functionally; but that apart from being capable of being interpreted functionally in a structural manner [i.e., the structure is understood to be correlated with other institutions], they can also be seen as arranged in long typological series, completely divorced from the social order in which any one link of the typological chain happens to have been composed.[29]

Munz's argument has been anticipated by the Russian scholars Ivanov and Toporov, who understood that typological study is the next logical extension of structuralism. In their programmatic article of 1962 written in cooperation with A.A. Zalizniak, "On the Possibility of Structural-typological Study of Several Modelling Semiotic Systems," they set forth an ambitious project for typological study of religious systems from every point of view, including the historical.[30]

Typological classifications can of course be made on the basis of any distinguishing characteristic. Munz proposes a straightforward classification for myths based on increasing specificity of the features. Noting that the simplest version of a mythical subject diverges only in small details, if at all, from a rational event or occurrence, Munz proposes a process of deflection and increasing complication of the myth through time.[31] While a typological classification will not allow us to fix the exact chronological relationship to the series of any given version of the myth, it will allow us to see the direction that the development of the myth took through time, or as Ivanov and Toporov put it, the chronological difference between the elements of the system appear in differences of a statistical character; it is therefore possible to speak of a probable determination of the direction of time.[32]

What the typological classification yields on the historical level is not fact but plausibility. What is arrived at by whatever series of operations the investigator performs is a statement that is itself a product of the system of operations. But that statement does have relevance, since presumably the operations were designed to answer a given question. If Propp had had at his disposal a scientifically constructed typology of the ritual, his finding of a ritual structure in the fairy tale would have more plausibility. As it is, the foundations of his comparison are shaky, since he used a structure of the ritual arrived at pragmatically by the combination of chance features. It has to be acknowledged that it seems likely that a scientifically constructed typology of the ritual will confirm in large part Propp's pragmatic construction and therefore will not advance the actual state of knowledge about the relationship between myth and fairy tale. But by making the relationship plausible, it can serve in turn for the construction of typologies on a higher level. The series can be extended in such a way as to answer some of our questions about the origins of the concept of fiction. Just such a typology could be constructed on the basis of the role of marriage as proposed earlier. The arrangement of a large number of specific versions in a series of increasing complexity would show the general direction that was taken by the motif of marriage in shaping fictional forms, or to restate it in the new terminology, we can construct a typology of the semantics of marriage as it serves to model the higher system of fiction. Such a series would have to be based on structural analyses of individual versions to reveal the distinctive features that must be taken into account in constructing the typological series.

Ivanov and Toporov have proposed that such constructions for cultural systems be based on the new theories of logic developed for information theory and semiotics. Any cultural system can be seen as composed of a number of layers of sign systems of varying complexity with each layer "modeling" or giving shape to the next higher stratum. In the foregoing example, marriage would be regarded as a less complex system for the purposes of the analysis, since it serves as a "language" or code through which information is conveyed about the primary system under analysis, fiction itself.

If we were to construct a typology of structuralist analysis of folk narrative, beginning with Propp and extending through Ivanov and Toporov, we would find that the historical direction of movement is away from the specific analysis of given genres toward the analysis of whole cultural systems, both in conceptual space and in actual historical time. Many current critics are dealing with works of literature as though they were of a piece with myths, that is, were products of the collective imagination. This is a movement that is disturbing to those who believe that the proper object of literary study is the text in the old sense of the word, that is, a specific work created by an individual author, rather than text in the new sense defined by Ivanov and Toporov as the "directly observable facts" which can be of different "substances": written or oral speech, graphics, paintings, architectural complexes, forms of human behavior, and so on.[33] The usefulness of this expanded definition of text for the reconstruction of a religious system is obvious. Its applicability to literary texts is more questionable. Critics of the new persuasion would do well to remember the distinction made by Jakobson and Bogatyrev in their seminal article of 1929. Folklore is distinguished from literature by its character as the collective product of the community. An individual recital of a folklore work is related to the actual existence of the work as Saussure's *la parole* is related to *la langue;* the work does not come into being until it has undergone community censorship and been adopted collectively. Works of literature are not submitted to this communal censorship. They have an objective being, and works rejected in one generation can be revitalized and accepted by succeeding generations. This opens the way for an individual creative imprint that cannot exist in folklore. Jakobson and Bogatyrev conclude:

> The typology of folklore forms must be built independently of the typology of literary forms. For example, compare the limited set of fairy tale plots typical of folklore with the diversity of plot characteristic of literature. Like structural linguistic laws, the general laws of poetic composition which result in a spontaneous likeness of plots are much more uniform and strict in their application to collective creativity than in regard to individual creativity.[34]

This does not exclude the possibility of constructing a typology of the typologies based on points of similarity and difference between the two systems, but it does argue for a scrupulosity of method that does not haphazardly confuse the qualities of two independent systems. The typology of the semantics of marriage proposed above would thus have to be constructed as a comparison of two independent typologies based on the special characteristics of folk narrative and literary narrative.

For the present, in the absence of carefully constructed typologies, we can nevertheless proceed on our intuition that literary narrative is related to folk narrative and that folk narrative is related to archaic mythologies. If the current project of the Russian structuralists proceeds to its conclusion, it will yield a logically plausible model of archaic mythology. It may also by the way yield a logically plausible model of the development of the concept of fiction. This may be the best that we can hope to achieve.[35]

Notes

1. E. Meletinsky, S. Nekludov, E. Novik, and D. Segal, "Problems of the Structural Analysis of Fairy Tales," *Soviet Structural Folkloristics*, ed. Pierre Maranda (The Hague/Paris, 1974), p. 75.

2. Claude Lévi-Strauss, "L'Analyse morphologique des contes russes," *International Journal of Slavic Linguistics and Poetics* 3 (1960): 134.

3. *Morfologiia skazki*, 2d ed. (Moscow, 1969), p. 21. All references in this paper will refer to this revised edition noted as *Morfologiia*. The revised edition is available in French translation (*Morphologie du conte suivi de Les transformations des contes merveilleux et de E. Mélétinski L'étude structurale et typologique du conte*, trans. Marguerite Derrida, Tzvetan Todorov, and Claude Kann, Paris, 1970). For an English version see *Morphology of the Folktale*, trans. L. Scott (Austin, 1968), which is a revised translation of the original English translation (Bloomington, 1958) of the first edition (Leningrad, 1928).

4. In his excellent survey "Strukturno-tipologicheskoe izuchenie skazki" printed as the afterword to the 1969 edition of Propp's *Morfologiia*, E.M. Meletinsky lists the numerous works devoted to Propp's theories. See the translation "Structural-Typological Study of Folktales" in *Soviet Structural Folkloristics*.

5. *Readings in Russian Poetics: Formalist and Structuralist Views*, ed. Ladislav Matejka and Krystyna Pomorska (Cambridge, Mass., 1971), p. 94.

6. Vladimir Propp, *Istoricheskie korni volshebnoi skazki* (Historical Roots of the Fairy Tale) (Leningrad, 1946), p. 7. Hereafter noted as *Istoricheskie korni*. Italian translation: *Le radici storiche dei raconti di fate* (Turin, 1949).

7. *Morfologiia*, p. 26.

8. See the work by A.J. Greimas: "Le conte populaire russe: Analyse fonctionelle," in *Sémantique structurale: Recherche de méthode* (Paris, 1966); "Eléments pour une théorie de l'interprétation du récit mythique," *Communications* 8 (1966). And by Claude Bremond: "Le message Narratif," *Communications* 4 (1964); "La logique des possibles narratifs," *Communications* 8 (1966); "Morphology of the French Folktale," *Semiotica* 2 (1970).

9. For a detailed critique of the French work from the point of view of Propp's school, see Meletinsky, "Problems of Structural Analysis."

10. Propp proposes the theory as though it were his own, but this may be due to reticence of a political nature. As a scholar whose work was associated with discredited Formalism, Propp may well have hesitated to identify his theories with those of English scholars.

11. *Istoricheskie korni*, p. 330.

12. For a discussion of other studies see Stanley Edgar Hyman, "The Ritual View of Myth and the Mythic," in *Myth: A Symposium*, ed. T.A. Sebeok (Blooming-ton, 1958).

13. *Istoricheskie korni*, p. 330.

14. See Clyde Kluckhohn's epoch-making article "Myths and Rituals: A General Theory," first published in the *Harvard Theological Review* 35 (1942), partially reprinted in *Myth and Literature*, ed. John B. Vickery (Lincoln, 1966).

15. "Introduction," *Morphology* (Austin, 1968), p. xi.

16. In *O teorii prozy* (On the Theory of Prose) (Moscow, 1929).

17. "L'Analyse morphologique," p. 136.

18. Ibid., p. 137. That Lévi-Strauss had some acquaintance with Propp's later work, at least by hearsay, is apparent from his article. It would seem that he had not read *Historical Roots of the Fairy Tale*.

19. Ibid., pp. 134–36.

20. *Istoricheskie korni*, p. 334.

21. "Problems of Structural Analysis," pp. 78–79.

22. Ibid., p. 76.

23. *Istoricheskie korni*, p. 16.

24. "Problems of Structural Analysis," pp. 74–75.

25. "Myth as Metastructure of the Fairytale," in *Soviet Structural Folkloristics*, p. 153.

26. "Marriage: Its Function and Position in the Structure of Folktales," in *Soviet Structural Folkloristics*, pp. 64–66.

27. Ibid., p. 68.

28. "Problems of Structural Analysis," p. 76.

29. *When the Golden Bough Breaks: Structuralism or Typology?* (London and Boston, 1973), p. 38.

30. "O vozmozhnosti strukturno-tipilogicheskogo izucheniia nekotorykh modeli-ruiushchikh semioticheskikh sistem," in *Strukturno-tipologicheskie issle-dovaniia*, ed. T.N. Moloshnaia (Moscow, 1962), pp. 134–42. Reprinted in *Texte des Sowjetischen Literaturwissenschaftlichen Strukturalismus* (Munich, 1971).

31. *When the Golden Bough Breaks*, p. 39.

32. "O vozmozhnosti strukturno-tipologicheskogo izucheniia," p. 142.

33. Ibid., p. 136.

34. Roman Jakobson and Petr Bogatyrev, "On the Boundary between Studies of Folklore and Literature," in *Readings in Russian Poetics*, p. 93. Written in 1929 and first published in *Łud Słowiański* 2 (1931), pp. 230–33.

35. Since this article was written, a number of books have appeared that extend the theories of Propp and his school. Among the most important of these are a posthumous volume of Propp's essays, *Fol'klor i deistvitel'nost'* (Moscow, 1976), a collection of essays in Propp's honor edited by Meletinsky and Nek-liudov, *Tipologicheskie issledovaniia po fol'kloru* (Moscow, 1975), and a major summation by Meletinsky of his theory, *Poetika mifa* (Moscow, 1976).

Eva Kushner

GREEK MYTHS IN MODERN DRAMA: PATHS OF TRANSFORMATION

To study the reappearances of myth in literature is to encounter the paradox of permanence and transformation. The haunting question that arises for the critic and the historian as well as for the theoretician of literature, and for those who study the anthropological, psychological, and sociological aspects of imagination, is that of the resilience of myths. How does it occur that these ancient narratives—very often Greek myths in the case of the literatures of the West—survive and revive with ever-renewed meaning for writers, readers, and spectators of subsequent periods? What is the source of their power of resurgence? It is not our ambition to give a direct answer to this question, but rather to suggest a method of analysis which, by attempting to shed a ray of light upon the manner in which classical myths renew themselves as they are transmitted from one literary version to another, may indirectly offer some pointers toward the sources of their viability.

Until the rise and development of structuralist studies, two main methods were applied to the study of myths in literature, which could both be subsumed under the heading of thematology. Thematology in general has the immense merit of fostering complete inventories of the becoming of mythical heroes and of the narratives that enshrine all their actions; and of requiring "reasoned" analyses with homogeneous criteria. Fourteen years after the publication of his book *Un problème de littérature comparée: les études de thème, essai de méthodologie*,[1] Raymond Trousson still maintains his exigency of completeness in the historical survey of any given myth, for fear that fragmentary studies distort the results through ignorance of past contexts, and of the modes of reception of myths in artificially isolated fragments of time.[2] If indeed the leading question is the question he asks at the end of his essay: "Pourquoi les mêmes mythes reviennent-ils de génération en génération?"[3] Trousson is right in considering the long-range history of each myth throughout the history of literature as a necessary field of investigation; and although in my view completeness of coverage is not a *sufficient* guarantee of success, it will at least preclude error in relating versions and interpretations of versions to one another.

Of the two forms of thematology referred to earlier, the first is thematology "avant la lettre": it prides itself upon following in an exhaustive manner all examples of a given myth in a given time of the history of literature or in a geographical area. It is based on a searching use of *Stoffgeschichte*. It therefore presupposes an original occurrence or set of occurrences of the myth in classical antiquity, and it probes modern literatures for examples of its recurrence. But, explicitly or implicitly, it always expects the modern creator to adhere to the past model. Thus, in chapter 23 of Gilbert Highet's *The Classical Tradition,* modern theatrical versions of ancient mythical stories are described with their various degrees of deviance from their prototypes. Characterization, variations in basic plots, and the use of colloquial language are all regarded as "anachronisms." Dream interpretation and Freudian slips in Cocteau's *La machine infernale;* the brutal language of the soldiers in Hasenclever's *Antigone;* the painfully real Electra complex, marked by attachment to the dead father, in Hofmannsthal's *Elektra,* are but examples of transgressions against that which such a conception of thematology regards as its true aesthetic norm: fidelity to the ancient model. It is our view that this manner of approaching modern literary texts should be reversed, and that the element of change should be viewed as a sine qua non of aesthetic success. This does not mean that change alone is a guarantee of success, but that it is a symptom of survival that will have to be taken into account with other factors of aesthetic success, such as coherence patterns in renewal and coherence between ancient signifier and modern signified.

Furthermore, Highet has a static view of myths as signifiers: "For century after century men have been captivated by the Greek legends, have told them in different ways, elaborating some and neglecting others, have sought different beauties and values in them, and when they gave them conscious interpretations, have educed from them many different kinds of truth."[4] It is as if myths were static containers into which various societies, at different times, infuse various meanings. The interpretation changes, but the basic myth remains the same, thanks to some "force" inherent in it. Because of this invariability it can be filled, so to say, with many meanings, as if it were itself a neutral form. The uniqueness of each new version, which is an exact symbiosis between the narrative structure, a moment, *and a literary work,* is lost from sight, and so is the fact that the myth, while remaining itself, undergoes substantive changes.

The second traditional approach consists in considering the various successive versions of a myth as variations upon a theme, after the fashion of musical variations. Here the myth is also taken as a static rather than a dynamic entity insofar as it is a passive object in the hands of the author who manipulates its forms and meanings according to his own idiosyncracies. The myth simply serves the literary critic as a touchstone for detecting these idio-syncracies; the author's intellectual horizon is measured purely in its relation to the myth rather than in its relation to historical and social context. All versions thus appear to exist in a perennial contemporaneity, and the comparing of versions is an intellectual exercise that does not enrich our knowledge of the myth itself. The critic's mind thus juggles with styles, movements, trends, even periods. His mind contemplates—and exaggerates—the per-manence of the mythical narrative and enjoys its transformations without analyzing their causes or their nature.

Let us take as an example the myth of Orpheus.[5] Is he not, from the depths of Hellenic times to our day, the founder of poetry and music, the civilizing hero pitched against all cruelty and barbar-ity? More or less directly, Virgil's hymn of harmony is heard in the *Auto sacramental del divino Orfeo,* where it merges with a Chris-tian vision; in Cocteau's witty *Orphée* of 1927 as well as in the film of the same name; in the cruel and dreamlike atmosphere of Kokoschka's *Orpheus and Eurydike,* and in the sordid meeting-places of Anouilh's *Eurydice.* In each case the historical moment acts as a prism producing a set of variations; the narrative structure seems unaffected. This can lead us to consider the unity it confers upon various versions as the sign of a permanent entity within the imagination. Trousson has reminded us that it is all too easy to extrapolate from this ontological considerations regarding the per-manence of human nature. He does admit that myths are enduring entities and refers to their *essence* and *pérennité;* but he regards as superficial the kind of extrapolation that would bridge centuries in order to associate into kindred families authors in whose thought a given myth occupies a central place.

"Le thème est un fil conducteur, éternel à travers la durée, qui se charge, au long des siècles, de tout le butin artistique et philosophique amassé, sur sa route illimitée, par l'aventurier humain; c'est pourquoi il préserve et restitue, à travers ses innombrables transmutations, quelques constantes, quelques préoccupations fondamentales, en un mot quelque chose de l'essentiel de la nature humaine.[6]

Thus we know that myth points toward enduring structures, but it neither identifies nor explains them. This indeterminacy is in itself a sign and a promise of vitality and prepares an answer for Trousson's following question, which is: "Pourquoi les mêmes mythes reviennent-ils de génération en génération?" We might venture to say that it is on account of the prehensile nature of myths as structures in Lévi-Strauss's sense of the word, that is, as sets of interrelationships in which, furthermore, the signifier absorbs the new signified every time and thus gives rise to a new signifier from which new signification emerges: a dialectic of the unfamiliar and the familiar is enacted in this way. It has been said over and over again that defamiliarization is the very crux of literariness. Thus in order to renew itself for new audiences the myth must adopt a new code and new code-breakers. But the thoroughly unfamiliar would not, contrary to this theory, produce the desired effect on the spectator's mind: *ostranienie* arises from the very familiarity of the mythical story made appealingly different by an element of divergence, but again familiar by a signification consequent with the more ancient meanings of the myth.

Thus the permanence of myths as they manifest themselves in modern literature lies not in fixity of narrative detail, nor in an ontological unity of the human mind as enshrined in the world of myths, nor again in the preservation of a classical flavor, but in the very dynamics of myth itself. The structuralist concept of myth sheds considerable light upon the so-called power that myths seem to possess towards reshaping themselves across time, space, and cultural contexts. Piaget's definition of structures as having the qualities of "totalité, auto-réglage et transformation"[7] is particularly basic to our study: if myths indeed are structures, they are not dependent upon one culture, one epoch, one specific narrative version, but have the ability of recombining elements of form and meaning through the very fact of transformation—whereas it used to be thought that they survived in some esoteric way, immutably, *despite* transformation.

But the structuralist explanation cannot thoroughly satisfy the literary critic and historian: it accounts for the survival of myth in imagination, individual and collective, as a referential reality, but not for a given author's grasp of it. We are still faced with another fact, which is the "reaestheticizing" of myth in a literary, and more particularly dramatic, work of art. As myth moves away from its religious or ethical role and is drawn into literary texts and contexts, the strict anthropologist may think that it loses its identity as myth.[8] Nonetheless, and perhaps for that very reason, myth is reactivated by the imagination as it becomes transformed into a literary work. This change should not be viewed as some sort of decay, lest we fall, by adherence to anthropological patterns, into the same attitude as that already described of the traditional literary historian. It should, in my view, be studied in the light of the unity of the realm of the imagination, in the manner most comprehensively described by Northrop Frye.[9]

Northrop Frye's system accounts for the common features and functions of literature and myth and thus explains the perennial presence (and present) of myth. Archetypal criticism begins by drawing individual myths out of their mysterious and mystifying isolation and makes of them the very pivots of a coherent conception, not only of the literary work itself, and of its literariness, but also of the entire community of literary works, that is, of literature. A deep and seminal link exists precisely between myth and literature: is not literature the modern form of myth, and would it not therefore appear that the modern playwright who chooses a mythical narrative, at the crossroads of literary tradition and of the collective imagination, makes, so to say, a double investment of his creation? Let us not conclude from this that a mythological play is necessarily a double success from the aesthetic viewpoint, in that it keeps the narrative structure of myth and reactualizes it in a historical and literary conjuncture. We are merely saying that it has an exemplary value toward explaining the kinship of myth and literature, since both forms of discourse are illuminated by being viewed in their mutual relationship. In both cases—and all the more when myth is given new literary life by a modern author—narration embodies and manifests its own meaning. Or, it can be said more simply that it affirms itself in its temporal rhythm and its recurrences; it carries reference to itself rather than to the surrounding reality, which does not mean that it is devoid of the real but rather the contrary: mythical narrative is prehensile to the extent that it transforms the historical moment into a new signifier, of which the signified is drawn from classical antiquity.

Returning to Northrop Frye, we can say that according to him myths form a language that has as its archetypal and central example the myth of the Quest with its cyclical character, manifesting the rhythm of the sun (day–night opposition) as well as the rhythm of life (life–death opposition) and that of dream (sleep–consciousness opposition). Thus every local myth, specific though it may be and to whatever culture it may belong, communicates with the major mythical formations, not through its ritual origins but through its actualized form. Obviously, in this respect, Frye draws upon such authors as Frazer and Jung to show the interdependence of the great symbolical formations.

It also appears that the autoregenerative capacity of the myth is linked to its narrative functioning, which in turn relates to its structural nature. Myths behave as structures, and this holds true of their literary manifestations; according to Piaget, whom we already quoted on this point, they act as wholes, regulate themselves and transform themselves. If we consider a mythological play in this perspective it is obvious that we do not expect it (as did Highet) to be the replica of an ancient, unsurpassable model, but to bring back to life, through an interplay of equivalences, that is, by transformation, the sum total of the mythemes that make up the "standard" myth. Every time such a transformation occurs, it should be received as wholly belonging to the myth by dint of the interplay of equivalences. "All accretions to the myth belong," says Harry Levin,[10] and Lévi-Strauss makes a similar statement: "Toutes les versions appartiennent au mythe." Our task is to discuss the manner in which radically new elements come to "belong."

One obvious locus of transformation is the "actantial" organization of a play. The concept of "actant" by far exceeds that of character, since it can subsume several characters whose effects are cumulative and complete one another, while also combining with nonhuman agents, which can be real, symbolical, or imaginary. At the beginning of Cocteau's *Orphée,* for example, the hero has a double—the horse—which according to him symbolizes his poetic inspiration and perhaps represents his subconscious. Later in the play the poet acquires a more exalted double: Hurtubise, the window repairman, who in fact becomes his guardian angel. Here are two projections of the poet's soul, opposed yet complementary. They are figures quite specific to Cocteau's play. The first could be said to express in eminently theatrical fashion, if only by using surprise, a perception of poetry touched by Freudianism and surrealism. The second reflects Cocteau's brief encounter with Maritain and Catholicism. The two *adjuvants* (helpers) through whom the character of Orpheus is both differentiated and corroborated are not only distinct from each other but opposite in nature; yet their main function in the actantial organization is together to oppose Aglaonice, the true enemy of poetry, an enemy all the more dangerous since she too claims to be a poet. But let us return to the two additional actants created by Cocteau: with Orpheus himself they establish at a specific moment in history (1927) the saving role of poetry among men.

Such enrichments of the actantial organization may at first sight appear heretical, at least in the eyes of the strict historicist. Are they not fanciful extrapolations on the part of the author, products of the imagination bearing much less relation to the myth than to the vagaries of contemporary taste? The point of our demonstration is that the very contrary is the case. The extrapolation is sometimes so extreme that one may wonder if it still belongs. There are two complementary manners of ascertaining whether it does. The first relates to the reception of the device by the reader or spectator. Reception is not our concern here, but it should be pointed out that the author necessarily seeks equivalent sources of religious emotion, philosophical thought, or aesthetic enjoyment to those conveyed by elements of earlier plays. Thus spectators of Tennessee Williams's *Orpheus Descending* would be more sensitized to the cruelty of the conservative merchants in a Southern town toward an unconventional traveling musician than to any other representation of the Bacchantes. The other test consists in examining whether an invented or superimposed actor can be considered by dint of his function as equivalent of an actor or actors in the standard myth. In Giraudoux's *Electre* the gardener creates no problem in this respect; although his fanciful discourses make him the mouthpiece of Giraudoux in the play and although he is not yet Electre's husband, he fulfills in the play the functions attributed by Euripides to the ploughman. But what about the beggar, a pure invention of Giraudoux, capable through his absurd intuitiveness of predicting the moment when a person declares himself, becomes himself, takes charge of his destiny? It would be too easy to say he corresponds to the chorus; at any rate, there are other secondary characters in the play who substitute for the chorus. However, the beggar shares an important function with the Corypheus in Aeschylus' *Choephori:* the truly maieutic function he fulfills as he elicits from Electra and Orestes the secrets of what is to follow. In *Mourning Becomes Electra,* this maieutic function belongs to Seth, the gardener, who plumbs the depths of all that is hidden in the hearts of the members of the Mannon tribe. Thus the function of Giraudoux's *beggar* is taken over in O'Neill's text by the *gardener,* who is, however, neither the betrothed nor the husband of Lavinia, the Electra in this play; Lavinia's fiancé is Peter, a childhood friend. In the intertextuality of the various versions a system of transfers can be seen to operate and to preserve the essential functions. What guarantees theatrical success, however, is the individuation and embodying of a function in a novel and unexpected character.

Certain actantial enrichments are due, no longer to the transformation of one character into another, but of an idea or a symbol into a character. In Cocteau's *Orphée,* death appears as an impressively efficient lady surgeon dressed in a laboratory coat and escorted by two assistants. In Anouilh's *Eurydice* death is also physically embodied, this time by a stranger in a raincoat whom Orpheus met on his way and who introduces himself as Mr. Henry. In both cases the presence of death is visually manifest so as to help along the expression of a mythologem through a mytheme which is the very mytheme of the classical story reactualized. In Cocteau's play, in which everything is *poésie de théâtre* and functions allegorically, Eurydice must die; the poet must be severed from an aspect of his own self before reunification of self is possible at a more sublimated level. Death counts, therefore, among the helpers (*adjuvants*), despite her very temporary collaboration with the wicked Aglaonice (the most perfidious embodiment of the shepherd Aristeus!); the resolution of the crisis involves a passage through death, but the end is in a manner quite opposite to that which Aglaonice had planned. In Anouilh's play, Mr. Henry is linked with the mytheme in which "Orpheus, by looking back, kills Eurydice a second time." Does this mean that death, as represented by Mr. Henry, is among the opponent forces? In order to answer adequately one would have to retrace the history of the *respectus* in relation to death through various periods and cultural outlooks.[11] In summary, though it is true that in Virgil's and Ovid's versions—whether the backward glance is motivated by a lapse into madness or by defiance of the gods of the underworld—the kingdom of death differs radically from that of life, Anouilh tenders an invitation to death, by endowing death with a friendly countenance and by inverting its traditional role. Anouilh is by no means the only modern artist in whose vision such a reversal takes place (Kokoschka in *Orpheus und Eurydike* provides another example); but the obsession with "purity" is specific to Anouilh and gives infinite value to death as opposed to life by casting a static and idealized image of Eurydice into the immutable mold, and the domain, of death.

These examples suffice to show that the transformation is a relational process, and that relations occur according to functions rather than according to symbolizations once and for all determined in the past. The concept of function is assuredly one of the key concepts we are seeking, since, necessarily, individual functional expressions correspond to the mythical function in man's imagination in general, while at the same time each of these individual expressions is capable of entering into the same global system. Through a function we can see the unfolding of the process that Northrop Frye calls "displacement," and which in some cases is coextensive with literary invention itself. Thus there exists in *Mourning Becomes Electra* a striking physical resemblance among all the members of the Mannon family, a kind of mask that becomes more forceful and compelling as each Mannon espouses his individual destiny. By dint of this literary strategy O'Neill adopts and emphasizes the motif of the accursed blood that weighs upon the household of Mannon as it did upon that of Atreus: the *fatum* of the Ancients, and in modern, and more specifically Freudian terms, guilt. In the Mannon family the motif of resemblance is the external and eminently theatrical manifestation of the guilt that dwells in the very blood of the Atreides.

Again the transformation which we are discussing, and the accompanying aesthetic realization, can have a symbol as its locus. Thus the sacrificial robe in which Clytemnestra traps Agamemnon in Aeschylus' play and which is then used by Electra and Orestes to kill Aegisthus becomes, among the Mannons, the family tool for suicide and murder: the gun, which in function is identical to Agamemnon's ritual robe.

Even the use of scenic space can be locus and occasion of renewal: in Tennessee Williams's *Orpheus Descending* the underworld is *above* the ordinary world represented by the confectionery store; in Kokoschka's *Orpheus und Eurydike* Hades is both a character and a place.

Last but by no means least, the locus of transformation and aesthetic realization can be the writer's vision impregnating the narrative structure. Here one could mention the psychologizing process that the myth of Electra and the myth of Antigone, among others, undergo in modern literature, as they evolve further and further from their religious and ethical origins. Perhaps the most striking example of distancing from the classical story, which nevertheless achieves unity with it, is the complete and radical reversal which Jean-Paul Sartre imposes on the story of Orestes in *The Flies*, since he illustrates his contempt of liberty by the very hero who was once, and long remained, the personification of nonliberty.

Aeschylus in his trilogy emphasizes the dependence of man and even of the gods themselves upon the laws of justice. Even if it takes several generations man must learn by suffering that crime must be punished and, more positively, that justice must be achieved. At the end of the trilogy it is implied that Orestes has atoned sufficiently for the crimes of the house of Atreus and that he might eventually be released. Athene declares him free of the blood-guilt. But the exercise of his freed will can only occur in Argos once again, within the laws of his city; Orestes vanishes so that his personal fate can be fulfilled in the collective peace that is now restored. Nothing could therefore be more different from the *Eumenides* of Aeschylus than Sartre's *Les Mouches* with its abhorrence for the acceptance of any guilt whatsoever. Electre, despite her earlier resistance to the morality imposed by Aegisthus upon the people of Argos, seems ready in the second act to give in to the Eumenides, symbolized by the flies. "Je suis libre, Electre. La liberté a fondu sur moi comme la foudre."[12] Electre, on the other hand, feels her past weighing upon her and determining her future: "Peux-tu empêcher que nous soyons pour toujours les assassins de notre mère?"[13] Orestes' reply is of course a manifesto of existentialist freedom pronounced in circumstances which Sartre has taken over from the trilogy, but to which he gives an opposite meaning. Orestes has assumed his act, taken it upon himself; he recognizes himself in it: "Crois-tu que je voudrais l'empêcher? J'ai fait *mon* acte, Electre, et cet acte était bon. Je le porterai sur mes épaules ... et j'en rendrai compte. Et plus il sera lourd à porter, plus je me réjouirai, car ma liberté, c'est lui."[14] Where Aeschylus had seen the unfathomable ways of fate to which man could only conform, at the cost of sufferings such as those of Electra and Orestes, Sartre's Oreste finds in the conquest of freedom the strength to rejoice in the very harshness of suffering. Whether we consider fate in the ontological manner of the Greeks or in the psychological manner of Racine, whose characters know that their fate is within and that it is an inner flaw that delivers them up to destiny ("Je me livre en aveugle au destin qui m'entraîne," says Orestes in *Andromaque*), the concept of fate, wherever it occurs, contradicts man's responsibility for the conduct of his life. Is not Sartre's Orestes, then, "unfaithful" to the myth? And why did Sartre choose, in order to give the most dramatic expression to the moral imperative of self-liberation, the very myth that had previously embodied unfreedom? Precisely because the reversal, the radical transformation, was bound to carry signification additional to the message of freedom, though related to it. By his choice Sartre attracts attention to the fact that it is precisely Orestes, traditional victim of fate, who now becomes the carrier of freedom. It has been said that Sartre may have used the mythological cover of the story of Orestes for the message of liberty as a cover against censorship by the German occupants. This explains the choice of *a* myth, but why precisely *this* myth? In my view it is because Sartre wishes to stress and polarize the extreme distance between his own Orestes and Aeschylus' Orestes. Mythology is a code. What is original and aesthetically satisfying, so that the spectator is most likely to perceive and receive it, is the very divergence from the classical story, the extreme tension within the familiar.

These are but a few examples of transformations of Greek myth in modern drama, along various categories of paths. They show the interdependence of that which endures (a pattern of functional relations) and that which changes (the actantial, or scenographic, or symbolical, or ideological translation, to which stylistic translation should be added in further studies); and this interdependence always rests upon a new pact between an author and a spectator according to a "horizon of expectation" and a given historical conjuncture. Every work is defined both by what it preserves and what it transforms, in an admixture unique to itself.

We have insisted, within the framework of our subject, upon paradigmatic relations established by a myth among a series of theatrical works. It was not our intention to reduce these dramatic texts to sets of relations but to indicate how each text becomes unique so that we may read it syntagmatically, as a very distinct phrase among others within the concert of literature.

Notes

1. Paris: Lettres modernes, 1965.
2. Cf. Proceedings of the Congress of the Société française de littérature générale et comparée, on Mythes, Images, Représentations, Université de Limoges, May 1977 (in press).
3. Raymond Trousson, *Un problème de littérature comparée: les études de thèmes, essai de méthodologie* (Paris, 1965), p. 92.
4. Gilbert Highet, *The Classical Tradition* (New York and London, 1949), p. 520.
5. Cf. Eva Kushner, *Le mythe d'Orphée dans la littérature française contemporaine* (Paris, 1961). I regard this book as an example of the kind of incomplete thematology that is under discussion here.
6. Trousson, p. 91.
7. J. Piaget, *Le Structuralisme*, collection *Que sais-je?* (Paris, 1968), p. 78.
8. This is the position taken by Professor Philippe Sellier, Université de Paris V, at the congress mentioned in note 2 above.
9. In *Anatomy of Criticism* (Princeton, 1957).
10. *Refractions: Essays in Comparative Literature (New York, 1966), p. 112.*
11. Kushner, chapter 1.
12. Jean-Paul Sartre, *Huis-Clos; Los mouches* (Paris, 1971), p. 163.
13. Ibid.
14. Ibid.

John B. Vickery

LITERARY CRITICISM AND MYTH: ANGLO-AMERICAN CRITICS

Ten years ago I brought together a number of the most significant and representative essays by contemporary scholars on literature and myth.[1] The aim was to provide a conspectus of views on the theories of myth current in literary circles and on the methods and problems of myth criticism. For a number of years readers and critics had been struck by and were calling attention to the connections between literary texts and ancient myths; some responded with interest and approbation, others with disbelief and vituperation. Yet, as with most civil wars, no one seemed to understand what all the scrapping was about or what precisely were the issues on which debate might fruitfully be joined. Since myth criticism was also becoming popular among students, it seemed even more important that incipient critics start thinking closely about definitions of myth, how myths enter literature, what roles they may have in specific works, whether they affect all or only some works, what connection they have with critical evaluation, and related questions. So far as I can tell, most people seem to feel that the effort was a valuable one and the collection both informative and provocative concerning contemporary theories and practices of myth criticism.

But now the situation is somewhat different. Around the 1950s a burgeoning of interest in myth as central to literature and criticism took place. As a result, many bathed in burning fountains while pursuing the quest for myth, in which they might find themselves with an older, more unified, mythic consciousness. Heroes bore a thousand faces, while gods wore masks to be pierced or at least scrutinized, and both were found to populate more literary works and more unexpected ones than had been dreamt of before. Now, however, the initial pioneering has been done, and the primary task becomes the extremely difficult one of consolidation and amplification of gains already achieved. Efforts in this direction seem to crystallize around two points: the need to refine the theoretical and methodological principles of myth criticism, and the importance of exploring in greater depth the roles of myth in particular genres and periods.

The purpose of this retrospective glance is to suggest that in the past decades we have both come a long way and have scarcely moved an inch, that our questions and approaches are more aware and sophisticated, and that our understanding is still fitful at best and confused or uncertain at worst. Such a paradoxical situation is scarcely unique in critical and scholarly circles; indeed, one can argue that such a development is not only inevitable but salutary. It marks the dropping away of spurious issues, the increased self-awareness of methodologies, and the concomitant recognition of the complexities inherent in asking questions, framing answers, and formulating theories. Advances in criticism, as in many other things, apparently consist as much of increased awareness as of alteration of objects or entities. Though it would doubtless be difficult to prove, I think that myth criticism is better today than a decade ago largely for the reasons mentioned. In addition, it has gained in direct proportion to its decline in amount or quantity and its movement away from the position it once occupied of critical fad. Yet it would be a serious mistake—one that would play directly into the hands of its opponents—to suggest that this improvement or refinement is not already evident in at least prototypical fashion in the work presented in *Myth and Literature*.

Since I have been asked to comment on its contents here and to offer some observations on the different perspectives and modes of myth criticism, perhaps it will be well to focus on those issues that are most obvious—both in themselves and for the development of the subject—so that they can be sharpened for future thinking about this critical enterprise. For simplicity's sake, these matters may be gathered under three headings: basic intellectual attitudes, postulates, and methodological traits. The first of these encompasses the view that myth criticism derives from historical Romanticism with its convictions of transcendental realities, diffuse religiosities, and symbolic or esoteric interpretations of verbal and existential realities. The most vociferous advocate of this view in *Myth and Literature* is Philip Rahv, though Wallace Douglas also makes the connection and finds a number of correlations between Nietzsche's *The Birth of Tragedy* and modern myth critics. Rahv's position on this point, and he is selected merely as a representative instance, consists of two ostensibly related claims. The first is that "the idea of myth has been invested in literary discourse with all sorts of intriguing suggestions of holiness and sacramental significance" so that "one can talk about it as if it were almost the same thing as religion, thus circumventing the all-too-definite and perhaps embarrassing demands of orthodoxy even while enjoying an emotional rapport with it."[2] The second facet of Rahv's polemic is that Romanticism continues to appeal to the modern mind because of "its enormous resourcefulness in accommodating the neo-primitivistic urge that pervades our culture, in providing it with objects of nostalgia upon which to fasten and haunting forms of the past that it can fill with its own content"; Romanticism, he feels, contains a "vision of the lost unities and simplicities of times past."[3]

In essence, his objections come down to charges of intellectual evasiveness or dishonesty, in the case of the myth-religion alignment, and of failure of nerve and psychic regression, in the case of myth's "revival of romantic longings and attitudes."[4] Insofar as he is accurately identifying a cultural tendency in certain writers and critics in the late 1940s and early 1950s, there is little to quarrel with in his first charge. As Douglas documents, a number of absurd and extravagant claims were made by some on behalf of myth, which was believed to be about to issue in a critical millennium and cultural salvation. Much of this was, of course, more a matter of the exuberant rhetoric attendant upon novelty than an issue of deep-seated and clearly apprehended belief or conviction. That is to say, the bulk of it was literary talk, a notoriously protean not to say chimerical commodity. The critical problem here, apart from Rahv's rather humorless polemical tone, is that this exposure of what he aptly calls "the cultism of myth" quickly ceases to be an exercise in critical discrimination and becomes instead an ideological attack with political, philosophical, and religious implications. In short, the critical baby is thrown out along with the cultic bathwater. Yet this is the crucial issue; for the serious myth critic, such as those represented in *Myth and Literature*, is neither evasive nor dishonest, no matter how mistaken he may be in interpretation or how simplistic in methodology. He is rather, as Philip Wheelwright suggests, trying to take seriously metaphor and literary meanings as a language with a sense and structure that are both determinable and translatable into the language of criticism.[5] It is for these reasons, and others, that I think Rahv's first charge is not pertinent to myth criticism.

Similarly, his argument from origins is vitiated by two flaws. First, to link modern literary interest in myths to the protracted influence of Romanticism does not in itself condemn that interest, any more than Rahv's passionate avowal of the importance of history is dismissible on the grounds of its derivation from the philosophy of Hegel with its assertory metaphysics and indefensible logic. Both are, or may be, facts of history, and their relationship (myth-Romanticism; history-Hegel) is intrinsically worth studying for the knowledge to be gained. Or so one would think, unless the study of history as distinct from the living of it is as culturally regressive as the exploration of myth. Second, to identify Romanticism with neoprimitivistic urges, nostalgic longings, and visions of lost unities and simplicities is to judge without adduced evidence and to pronounce guilt by association. It is, in brief, to flee history not through esoteric or archaic myth but via a contemporary stereotype that fixes a temporal period of great flux and complexity in what Eliot called "a formulated phrase." It may be that this characterization of the appeal of Romanticism is correct, though I am more than a trifle inclined to doubt it. But whether so or not, it is clear that we need more than one map of misreading, given the evident dangers of misjudging our topography of literary and cultural history.

Other attitudes frequently held to be relevant to the so-called myth criticism are held by those who argue that it is unhistorical or even antihistorical, and those who insist that its study or practice calls for a particular philosophical position. The first charge is made most vigorously in *Myth and Literature* by, again, Philip Rahv, but it is one that a number of others have raised in one way or another almost since its practitioners were dubbed a "school." Here again there are essentially two facets to the criticism; one is a matter of methodology, the other of motivation. For Mr. Rahv the basic concern is that the modern intellectual's interest in myth is due to a fear of history, by which he means a "fear of the hazards of freedom."[6] But by history it is clear that he means the present, the modern world, which for him is marked essentially by changes that are both enormous and fast as well as virtually ununderstandable and uncontrollable. This is scarcely the place to debate or explore in detail the nature and characteristics of the modern world. Yet one can speculate that the upsurge of change as a historical phenomenon may be more illusory than we are ordinarily inclined to think. Just possibly it is a function of increased personal and cultural self-awareness as a result of technological overlap and multiplied communication resources, which seem to annihilate time by destroying space. And we may even grant, as I think we are in honesty bound to do, that Rahv is correct insofar as some intellectuals (and nonintellectuals too for that matter) do find the world around them disquieting and even threatening. As a result, they may seek a more stable and psychically secure existence through a variety of mental adjustments ranging from myth, yoga, the Constitution, fortress America, benevolent father figures, cultural brotherhood, and World Federalism to Transcendental Meditation and vegetarianism. In doing so, however, they are one with mankind generally, including Rahv, in generating for themselves methods of coping with, comprehending, and enduring the present and the world they inhabit.

The difference between "mythicists" and Rahv is that they take as operative concepts and perhaps as heuristic devices the notions of myth and ritual, while he seizes upon ideas like dialectical freedom and objective history. His criticism of the former indicates two things. One is that he is unwilling to endorse a critical policy of free choice being contingent on paying one's money (or value equivalent). And the second is that his approach is not so much historical as it is moral or evaluative. "Myth-fixity-conservative" predilections are bad and to be eschewed; "history-flux-radical" are good and to be embraced.[7] The interesting thing about this, apart from both the questionable validity of the dichotomy and the correctness of the judgment and recommendation, is that it reveals quite clearly that Rahv's interest in history does not extend to its method. Close and extended study of the dynamics and development of the modern interest in myth in conjunction with literature is rejected in favor of doctrinaire reductions in the scope of history as a subject. In short, the method implicit in the argument is not so much historical as rhetorical and ideological.

The common charge often leveled against myth criticism, that it is unhistorical in its method, is a more serious one, but ultimately no less answerable. The real focus of the problem lies in two related matters. The first is the lack of a critical language or syntax for dealing with issues involving myth and literature. Too often as a result, the early critics who attempted the task wrote in terms of identifications, quasi-allegorical equations, and other essentialist locutions. The result was that major and significant differences between the mythic patterns or schema and specific texts were apparently ignored. Osiris as he appears in Egyptian religious texts and as he is presented in *Finnegans Wake*, say, was, or so the critics' language suggested, one and the same. To the extent that some critics intended or accepted the consequences of their essentialist language, they were unhistorical in that their speech habits showed them to be asserting temporally impossible statements. Most, however, were guilty only of flawed, because unrefined, uses of language. And this, as in any critical methodological and linguistic lapse, can be remedied. Indeed, if a critical method were to be indicted and abandoned because some practitioners made statements that were historically inaccurate or impossible, then even those consciously espousing the historical method itself would be culpable and the method jeopardized.

The second question with a central bearing on the problem is the nature of the mythic method and its relation to historical perspectives. Here we have to recognize that the two methods are not so contradictory as complementary. They embody differences in emphasis and demand of the critic distinct acts of attention. Given the extensive attention directed in recent years to the nature of history and the problem of its method, it would be impossible to pursue the matter to anything resembling a definitive conclusion.[8] Indeed, it is precisely a detailed and sustained exploration of the possibilities inherent in both critical methods that one might hope would soon engage the attention of interested persons. To differentiate myth and history or to delineate their interrelationships may be an impossible task, but to develop a theory that would specify compatible assumptions, laws of inference, criteria of evidence, and the like for mythic and historical methods looks much more manageable if contemporary techniques of theory construction are to be believed.

In the meantime, a few simple observations are possible and perhaps pertinent. One is that the historical method operates in terms of temporal progression, causation, and cultural context, whereas the mythic method is concerned with comparative structures, functions, and individual complexes of traits or qualities.[9] The important thing about these characterizations is not their rudeness but their interdependence. Thus a historical critic may place *Paradise Lost* in its historical milieu, compare it with other Renaissance and classical epics, assert the resemblances to be due in some measure at least to the impingement of the earlier on the later author, and still endeavor to say something about the distinctive features of *Paradise Lost*. Similarly, a myth critic may compare the structure of works or characters with a common quality (as in Stanford's *The Ulysses Theme* or Galinsky's *The Herakles Theme*) and may differentiate the function of the motif in the works.[10] At the same time he may study the influence of the earlier upon the later or of the importance for a particular author of contemporary works using myth. Instances of these would be such investigations as *Ulysses'* effect on *The Waste Land* or John Barth's awareness of the mythopoeic bent of Yeats, Eliot, Mann, and Joyce in his shaping of *Giles Goat-Boy* and *Chimera*. That is to say, these traits singled out for each method are not mutually exclusive. What they do essentially is delimit the kinds of questions each is interested in asking and the kinds of answers each is prepared to accept. Only when the questions are the same and the answers contradictory are the methods irreconcilable. Differing answers may result from different questions, from ostensibly similar but actually insufficiently delimited and precise questions, or from the same questions. In the first two instances, no conflicts are possible between the two methods, and in the last case, they are more likely to occur between adherents of one method rather than between advocates of the two methods, and this only when the critic claims exclusive and fundamental correctness for his formulation.

From this it is clear that the ostensible conflict between mythic and historical methods derives from two essential misunderstandings. One is a matter of logic and revolves largely around critics' misconstruing the function and implications of the law of contradiction and the means of establishing logical truth. While it is not logically possible to affirm simultaneously that "x is a" and "x is not a," it is quite possible to affirm "x is a" and "x is b" so long as the value of b is not $-a$. And in neither sense are the assigned values (or meaning, if you prefer) of these terms identical. Similarly, the logical establishment of the truth of a proposition is not a matter of proving the proposition but of establishing that the denial of its contradictory is valid. Consequently, a historical critic talking about the form of *The Faerie Queene* in terms of Renaissance literary and intellectual traditions and conventions and a myth critic discussing the same work as shaped by the formal requirements of congruence with a mythic model are not contradicting one another, since each is making but one of many possible statements about the work.

This brings us to the second misunderstanding, which is a question of language choice and the confusing of syntactic exclusion with ontological denial. Some years ago R.S. Crane showed us how criticism possesses a variety of languages in which to couch its perceptions and urged that as critics we be aware of which language it is that we are electing and of the implications of that choice. But because critics, like other human beings, speak out of passions and perceptions and attitudes rather than out of a rigorous concern for the parameters of a theory and the sorts of statements logically possible in the chosen kind of discourse, their utterances linguistically resemble a composite of several languages, a kind of conceptual cross between pidgin English and the verbal resources of *Finnegans Wake,* a critical speaking with tongues as it were. As a result, the purported selection of a critical method (which is usually more of an inclination or a disposition than a rational choice) rarely entails the actual use of a language wholly congruent with the method.

Yet even if critics sought, in neopositivist fashion, to formulate artificial or ideal languages that would accord with the assumptions, axioms, and rules of inference of each method, a problem would remain. (Though the failures or limited successes of such constructions in philosophy suggest caution, an attempt by critical theorists to work out the range of possible kinds of statements available to any method nevertheless seems an interesting and productive activity if only so that we might clarify the difficulties involved, such as the logical limitations of the enterprise.) That is, assuming that critics grew more aware either by logical or empirical means of the nature and impurities of their language, they would still have to face the implications and nonimplications of that choice. There is a curious phenomenon of literary criticism that extends also into such ancillary pursuits as reviewing, editorial choices, and manuscript appraising. It is that so many persons appear to assume that a critic's making of a certain set of statements entails a denial of the value or ontological existence referred to in other statements that are conceivable or possible but not uttered. In other words, to use either historical or mythical language (that is, language congruent with the historical or mythical methods) is not to deny the possibility of using the other. The use of one entails only the nonuse of the other. And even this is true only insofar as the two are construed as distinct, though complementary, rather than as logically interrelatable. In point of fact, the two languages may be used either singly or together, for both are subject to the same laws of linguistics and logic, though as one

would naturally suspect, the use of both together is a more difficult undertaking since variables, rules of syntax, and other factors
compound the chances of error. Nevertheless, it is clear that
mythic criticism is not inherently unhistorical, though like a formalism of any persuasion (philological, contextual, phenomenological, or structural) it may opt in any given instance not to make
historical statements. As Stanley Hyman pointed out some years
ago, because it "does not claim to be a theory of ultimate significance, but a method of study in terms of specific significance, it
can cohabit happily with a great many other approaches."[11]

From this last point, it follows that the suggestion, made by
Hyman as well as Richard Chase and others, that myth criticism
requires a particular philosophical position is quite erroneous.
Neither the "rational materialism" advocated by Hyman, the pragmatic naturalism stressed by Chase, nor the neo-Kantian idealism
that Bidney finds in back of Northrop Frye and Philip Wheelwright is essential to their writing myth criticism, though their
metaphysical or philosophical positions may indeed influence the
tone and emphasis of that criticism. The arguments against align-
ing this critical mode with a specific philosophical ambience are
several. First, it is unnecessary; the possibility of writing such
criticism is not dependent upon any metaphysical position consciously held, much less a particular one. The evidence for this
lies in the existence of such criticism written from a variety of
positions. Materialists, empiricists, idealists, and undecideds all
produce myth criticism of differing emphasis but equivalent quality. Second, while a writer's language may presuppose and even
imply a particular metaphysics, the opposite is difficult to insist
upon empirically or observationally. A metaphysics does not entail
a particular language or method for literary criticism. (This may be
due, as some would argue, to the lack of rigor or precision in
critical thought or language. Another possibility is that what metaphysics entails is not so much a particular language as a set, one or
more instances, of nonuses—that is, refrainments from using—of
particular languages. Such a set's limiting role would not, however, produce the single possibility required for a necessitarian
argument.) Indeed, what is most striking in this connection about
the twenty-odd essays of practical criticism in Part 3 of *Myth and
Literature* is precisely the impossibility of determining the philosophical positions of their authors or even whether they have any
such consciously articulated positions.

The second major area of essential issues for myth criticism is that revolving around the presumed postulates upon which its critics develop their arguments. The three principal points raised here over the years are: first, that myth critics identify myth and literature; second, that myth is regarded as a particular form of knowledge, a kind of philosophy, a repository of esoteric or transcendental wisdom; and third, that the presence of myth in literature confers a special value and preternatural power or mana on those instances of its occurrence. In each case, two aspects figure: first, whether historically myth critics have made these assumptions attributed to them; and second, whether they need logically make such assumptions in order to infer from them a viable theory of myth criticism and to practice such a critical mode. On the basis of the essays in *Myth and Literature* alone, it is clear that critics have, at least ostensibly, in some instances adopted such postulates. For instance, in his essay on *Finnegans Wake*, Marvin Magalaner remarks that "James Joyce had greater need than most writers to construct for himself a myth which would offer some degree of stability in a disintegrating modern world."[12] At the same time, in the course of indentifying some of the mythic and legendary materials used by Joyce, he makes it clear that he also regards that work as a novel, thereby developing an at least implicit equation of myth and literature. The same kind of identification is suggested by John Hart's remark that "as one way of reexamining *The Red Badge of Courage*, we would want to read it as myth and symbolic action,"[13] and John Lydenberg's assertion concerning William Faulkner's "The Bear" that "the story is essentially a nature myth."[14] The most unequivocal assertion in this regard is that of Richard Chase who says flatly: "Myth is narrative or poetic literature."[15]

The relationships between myth and literature are far too complicated to be developed in adequate detail here. But it is possible to suggest that this identification at the very least appears to contradict our ordinary understanding of the word "literature." Insofar as anthropologists, classicists, comparative religionists, and field-trained psychologists agree on anything, they seem to converge on the conviction that myths are sacred tales usually about gods, that they entail the teller's or celebrator's belief in the objective reality of the story's narrative, and that they are the product of communal and therefore anonymous authorship.[16] But clearly each of these characteristics is at odds with our notion of the nature of literature and its cultural role, for on the most literal level it as a whole is neither sacred, believed, nor anonymous. For this reason, if for no other, the equating of myth and literature is, in one sense, not only erroneous but critically misleading and dangerous.

Yet if some critics have made such an identification, others, such as Stanley Edgar Hyman, David Bidney, Philip Rahv, and Northrop Frye, have not. The implication is clear: the identification is not necessary to myth criticism or its theories, for if it were, their work would not have been possible. What this conclusion actually raises is less the correctness of the issue than the actuality or reality of it. That is to say, it is true that many critics, including those we mentioned earlier, have talked as though they identify myth and literature. But while technically imprecise and inaccurate in handling those two protean words, such a use appears more a rhetorical and suasive device than an ontological assertion. While we need not agree completely with the thrust of his argument, we can nevertheless feel the validity of Douglas's observation that "in general, 'myth' seems to be less an analytical than a polemical term, calling attention rather to a critic's mood or moral attitude than to observed facts under discussion."[17] A more charitable view might suggest that this use of "myth," while vague and ill-defined, is functionally deliberately so, arising out of the critic's (and indeed any writer's) need for terms that are loosely encompassing and semantically connective rather than referential and whose function is to maintain syntactic movement instead of semiotic definition.[18] One danger of sowing terms like "myth" and "mythic" in a cavalier and broadside manner through critical articles is indeed the generation and proliferation of confusion about concepts and entities. But a much greater danger is the production of stylistic inanition and imaginative complacency in the critic and fatigued boredom and indifference in the reader.

The second issue of a postulational order is that which holds, as Richard Chase puts it, "that myth is philosophy—that it is a system of metaphysical or symbolic thought, that it is a theology, a body of dogma, or a world-view."[19] Chase, Hyman, and Rahv all insist vehemently that such a postulate is erroneous and productive of intellectual inflation and critical excesses, which are ultimately self-defeating because impossible of fulfillment and thereby stultifying. And in a general sense they would seem to be right, at least in that not all myths of a particular culture, much less all the myths of all cultures, are of this order. One thing is clear both from the later work of Northrop Frye on the literary side, and on the anthropological, from the studies of two, to take but two, such representative and differing authorities as Melville Herskovits and Cliffort Geertz. This is that myth is not propositional, it does not make assertions, either true or false. Yet it is equally undeniable that all myths—at least in their verbal form—employ declarative statements and so *seem* to possess assertory power. It was this fact together with the conviction that myths coud be explained in essentialist terms and univocal meanings assigned that led to such things as the solar theories of mythology in the mid-nineteenth century and vegetation theories such as those of Mannhardt and Frazer.

With this we are in a position to see that the real issue implicit in the affirmation or denial of this postulate is linguistic and functional or contextual rather than ontological or empirical. Myth may not be philosophy but it may be philosophical; it may not be a system of symbolic thought but it may be a symbolizing activity. In the former case, its family resemblance (as the Wittgensteinians would say) is with the likes of Plato's *Dialogues, Thus Spake Zarathustra,* and the anecdotes of Zen Buddhism. In the latter instance it has affinities with poems, novels, paintings, and all the other art forms. Myth, on one level, is a story about story-telling.[20] As a result, its function is interpretive of entities and relationships and of the linguistic forms in which they are couched, such as image, metaphor, and narrative. But its interpretative technique and premises are not those of facticity but of perspective, not those of declarative absolutes but of expressive capacities and ranges of relevance. So seen, myth emerges less as something that does or does not "contain" abstract thought or symbolic referents, whether explicit or tacit, than as something susceptible to and eliciting conceptual interpretation, which itself is couched in expressive terms. Consequently, remarks like that of Chase cited above or Hyman's observation that myth "neither means nor explains anything" do not call for assent or denial.[21] They call for interpretation or qualification, since in some measure they are misconstruing the issue or problem, though admittedly for largely unexceptionable historical reasons. As Hyman makes clear, the rejection of philosophy or symbolic thought in myths is actually a disclaimer directed at what he calls "the worst excesses of speculative research," by which he means the learned but eccentric ingenuities of Robert Graves, Flavia Anderson, and others like Desirée Hirst and assorted mages and spiritualists.[22]

The key issues raised by Chase and Hyman are those of "system" and explanatory meaning, but these as they stand in their original formulations are not quite to the point, though in different ways. Any acquaintance whatsoever with specific collections of myths reveals that they do not constitute systems—though they are possessed of differing degrees of coherence as a group—but that at least some purport to be explanatory, though today we are inclined for a variety of reasons to reject them as true or adequate. What may be systematic are the sundry accounts of the significance of myths, whether anthropological, philological, psychological, or chimerical in character. And what is pertinent is the function of these systematic explanations, or rather the discriminating among possible explanations and the determining of which function is operative in which explanation. Such a catholic strategy renders Chase's strictures inoperative, for it locates the systematic (at least the explicitly so) where it actively exists, namely, in the allegorical activity of the critic or commentator or explainer, not in the texts themselves.[23]

At the same time, it frees us of the necessity—implicit in Hyman's rejection of explanatory meaning—of running a censor bureau for intellectual research efforts. That is, even the zanier treatments of myth may fulfill a human need and hence a function. From Jacob Bryant and Richard Payne Knight to Robert Graves and D.H. Lawrence, we are continually struck by the fascination resident in improbable hypotheses and evidentiary leaps of faith and by the diminishment of rage and fear over these views with the passage of time. The sifting of history is more than adequate for the discrimination of theories and interpretations and needs no real help from time- and culture-bound individuals, though, of course, the position just sketched also dictates that we leave these last free to pursue their strictures if they so desire. All that is required is that we recognize the results as belonging to the genre of the jeremiad rather than that of criticism.

We can do so with equanimity when we realize that the explanatory meaning with which Hyman is concerned is for myth and myth criticism both more complex and also less an issue than ordinarily thought. For if myth is a story and an interpretive perspective, it would seem to follow that it (and myth criticism too) operates on a model far different from that regularly attached to it. The generally accepted model is that of precise empirical observation, codified in laboratory report descriptions of observed particulars, and operative equally, though differently, in Freud's view of Oedipus, Malinowski's view of Trobriand myths, and Kerényi's sense of Prometheus. Yet the pertinent model for myth and myth criticism (as well as many other intellectual enterprises) may well be something like that of literature itself and expressive forms in general with their devices of allusion, image, metaphor, symbol, irony and their attitude of constructing, rendering, representing, and entertaining for specific purposes and limited scopes.[24] The scholar who remarked that the gist of Plato lies in his having added "in a sense" to all Sophist arguments and texts was saying something very much to our purposes here. Myth and myth criticism function by subscribing "in a sense" to the story told and the comments on it. In a very interesting and suggestive sentence, Clifford Geertz recently observed that "any expressive form works (when it works) by disarranging semantic contexts in such a way that properties conventionally ascribed to certain things are unconventionally ascribed to others, which are then seen to possess them."[25] Assuming what seems difficult to deny—at least linguistically—that myth and myth criticism may both be "expressive form," it would follow that their role or function is the purposive disarranging of semantic contexts in order to effectively bring out features of their subject that otherwise would be obscured. In this event, the difference between them would be, of course, that myth is an implicit, mediate disarrangement and myth criticism an explicit, immediate one.

If we now ask ourselves why activities such as myth criticism are pursued, we find ourselves simultaneously confessing ignorance and murmuring about the discovery and elucidation of values. It is the latter that constitutes the final postulate frequently ascribed to myth criticism. Most baldly it is equated with the conviction that, as Rahv put it, "to identify a mythic pattern in a novel or poem is tantamount to disclosing its merit."[26] One cannot deny that some critics, particularly in the first wash of enthusiasm for myth criticism, certainly wrote as if they thought this to be true. All one can say is that if they did indeed think this and were not merely engaging in exuberant professional rhetoric; they were both wrong and insufficiently acquainted with the effusions of, say, R.C. Trevelyan, Alfred Noyes, Charles Mackay, Edmund Gosse, and others of the same order scattered throughout the history of literature. Thus we can say with Haskell Block that "no method or combination of methods can mean anything in the hands of those who are insensitive or indifferent to art."[27] But this, while tempting, shifts the problem back into the region of individual psychology and personal taste and sensibility. It threatens to dismiss critics whose failure is not so much personal incapacity as it is a category mistake or inferential lapse. Preferable perhaps is to acknowledge the relevance of Gilbert Ryle's remark that intelligent theory always holds out the possibility of unintelligent practices.

The pertinence of this approach is that it allows us to improve the practices of myth criticism by clarifying its theoretical base. Central in this effort is the elimination of the equating of literary value with mythic patterns. The reasons for this extend beyond the mere demands of efficiency and expediency. They also involve the factual and logical. If we equate literary merit and mythic pattern, logically we have to do one of two things. Either we have to approve works that in fact we cannot approve, or we have to adjudge certain works nonliterary because no mythic pattern is discernible. And as a secondary issue there is the problem of quantifying the measure or extent of "mythicness" possessed by various works in order to determine the extent of their merit. But if Northrop Frye is correct, as I think he is, in suggesting that myth is a structural principle of literature, then there are no literary works unrelated to myth.[28] Clearly what is called for is a working out of the nature and kinds of relationship obtaining between: (1) the class or classes of specific myths, (2) the concept of myth as a structural principle, (3) literature as a class of verbal constructs, and (4) specific literary works. Obviously this is an ambitious undertaking and one that may well prove impossible. Yet what is important is that such an activity would mark a shift from axiological or evaluative issues to methodological and taxonomic ones. "Value," like formal cause for the physicist, would be neither invoked nor explored, so that attention could be focused on other explanatory ends and designs. One such would be the reconciliation of what some people today call "high" literature with popular or folk literatures, so that a common critical grammar might be developed.

The question of structure touched on above suggests a curious fact about the criticisms of approaching literature by attending to myth. This fact is the existence of a sharp disjunction between the strictures placed on its intellectual attitudes and postulates, on the one hand, and its method on the other. The former are stigmatized as vague, diffuse, and imprecise, while the latter is castigated for its rigidity and arbitrariness. In examining the former, I have been at pains to distinguish between adventitious and logically essential beliefs and postulates and to suggest that the former are relevant only to the history of myth criticism and not to its theory, which is, or should be, concerned with issues of logical necessity.

The same emphasis is called for in connection with methodological issues, though here greater attention to reformulation and clarification of techniques and strategies may be called for.

Whether all or the majority of myth critics employ the same method is difficult to say, but there seems no doubt in the minds of many that certain uniform methodological traits are determinable and are of a negative order. In the main, the criticisms of the use of myth in literary interpretations are four in number. First, the method involves an arbitrary imposition of a pattern found in myth on works of literature. Second, the method entails an indifference to and a disregard for the uniqueness of individual works. Third, it exaggerates the role of and so misuses analogy in the interpretive effort. Finally, it ignores, distorts, and otherwise violates historical facts and pays little or insufficient attention to the kinds of evidence relevant to determining the presence of mythic dimensions in literary works. That all of these may be justified with regard to a particular piece of myth criticism goes without saying, just as the common strictures made of historical, formalist, or psychological criticism hold for certain instances. But what is of real concern is whether these assertions describe errors or inherent and inevitable features of myth criticism. The former are correctable or avoidable; the latter are not, and their reality would render the approach suspect for all save the hopelessly eccentric. It is my contention that these strictures do not speak to anything inherent in the critical mode but are based on lapses in practice and misunderstanding of vital concepts and of the nature of interpretation itself.

The first charge consists of two related complaints: one, that the pattern is imposed from without, from an area or discipne other than literature; and second, that its application is arbitrary rather than inevitable or necessary. Two questions may help us to get at the central issues of the first complaint: is the pattern externally imposed in fact? and if it is, is this unusual or inevitable? The first question leads us into very complex historical and formal issues that would take a volume or several to unravel. Put most succinctly, it raises the issues of origins and definition. A number of scholars, including Ernst Cassirer, point out that in the history or prehistory of human culture myth precedes "high" or formal literature, but that the latter is one of the cultural forms deriving from or emerging out of myth by a process of functional self-clarification. In other words, the distinction between myth and literature may be a matter of degree rather than of kind. It may be a matter of temporal degree in that the two become differentiable only at a particular point, period, or stage in history. Or it may be a case of social status or cultural evaluation and awareness, in that myth is regarded as sacred and literature as secular, and that literature becomes aware of itself as literature only when it recognizes its differences from myth.

Now if myth and literature do have essentially this kind of historical relationship, is it reasonable to assert that the patterns of the former are "imposed" on the latter by one mode of literary criticism? Or is it more appropriate to say that the structural forms of the one are carried over into the other but with the inevitable alterations in their nature that time, medium, function, and role play in all such human situations? In short, the patterns in literature discernible to the critical intelligence bear a family resemblance to those in myth, so that the relationship between them is not so much of imposition as of association. To the extent that the critic does impose the patterns of myth on the text before him he is participating in a common enough and, indeed, an inevitable activity.[29] Critics draw patterns or frameworks from history, philosophy, psychology, theology, sociology, and politics, to mention only the obvious ones, on the grounds of historical influence, cultural diffusion, philosophical truth, pragmatic relevance, or structural resemblance. And depending on the skill, wit, daring, logic, and ingenuity of the critic, the results are applauded or hooted, accepted or rejected. The same opportunity is logically available (or should be) to the myth critic.

In other words, the term "imposition' itself is the troublemaker so long as it is allowed to carry a quasi-authoritarian association instead of an inferential or implicative one. The latter recognizes that the choice of pattern is postulational and the application a matter of drawing the conclusions possible from the pattern elected. In one sense, all critical structures or patterns are "imposed" from without, even those that purport to use something called the language of literature itself. Terms like character, theme, action, plot, image, belief, convention are often thought to guarantee the autonomous, literary-based character of a critical mode. Yet they themselves occur as part of many, many other nonliterary patterns or frameworks including the existential one of ordinary everyday living. It is a moot point as to whether such terms originated in literary or nonliterary discourse, but while the particular answer may somewhat alter the problem—as to, say, whether literature is being regarded existentially or existence literarily—the dichotomy in any case remains between forms and uses of discourse. Insofar as myth is not literature, a mythic pattern is external to literature, but then so is every other critical pattern employed. Though the use of such patterns, conceptual structures, or terminological constellations may be impositional in the negative sense and hence arbitrary, they need not be. The arbitrariness that is unacceptable is the result of willful rejection or obliviousness to the canons of logical and historical possibility, as when one tries to argue that James Thomson's *The Seasons* influenced *Beowulf* or the *Aeneid*. The arbitrariness that is acceptable follows from the recognition that a choice among a plurality of patterns is implicit in the act of criticism and the use of language.

About all that one can say is that given the closeness of the presumed origins of myth and literature, the use of the patterns of the former in connection with the latter seems to possess greater inherent reasonableness and viability than the applications of patterns from other areas more remote from literature, such as political thought. And if one looks closely at specific myths and specific literary works, it is possible to find oneself perplexed as to which is which. Even the most casual glance at the tales in Herskovitz's *Dahomean Narrative* or Radin's *The Trickster* and those in Jerome Rothenberg's *Technicians of the Sacred* leaves us uncertain as to which we want to define as myths and which as literature. This suggests that formally at any rate, if not in terms of historical knowledge and scholarship, at least some myths may be indistinguishable from and hence classifiable as literature using that term in its broadest sense to include so-called popular manifestations. If that is so, then it is difficult to see how the critical use or application of a pattern found in myths indistinguishable from literature to works of literature indistinguishable from myths is a case of imposition, much less arbitrariness.

The second of the charges made against the method of myth criticism is that it ignores the individuality and uniqueness of the literary work. Haskell Block formulates the matter clearly when he says: "A good deal of literary anthropology takes no account of the uniqueness of individual works of art, or indeed, of the fact that the value of a work of art transcends its documentary function. The mere presence of anthropological material in a novel, play, or poem does not help us differentiate between masterpieces and drivel."[30] And more specifically we have Charles Moorman's detailed animadversion on Heinrich Zimmer's approach to *Sir Gawain and the Green Knight* by way of the archetype of death and rebirth: "While no one would deny that the poem involves testing and initiation, it is difficult to understand in reading Zimmer's analysis just how this general statement of theme, applicable surely to a great many myths, is entirely and consistently relevant to a particularly finished and beautifully articulated fourteenth-century poem."[31] Zimmer, Moorman complains, focuses more on the myth pattern's appearance in the poem's sources than on the poem itself. Hence, he concludes:

> In short, Zimmer refuses to deal with the poem on its own terms; if Morgan le Fay, or if anything else for that matter, does not fit in with the myth and the archetype, then it is denounced as a late addition or put down as an example of the poet's failure to understand the myth involved, and so done away with as irrelevant to the proper study of the poem. This, it seems to me, is to underestimate gravely the skill, the understanding, and the intent of the poet and, worse than this, to ignore completely the literary qualities and the integrity of the text itself.[32]

Moorman's strictures are cogent and, as we see from his remarks concerning John Speirs's reading of the same poem, identify a danger of which the myth critic must always be aware. This danger, however, is not pertinent only to one critical mode; it bears directly and immediately on every method that utilizes the concept of a model or paradigm.

Yet as Moorman himself goes on both to argue and to demonstrate in the remainder of his essay, it is possible for the myth critic to use the models he locates in myth to identify the distinctive traits and combination of traits in specific works. As he succinctly observes:

> The critic can thus use myth both as a point of entrance and as a means of analysis; myth becomes (1) a means of coming directly and with dispatch to the structural and thematic core of a literary work and (2) a yard-stick by which the critic can measure the uses to which the poet puts the myth in terms of a specific metaphor and theme. In short, having discovered the myth core of a piece of literature, the critic must go on to examine in their own right the other literary aspects of the work, most of which he will find to be determined by the central archetype.[33]

That this method is more than mere wishful thinking is demonstrated both by Moorman's own essay and others in *Myth and Literature*. One instance is Charles Eckert's careful effort to reveal the initiatory paradigm in the *Odyssey* and also to show how Homer functionally departs from the mythic paradigm, a departure that he suggests is "the product of a shift from seeing traditional story as a sequence of acts to be understood in the context of ritual, to seeing the story as a general paradigm from which many meanings may be derived."[34] Or there is Herbert Weisinger's treatment of Shakespeare's tragedies, which is almost exclusively devoted to assessing the varying extent to which individual plays realize the pattern of myth as amended by the needs of tragedy as an art form. Countless other examples attest to the fact that Moorman's proposal about the methodology of myth criticism is not idle theory and speculation.

It is curious in view of the evidence that such a stricture should have so long persisted as a critical commonplace. The explanation may lie both in the notion of models and also in the lack of clarity as to the methodology of myth criticism on the part of many of its practitioners.[35] The role of models is greater or at least more explicit in disciplines such as psychology and sociology, so that its function and effect are better understood there than by literary critics. In literary matters models tend for a variety of reasons to be associated with sterile copying of originals in response to cultural mandates of varying weights; hence the critical equivalent is taken to be the imposing of an outmoded, foreign, and distorting grid upon a helpless victim. The model of a model in critical circles appears unfortunately to be a cookie-cutter rather than a telescope or microscope. The function of a model is to provide a structure, a set of related elements or features in which the relationships are as significant as the elements, whose structuring role may stimulate those examining fresh, different, or hitherto unexamined, that is, unanalyzed, entities, situations, or texts to recognize a structure with elements or relationships *similar* (not identical) in some sense to those possessed by the model. The aim of this activity of model study is not, as some seem to think, to discover the nonexistent but to provide an implicit conspectus of features to be attended to, of questions to be asked, and of answers to be accepted. It is in short an eliminative but not an annihilatory device for perception and discourse, a methodological strategy for focusing by sorting and ordering in accord with something more than unaided intuition.[36] Because critics, both mythic and nonmythic, have been uncertain as to the role of models in their activity, they have tended to behave as though the model was doing something it was not actually performing. Some myth critics endorsed the model because after all it was their cookie-cutter and the shapes produced were in a sense their creation. Some non-myth critics sought to destroy the model because they wanted gingerbread men, not cookies. Between these two positions there is little to choose, but fortunately with a clear grasp of the aim and function of the concept of a model, such a decision is unnecessary.

This vagueness and uncertainty about models contributes also, I believe, to the third criticism of the method of myth criticism, namely, that it relies upon analogy almost to the total exclusion of other modes of argument and reasoning. When Block says that "too often, anthropological criticism has substituted the discovery of analogies for the examination of artistic structures,"[37] he reflects the feeling of many readers from R.S. Crane to the present. But he does something else as well, something worth attending to. At least implicitly, his sentence distinguishes between two activities—analogy-finding and structure study—and finds them mutually exclusive. Surely, however, this is not the case. Clearly framing analogies need not involve attending to literary texts, and engaging in literary criticism need not entail the perceiving of and the use of analogies, though I think many would be surprised at how often analogy figures prominently and even centrally in the critic's thinking and argument. But that they are logically compatible is certain.

What Block is getting at here is really the question of the ontological status of critical statements. If we postulate an objective nature for artistic structures and a defined terminology and an understood syntax for the critic's language, it is often thought that resulting declarative statements possess something called facticity and descriptive accuracy. In a curious fashion, the truth of the statement gets mixed up with the reality of the attributes, so that furious arguments result over such matters as whether *Death of a Salesman* really is a tragedy. Yet the fact of the matter is that the critic's statements are basically interpretive, not factual, and inferential, not descriptive, with the result that their "truth" is social rather than scientific, logical rather than empirical. Once it is recognized that the assertory weight of critical statements is lighter than those of literal propositions, we are in a better position to appreciate the role of analogy and its relation to the concept of a model in the method of myth criticism.

The commonest view of analogy's role in myth criticism (and indeed of analogy's nature generally) is that enunciated by R.S. Crane in the course of discussing the critical suggestion that the death of a character in Conrad's *Victory* is an expiation ritual. He says:

> We are stating, in short, not a relationship of effect to cause, but of like to like—that is, of analogy merely; our proposition is a kind of proportional metaphor in which, because of the parity of relations we perceive between the parts of the incident in *Victory* and the parts of the ritual, we transfer to the incident the words, and their connotations, which anthropologists have employed to state the significance of the ritual.[38]

So far as it goes, this is instructive, but its limitations are ones that go to the very heart of an understanding of analogy as a methodological principle in myth criticism. It is true that anthropology or comparative religion or psychology or some synoptic metavariant of all may suggest interpretive significance not as readily apparent by examination of the text alone. But then so does history or philosophy or art history or literature itself, and it is no more a part of the method of the former than it is of the latter in critical contexts merely to "transfer" words, connotations, and significance from the one intellectual realm to another. Rather, as I remarked some years ago about myth criticism in particular, though the notion applies to virtually all criticism, it espouses "the necessity of extraliterary knowledge for the critic while reserving the right to adapt that knowledge in accord with the needs of literary study."[39]

It is true that the critical act of attention may involve the drawing of analogies between distinct sets of material, and it is also true that the effectiveness of the perception depends on whether the analogies are superficial or fundamental. For as logicians have known for a very long time, everything is similar to every other thing in at least some respect. Because the character of the analogies noted is central, a testing or verification procedure is usually employed. Thus the perception of similarities between a myth or myths and a literary text's imagery, themes, structure, or cultural role has led to such conclusions as that the similarities are due to the constancy of the mind's modes of functioning, to the historical transmission and cultural diffusion of the one to the other, or to the operation of some such conceptual postulate as racial memory. Such conclusions are admittedly not experimentally verifiable, but that does not nullify their interpretive significance, however much it may qualify it. By bringing the available historical and psychological evidence to bear on the conclusion, the critic can determine whether he has a postulate that is strongly, moderately, or weakly defensible. And in point of fact that is what has historically happened to the three explanatory conclusions mentioned above; each has been adjudged evidentially limited and less than universally referential. As a result, now critics are in a position to weigh these postulates' explanatory power against their defensibility in order to determine their inclusion or exclusion from the critical system underlying their individual efforts. The striking thing about these premature postulates of myth criticism is that they all are historical or factual, or at least presuppose and encourage such a context for validation, and they all utilize concepts or entities for explanation that lie outside the original areas of inquiry and resemblance, namely, myth and literature. None attempts a formal or logical formulation of the resemblance such that the immediate, particular, or quasi-empirical statements of the critic may be systematized into a theory that determines the methodology of myth criticism. And yet such an approach appears to be not only the most obvious means of avoiding problems already encountered but also the most potentially productive for the ongoing critical enterprise.

Why this tack was not adopted at the outset is puzzling, though the passage cited above from Crane affords some clues. Part of the reason may be the habituation of critics to the model of causal explanation.[40] Another and even more significant reason may be the assumption that the method of myth criticism consists of analogical argument exclusively.[41] Certainly this assumption appears implicitly to underlie Crane's remarks. These suggest that once the initial relationship is noticed, the interpretive argument concerning the significance of the literary text in question is merely read off the mythic ·or anthropological side of the equation. Actually, myth criticism's method only commences with the perception of analogy, which, as has been suggested, generates the need for a postulate or set of postulates. This in turn serves as the implicative basis for an interpretive method. To obviate the problems occasioned either by knowledge inclining to contradict or weaken the postulates mentioned earlier as historically entertained by myth critics or by the lack of sufficient information to endorse such postulates, it follows that the patterns of myth have to be nonextraneous to literature. One course is to identify myth and literature, but this we have seen is impossible to sustain without a greater measure of semantic disarrangement than is productive. A preferable alternative is to treat myth and literature not as historical entities, as antecedent and consequent, though indeed they may have that relation historically, but as formal structures related by virtue of myth's being the structural principle of literature. Such, I take it, is the central thrust of the later theoretical or integrative work of Northrop Frye, most notably in *Anatomy of Criticism*, certain of the essays in *The Stubborn Structure*, and more recently in *The Secular Scripture*. Rather than summarize or elaborate on it, I shall explore what I take to be the methodological consequences and implications of regarding myth in this way.

The first result of this formulation is that the myth critic no longer needs to treat his interpretive remarks as analogies correlating unrelated sets of material. Instead his method at this point, after the initial perception of resemblance—which is an instance of analogical recognition—becomes homologous. It is directed to the examination of correspondences in *structure* between a particular literary work and a myth or myths or portions of myths, or among several works of literature in terms of the structure of a myth or myths. The first of these is what we ordinarily think of as myth criticism, while the latter moves in the direction of genre criticism, thereby suggesting both the continuity and the unity of criticism in general. It is important in this context to emphasize that the structural congruence may involve more than a single myth and also less than the complete myth or myths; it may also, if the critic's conscious purpose dictates, involve a metamyth or idealized pattern of the sort that we find Weisinger and Campbell referring to or of the sort that *The Golden Bough* implicitly develops under such famous rubrics as the dying and reviving god. What is important is that the critic keep clearly in mind the materials being examined for homologous relations, for the interpretive remarks possible will vary in scope and character, depending on whether the paradigmatic materials of myth are single or multiple, and actual or artificial.

In the actual process of identifying the homologous relations, the critic is also likely to be asking or entertaining functional and possibly motivational questions as well. But for methodological simplification and clarity it is probably better to regard these issues as constituting a separate level of investigative discourse. It is also an essential level if myth criticism is to avoid the methodological flaws that issue in the charges that it disregards the literary work's unique individuality and is reductive in intent and effect. For assuming the critic has identified and noted the homologous relationships between such a mythic figure as the scapegoat and characters in literature such as Euripides' Pentheus, Strindberg's Libotz, and Faulkner's Joe Christmas, he has now to consider functional issues pertinent to the individual work, literary tradition, and culture of which it is a representative instance. The structural model of myth and ritual may determine the majority of critical questions asked at this juncture, but the answers will be in terms of the literary work's individual imaginal design, character alignment and representation, thematic conspectus, narrative movement, and the like. The homologous relationships noted generate in conjunction with the scapegoat model such paradigmatic questions as why these particular characters were chosen as scapegoats, what communal sins they are to remove, what form or forms their suffering and expulsion take, what attitude to the model is implicit in the work, and what cultural conventions contribute to these and other determinations that constitute the individual literary structure. In the answering of these questions, the myth critic magically shakes off his Mr. Hyde-like accoutrements and appears as Dr. Jekyll trying earnestly to penetrate the same mystery of human personality and its products as all other literary critics who essay different methods and espouse different systems.

The fact that the myth critic does function in much of his work in a manner common to all critics suggests the logical response to the fourth and final methodological challenge leveled at him. To those who say myth criticism ignores or distorts historical and other evidence in interpreting texts, we can point out that this is scarcely applicable as a methodological issue. Not to use certain kinds of evidence even where available is a decision based on the kinds of questions being asked. So that to ask nonhistorical questions precludes the necessity of using historical arguments. At the same time, this formalist dimension of the enterprise does not rule out the critic's exploration of the historical dimension of myth criticism any more than it does in any other species of formalism. The involvement in historical questions and the resultant use of its evidence is an operational determination made by the critic in the light of his interests, convictions, skills, and other criteria. Whether these criteria meet the metacriteria for theoretical adequacy is a valid inquiry, but not one that bears on the performative level of the enterprise qua criticism. To raise such issues is to inquire into the coherence, completeness, and validity of the individual's theory of criticism implicit in the performance. Similarly, to place strictures upon the evidence adduced is to question or challenge the performance as realized; it does not speak to the possibilities or inherent capacities of the method itself. And that the method of myth criticism has the capabilities of answering the questions it asks follows from the fact that it, like all other species of criticism, is generated from a quasi-logical, paradigmatic model in which questions and answers are ordered in accordance with an inferential structure that precludes the possibility of irrelevant though not of mistaken answers issuing from its instigative questions. And for more than that myth criticism neither wishes nor has a right to ask.

Notes

1. *Myth and Literature*, ed. John B. Vickery (Lincoln, 1966), p. 390. Bison ed., 1969.
2. Philip Rahv, "The Myth and the Powerhouse," in *Myth and Literature*, p. 110.
3. Ibid.
4. Ibid.
5. Philip Wheelwright, "Notes on Mythopoeia," in *Myth and Literature*, p. 66.
6. "The Myth and the Powerhouse," p. 117.
7. This type of argument readily lends itself to the analyses of emotive ethics first demonstrated in detail by C.L. Stevenson, *Ethics and Language* (New Haven, 1944).
8. Some of the relevant works whose arguments and insights need application to the problems of literary history and critical theory are: Morton G. White, *Foundations of Historical Knowledge* (New York, 1065); *Theories of History*, ed. Patrick Gardiner (Glencoe, Ill., 1959); William Dray, *Laws and Explanation in History* (Oxford, 1957); *Philosophy and History*, ed. S. Hook (New York, 1963); Isaiah Berlin, *Historical Inevitability* (London, 1954); Patrick Gardiner, *The Nature of Historical Explanation* (Oxford, 1952); M. Mandlebaum, *The Problem of Historical Knowledge* (New York, 1938); M.G. Murphey, *Our Knowledge of the Historical Past* (New York, 1973); A.C. Danto, *Analytical Philosophy of History* (Cambridge, 1968); W.B. Gallie, *Philosophy and the Historical Understanding* (New York, 1964); F.J. Teggart, *Theory and Processes of History* (Berkeley, 1960); H. Fain, *Between Philosophy and History* (Princeton, 1970).
9. I use "cause" or "causation" here to cover the scholarly interpretive statements of historians in order to point up the difference in emphasis between the two methods and to suggest what many regard as the historical enterprise. On the problems of causal explanation in history, see White, *Foundations*, chapter 4. N.R. Hanson, *Perception and Discovery* (San Francisco, 1969), p. 280, suggests that "explanation" is preferable to "cause" as a translation and concept even in the case of Aristotle.
10. Neither of these works is usually equated with what we ordinarily think of as

myth criticism. This attitude may, however, be as much a function of the limitations of our casual or conventional assumptions as of anything else. In any event, they exemplify the kind of topic to which such criticism is appropriate. Though she does not focus on a single figure or motif, a good instance of what I would call thematic myth criticism is Lillian Feder's *Ancient Myth in Modern Poetry.*

11. Stanley Edgar Hyman, "The Ritual of Myth and the Mythic," in *Myth and Literature,* p. 51.
12. "The Myth of Man: Joyce's 'Finnegans Wake,' " in *Myth and Literature,* p. 201.
13. " 'The Red Badge of Courage' as Myth and Symbol," in *Myth and Literature,* p. 221.
14. "Nature Myth in Faulkner's 'The Bear,' " in *Myth and Literature,* p. 257.
15. "Notes on the Study of Myth," in *Myth and Literature,* p. 70.
16. This last point is not meant to reject the point made by Clyde Kluckhohn and others that certain myths may originate in an individual's dreams, fantasies, or habit formations. It only emphasizes that when recognized or accepted as myths, these tales are bereft of individual, identifiable authors. To the extent that they are linked with an author, it turns out to be an individual functioning either as a scholar or compiler (Apollodorus) or as a creative artist (Sophocles, Ovid), neither of whom is the originator of the tale. As Reuben Brower, "Visual and Verbal Translation of Myth: Neptune in Virgil, Rubens, Dryden," in *Myth, Symbol, and Culture,* ed. C. Geertz (New York, 1971), p. 155, astutely remarked, "There are no myths, only versions . . . only texts for interpretation."
17. Wallace W. Douglas, "The Meaning of 'Myth' in Modern Criticism," in *Myth and Literature,* p. 127.
18. If we adopt a philosophical position of semantical realism, "myth" in this use may be a theoretical concept marked by "openness" or "surplus meaning" following from indeterminate definitions. See R. Tuomela, *Theoretical Concepts* (Vienna, 1973), pp. 93, 118–19.
19. "Notes on the Study of Myth," p. 68; italics omitted.
20. This notion is developed in greater detail in my " 'The Centaur': Myth, History, and Narrative," *Modern Fiction Studies* 20 (1974): 29–43.
21. "The Ritual of Myth," p. 54.
22. Ibid. Cf. B. Malinowski, *Magic, Science and Religion* (New York, 1955), p. 101.
23. "Allegorical" is used here in Northrop Frye's sense. See *Anatomy of Criticism* (Princeton, 1957), pp. 89–90. The assertion does not entail adoption of an affective stylistics theory such as Stanley Fish, *Self-Consuming Artifacts* (Berkeley, 1972), pp. 383–427, has developed.
24. Cf. Tuomela's remark: "Aspects of reality can in general be 'modelled' and represented in indefinitely many ways. Different ways of representing result in different formulations of theories and this often affects the meanings of concepts. A certain representation of an aspect of reality may be semantically clearer than another one." *Theoretical Concepts,* p. 127.
25. "Deep Play: Notes on the Balinese Cockfight," in *Myth, Symbol, and Culture,* p. 26.
26. "The Myth and the Powerhouse," p. 118.
27. "Cultural Anthropology and Contemporary Literary Criticism," in *Myth and Literature,* p. 136.

28. *The Stubborn Structure* (Ithaca, 1970), p. 18.
29. To speak in terms of such impositions, either affirmatively or negatively, is, of course, to oversimplify grossly. On problems of observation, fact, and theory-laden language, see N.R. Hanson, *Patterns of Discovery* (Cambridge, 1958), chapters 1 and 2, and *Perception and Discovery*, chapters 10, 11, and 18.
30. "Cultural Anthropology," p. 136.
31. Charles Moorman, "Myth and Medieval Literature: 'Sir Gawain and the Green Knight,'" in *Myth and Literature*, p. 172.
32. Ibid. In fairness to Zimmer it should perhaps be pointed out that his central interest is with psychological issues, which preempts a sharp, detailed focus on matters vital to the literary critic.
33. Ibid., p. 186.
34. "Initiatory Motifs in the Story of Telemachus," in *Myth and Literature*, p. 169.
35. The concept of models is closely bound up with mathematics, symbolic logic, and philosophy of science. See, for example, A. Robinson, *Introduction to Model Theory* (Amsterdam, 1963); H. Blalock, *Theory Construction* (Englewood Cliffs, N.J., 1969); R.B. Braithwaite, *Scientific Explanation* (Cambridge, Eng., 1953); I. Scheffler, *The Anatomy of Inquiry* (New York, 1963).
36. Cf. Hanson's remark, *Perception and Discovery*, p. 217: "The facts are what our hypotheses call to our attention. Our questions determine, to a large extent, what will count as answers."
37. "Cultural Anthropology," p. 155.
38. *The Languages of Criticism and the Structure of Poetry* (Toronto, 1953), p. 128.
39. *Myth and Literature*, p. x.
40. For a succinct discussion of possible modes of reasoning, see P. Achinstein, *Law and Explanation* (Oxford, 1971), pp. 110–41.
41. Cf. Achinstein, pp. 132–33, 153–55.

Klaus Weissenberger

MYTHOPOESIS IN GERMAN LITERARY CRITICISM

In order to give a meaningful account of the treatment of mythopoesis in German literary criticism, which could result in tentative guidelines toward a deeper understanding of this central aspect of poetry, it is necessary to grasp the problem in its entirety. As the very concept indicates, mythopoesis is based on the synergetic interplay and reciprocal relationship between the principles of literature and myth. However, with respect to the specific quality of this relationship, due to the holistic character of literature and its resultant autonomy, myth can be realized only as a literary category—that is, in a literary function—with respect to mythopoesis. This fundamental aspect of our problem has been, however, for the most part neglected by modern scholarship.

This situation has been brought about in part by myth scholarship itself, which is drawn from the most various academic disciplines; yet another reason lies in the fact that almost all myths have come to us in their literary form only. The result was that even nonliterary hermeneutics of myth pretended to be genuine literary criticism, and in many cases its findings were not transformed into literary categories. This led to the present confusion about the concept of mythopoesis, for which one has to blame the Romantic hermeneutics that founded modern myth scholarship; for, despite its pioneering discoveries, it did not carry out its scholarship on myth and mythopoesis for purely scholarly reasons, but rather for epistemological self-justification. Since then, the "intentional fallacy" generated by the Romantic outlook has burdened and dis-

I am especially indebted to James Rolleston for his assistance in improving the English translation.

torted the concept of myth, because scholars, without being aware of it, confused categories and obscured definitions.

The dilemma of current myth scholarship and consequently of the understanding of mythopoesis can be seen in the various volumes of collected essays on this subject that have appeared during the past ten years; they consist in most cases of a compilation of articles from the various disciplines and lack an overriding concept that would be binding for all. Some do not attempt to establish such a concept; others subsume the essays under a questionable one.[1] On the other hand, due to the lack of understanding of mythopoesis, various interpretations of individual authors and their works treating the problem of myth are based on the erroneous assumption that they can do justice to this problem from their limited perspective. In contrast to these, there are so far only a few investigations that are based on a purely literary concept of myth and from which one can expect to derive a definition of mythopoesis and a clarification of the contradictory theories.

The strong criticism of Romantic myth scholarship is primarily directed against its subsequent exploitation and falsification, which was achieved by unscrupulously ignoring its premises. For in principle, Romantic myth scholarship represents the historical-etiological method of investigation, which, by way of the "hermeneutic cycle," makes it possible to investigate the historical concept of myth and its development; and the main merit of Romantic myth scholarship lies in the fact that such differing sciences as classics, religious science, ethnology, psychology, cultural anthropology, and philosophy all derive their myth theories from the Romantic ones. However, it is precisely these sciences which have reduced literature to a reservoir of evidence in order to document their nonliterary theories.

Using the autonomy of the literary work of art as a point of departure, it has become now the task of literary criticism to convert the historical-etiological aspect of myth, in all the modes of concretization discovered and yet to be discovered by the different scientific branches of myth scholarship, into a morphopoetic concept of myth. Mythopoesis can be related to the corresponding levels of the literary work of art only on the basis of this methodological approach. Accordingly, it is the intention of this investigation to derive criteria for the analysis and evaluation of the various contributions to German myth hermeneutics and especially mythopoesis from a model-like definition, which can lay claim to universal validity; such criteria can, it is hoped, provide a basis for future scholarship.

The definition of myth given by Wellek and Warren may serve as a point of departure, since it is not affected by the German tradition and therefore can be considered as an "objective" locus of discussion. Wellek and Warren speak about the peculiar nature of a myth, "if its authorship is forgotten, not generally known, or at any event unimportant to its validation—if it has been accepted by the community, has received the 'consent of the faithful.' "[2] This definition presupposes the concretization of myth in a specific phenomenological mode of presentation and relates it to a functional level, which must have the quality of universal validity.

With the few exceptions of the dance or the rite, the only level of concretization of myth still accessible today is the literary one; it is therefore constituted by the polarity of form and content (*Gehalt*) inherent in literature. In contrast, myth presents itself on the functional level as an ontological totality, by declaring its claim to universal validity through dimensions that exceed spatial and temporal limits; this claim is confirmed and realized by deploying literary means. Such could have been the original relation between myth and poetry at a time when the latter was still occupying a subordinate role to the former; in the course of the secularization of myth and the emancipation of literature from it, this relation must have reversed itself, for at this point literature makes use of myth, strives to be effective on the functional level of myth, or creates new myths. This affinity of literature for myth is based on the ontological universalism of the functional level of myth, which constitutes the substantive basis for the formalistic claim of literature to autonomy.

From these preliminary considerations one has to conclude that a definitive understanding of mythopoesis can necessarily be achieved only from a model of literary myth. In pursuing this goal, the analysis and evaluation of the previous scholarship serves to clarify the critic's understanding of his own approach and helps not only to uncover basic fallacies, but to continue promising approaches as well.

THE HISTORICAL-ETIOLOGICAL MYTH HERMENEUTICS

Romantic Myth Scholarship

As already mentioned, the beginnings of an independent myth hermeneutics and a corresponding understanding of mythopoesis are to be found in Romanticism. The basically historical-etiological character of Romantic myth scholarship is caused by the state of research of that time, which, on one hand, consisted of collecting and evaluating the myths, and, on the other, made inevitable the use of Greek mythology as model. However, the historical-etiological character was obscured by some of the Romantic assumptions that operated on the functional level of myth, but this characteristic became evident again later after these assumptions had become obsolete. For epistemological reasons, Romanticism could maintain the claim of myth to totality on the functional level only by "sublimating" the reality factor in a polarity between logically verifiable actuality and man's cosmic context. The subsequent countermovement has led to a reverse claim of totality for the reality factor itself and has again made obvious the historical-etiological character of this myth concept.

The veneration of myth, so characteristic of Romanticism, is not based primarily on a subordination of the objective-empirical mind to a subjective-mythical one but rather on a separation into the two areas of cognition and experience. Although due to this fact the reality content of myth appears relative and subjective, it nevertheless remains unchallenged and can expand to encompass dimensions of the collective and historical by way of the genetic derivation of myth from the original proximity of man to nature preserved by the individual in his imagination and fantasy. Thus the myth-creating imagination is related directly to the priests' caste or to the original classes of society and is derived from the historical development of a nation or from the "divine" origin of all mankind. In this case, the creation of myths takes place with the "inevitability and lawfulness of a 'natural' instinct,"[3] due to its placement in the subconscious.

The dominance of transcendental mythical truth over the empirical manifests itself in the historicotheological aspect of myth. This is possible because it obtains general metaphysical-religious traits by way of its historicometaphysical interpretation and in turn imposes the quality of relativity and dependence on historical reality. The creation of myths is shifted into the prehistorical beginnings of man and is interpreted as the primal relevation of the divine, as well as the expression of the self-renewing revelation of the divine at all times in history. This corresponds to the historicometaphysical derivation of myth from nature as natural poesy, since nature is considered in the Romantic natural philosophy to be an emanation of the divine, so that nature and not man has to be considered the creator of myth. This theory is corroborated by the empirical-historical fact that the analogies of myths among all nations can be explained only by a collective unconscious, a fact that has led in some instances even to postulating a primal myth.

Myth, however, is not only the object of the divine but also the manifestation of the divine, and it therefore combines in a metaphysical-religious sense the personification of the power that animates and inspires all of nature with the concept of the "eternal harmony and security, full of love and mercy" (Ziegler, p. 577).

In this self-contained philosophical-religious system, the understanding of the level of myth's aesthetic concretization undergoes a specific development. Although the Romantics were aware of the essentially symbolic character of myth, they did not interpret it as being exclusively literary, but rather subordinated it to their eschatological intentions; the understanding of literature and art was based on these intentions, so that the "intentional fallacy," which underlies all the Romantic myth scholarship, became prevalent also in this respect.

Friedrich Schelling was the first to proclaim the intrinsic affinity between the mythic and the aesthetic as an inevitable consequence and confirmation of his pantheistic nature philosophy. In his *Philosophie der Kunst* (Philosophy of Art, 1802), he "constructed" the universe along aesthetic lines by labeling the gods of mythology as the artistic manifestations of absolute ideas and by declaring the gods therefore to be the primary and dominant subject of all art. By defining the absolute as manifesting itself in reality through a total indifference toward the distinction between the universal and specific, Schelling derived the necessary truth that the presentation of the absolute in mythology can be only symbolical. Thus a direct mythic quality is attributed to the literary symbol, and for the first time its structure is equated with a primarily emotionally and irrationally structured imagery; this view became prevalent for the entire Romantic aesthetics from Creuzer, Kanne, and Grimm to Bachofen, and it has also experienced a revival in the twentieth century.

Friedrich Creuzer already implies the correlation between the mythic and the aesthetic with the title of his major work, *Symbolik und Mythologie der alten Völker* (Symbolism and Mythology of the Ancient Peoples, 1810–12). Even though his myth hermeneutics had become outdated during his own lifetime—for example, his conviction that the earliest stage of myth is embodied in the symbol, which the priests' caste then used to organize the myth—he nevertheless recognized the emblematic power that connects the mythic and the aesthetic and, viewing myth as a legendary explication of the symbol, considered the joining of form and content to be an intrinsic and fundamental criterion of myth. Arnold Kanne, in comparison, has to be considered much more penetrating in his ideas; on the basis of his eschatological concept of history, he attempts to reconcile speculative myth theories with historical-empirical myth scholarship. Kanne postulates a protomyth, which manifests its historical reality as well as the presentation and realization of the absolute idea in a protolanguage. In the mythical "name word," the divine *pneuma* and the phonological shape, the latter inspired anew by the former each time, unite and constitute a symbolic form; its mythical content and meaning become evident in its phonetic realization. Kanne utilized this concept as a starting point to develop his etymological mythology, which, although it lacks the scientific foundation of Grimm's subsequent *Deutsche Grammatik* (German Grammar), already contains results vital for literary mythopoesis. The structure, relating all words in a poem to each other by creating the lyrical *Ineinander* (interplay) or by constituting in a less self-contained form the unity of the epos or the drama, is based on the identity of form and content (*Gehalt*) already postulated by Kanne; he deduces this identity from an original unity derived on speculative grounds, which realizes itself anew each time. If one excludes Kanne's soteriological-eschatological interpretation of myth, this process has remained the basic principle of post-Kantian idealistic aesthetics and manifests itself as literary poesis in each literary work of art.[4]

Arnold Kanne has been unjustly forgotten, for he represents the crosspoint of the two schools of Romantic myth scholarship. Although Jakob Grimm later on discards Kanne's etymological postulations of an original language as not philological, he nevertheless was inspired by Kanne's mythological concept of history and language. Still in reference to Kanne, Grimm refers to the "(revealed) proto-language," the "general language," the "general mythology";[5] however, he considers the protohistory of man not to be accessible to scientific investigation, just as the protohistorical "Adam is removed from our sorrow as well as from our joy" (p. 84). The "divine truth," however, can be grasped in the myths and epics of a nation, since in them myth (equal to legend) and history form a union as the divine and earthly aspect of man or as divine and historical truth.[6] With this, Jakob Grimm too refers to the two-sidedness of myth. However, he regards the idea and the fact of a myth as related to each other; they should not be separated from each other because they contribute to the necessary historical development toward freedom (*Kleine Schriften,* 4:85). Grimm regards the nation as the bearer of myths and the creator of the epics that convey the myths, for in a nation the divine and general nature of man coincides with the human and individual one; this explains why Grimm interprets the Romantic *natural poesy* as *national poesy.*

This mythicizing of the nation, and especially of the German nation, represents for Grimm the "consolation of history," since because of the "community and identity with the past people" (p. 75) a nation can become aware of the divine part of its human nature; however, this interpretation of a nation, when translated into an organic world view, served as the pseudoreligious basis for the national-socialistic racial theory. Yet, on the other end of the spectrum of myth hermeneutics, Grimm's myth theory served for André Jolles as the point of departure for his morphological analysis of the *Mythe* as a poetological form.

Johann Jakob Bachofen completes the Romantic contribution to literary mythopoesis by expanding the concept of myth to include its ethnological and anthropological component. The naiveté and absence of qualifications with which Bachofen deduces the historical development of mankind from myth, starting from barbaric social forms and moving through matriarchy to patriarchy, is based on his speculative theory about gynecocracy as the paradisal stage of mankind or as the poesy of history. However, his theory is founded factually on symbolism, especially the tomb symbolism as it is handed down in myth as the exegesis thereof. In myth, history and religion united to form the cultic origin of human existence, which for Bachofen is characterized by the maternal being the all-embracing principle. Bachofen's contribution to the understanding of literary mythopoesis can be seen in the interaction of content and form in his myth concept. The transposition of the creation of symbol and myth into the subconscious and collective and their connection to metaphysical, religious, and ethical values coincide on the formal level with the primarily sensual— and therefore holistic—perception and comprehension of symbol and myth; thereby a quality of inevitability and a character of universal validity is attributed to them, which is rationally incomprehensible and can be reconstructed only emotionally. This corresponds with the aesthetic intention to express, through the suprapersonal (*überpersönlich*) and extrapersonal (*ausserpersönlich*) quality of symbol and art, the claim of universal validity of the literary work of art and its resultant autonomy.

However, Romanticism was still far away from such an application of its myth theory to aesthetics. Instead, Richard Wagner and Friedrich Nietzsche gave it a turn that allowed the subsequent transfer of Romantic myth concept to the social-political level and the rooting of it in a nationalistic-racial subsoil. Wagner's glorification of myth in the *Gesamtkunstwerk* (total work of art), which has its negative correlative in a direct antihistoricism and a criticism of civilization, has as its goal to demonstrate the elements of salvation that distinguish the mythic through its organic foundation in the collective, extra-, and suprapersonal totality of a nation's community. This veneration has the effect that the interpretation of myth—and of all genuine religion and art—is transfered from a cognitive understanding of the physical world to the transcendence of the world via images and figures. Despite the Romantic traits, particularly, the reciprocal interrelations of myth and the metaphysical-religious and of myth and the aesthetic, Wagner has prepared the way for the expansion of the functional realm of myth toward the organic and social-political and has given an artistic form and thus an apparent justification to the generally prevalent "hunger for myth."[7]

In basic harmony with Wagner's ideas but with much greater impact, Nietzsche denounced the intellectual and cultural shallowness of his time. Starting with his work *Die Geburt der Tragödie aus dem Geiste der Musik* (The Birth of Tragedy out of the Spirit of Music) he proclaimed, in contrast to Wagner, the myth of the Dionysian, which heralded the overcoming of individuation and salvation in eternal unity. Nietzsche attributed Western intellectual development to the increasingly absolute role of the Apollonian counterprinciple to the Dionysian; the Apollonian confronted the original irrational heroic and tragic Greek philosophy of life with an optimistic and harmonic world view in the form of enlightened rationalism originating with Socrates and found its continuation in the "slave morality" of Christianity. Nietzsche's celebration of the Dionysian, which had already experienced a revival in Schopenhauer's philosophy and in Wagner's tragic music drama, culminates in an ecstatic inebriation, a cult that, due to its foundation in the similarly organic concept of a nation, has become the guiding principle for the nationalistic-racial movement in the twentieth century. However, this specific development takes place outside of our area of investigation and therefore does not have to be taken into account.[8]

On the other hand, the mythicizing of literary criticism and of the science of history by the George-Kreis devotees (the circle of poet Stefan George) had direct consequences for literary mythopoesis; its most representative contributions were Friedrich Gundolf's book on Goethe (1916) and Ernst Bertram's on Nietzsche—the latter bears the significant subtitle, *Versuch einer Mythologie* (Attempt at a Mythology). In direct reference to Wagner and Nietzsche, the artistic and heroic man is declared to be the intellectual leader of mankind and the apex of history. Correspondingly, the task of literary criticism has to be seen in a mythic presentation, the "legend of his glory," in which the poet is acknowledged as the mythic shaper of life, giving meaning to it.

In summarizing the Romantic concept of literary mythopoesis, one can say that the symbolic quality of the mythic forms of concretization was not directly derived from the literary function of myth but rather indirectly by way of the soteriological dimension of myth's preliterary functional level. Because of this, Romanticism never had to define the specific quality of literary mythopoesis; the ambiguity has resulted in the equation of the literary functional level with all others for the purpose of a monistic etiological theory of myth. The fascination with such a homogeneous concept of myth has remained until today. Even the soteriological-eschatological aspect was saved in an only slightly secularized way, particularly in the area of the *Germanische Altertumswissenschaft* (science of Germanic antiquity), since Romantic wishful thinking could assert itself quite easily due to the lack of historical evidence. With regard to the criticism of modern literature, scholars relinquished the explicit evidence of a specific religious governing concept (*Überbau*). However, the continued implicit privileging of the unity of all functional levels at the same time led to the reduction of literature to the demonstration of mythologomena. This tendency was already an intrinsic characteristic of the Romantic historical-etiological approach to myth hermeneutics, because it encouraged the establishment of only normative guidelines for literary mythopoesis, and at most provoked a view of literature as mythicizing and using mythologomena. Correspondingly, notwithstanding its value as an introduction into the subject matter, Fritz Strich's comprehensive survey of the *Mythologie in der deutschen Literatur von Klopstock bis Wagner* (Mythology in German Literature from Klopstock to Wagner)[9] is based only on an unreflected myth concept derived from the Romantic monistic concept and consists of the demonstration of myth theories in literature instead of pursuing the problem of mythopoesis.

Myth Scholarship in the Footsteps of Romanticism

Romantic mythological literary criticism experienced its first principal rejection at the onset of the twentieth century by Andreas Heusler and Hermann Schneider, who approached the literary documents of Germanic antiquity with purely literary-aesthetic and literary-historical criteria. However, Heusler's thesis, "heroic legend is heroic poetry," was formulated in such an exaggerated way that it necessitated modification by progress in the fields of ethnology and cultural anthropology. In the process it had to give ground again to the erroneous alternative of tracing back the heroic lays, epics, and fairy tales to religious functions. Thus Germanic shamanism, Germanic initiation covenants, Germanic cult games, and Germanic *Königsheil* (kingly hail) represented—similar to the earlier concepts of etiology and homogeneity—the substratum of myth to which the forms of poetry were reduced by producing the evidence of mythic and fairy tale-like derivatives.

The entire fairy tale scholarship of Friedrich von der Leyen and his followers belongs to this romanticizing school. In their attempt to trace back fairy tale and myth to cultic rituals, they try to understand the history of the fairy tale by producing evidence of higher and lower mythologomena, heroic environment, bourgeois milieu, and robber Romanticism, although these only represent levels of the fairy tale.[10] The same criticism of a one-sided mythologizing of Germanic heroic poetry applies to Jan de Vries, whose works have been canonized by his disciples. His interpretation of the *Hildebrandslied* may serve as an example for his distortion of the work of literature; he explains the father-son battle as literary evidence of a myth about the god who sacrifices his own son.[11] Correspondingly, Franz Rolf Schröder derived the legend of Siegfried and his demise from the myth about the battle between a light and a dark god.[12] Using the historical elements of the legend as a point of departure, Otto Höfler interpreted in a similar way the mythicizing of Theodoric the Great as a direct outgrowth of the Germanic *Sakralkönigtum* (Divine Kingship) and attempted to document by that the subordination of history and literature under the history of religion.[13] Karl Helm is of a similar opinion, when he considers mythology as religion in a historical setting.[14]

The festschrift *Märchen, Mythos, Dichtung* (Fairy Tale, Myth, Poetry), in honor of Friedrich von der Leyen's ninetieth birthday, may serve as proof for the fact that even the investigation of modern literature, according to panreligious criteria, ends up as a mere demonstration of the existence of mythologomena.[15] A prime example is Wolfgang Danckert's book, *Goethe. Der mythische Urgrund seiner Weltschau* (Goethe: The Mythic Origin of His Worldview),[16] in which the author relates Goethe's symbolism and philosophy to the "chthonic proto-religion of the Pelasgians" (p. 171) in connection with Bachofen's transfer of the mythic "protohomeland" to Asia Minor and to Klage's treatise, "The World View of the Pelasgians." Goethe was supposed to have reinvoked the cosmic philosophy of a "prehistorical chthonism and tellurism" (p. 5) in the form of a palingenesis. Herbert Singer is also guilty of such an ahistorical generalization and equation of symbols and mythologomena; in his *Antrittsvorlesung* (first lecture as full professor), he places Gerda Buddenbrook and her son Hanno, together with Helena and Euphorion from Goethe's *Faust*, on the same mythological level.[17]

The only still-acceptable methodological aspect of the Romantic theory of literary mythopoesis remains the understanding of myth as the articulation of exemplary life experiences, which may result in a new literary concretization in each poet. Thus literary mythopoesis would manifest itself as the meeting point of a universally valid symbolic structure and its individual concretization. Johannes Kleinstück understands literary mythopoesis to be such a concurrence in his presentation *Mythos und Symbol in englischer Dichtung* (Myth and Symbol in English Literature),[18] and also Walther Killy attributes exactly this meaning to the element of the mythic in lyric poetry.[19] However, both limit themselves to the proof of mythologomena and their evocative function without doing justice to the creative aspect of language and the multidimensionality of the mythic in poetry.

Klaus Ziegler's article, "Mythos und Dichtung" (Myth and Poetry) in the *Reallexikon*, on the other hand, differs from this, since he investigates Romantic myth theory, traces its consequences for literature and myth theory of the twentieth century and therefore includes only "mythicizing" literature in his discussion. Within this framework, Ziegler's concluding statement remains fully valid:

> The myth theory of the later modern times serves, so to speak, as a mode of self-understanding for the mythicizing literature of the same period, as a conceptually refracted understanding

of one's own essence and wishes. For that reason, it is hardly possible to arrive at a truly adequate understanding of the central position that the idea of myth and the mythic has occupied in German poetry since the beginning of the Goethe period without productively drawing upon and incorporating contemporary mythology. (p. 584)

Myth Scholarship in a Narrower Sense

Since the problem of literary mythopoesis does not concern the majority of myth scholars, we can confine ourselves to the discussion of their two most important representatives in the twentieth century, Karl Kerényi and Walter F. Otto, who, in reference to Romanticism, consider the artistic representation of myth a correlative to and a compensation for the loss of myth embodying a "coherent world." Only the most representative of the large number of writings by both scholars will be referred to.

In the article "Gesetz, Urbild und Mythos" (Law, Prototype and Myth), Otto places man in a philosophical world system, which is realized most in myth as the highest prototype down to the details of all human laws and forms of intellectual and practical activities.[20] In this framework poetry above all is distinguished by the dynamic-creative power of *Gestalt-Offenbarung* (revelation of form), in which myth experiences a momentary epiphany not unlike the realization of the divine in the ritual. Otto speaks even more pointedly in another article about the "pure, original myth," which represents as "cult the ascendence of man to the divine" and in the word "the incarnation of the divine in the human."[21] However, poetry and art in general differ from the concretization of myth in the words insofar as they are able to represent the divine height only for moments, as they do not have the power to "create us in their image, to change our lives entirely" (p. 275). Therefore Otto does not want to see the concept of the creative applied to poetry or art, but ascribes it to language as such, which is identical to myth in its primary ability to actualize the higher essence of the objects. Correspondingly, Otto sees the poet as the listener "who makes known with his voice what the inner ear has perceived," that with which language or, as the Greeks called it, the muses have inspired him.[22]

It is significant that Otto's ontologizing of the relation of sign and thing signified in myth has supposedly been confirmed by philosophy. Heidegger's interpretations of Hölderlin and Trakl represent, on the existential-philosophical level, the equivalent of

Otto's myth concept, and they make obvious the problems that are created due to the absence of the literary-historical constituents and the privileging of the ontological problem.

In comparison to Otto, Karl Kerényi's myth research is much more subject-oriented and descriptive. For that reason, Kerényi's main merit lies in the discovery and analysis of detailed material from Greek mythology. On the basis of this, Kerényi has undertaken investigations on the theory of myth, which, despite their spiritual relationship to Otto, followed their own direction.[23] Kerényi sees the primary quality of mythology in the fact that it explains itself and everything else in the world because it represents an organized human response to the autonomous subject matter of myth. In its narration, as well as in its presentation, myth reveals "man's return to his origin and hence the realization in proto-types, proto-mythologomena, and proto-rituals of that which is at all humanly attainable" (Über Ursprung und Gründung in der Mythologie," p. 26). Therefore mythology constitutes as "subject-related action plan" (p. 43) a supplementary framework to the overall structure of the poetic work that Kerényi calls "archetypal" and by which he described the "extension from the historical to the universally human" (p. 51). He thereby made the connection to Jung's theory of archetypes, but he went further by implying that scholars should reduce literature to the status of evidence for the etiological mythologomena established by him. (See in the following section the criticism of the reductionism that characterizes German mythological criticism.)

Psychoanalytical Myth Scholarship

Although Carl Gustav Jung is generally considered to be the founder of the so-called mythological literary criticism, the other modern psychoanalysts too, who have established a correlation between the manifestations of the condition of the human soul and the symbolic character of poetry, have occupied themselves with myth scholarship. Historically one can trace a line of development from the Romantic psychologists Schubert and Carus via Wundt to Freud; aside from this, Jung had been influenced directly by Creuzer.

For Freud, myths served to interpret the subject matter of poetry in terms of the history of its development, from the standpoint of his theory of psychoanalysis. By speculating about the origin of myths "that they correspond to the distorted remains of wish fantasies of entire nations, to the secular dreams of early mankind," Freud is making Wundt's idea of an ethnopsychology more concrete.[24] Therefore Freud sees the cultural-historical interest in psychoanalysis "in the transfer of the psychoanalytical insights gained from dreams on to products of nations' fantasies such as myth and fairy tale."[25]

Freud directly applied this theory in his treatise "Der Mann Moses und die monotheistische Religion" (The Man Moses and Monotheistic Religion).[26] In it he establishes an analogy between the stages of a traumatic neurosis—from the early trauma to defense, latency, outbreak of the neurosis, and the compulsion to repeat the thing repressed—and the religion founded by Moses by referring to his theory of the killing of the tribal father by his sons. The importance of the religion founded by Moses and of its specific mythic foundation is based on surmounting the original terrifying aspects of Jahwe. "In the long run, it does not matter that the people most likely rejected the teachings of Moses after a short time and eliminated him. The tradition and its influence remained, and it accomplished, though gradually and only after many centuries, what had been denied to Moses himself" (p. 152).

The principle of the compulsion to repeat tradition, which has been repressed into latency and revived later, manifests itself according to Freud in the concretization of the myths in Greek poetry: "We recognize the following condition: a section of prehistory, which immediately afterwards had to appear as significant, important, and remarkable, perhaps always as heroic, but which has happened so long ago, belongs to such far-removed times that only an obscure and incomplete tradition can inform later generations about it" (p. 175). Even if Freud has realized and explained a basic structure of myth by applying the notion of repetition and anamnesis, the artificiality of an anology to neurosis distorts the creative aspect in each new poetic concretization into a repressed complex, which "emerges" again; moreover, the analogy excludes a conscious allusion in a modified form or ironic treatment. And since Freud, and especially his followers, primarily use literature to provide themselves with evidence for their theory of psychoanalysis, the practical application of their theory for literary analysis has led merely to a reduction of the literary work of art and its myths to a mechanistic causality principle. The main impulse of this principle supposedly originates with libidinal drives, which themselves are for the most part of infantile origin. Among the German scholars, it was especially Otto Rank who carried the application of Freud's theory to literature to the extreme: he attempted to prove Freud's Oedipus complex to be the main myth of world literature by relating the incest motif to the myth of the birth of the hero.[27]

C.G. Jung was able to overcome the one-sidedness of Freud's libidinal drive theory with his theory of archetypes, which probably has to be considered the most valuable contribution of psychoanalysis to the understanding of myth. Jung expands Freud's pathological concept of the complex and subordinates it to the archetype, which constitutes the collective subconscious as invisible "converging point" or "core of meaning charged with energy." In its potentiality, the archetype represents a reaction and contingency system, which is given concrete form only through its conscious realization as symbols and their collective expansion into myths.[28]

On the basis of his theory of archetypes, Jung points also to the poetic creative process and differentiates between "psychological" and "visionary" creativity;[29] the former deals with the multiplicity of human experiences and is accessible to the general consciousness, while "visionary" creativity, on the other hand, transcends the limits of immediate human comprehension and becomes accessible to the artist subconsciously out of the collective unconscious as primeval experience. The greatness of an artist depends solely on the power of his sensitivity to give artistic form to the potential prototypes, so that Jung can formulate pointedly: "Not Goethe creates Faust, but Faust creates Goethe" (p. 329).

Because of its simplifying model, which, in addition, is not based on the aesthetic aspect of the work of art, this typology of poetry has not been widely accepted, and Fritz Strich had pointed already to the fallacy of this approach in his lecture "Das Symbol in der Dichtung" (The Symbol of Poetry, 1939),[30] by contrasting Goethe's specific symbolism with Jung's archetypes. Hermann Pongs expressed a similar criticism from the viewpoint of poetic morphology.[31] These reservations against the application of Jung's theory of archetypes to the analysis of literature have been confirmed by the writing of Jung's followers in literary criticism. For just as in the case of Freud's psychoanalysis, they became guilty of a reductionism by tracing back the literary work of art to a select group of myths and by establishing entirely ahistorical analogies between art and religion. Aniela Jaffé's analysis of E.T.A. Hoffman's fairy tale, *Der goldene Topf*,[32] or the book on the *Graalslegende in psychologischer Sicht* (The Grail Legend in Psychological Terms),[33] started by Emma Jung and completed by Marie-Louise von Franz, are representative of this particular practice. In both primary works the archetypal character of symbols and myths cannot be denied; however, the authors fail to apply insights gained with the help of the theory of archetypes to the aesthetic understanding of a specific work of art as a historically rooted yet autonomous entity. It does not suffice simply to give evidence of the existence of an alchemistic imagery; only its integration into the specific poetic functional frame will lead to the "poetic philosophers' stone."

In his mythological investigations, Alfredo Dornheim also made the mistake of establishing analogies between mythological and poetic symbols, which developed into an empty ahistorical identification. Thus he equates Goethe's Mignon and Thomas Mann's Echo with the mythologomenon of the "Divine Child" taken from Jung's and Kerényi's writings and applies this approach to additional works of literature from the time of Goethe to the present.[34]

The difficulty in finding poetic correlatives for the archetypal symbols and myths, or in understanding the latter on the basis of their poetic forms of concretization, can be seen in the fact that until now, German "mythological" literary criticism has produced constructive insights only when the nature of the literary subject matter refers directly back to an archetype. In this respect, Hedwig von Beit has been able to contribute to the understanding of the symbolism of the fairy tale with extremely innovative ideas by establishing its "magical space," "its magical main figures," and the model of human awareness in the figure of the hero as archetypically based criteria.[35] However, even Hedwig von Beit commits the mistake of attributing a normative quality to the Jungian concepts of anima, animus, shadow, self, I, persona, or great Mother, which quality supposedly constitutes the fairy tale in an absolute manner, instead of analyzing on the one hand the psychic reality that stands behind these concepts and on the other their literary function. Unfortunately, this tendency increased in her later works to such a degree that the recognized structure of the fairy tale falls prey to a speculative psychologism.[36]

The school of psychoanalytical fairy tale research, which sees psychic or psychosomatic maturation processes as reflected in individual fairy tales, leads even further away from a genuine understanding of literary mythopoesis, since these scholars confine their investigation to the maturation experience of puberty.[37] Instead it would be much more meaningful, following the suggestions made

254   KLAUS WEISSENBERGER

by Mircea Eliade or Lutz Röhrich, to relate the symbolism of transformation in the fairy tale to initiation rites in general, "which extend from the transformation rites of primitive nations still close to
nature all the way to the mystery cults and initiation rites of established religions."[38]

In contrast to the reductionism caused by the exclusivist claims
of Freud's and Jung's aesthetics, Erich Fromm uses the universal
and original symbolic language common to both dreams and
myths as the level of comparison in his investigation, *Märchen,
Mythen, Träume. Eine Einführung in ihre vergessene Sprache*
(Fairy Tales, Myths, Dreams: An Introduction to Their Forgotten
Language).[39] Despite the brevity of his analyses—for example, on
such diverse works as Sophocles' *Oedipus* trilogy or Kafka's
Trial—it is obvious that Fromm proceeds from and refers back to
the work as an autonomous entity when he interprets its mythological symbolic language in "psychological" terms. Already in
1951, he related the conflict in Kafka's *Trial* to the mythic contrast
of two levels of human awareness; Walter Sokel transposed this
conflict onto Kafka's entire work and analyzed it in detail in his
pioneering book, *Franz Kafka. Tragik und Ironie.*[40] Sokel's book,
which had been discounted by some critics as just a "psychological" study, actually has to be considered as one of the great achievements in understanding mythic style and structure phenomena by
way of psychological categories without becoming a victim of their
totalizing claims.

It is significant, however, that these last two contributions to
literary mythopoesis were made by German-speaking emigrants to
America, while in Germany the emphasis still remains on the psychological approach, in contrast to a strictly literary one. A good
example is Norbert Groeben's *Literaturpsychologie* (1972),[41] in
which the hermeneutics and textual practice of literary criticism
are classified according to a psychological model, and the aesthetic holistic aspect of the literary work of art is not considered at
all.

Marxist and Ideological Myth Scholarship

Marxist myth theory developed out of the Romantic concept, although with the decisive modification that it exchanges the es-
chatological-soteriological orientation of myth for a dialectical-
materialistic one and substitutes for a suprahuman framework
norms derived from social reality. In general, Marx derives myth

from early developmental stages of individual societies, in which it served to "overcome" the natural forces, to "dominate" them and to "concretize them in the imagination and by way of the imagination."[42] As soon as human beings have control over natural forces, myth loses its *raison d'être* and, according to Marx, must be dissolved totally under capitalism, where at most it is used as an instrument of the ruling class. In this sense, myth is interpreted as "a stage that never returns" (p. 31), which has to be followed by one of "realism"; a reasoning that is based on the oversimplification of the function of literature, but that is consistent with the realization of the dialectical economic process. Georg Lukácz based his theory of realism on this axiom and, for some time at least, it was recognized as the standard aesthetic guideline within the school of Marxist literary criticism.

On the other hand, the new departures of Ernst Fischer and Robert Weimann, despite their adherence to Marxist premises, attribute a genuine validity to myth even in modern literature. In his criticism of the present theory and application of "socialist realism," Fischer considers "literature and art to be in search of a deeper 'authenticity', of a mutual intensity and concretization," that is, principles related to those of myth.[43] However, it should be obvious that this "modern" myth lacks all mystification or transcendental reference. In it the "authenticity of the invisible," the historical potentiality that "documents itself in the interweaving of nature, history, and human existence" should take effect. The secularized myth is supposed to make evident the model of the Marxist humanist vision of the future in an exemplary form; however, with regard to its genuine literary function, it can only be considered as another version of the ideology of dialectical materialism in pseudoliterary terms.

Weimann, on the other hand, appears to proceed with more caution when he approaches the relation between myth and poetry by way of a discussion of the respective theories. Weimann derives the importance of myth even for modern literature from the historical-materialistic approach, but only by separating myth and poetry into their historical-social functions. Therefore he is able to discard the "idealistic claim to the autonomy of the 'inner form'" for the sake of the "concept of historical function" and supposedly recognizes the essence of literary mythopoesis in the dialectic relationship of rite and myth and its artistic reception.[44] Due to that fact, he can also give special recognition to Maud Bodkin's book *Archetypal Patterns in Poetry*,[45] which, according to him, establishes a psychological-literary typology out of the spirit of the "collective-mythical" (p. 408); however, he has to eliminate the differences between the autonomy of the artistic realization and the collective tradition and reduces the literary work instead of "differentiating" it, despite his expressed intentions not to do so (p. 410).

In evaluating historical-etiological myth hermeneutics as a whole, the two main reasons for its conceptual and methodological imprecision, which are inherent in this approach and impair the understanding of literary mythopoesis, have to be pointed out. One of the reasons concerns the erroneous epistemological relation of myth and truth implied by historical-etiological myth hermeneutics. However, Walter Benjamin states in his interpretation of Goethe's *Wahlverwandtschaften* (Elective Affinities) that the possibility of a presence of truth exists "only on the basis of a cognitive comprehension of myth, that is, a cognitive comprehension of its annihilating indifference towards truth."[46]

The second main reason for the conceptual and methodological ambiguities is based ultimately on the extensiveness of the general and scholarly interest in myth; the cultural anthropologist Ernst Mühlmann concludes therefore: "Such an extensive interest is hardly possible without a collective emotional undercurrent; this, however, is permeated by intellectual values which do not always have a favorable effect on the cognitive comprehension of mythic reality."[47] Although Mühlmann confirms in principle the validation of Jung's theory of archetypes by the empirical evidence of his science, he cautions against overinterpreting myths from the viewpoint of an etiological and homogeneous concept. Rather, by taking a position not unlike Benjamin, he demands the understanding of myth out of "the context of the interrelation of human actions" (p. 175), since it would receive its meaning only "through the act of narration or mimesis." As a consequence, any advances in the understanding of literary mythopoesis can emerge only from its interpretation within a functional literary context.

MORPHOPOETIC MYTH HERMENEUTICS

The entire preceding discussion of the historical-etiological myth hermeneutics has served the purpose—aside from the historical-systematical survey of myth scholarship since Romanticism—to point out the principal shortcomings or only conditionally valid perceptions for the understanding of literary mythopoesis inherent in this methodological approach. Nevertheless, it should not be implied that the problem already has been solved by German morphopoetic myth hermeneutics. The contributions, which will be discussed, were inspired by the criticism of the German historical-etiological school; however, they represent only solutions to special problems of literary mythopoesis or initial steps toward understee understanding it in its entirety, and only seen as a whole do they indicate what a systematic morphopoetic theory should accomplish.

There are two historical reasons for the lack of such an all-inclusive myth theory in German literary criticism. One can be seen in the dominance of "intellectual history," which in all its variations represented the only synthesizing criticism in Germany after Dilthey until it degenerated during the Third Reich. The second reason is found in the "intrinsic," phenomenologically oriented poetics of Staiger and Kayser, who restored to German literary criticism of the postwar period a solid foundation; they excluded, for understandable reasons, but also as a result of their theory, the treatment of myth. In this respect American criticism, represented by the great writings of Northrop Frye and Philip Wheelwright, is much more advanced, and it would be only to the advantage of the German critics if they were to acknowledge this fact.

In the case of German morphopoetic myth theories, one can distinguish between two principal trends: while the scholars, on the one hand, want to understand literary myth exclusively on the basis of its integration into the functional frame of the individual work, the others proceed from myth as a depth dimension, which reveals itself functionally through the typologies of poetry, style, genre, or period style. Already the few attempts to integrate the results of both schools into an all-encompassing concept are an indication that a breakthrough leading out of the dilemma of myth hermeneutics for literature can be accomplished only this way.

The first step toward a morphopoetic myth concept can be recognized in André Jolles's definition of *Mythe* as a preliterary subform of genre. Jolles differentiated clearly between myth in poetry and *Mythe* as a separate elemental form of language prior to all literary concretization; this latter has its own "linguistic gesture," which responds to a "preoccupation of the human spirit" that has presented itself as a question, and that finds its subsequent literary realization in each single myth.

The question is directed towards the essence and condition of all that we observe in the world as constant and manifold. The answer combines all this into the event which embodies both manifoldness and constancy as a unity by means of its absolute singularity and models this unity in a firm and flexible way, in an event, which becomes destiny and fate.[48]

The "linguistic gesture" of *Mythe*, however, has to be understood as being beyond all cultural- and literary-historical facts, and its universal acceptability has to be questioned as long as this connection has not been established, although one could expect precisely from it insights into the linguistic quality of myth and its potential for literary realization. Also, the consequences that Jolles draws from this approach appear to be problematical, since on the basis of the criterion of conclusiveness, which he attributes to the truth-giving quality of *Mythe*, he declares *Mythe* to be the expression of a serene world or of a world that can heal itself, where important questions do not remain unanswered. This notion, however, reunites *Mythe* with the Romantic myth concept, the essence of which can be shown to derive from the etiological theories of a later historical period. Only with respect to his cultural-historical derivation of the symbol saturated with *Mythe* did Jolles constantly adhere to his proposed division of mythology and *Mythe* and thus contribute to the understanding of a genuine aspect of the symbol.

Hugo Kuhn uses the uncertainty of Jolles's ahistorical and supralinguistic language formulas or *Sprachgebärden* as a point of departure in order to establish instead a typology of the oral literary documents of Germanic antiquity by gaining insight into the cultural function, which can be recognized only separately in each case.[49] In pursuing this goal he indirectly arrives at fundamental insights in the relationship between myth and poetry. The divergence of *Gestalt* and function, which cannot be reconciled, especially in prehistorical and primitive cultures, constitutes art until our own time and is evident especially today as the "revolution" in the arts. Kuhn explains the matter as "complementarity between life processes and *Gestalt*" (p. 28), which in the case of poetic mythopoesis makes it necessary to classify its *Sprachgestalt* first on the basis of its sociologically and historically definable area of effectiveness and to establish in this way the twofold aspect, that is, the interplay of the relative autonomy of the *Sprachgestalt* with the function of usage resulting in a symbolic system.

Kuhn has demonstrated the practical implementation of his the-

ory in his article "Parzival. Ein Versuch über Mythos, Glaube und
Dichtung im Mittelalter" (Parzival: An Attempt toward Myth,
Faith and Poetry in the Middle Ages).[50] Avoiding the reductionism of the Jungian school, and using rather the functional context
of the German Arthurian romances as the basis for his investigation, Kuhn develops the structural principle of antithesis as the
basis of *Parzival;* the antithesis manifests itself "between mythically collective commitment and personal action, between an almost paradoxical final stage of mythicizing, indeed with Christian
overtones, and an almost paradoxical demythologization, freeing
the individual to be his own self!" (p. 176).

Similar to Kuhn's theory on the typology of oral texts of the
German antiquity, Klaus von See demonstrated that it is impossible to prove the mythic and cultic origin of the heroic legends.[51]
Rather, a careful analysis of the texts in question provides the
evidence that the fairy tale-like and mythic aspects of the heroic
legends have to be attributed to later insertions, and the "unusual,
dubious, frightening events—events, which demanded questions,
which . . . provoked rumors" (p. 94), are in the center of these
legends.

Wilhelm Emrich deserves the credit for having exemplified the
principal prerequisites of literary mythopoesis for modern German
literature. By investigating in his article "Symbolinterpretation
und Mythenforschung" (Interpretation of Symbols and Myth Scholarship, 1953) mainly the symbolism in Goethe, he was able to
reject the totally ahistorical identification of symbols in Goethe
with the myth of the Divine Child or the Pelasgian telluric
myths.[52] On the basis of an interpretation of the Mignon and Euphorion figures, he demonstrated how Goethe intentionally altered the function of the mythic symbols into autonomous poetic
ones, giving them a new meaning. By using Kafka as an example,
Emrich was later able to prove how the imagery of a poet might
expand to mythic proportions, due to the poetic realizations of its
absolute claim, a process that cannot be explained by way of identification with or reduction to established myths.[53] However, Emrich's myth concept loses some of its conciseness when he defined
Kafka's imagery as a myth without explicitly demonstrating how
Kafka establishes the functional context for a *Sprachgestalt* with
his self-reflective world of images.

Several works related to Jolles's approach have postulated a
supratemporal function of usage of myth without, however, differentiating conceptually between practical function and *Sprach-*

gestalt. In his *Morphologie der metaphorischen Formen* (Morphology of Metaphorical Forms), Hermann Pongs distinguishes in principle between the poetic attitude that, on the one hand, animizes the outer world or annexes it by projecting personality upon it and, on the other hand, the poetic attitude that subordinates itself to the outer world by way of empathy or absorption of self into process.[54] The former manifests itself in a mythic imagery of anthropomorphization, the latter in a magical or mystical one of self-transfiguration. While Pongs's typology was a purely phenomenological one and remained somewhat imprecise conceptually, Walter Muschg has tried to establish this approach ontologically and by way of a typology of poetry. He establishes as a basis for a fundamental poetics the correlation between poetic imagination and representation in general. In this he makes use of the insights of psycholanalysis into the heightened powers of fantasy and imagination of the artist and reduces them, in his attempt to give order to the poetic images, to three basic anthropological types or stages: the magical stage, "at which the individual soul finds itself in everything and expands itself towards the universe"; the mythical one, "at which the individual considers himself secure in a natural community"; and the mystical one, at which one recognizes "in all of sensuous reality the reference to an invisible divine."[55] These basic anthropological types have correlatives in the personal "I" as magical, "thou" as mystical, and "it" as mythical poetic attitudes, as well as in the poetic types of the magical, mystical, and mythical poet and their poetry corresponding to these attitudes.

Muschg calls the mythical poet the singer who is filled with hunger for the objects of this world. This poetic attitude is based on the recognition of the beauty and greatness of life as it apparently reveals itself in the organic makeup of all phenomena. Therefore the "mythical" poet attempts to recognize the coherence of the external world and establishes classical forms or reverts to them. Muschg has been able to relate his models of poetic attitude also to specific genres and genre subforms and, by establishing them in an archetypal framework, he stimulated scholarship to relate those in turn to stylistic periods. In that respect, mythical poetry fulfills once again the criterion of sociocultural utility in a poetically charged transformation of function, determining both genre and period style.[56] However, one has to object to some of the examples Muschg selected in order to demonstrate the correlation of poetic attitude and period style, as they are not always conclusive, due to the fact that Muschg's starting basis is too limited.

In addition to Muschg's definition, mythical poetry can be defined much more fundamentally from the viewpoint of literary sociology and cultural anthropology. In his *Sozialgeschichte der Kunst und Literatur* (Social History of Art and Literature), Arnold Hauser has established a relationship between the art of the Old Stone Age and its monistic world view based on magic and thus has understood the fusion of identiy, which the artist established between the animal and its pictorial representation and which should lead to the killing of the animal, to be a magical-realistic one.[57] This monistic world view is followed by the dualistic animism of the Neolithic Age, in which man experiences himself as being apart from the world and in which he differentiates between a reality and a suprareality. The tangible richness of life is replaced by the notion of the essence of the things in the Neolithic Age, by the organizing principle of idea and concept and correspondingly by the symbol in art. This is the birth of myth, which in these terms represents a sublimation of the magical world view of the Paleolithic Age, since in myth the dualistic world view is drawn together into a totality. Man and world, idea and thing, reality and suprareality integrate into an order that claims to combine all ontological aspects in their multiplicity and paradoxical nature into a unity.

Joseph Strelka has already pointed out this historically hard to prove yet captivating connection between the origin of myth and the transitional stage of humanity from the Paleolithic to the Neolithic Age. In his literary sociology, *Die gelenkten Musen* (The Manipulated Muses), he postulated the original integration of myth and mythic into this literary-sociological framework.[58] According to this view, the origin of myth and mythic is signified by characteristics of transition that distinguish the stylistic change from the Paleolithic naturalism to the Neolithic stage, whose corresponding features are marked by a stylization and schematization of the naturalistic forms. From there one can trace the development to expressive classicism, which is based on the synthesis of the "magical-realistic" and the "mystical-romantic" modes of literature, "in which the realistic component embodies the aspect of the search for reality and the idealistic component the aspect of elevation, of the anagogic in the broadest sense" (p. 274).

This two-fold heritage—the sublimation of a monistic world view into a dualistic one—explains the ambivalence or even antinomic structure of myth, which characterizes its level of function and is, however, analogous to the essence of poetry; for in poetry too the heterogenous elements and heterogeneous aspects are integrated into a holistic entity. Therefore it is possible that the poetic and mythic levels of function can be shown to overlap in poetry.

This typological definition of a "classical" style on the basis of a typology of mythic content can also help to clarify the ambiguous term "realism," which Muschg, due to the lack of sociocultural foundation in his typology, wants to equate with mythic poetry. Realism can be derived primarily from the utilitarian magical-realistic identity between the thing and its pictorial representation in Paleolithic art, and only secondarily from the mythical stance that emerged in the transitional phase to the Neolithic Age. At this time, the naive-magical naturalism, now understood as consciously reverting to tradition, must have become subjected to a social collectivization, and the realistic artist must have adopted the attitude that Muschg calls the hunger for the things of this world. Therefore, like mythic poetry, realism also is characterized, in its typologies of both style and content, by a two-fold heritage of the magical and mythical cultural stage.

The mythic aspect of realism reveals itself in the expansion of the magical striving for identity toward the typical and symbolical. It even resembles the strivings for a classical style, so that Hans Mayer, as an advocate of socialist realism, can consider Goethe's concept of classicism to be a realistic one.[59] However, it is exactly the mythic aspect of realism that may have led to its artistic decline into a utilitarian naturalism, by way of a total rationalization of realism on the part of the later bourgeoisie. This ambivalent tension between magical identification *with* the outer world and mythical animation *by* the outer world explains the entire spectrum of realism, from the magical and idealistic variant to the socialistic one. While Keller's and Storm's transfiguring, fairy tale-like, and sensuous style is based on the strong emphasis on the magical component, one can ascribe, even while using different criteria, Stifter's idealistic realism and Fontane's novels, with their strong element of social criticism, to the mythic strivings for a balance between the magical and mythical, or to the transition from one to the other. Stifter tries to keep the classical world view intact by stylizing reality, whereas Fontane, from the opposite pole of the spectrum and despite his objective rationalization of man and society and his factual, detached attitude, recognizes the subjective right to self-preservation. In comparing the later writings of Raabe to those of Fontane, the third principal aspect of the mythic attitude becomes apparent, that is, the anagogic aspect, which follows from the self-establishment of the "I" against all imperatives and rationalist codes that might limit the "I."

A similar combination of basic poetic attitudes characterizes the period of New Objectivity, which includes aspects of expressionism as a prerequisite for its attempts to counterbalance it. Even socialist realism is characterized by this type of combination. However, due to the materialistic world view, the magical and mythical attitudes cannot be clearly differentiated, and the mimesis of reality is necessarily reduced to a schematization and mechanistic realization, instead of being enhanced by the symbol-like character of the mythic poetic attitude.

Käte Hamburger and Rolf Tarot must be credited with having grasped analytically the literary phenomenon of the mythic attitude, seen in terms of the logic of poetic language, without, however, establishing the correlation to its literary-typological and literary-aesthetic aspect. According to Käte Hamburger, the mythic attitude corresponds on the logical level to the mimetic or fictional genre, which does not originate from a narrator's realm of experiences but has to be considered as the product of the mimetic narrative function of the representation of reality.[60] In addition to the third-person narrative, Käte Hamburger counts also the drama among the mimetic genres by postulating a surrogate mimesis, which consists in the drama's being performable on stage; lyric poetry and the first-person narrative, on the other hand, represent, as statements of an I-origin, a statement of directly experienced reality.

Rolf Tarot expands this system of the logic of literature by including the concept of *imitatio,* which he develops in the course of an analysis of Brecht's epic theater from the viewpoint of the logic of literature. In reference to the statement system of language, Tarot understands *imitatio* to be a feigned reality statement.[61] With this concept of *imitatio,* Tarot is able to go beyond the dramatic genre and is able to assign the first-person narrative to the epic presentational form with imitative structure, or to designate on the other hand the ballad as "mimetic structure in the lyrical presentational form" (p. 133); this way he is able to effect a meaningful classification of literary forms, a problem which Käte Hamburger resolved unsatisfactorily.

Thus we are presented with a model aiding us in the comprehension of the problem of literary mythopoesis in terms of the logic structure, which need not be confined exclusively to the mimetic presentational form but can also possess *imitative* traits. This applies especially to the first-person narrative or the entire body of mimetic lyric poetry, which, according to the twofold heritage of mythic poetry, represents an amalgamation or cross-fertilization of mimetic and imitative lyric poetry, while the purely imitative lyric poetry or *Erlebnislyrik* tends to use mythologomena without representing a myth, because of the feigned quality of the statement-subject. The combination of mimetic and imitative presentational forms manifests itself also in the narrative structure of realistic literature; the epic fiction signifies the mimetic presentational form and the feigned reality statement the imitative one. This differentiation in turn corresponds to the previously demonstrated division of realism into mythical literature on the one hand and magical and mystical on the other: in Meyer and Fontane, the aspect of epic fiction prevails, whereas Keller, Storm, and Raabe (in his later writings) emphasize the feigned reality statement.

In addition to an analysis of literary mythopoesis in a literary-sociological context and a transferring of the findings to the theoretical and logical categories of poetic language, myth has also been interpreted in its relation to poetry from a historical-philosophical viewpoint, which apparently confirms the sociocultural basis discussed thus far. When Hermann Broch in his later works considers Homer's writing to represent the threshhold at which the mythic becomes poetry and Tolstoy's writings that at which the poetic becomes again mythic, he wants to evaluate the integration of the mythic from the viewpoint of the historical development of its sociocultural utilization and wants to draw conclusions about the contemporary intellectual situation of mankind on the basis of the change in such utilization.[62] In the cycle of the continuing disintegration of values and the resultant rationalization of all artistic means, the time of the total depletion of myth and rigidity of art has come; originally art lived off its mythic heritage, which can be traced back to the diminutive formulas of fairy tale and song and which interprets human existence without reference to temporal change.[63] The "apocalyptic feeling of a general disintegration of values,"[64] starting with Dostoevsky, has been confirmed by historical events in the twentieth century and demands a transcending of the aesthetic function of myth into timelessness and its expansion into a renewed *Totalitätsverständnis* (absolute meaning).

Broch has already attempted to achieve his goal in his mountain novel *The Tempter*, by including death as an epistemological aspect and thus pointing toward a new dimension of depth in humanity, which is to be realized poetically through the device of simultaneity. While Broch does justice to his request only on the level of imagery in *The Tempter*, he succeeds in *The Death of Virgil* in finding a poetic representation of a new cosmogony by expanding the form of the novel toward the lyrical, which in turn enables him to create a realization of totality as an epiphanic breakthrough into simultaneity. In this synergetic interplay of content and form in myth, which for Broch is ultimately based on the unity of mythos and logos, he recognizes the relationship to Jung's archetypes, as both "are nothing else but the essence of humanity itself" ("Die mythische Erbschaft," p. 239). However, contrary to Jung's theory of archetypes, Broch's theoretical writings and the two novels do not demonstrate a regression to an archaic myth, but rather its sublimation into a mystical poetic realization. A similar culmination of mythic references in an imagery of mystical elevation is characteristic of the poetry of Nelly Sachs and Paul Celan.[65]

Contrary to Broch, Hans Blumenberg develops his historical-theoretical model for a myth theory out of the conviction that myth can be interpreted only "as an unretrievable potential of meaning in an ever-changing function,"[66] that is, solely out of its reception. Blumenberg attempts to explain the reality of the mythic in the urge to combat the power of everything frighteningly omnipotent and in the resultant stimulus toward an imaginative creation of an autonomous outlet in the poetic realm. From the original antinomic structure of myth, which Blumenberg perhaps oversimplifies in his formula "terror and play," two principal morphopoetic consequences result, which he believes can be transferred to the "received" myth: the elements of freedom and distance on the one hand and of repetition and circumstantiality on the other. Blumenberg thus interprets the power of myth to "de-fang, uncover, untie, unmask, and to translate into play" (p. 24) as a fundamentally poetic-aesthetic power, which, however, does not want to deny its original heritage. "Without the memory of the terror and forces, which the freedom of myth overcame, its specificity— as joy of the variation vis-à-vis the power of repetition—is meaningless" (p. 34). Therefore myth can function only as a pattern, as a frame within which the freedom of circumstantiality can realize itself vis-à-vis the coercion of repetition, which confronts this freedom with a basic cyclical structure. The dogmatism of the Chris-

tian late antiquity and the rationalization of the historical consciousness have distorted this original function of myth and made
it serve their own ends.

At first glance, Blumenberg's model appears to be extremely
convincing; however, certain reservations and doubts must be
raised concerning the privileging of the two basic mythical attitudes, terror and play, as the fundamental alternatives and concerning the consequences for the poetic deduced therefrom. It
appears, to be sure, that the preliterary language gesture of the
mythic, which Jolles postulated, has found here a much stronger
confirmation; however, to establish his theory, Blumenberg sacrifices the comprehension of a specific literary mythopoesis derived
from an individual work, as well an independent concept of poetry
as an entity in itself. The cosmogonic mission of poetry, which
Broch derives from its mythic heritage and which he tries to realize anew, cannot be analyzed in terms of the joy of the "variation
vis-à-vis the power of repetition."

Thus far, all the discussed models of a morphopoetic myth concept are characterized by overemphasizing either the intrinsic definition of myth, or the typological definition of myth, and of the
mythic in poetry. Gerhardt Schmidt-Henkel is among the few
whose principal aim it is to reconcile both schools. However, with
regard to the practical consequences of his approach, he confines
himself in his book *Mythos und Dichtung* (Myth and Poetry) to the
discussion of mythologomena in the works of Büchner, Eichen-
dorff, Spitteler, Holz, Döblin, and Jahnn and evades the issue of
mythopoesis.[67] Conversely, his theoretical summary is not based on
any systematic concept, which could integrate all partial aspects
into a whole; therefore the partial insights either disintegrate into a
mechanically applied positivism, or they result in an amorphous
potpourri due to the confusing of concepts and their imprecise definition. This becomes especially apparent when Schmidt-Henkel
rightly proclaims the superiority of the mythic over the myths
within poetry, but at the same time he wants to trace the evidence
of the mythic as far back as the stylistic figures of metonymy and
synecdoche because of their similarity, as modes of repetition, to
the self-confirming rhythms of mythic repetition. Peter Kobbe's
reconciliation attempt between the two mythopoetic concepts has a
much more secure methodological basis. However, his book *Mythos und Moderne* (Myth and the Modern) is characterized by such
a high degree of rationalization that the mythic has lost all of its
suprarational qualities.[68] Furthermore, Kobbe has not understood

the aspect of the depth dimension of the mythic, the importance of which has been argued here. Nevertheless, this book deserves our special attention on the basis of its intention.

Kobbe analyzes very concisely and to the point the spectrum of contemporary myth theories and attributes the conceptual confusion to the different frames of reference of the practical application of the myth concept within which each discipline operates without being aware of these differences. In the case of poetry, therefore, myth can no longer be understood in its original frame of usage, but only in its poetic function as subject matter. In principle, two possibilities offer themselves for the integration of myth into poetry and its resultant poetic function. One such possibility is the allusion or citation that is based on the reference to the model (p. 44) and has to be understood as poetic reception of mythology; the other is the mythic per se, which appears as depth dimension, not patternlike, but as an event. In the mythic, the aspect of the transempirical and of its potential to become evident, which the individual myth lost along with its utilitarian function, reasserts itself. Therefore Kobbe differentiates again between the transempirical presentational form, by means of which the fictive-historical surface reality is penetrated, and the poetic expressive function through which the surface reality is questioned, expanded, and deepened. With this double aspect of the mythic, he defines the "correlation of poetic positing and poetological grounding" (p. 46) peculiar to the mythic. Beyond that, Kobbe considers the mythic to be correlated with presentational and epistemological problems within poetry, "because a sanctioned transcendence or transempiry is not pre-established for poetry, but has to be redefined each time" (pp. 46f.) so that the poetic representation of the mythic is closely related to the claim to its truthfulness. This explains the direct correlation of philosophical myth interpretation with poetic ones, which the disciplines of religious and historical-theoretical sciences and the aesthetic, epistemological, and ontological disciplines have undertaken without recognizing their strictly poetic functions.

Kobbe arrives also at an explanation for the apparent affinity of the mythic and mythological to the subconscious, which has to be accounted for on purely poetic grounds. With respect to the poetic realization, the transempirical dimension of the mythic, as well as the partial thematization of the mythological, presuppose a relatively autonomous depth dimension of the conscious or relatively autonomous typicality in communication and interaction. In this light, attempts at explaining the mythic on the psychoanalytical or ideological grounds appear self-evident.

With his explication, Kobbe undoubtedly presents the most far-reaching methodological model of literary mythopoesis and provides corresponding criteria for its definition. However, the condensed technical language and the programmed mechanical thought development are already an indication that for Kobbe, myth and poetry can be totally rationalized, without the epistemological aspect of aesthetic experience, which Roman Ingarden demands for the recognition of the literary work of art.[69] Therefore one misses also the incorporation of Kobbe's results into a holistic theory of poetry, which would do justice to the *seins-heteronome Eigenwürde* (autonomous value) of the poetic.

Using these criteria, the two last scholars discussed in our survey approach the problem of literary mythopoesis. For the German-Russian Wladimir Weidlé, the holistic character of art and poetry originates from the same root common to religion and art, and he therefore interprets the artistic creative process through analogical comparisons with the religious concepts of the incarnation and transfiguration: "The incarnation of a content into a form and the transfiguration of the real into the imaginary are the acts which produce the work of art, which have it as their goal, and which create it."[70] This religious depth dimension of the work of art extends into the presentational form, which emerges as "antinomic identity" according to its "transcendental relation to the law of contradiction" (p. 381). It is now typological for the history of the development of poetry and art in general, which Weidlé considers to be directly dependent on the increasing process of intellectualization and differentiation of the culture of humanity, that due to this process, art has removed itself more and more from its actual roots and has fallen in our time into the danger of total sterility and aridness. The intellectual, sociological, and general cultural position of the modern artist is one of a "priest who sacrifices without a community" (p. 121), since the "uprootedness" and isolation of the modern man leave also the modern artist to himself and favor an artistic solipsism, which can only result in pure formalism. Therefore Weidlé demands that art, according to its origin, should develop again out of the realm of imagination and mythic thinking, which he calls "the natural intersection of art and religion" (p. 357).

In his later essay "Die zwei 'Sprachen' der Sprachkunst" (The Two 'Languages' of the Art of Language), Weidlé characterized in most appropriate terms the presentational mode of poetry, which is based on the antinomic identity of sign and thing signified, using the concept of mimesis in its pre-Socratic meaning.[71]

> Mimesis is a practice which leads to a poiesis and remains recognizable in it; an act, by which something is made visible by expressing it through its presentation and having it merge or coincide with what is expressed and presented (it is the same). The important difference between the mimetic sign and all others consists primarily in the fact that it designates only what it expresses and does not refer to something not presented in it; and secondly, that what is expressed and presented is perceived in the sign itself, and appears therein. (pp. 163f.)

This mimetic language, the essence of all arts, understood in these terms, has originally served religion and still receives, by way of this mythic relation, its metaphysical impulses and its transcendental dimensionality. With respect to poetry, Weidlé distinguishes between two modes of realization of this mythic relation: that of the *Wortkunst*, which consists principally of the epic and dramatic genre, and that of the *Dichtkunst*, which characterizes the lyric genre.

> The difference between the two mimetic languages consists in the fact that the mimetic expressive presentation or the mimetic expression in a mode of presentation, takes place, on the one hand, in the phonetic forms and verbal resonances of poetic speech; on the other hand, however, it takes place in the events and actions being described by a speech, which might be more or less poetic, but does not have to be. (p. 176, footnote 26)

Weidlé's conceptual differentiation between the two mimetic languages makes it possible to recognize why the mythic dimension in epic and drama has attained the form of myth as fable in the Aristotelian sense in order to fulfill the poetic demands of the mimesis as *Wortkunst* by way of the presentation of actions and acting persons. The fundamental displacement of the fable in lyric poetry has resulted in the mythologomena being the only link to the mythic for lyric poetry. However, the potential for repetition of the narrated myth, including the aspects of rigidity and variation, corresponds to the relation of meter and rhythm and the phonetic and prosodic elements in lyric poetry; the meter serves, just like the myth as fable, to guarantee the supratemporal and supraspatial dimension of poetry. Only the veneration of Aristotle's definition of myth has caused scholarship not to recognize the all-encompassing mythic relation common to all of art in the mimesis (in its pre-Socratic meaning) of lyric poetry. This theory has been confirmed in Wolfgang Schadewaldt's lecture "Das Wort in der Dichtung. Mythos und Logos" (The Word in Poetry: Mythos and Logos).[72]

The function that establishes the essence of poetry is based for Schadewaldt on the "model of a living ontological reference system imposed on the chaos of being" (p. 94). This demand for mastery of the world characterizes language in its original function and also grants poetry at least the same right as the sciences, which express the same claim. It finds its realization in the iconographic signification of poetic images, which Schadewaldt equates with the *mytheisthai* of the Greeks. In the *"threefold totality:* of the *world,* of *man* and of the musical-rhythmic *body of resonance"* (p. 121), poetry transcends the level of language as formula and presents itself as a "piece of nature," as "one and whole." While science can maintain its demand for precision with the help of the *logos,* the poetic mythopoesis, in contrast to the *logos,* aims at a world totality, which allows each individual poetic work to establish itself as an autonomous cosmos and to correspond to a new creation. Therefore the poet can only be someone who is inspired by the world and the divine at the same time, someone who speaks as an "enthusiast."

In contrast to the theories that fragment the mythic into the different sociocultural frames of usage or into the intrinsic relations of a work, Schadewaldt and Weidlé offer a total concept of poetry, which is based on the reciprocal penetration of the mythic and poetry, which established the *seins-heteronome Eigenwürde* (autonomous value) of poetry, and which offers criteria for the definition of the main genres on the basis of the different realizations of literary mythopoesis. It is only regrettable that theories with such far-reaching consequences hardly find any echo nowadays in Germany.

Notes

1. Cf. *Die Wirklichkeit des Mythos,* ed. Kurt Hoffmann (Munich and Zürich, 1965); *Die Eröffnung des Zugangs zum Mythos, Wege der Forschung,* vol. 20,

ed. Karl Kerényi (Darmstadt, 1967); *Terror und Spiel. Probleme der Mythen-rezeption*, ed. Manfred Fuhrmann, *Poetik und Hermeneutik*, vol. 4 (Munich, 1971).

2. René Wellek and Austin Warren, *Theory of Literature*, 3d ed. (New York, 1956), p. 191.

3. Klaus Ziegler, "Mythos und Dichtung," in *Reallexikon der deutschen Litera-turgeschichte*, ed. Werner Kohlschmidt and Wolfgang Mohr (Berlin, 1965), 2:574.

4. Cf. the excellent investigation by Dieter Schrey, *Mythos und Geschichte bei Johann Arnold Kanne und in der romantischen Mythologie, Studien zur deutschen Literatur*, vol. 14 (Tübingen, 1969).

5. "Gedanken über Mythos, Epos und Geschichte," in *Kleinere Schriften* (Berlin, 1869), 4:84.

6. Jakob Grimm, "Vorrede zur 'Deutschen Mythologie,'" in *Kleinere Schriften* (Gütersloh, 1890), 8:148–71.

7. Cf. Theodore Ziolkowski, "Der Hunger nach dem Mythos. Zur seelischen Gastronomie der Deutschen in den Zwanziger Jahren," in *Die sogenannten Zwanziger Jahre*, First Wisconsin Workshop, ed. Reinhold Grimm and Jost Hermand (Bad Homburg v.d.H., Berlin, and Zürich, 1970), pp. 169–201.

8. Cf. Ibid., pp. 192ff.

9. 2 vols. (Halle a.d. Saale, 1910).

10. Cf. Friedrich von der Leyen, "Mythus and Märchen," *Deutsche Vierteljahrs-schrift für Literaturwissenschaft und Geistesgeschichte* 33 (1959): 343–60.

11. Jan de Vries, "Das Motiv des Vater-Sohn-Kampfes im Hildebrandslied," *Ger-manisch-Romanische Monatsschrift* 34 (1953): 257–74.

12. Franz Rolf Schröder, "Ursprung und Ende der germanischen Heldendich-tung," *Germanisch-romanische Monatsschrift* 27 (1939): 325–67.

13. Otto Höfler, *Der Runenstein von Rök und die germanische Individualweihe. Germanisches Sakralkönigtum*, vol. 1 (Tübingen, 1952).

14. Karl Helm, "Mythologie auf alten und neuen Wegen," in *Beiträge zur Ge-schichte der deutschen Sprache und Literatur*, 77 (Tübingen, 1955), pp. 333–65.

15. Ed. Hugo Kuhn and Kurt Schier (Munich, 1963).

16. Berlin, 1951.

17. "Helena und der Senator. Versuch einer mythologischen Deutung von Tho-mas Manns 'Buddenbrooks'" (1963), in *Thomas Mann*, ed. Helmut Koop-mann. *Wege der Forschung*, 335 (Darmstadt, 1975), pp. 247–56.

18. *Sprache und Literatur*, 18 (Stuttgart, 1964).

19. *Elemente der Lyrik* 2d ed. (Munich, 1972), pp. 66–93.

20. In *Die Gestalt und das Sein. Gesammelte Abhandlungen über den Mythos und seine Bedeutung für die Menschheit* (Düsseldorf and Cologne, 1955), pp. 25–90.

21. "Der ursprüngliche Mythos," in *Die Eröffnung des Zugangs zum Mythos*, pp. 271–78.

22. "Die Sprache als Mythos," in ibid., p. 287. Cf. also Otto, *Die Musen und der göttliche Ursprung des Singens und Sagens* (Düsseldorf and Cologne, 1954).

23. "Was ist Mythologie?" in *Die Eröffnung des Zugangs zum Mythos*, pp. 212–33; "Wesen und Gegenwärtigkeit des Mythos," in ibid., pp. 234–52; "Über Ursprung und Gründung in der Mythologie," in Karl Kerényi and Carl Gustav Jung, *Einführung in das Wesen der Mythologie*, 4th ed. (Zürich, 1951), pp. 9–

104; *Umgang mit Göttlichem. Über Mythologie und Religionsgeschichte*, Vandenhoeck-Reihe 18, 2d ed. (Göttingen, 1961).

24. "Der Dichter und das Phantasieren," in *Gesammelte Werke*, ed. Anna Freud et al. (London, 1941), 7:2.

25. "Das Interesse an der Psychoanalyse," in *Gesammelte Werke*, 8:41.

26. *Gesammelte Werke*, 16:101–246.

27. *Der Mythos von der Geburt des Helden. Versuch einer psychologischen Mythendeutung* (Leipzig, 1922).

28. For Jung's theory of archetypes, cf. the excellent compilation by Jolande Jacobi, *Komplex, Archetypus, Symbol in der Psychologie C.G. Jungs* (Zürich and Stuttgart, 1957).

29. "Psychologie und Dichtung," in *Philosophie der Literaturwissenschaft*, ed. Emil Ermatinger (Berlin, 1930), pp. 331–75.

30. In *Der Dichter und die Zeit. Eine Sammlung von Reden und Vorträgen* (Bern, 1947), pp. 13–39.

31. "Psychoanalyse und Dichtung," *Euphorion* 34 (1933): pp. 38–72.

32. "Bilder und Symbole aus E.T.A. Hoffmanns Märchen 'Der goldene Topf,' " in C.G. Jung, *Gestaltungen des Unbewussten* (Zürich, 1950), pp. 237–616.

33. Zürich, 1960.

34. *Vom Sein der Welt. Beiträge zur mythologischen Literaturgeschichte von Goethe bis zur Gegenwart*. Veröffentl. No. 3 of "Argentinischen Goethegesellschaft" (Mendoza, 1958).

35. *Symbolik des Märchens. Versch einer Deutung* 2 vols. (Bern and Munich, 1952–1956).

36. *Das Märchen. Sein Ort in der geistigen Entwicklung* (Bern and Munich, 1965).

37. Cf. Josephine Bilz, *Menschliche Reifung im Sinnbild*, vol. 5, *Beiheft zum Zentralblatt für Psychotherapie* (1943); "Märchengeschehen und Reifungsvorgänge unter tiefenpsychologischem Gesichtspunkt," in Charlotte Bühler and Josephine Bilz, *Das Märchen und die Phantasie des Kindes* (Munich, 1958); Gustav Hans Graber, "Märchengestalten bei Jugendlichen," *Schweizerische Zeitschrift für Psychologie* 5 (1946): 53–59; Bruno Jöckel, "Das Reifungserlebnis im Märchen," *Psyche* 1 (1948): 382–95.

38. Wilhelm Laiblin, "Einleitung," in *Märchenforschung und Tiefenpsychologie*, ed. Wilhelm Laiblin, *Wege der Forschung*, vol. 102 (Darmstadt, 1972), p. xxii.

39. Stuttgart, 1957; first in English, New York, 1951.

40. Munich and Vienna, 1964.

41. *Literaturwissenschaft zwischen Hermeneutik und Empirie, Sprache und Literatur*, vol. 80 (Stuttgart, 1972).

42. Karl Marx, "Einleitung," in *Grundrisse der Kritik der politischen Ökonomie* (Berlin, 1953), p. 30.

43. *Kunst und Koexistenz. Beitrag zu einer modernen marxistischen Ästhetik* (Reinbek b. Hamburg, 1966), p. 199.

44. Robert Weimann, *Literaturgeschichte und Mythologie. Methodologische und historische Studien* (Berlin and Weimar, 1974), p. 392.

45. *Psychological Studies of Imagination* (Oxford, 1934).

46. "Goethes Wahlverwandtschaften," in *Schriften* I (Frankfurt, 1955), p. 96.

47. *Homo Creator. Abhandlungen zur Soziologie, Anthropologie und Ethnologie* (Wiesbaden, 1962), p. 162.

48. *Einfache Formen*, 4th ed. (Tübingen, 1902), p. 115.

49. "Zur Typologie mündlicher Sprachdenkmäler," *Sitzungsberichte der Bayerischen Akademie der Wissenschaften, Philosophisch-historische Klasse, Jahrgang 1960,* vol. 5 (Munich, 1960).
50. *Dichtung und Welt im Mittelalter. Klein Schriften,* vol. 1 (Stuttgart, 1959), pp. 151–80.
51. *Germanische Heldensage. Stoffe, Probleme, Methoden* (Frankfurt am Main, 1971), p. 52.
52. In *Protest und Verheissung. Studien zur klassischen und modernen Dichtung* (Frankfurt am Main and Bonn, 1960), pp. 67–94.
53. Ibid., pp. 249–63.
54. *Das Bild in der Dichtung,* vol. 1, 2d ed. (Marburg, 1960).
55. *Die dichterische Phantasie. Einführung in eine Poetik* (Bern and Munich, 1969), p. 23.
56. Cf. Klaus Weissenberger, "A Morphological Genre Theory: An Answer to a Pluralism of Forms," in *Theories of Literary Genre. Yearbook of Comparative Criticism,* vol. 8, ed. Joseph Strelka (University Park, Pa., 1977), pp. 239–52.
57. Munich, 1953, 1: 2–8.
58. *Dichtung und Gesellschaft* (Vienna, Frankfurt, and Zürich, 1971), pp. 249–75.
59. Hans Mayer, "Goethe und Hegel," *Von Lessing bis Thomas Mann. Wandlungen der bürgerlichen Literatur in Deutschland* (Pfullingen, 1959).
60. *Die Logik der Dichtung,* 2d ed. (Stuttgart, 1968).
61. "Mimesis und Imitatio. Grundlagen einer neuen Gattungspoetik," *Euphorion* 64 (1970): 125–42.
62. "The Style of the Mythical Age," in *Dichten und Erkennen. Esays Vol. 1, Gesammelte Werke* (Zürich, 1955), 6: 249.
63. Hermann Broch, "Einige Bemerkungen zur Philosophie und Technik des Übersetzens," in ibid., pp. 277–94.
64. Hermann Broch, "Die mythische Erbschaft der Dichtung," in ibid., p. 246.
65. Klaus Weissenberger, *Zwischen Stein und Stern. Mystische Formgebung in der Dichtung von Else Lasker-Schüler, Nelly Sachs und Paul Celan* (Bern and Munich, 1976).
66. This formulation served as a consensus formula for the contributions to the colloquium, which have been published under the title *Terror und Spiel,* note 1; cf. ibid., p. 9.
67. *Zur Begriffs- und Stilgeschichte der deutschen Literatur im neunzehnten und zwanzigsten Jahrhundert* (Bad Homburg v.d.H., Berlin, and Zürich, 1967).
68. *Eine poetologische und methodenkritische Studie zum Werk Hans Henny Jahnns. Studien zur Poetik und Geschichte der Literatur,* vol. 32 (Stuttgart, Berlin, Cologne, and Mainz, 1973).
69. *Vom Erkennen des literarischen Kunstwerks* (Tübingen, 1968).
70. *Die Sterblichkeit der Musen. Betrachtungen über Dichtung und Kunst in unserer Zeit* (Stuttgart, 1958), p. 381.
71. In *Jahrbuch für Ästhetik und allgemeine Kunstwissenschaft* 12, no. 2 (1967): 154–91.
72. In *Gestalt und Gedanke,* 6 (Munich, 1960), pp. 90–128.

LIST OF CONTRIBUTORS

ADOLF, HELEN

Born: December 31, 1895, in Vienna, Austria.

Education: Ph.D., University of Vienna, 1923.

Present position: Professor Emerita of German, Pennsylvania State University.

Books: *Wortgeschichtliche Studien zum Leib/Seele-Problem* (1937); *Visio Pacis: Holy City and Grail* (1960); *Werden und Sein* (1964); *Therese von Avila* (translation with introduction, 1929).

Editor: *Dem Neuen Reich Entgegen, 1850–1871* (1930); *Im Neuen Reich, 1871–1914* (1952).

BLOCK, HASKELL MAYER

Born: June 13, 1923, in Chicago.

Education: Docteur D'Université, 1949, Université de Paris.

Present position: Professor of Comparative Literature, State University of New York at Binghamton.

Books: *Mallarmé and the Symbolist Drama* (1963); *Naturalistic Triptych* (1970); *Nouvelles Tendances en Litterature Comparé* (1970);—with Herman Salinger: *The Creative Vision* (1960);—with Robert G. Shedd: *Masters of Modern Drama* (1962).

CARDEN, PATRICIA

Born: October 11, 1935, in Burlington, North Carolina.

Education: Ph.D., Columbia University, 1966.

Present position: Chairman, Department of Russian Literature, Cornell University, Ithaca, New York.

Books: *The Art of Isaac Babel* (1972).

DÖRRIE, HEINRICH

Born: November 27, 1911, in Hanover, Federal Republic of Germany.

Education: Ph.D., Göttingen, 1935.

Present position: Professor of Classical Philology, University of Münster, Federal Republic of Germany.

Books: *Passio SS. Machabaeorum, die antike Übersetzung des IV. Makkabärbuches* (1938); *Hypostasis. Wort und Bedeutungsgeschichte* (1955); *Leid und Erfahrung* (1956); *Drei Texte zur Geschichte der Ungarn und Mongolen* (1957); *Untersuchungen zur Überlieferungsgeschichte von Ovids Epistulae Heroidum* (1960); *Der Königskult des Antiochos von Kommagene im Lichte neuer Inschriften-Funde* (1964); *P. Ovidius Naso: Der Brief der Sappho an Phaon*(1975); *Platonica Minora* (1976); *Sinn und Funktion des Mythos in der griechischen und der römischen Dichtung* (1978);—with J.H. Waszink and Willy Theiler: *Porphyre* (1966).

DRESDEN, SEM

Born: 1914, in Amsterdam, the Netherlands.

Education: University of Amsterdam and the Sorbonne.

Present position: Professor of French Literature and Comparative Literature, University of Leiden.

Books: *The Artist and the Absolute: Valéry and Proust* (1941); *Well-Considered Adventures: Bergson, Proust, Vaéry, Camus* (1949); *Montaigne: The Playful Philosopher* (1952); *The World in Words: Considerations on the Art of the Novel* (1965); *Humanism and the Renaissance* (1968); *Biography and Literature* (1972).

DUMÉZIL, GEORGES

Born: March 4, 1898, in Paris.

Education: Agrégé des Lettres, Docteur des Lettres.

Present position: Honorary Professor at the Collége de France, Paris.

Books: *Recherches comparatives sur le verbe caucasien* (1933); *Ouranos-Varuna* (1935); *Flamen-Brahman* (1935); *Textes arméniens* (1937); *Contes lazes* (1937); *Mythes et dieux des Germains* (1939); *Mitra-Varuna* (1940); *Horace et les Curiaces* (1942); *Servius et la fortune* (1943); *Naissance de Rome* (1944); *Naissance d'archanges* (1945); *Tarpeia* (1947); *Les mythes romaines* (1947); *Loki* (1948); *Jupiter, Mars, Quirinus* (1948); *L'héritage indo-européen à Rome* (1949); *Le troisiéme souverain . . .* (1949); *Les dieux des Indo-européens* (1952); *La saga de Hadingus* (1953); *Rituels indo-européens à Rome* (1954); *Aspects de la fonction guerriére chez les Indo-européens* (1956); *Contes et légendes des Oubykhs . . .*

(1957); *Les dieux des Germains* (1959); *Etudes oubykhs* (1959); *Documents anatoliens sur les langues et les traditions du Caucase* (1960); *Le livre des héros* (1965); *La religion romaine archäique* (1966); *Mythe et épopée* ... (1968); *Du mythe au roman* (1970); *Fêtes romaines d'été et d'automne* (1975); *Le verbe oubykh* (1975); *Romans de Scythie et d'alentour* (1978).

FEDER, LILLIAN

Born: July 10, 1923, in New York.

Education: Ph.D., University of Minnesota.

Present position: Professor of English and Comparative Literature, Queens College and the Graduate School, City Univerity of New York.

Books: *Crowell's Handbook of Classical Literature* (1964); *Sermon or Satire: Pope's Definition of His Art* (1967); *Ancient Myth in Modern Poetry* (1971).

KUSHNER, EVA

Born: June 18, 1929, in Prague.

Education: Ph.D., McGill University.

Present position: Chairman, Department of French Literature, McGill University, Montreal.

Books: *Saint-Denys-Garneau* (1967); *Rina Lasnier* (1969); *Mauriac* (1972).

VICKERY, JOHN B.

Born: August 20, 1925, in Toronto.

Education: University of Toronto, Colgate University, University of Wisconsin, Harvard University.

Present position: Professor of English, University of California, Riverside.

Books: *Robert Graves and the White Goddess* (1972); *The Literary Impact of "The Golden Bough"* (1973).

Editor: *Myth and Literature* (1966); *Goethe's "Faust: Part One": Essays in Criticism* (1969); *The Shaken Realist: Essays on Modern Literature* (1970); *"Light in August" and the Critical Spectrum* (1971); *The Scapegoat: Ritual and Literature* (1971).

WEINBERG, KURT

Born: February 24, 1912, in Hanover, Federal Republic of Germany.

Education: Ph.D., Yale University.

Present position: Professor Emeritus of French, German and Comparative Literature, University of Rochester (New York).

Books: *Henri Heine, "romantique défroqué," héraut du symbolisme français* (1954); *Kafkas Dichtungen: Die Travestien des Mythos* (1963); *On Gide's "Prométhée": Private Myth and Public Mystification* (1972); *The Figure of Faust in Valéry and Goethe. An Exegesis of "Mon Faust"* (1976).

WEISSENBERGER, KLAUS

Born: November 15, 1939, in Sydney.

Education: Ph.D., University of Southern California.

Present position: Chairman, Department of German Literature, Rice University, Houston.

Books: *Formen der Elegie von Goethe bis Celan* (1969); *Die Elegie bei Paul Celan* (1969); *Zwischen Stein und Stern. Mystische Formgebung in der Dichtung von Else Lasker-Schüler, Nelly Sachs und Paul Celan* (1976).

WHITE, JOHN J.

Born: June 18, 1940, in St. Austell, England.

Education: Universities of Leicester and Alberta, Freie Universität Berlin, and University College, London.

Present position: Reader in German at King's College, London.

Books: *Mythology in the Modern Novel. A Study of Prefigurative Techniques* (1971)

Co-editor: *August Stramm. Kritische Essays und unveröffentlichtes Material aus dem Nachlass* (1978); *German Life and Letters*.

INDEX OF NAMES